Sustainable Tourism VI

WITPRESS

WIT Press publishes leading books in Science and Technology.
Visit our website for the current list of titles.
www.witpress.com

WITeLibrary

Home of the Transactions of the Wessex Institute.
Papers presented at Sustainable Tourism VI are archived in the WIT eLibrary in volume
187 of WIT Transactions on Ecology and the Environment (ISSN 1743-3541).
The WIT eLibrary provides the international scientific community with immediate and
permanent access to individual papers presented at WIT conferences.
Visit the WIT eLibrary at www.witpress.com.

SIXTH INTERNATIONAL CONFERENCE
ON SUSTAINABLE TOURISM

Sustainable Tourism VI

CONFERENCE CHAIRMEN

C.A. Brebbia
Wessex Institute of Technology, UK
S. Favro
Hydrographic Institute of the Republic of Croatia, Croatia
F.D. Pineda
The Complutense University, Spain

INTERNATIONAL SCIENTIFIC ADVISORY COMMITTEE

I. Jurincic
I. Navis
Y. Ohe
T. Oyabu
U. Probstl-Haider
J. Urciaga
K. Valencia
S.S. Zubir

Organised by
Wessex Institute of Technology, UK
The Complutense University, Spain

Sponsored by
WIT Transactions on Ecology and the Environment
International Journal of Sustainable Development and Planning

WIT Transactions

Transactions Editor

Carlos Brebbia
Wessex Institute of Technology
Ashurst Lodge, Ashurst
Southampton SO40 7AA, UK

Editorial Board

J-T Chen National Taiwan Ocean University, Taiwan

A H-D Cheng University of Mississippi, USA

J Chilton University of Lincoln, UK

C-L Chiu University of Pittsburgh, USA

H Choi Kangnung National University, Korea

A Cieslak Technical University of Lodz, Poland

S Clement Transport System Centre, Australia

M W Collins Brunel University, UK

J J Connor Massachusetts Institute of Technology, USA

M C Constantinou State University of New York at Buffalo, USA

D E Cormack University of Toronto, Canada

D F Cutler Royal Botanic Gardens, UK

W Czyczula Krakow University of Technology, Poland

M da Conceicao Cunha University of Coimbra, Portugal

L Dávid Károly Róbert College, Hungary

A Davies University of Hertfordshire, UK

M Davis Temple University, USA

A B de Almeida Instituto Superior Tecnico, Portugal

E R de Arantes e Oliveira Instituto Superior Tecnico, Portugal

L De Biase University of Milan, Italy

R de Borst Delft University of Technology, Netherlands

G De Mey University of Ghent, Belgium

A De Montis Universita di Cagliari, Italy

A De Naeyer Universiteit Ghent, Belgium

P De Wilde Vrije Universiteit Brussel, Belgium

D De Wrachien State University of Milan, Italy

L Debnath University of Texas-Pan American, USA

G Degrande Katholieke Universiteit Leuven, Belgium

S del Giudice University of Udine, Italy

G Deplano Universita di Cagliari, Italy

I Doltsinis University of Stuttgart, Germany

M Domaszewski Universite de Technologie de Belfort-Montbeliard, France

J Dominguez University of Seville, Spain

K Dorow Pacific Northwest National Laboratory, USA

W Dover University College London, UK

C Dowlen South Bank University, UK

J P du Plessis University of Stellenbosch, South Africa

R Duffell University of Hertfordshire, UK

N A Dumont PUC-Rio, Brazil

A Ebel University of Cologne, Germany

G K Egan Monash University, Australia

K M Elawadly Alexandria University, Egypt

K-H Elmer Universitat Hannover, Germany

D Elms University of Canterbury, New Zealand

M E M El-Sayed Kettering University, USA

D M Elsom Oxford Brookes University, UK

F Erdogan Lehigh University, USA

D J Evans Nottingham Trent University, UK

J W Everett Rowan University, USA

M Faghri University of Rhode Island, USA

R A Falconer Cardiff University, UK

M N Fardis University of Patras, Greece

P Fedelinski Silesian Technical University, Poland

H J S Fernando Arizona State University, USA

S Finger Carnegie Mellon University, USA

E M M Fonseca Instituto Politécnico de Bragança, Portugal

J I Frankel University of Tennessee, USA

D M Fraser University of Cape Town, South Africa

M J Fritzler University of Calgary, Canada

T Futagami Hiroshima Institute of Technology, Japan

U Gabbert Otto-von-Guericke Universitat Magdeburg, Germany

G Gambolati Universita di Padova, Italy

C J Gantes National Technical University of Athens, Greece

L Gaul Universitat Stuttgart, Germany

A Genco University of Palermo, Italy

N Georgantzis Universitat Jaume I, Spain

P Giudici Universita di Pavia, Italy

L M C Godinho University of Coimbra, Portugal

F Gomez Universidad Politecnica de Valencia, Spain

R Gomez Martin University of Granada, Spain

D Goulias University of Maryland, USA

K G Goulias Pennsylvania State University, USA

F Grandori Politecnico di Milano, Italy

W E Grant Texas A & M University, USA

S Grilli University of Rhode Island, USA

R H J Grimshaw Loughborough University, UK

D Gross Technische Hochschule Darmstadt, Germany

R Grundmann Technische Universitat Dresden, Germany

A Gualtierotti IDHEAP, Switzerland

O T Gudmestad University of Stavanger, Norway

R C Gupta National University of Singapore, Singapore

J M Hale University of Newcastle, UK

K Hameyer Katholieke Universiteit Leuven, Belgium

C Hanke Danish Technical University, Denmark

K Hayami University of Tokyo, Japan

Y Hayashi Nagoya University, Japan

L Haydock Newage International Limited, UK

A H Hendrickx Free University of Brussels, Belgium

C Herman John Hopkins University, USA

I Hideaki Nagoya University, Japan

D A Hills University of Oxford, UK

W F Huebner Southwest Research Institute, USA

J A C Humphrey Bucknell University, USA

M Y Hussaini Florida State University, USA

W Hutchinson Edith Cowan University, Australia

T H Hyde University of Nottingham, UK

M Iguchi Science University of Tokyo, Japan

D B Ingham University of Leeds, UK

L Int Panis VITO Expertisecentrum IMS, Belgium

N Ishikawa National Defence Academy, Japan

J Jaafar UiTm, Malaysia

W Jager Technical University of Dresden, Germany

Y Jaluria Rutgers University, USA

C M Jefferson University of the West of England, UK

P R Johnston Griffith University, Australia

D R H Jones University of Cambridge, UK

N Jones University of Liverpool, UK

N Jovanovic CSIR, South Africa

D Kaliampakos National Technical University of Athens, Greece

N Kamiya Nagoya University, Japan

D L Karabalis University of Patras, Greece

A Karageorghis University of Cyprus

M Karlsson Linkoping University, Sweden

T Katayama Doshisha University, Japan

K L Katsifarakis Aristotle University of Thessaloniki, Greece

J T Katsikadelis National Technical University of Athens, Greece

E Kausel Massachusetts Institute of Technology, USA

H Kawashima The University of Tokyo, Japan

B A Kazimee Washington State University, USA

S Kim University of Wisconsin-Madison, USA

D Kirkland Nicholas Grimshaw & Partners Ltd, UK

E Kita Nagoya University, Japan

A S Kobayashi University of Washington, USA

T Kobayashi University of Tokyo, Japan

D Koga Saga University, Japan

S Kotake University of Tokyo, Japan

A N Kounadis National Technical University of Athens, Greece

W B Kratzig Ruhr Universitat Bochum, Germany

T Krauthammer Penn State University, USA

C-H Lai University of Greenwich, UK

M Langseth Norwegian University of Science and Technology, Norway

B S Larsen Technical University of Denmark, Denmark

F **Lattarulo** Politecnico di Bari, Italy

A **Lebedev** Moscow State University, Russia

L J **Leon** University of Montreal, Canada

D **Lesnic** University of Leeds, UK

D **Lewis** Mississippi State University, USA

S **Ighobashi** University of California Irvine, USA

K-C **Lin** University of New Brunswick, Canada

A A **Liolios** Democritus University of Thrace, Greece

S **Lomov** Katholieke Universiteit Leuven, Belgium

J W S **Longhurst** University of the West of England, UK

G **Loo** The University of Auckland, New Zealand

J **Lourenco** Universidade do Minho, Portugal

J E **Luco** University of California at San Diego, USA

H **Lui** State Seismological Bureau Harbin, China

C J **Lumsden** University of Toronto, Canada

L **Lundqvist** Division of Transport and Location Analysis, Sweden

T **Lyons** Murdoch University, Australia

Y-W **Mai** University of Sydney, Australia

M **Majowiecki** University of Bologna, Italy

D **Malerba** Università degli Studi di Bari, Italy

G **Manara** University of Pisa, Italy

S **Mambretti** Politecnico di Milano, Italy

B N **Mandal** Indian Statistical Institute, India

Ü **Mander** University of Tartu, Estonia

H A **Mang** Technische Universitat Wien, Austria

G D **Manolis** Aristotle University of Thessaloniki, Greece

W J **Mansur** COPPE/UFRJ, Brazil

N **Marchettini** University of Siena, Italy

J D M **Marsh** Griffith University, Australia

J F **Martin-Duque** Universidad Complutense, Spain

T **Matsui** Nagoya University, Japan

G **Mattrisch** DaimlerChrysler AG, Germany

F M **Mazzolani** University of Naples "Federico II", Italy

K **McManis** University of New Orleans, USA

A C **Mendes** Universidade de Beira Interior, Portugal

R A **Meric** Research Institute for Basic Sciences, Turkey

J **Mikielewicz** Polish Academy of Sciences, Poland

N **Milic-Frayling** Microsoft Research Ltd, UK

R A W **Mines** University of Liverpool, UK

C A **Mitchell** University of Sydney, Australia

K **Miura** Kajima Corporation, Japan

A **Miyamoto** Yamaguchi University, Japan

T **Miyoshi** Kobe University, Japan

G **Molinari** University of Genoa, Italy

T B **Moodie** University of Alberta, Canada

D B **Murray** Trinity College Dublin, Ireland

G **Nakhaeizadeh** DaimlerChrysler AG, Germany

M B **Neace** Mercer University, USA

D **Necsulescu** University of Ottawa, Canada

F **Neumann** University of Vienna, Austria

S-I **Nishida** Saga University, Japan

H **Nisitani** Kyushu Sangyo University, Japan

B **Notaros** University of Massachusetts, USA

P **O'Donoghue** University College Dublin, Ireland

R O **O'Neill** Oak Ridge National Laboratory, USA

M **Ohkusu** Kyushu University, Japan

G **Oliveto** Universitá di Catania, Italy

R **Olsen** Camp Dresser & McKee Inc., USA

E **Oñate** Universitat Politecnica de Catalunya, Spain

K **Onishi** Ibaraki University, Japan

P H **Oosthuizen** Queens University, Canada

E L **Ortiz** Imperial College London, UK

E **Outa** Waseda University, Japan

A S **Papageorgiou** Rensselaer Polytechnic Institute, USA

J **Park** Seoul National University, Korea

G **Passerini** Universita delle Marche, Italy

F **Patania** University of Catania, Italy

B C **Patten** University of Georgia, USA

G **Pelosi** University of Florence, Italy

G G **Penelis** Aristotle University of Thessaloniki, Greece

W **Perrie** Bedford Institute of Oceanography, Canada

R **Pietrabissa** Politecnico di Milano, Italy

H **Pina** Instituto Superior Tecnico, Portugal

M F **Platzer** Naval Postgraduate School, USA

D **Poljak** University of Split, Croatia

H **Power** University of Nottingham, UK

D **Prandle** Proudman Oceanographic Laboratory, UK

M **Predeleanu** University Paris VI, France

I S **Putra** Institute of Technology Bandung, Indonesia

Y A **Pykh** Russian Academy of Sciences, Russia

F **Rachidi** EMC Group, Switzerland

M **Rahman** Dalhousie University, Canada

K R **Rajagopal** Texas A & M University, USA

T **Rang** Tallinn Technical University, Estonia

J **Rao** Case Western Reserve University, USA

J **Ravnik** University of Maribor, Slovenia

A M **Reinhorn** State University of New York at Buffalo, USA

G **Reniers** Universiteit Antwerpen, Belgium

A D **Rey** McGill University, Canada

D N **Riahi** University of Illinois at Urbana-Champaign, USA

B **Ribas** Spanish National Centre for Environmental Health, Spain

K **Richter** Graz University of Technology, Austria

S **Rinaldi** Politecnico di Milano, Italy

F **Robuste** Universitat Politecnica de Catalunya, Spain

J **Roddick** Flinders University, Australia

A C **Rodrigues** Universidade Nova de Lisboa, Portugal

F **Rodrigues** Poly Institute of Porto, Portugal

G R **Rodríguez** Universidad de Las Palmas de Gran Canaria, Spain

C W **Roeder** University of Washington, USA

J M **Roesset** Texas A & M University, USA

W **Roetzel** Universitaet der Bundeswehr Hamburg, Germany

V **Roje** University of Split, Croatia

R **Rosset** Laboratoire d'Aerologie, France

J L **Rubio** Centro de Investigaciones sobre Desertificacion, Spain

T J **Rudolphi** Iowa State University, USA

S **Russenchuck** Magnet Group, Switzerland

H **Ryssel** Fraunhofer Institut Integrierte Schaltungen, Germany

S G **Saad** American University in Cairo, Egypt

M **Saiidi** University of Nevada-Reno, USA

R **San Jose** Technical University of Madrid, Spain

F J **Sanchez-Sesma** Instituto Mexicano del Petroleo, Mexico

B **Sarler** Nova Gorica Polytechnic, Slovenia

S A **Savidis** Technische Universitat Berlin, Germany

A **Savini** Universita de Pavia, Italy

G **Schmid** Ruhr-Universitat Bochum, Germany

R **Schmidt** RWTH Aachen, Germany

B **Scholtes** Universitaet of Kassel, Germany

W **Schreiber** University of Alabama, USA

A P S **Selvadurai** McGill University, Canada

J J **Sendra** University of Seville, Spain

J J **Sharp** Memorial University of Newfoundland, Canada

Q **Shen** Massachusetts Institute of Technology, USA

X **Shixiong** Fudan University, China

G C **Sih** Lehigh University, USA

L C **Simoes** University of Coimbra, Portugal

A C **Singhal** Arizona State University, USA

P **Skerget** University of Maribor, Slovenia

J **Sladek** Slovak Academy of Sciences, Slovakia

V **Sladek** Slovak Academy of Sciences, Slovakia

A C M **Sousa** University of New Brunswick, Canada

H **Sozer** Illinois Institute of Technology, USA

Sustainable Tourism VI

Editors

C.A. Brebbia
Wessex Institute of Technology, UK

S. Favro
Hydrographic Institute of the Republic of Croatia, Croatia

F.D. Pineda
The Complutense University, Spain

WITPRESS Southampton, Boston

Editors:

C.A. Brebbia
Wessex Institute of Technology, UK

S. Favro
Hydrographic Institute of the Republic of Croatia, Croatia

F.D. Pineda
The Complutense University, Spain

Published by

WIT Press
Ashurst Lodge, Ashurst, Southampton, SO40 7AA, UK
Tel: 44 (0) 238 029 3223; Fax: 44 (0) 238 029 2853
E-Mail: witpress@witpress.com
http://www.witpress.com

For USA, Canada and Mexico

Computational Mechanics Inc
25 Bridge Street, Billerica, MA 01821, USA
Tel: 978 667 5841; Fax: 978 667 7582
E-Mail: infousa@witpress.com
http://www.witpress.com

British Library Cataloguing-in-Publication Data

A Catalogue record for this book is available
from the British Library

ISBN: 978-1-84564-800-8
eISBN:978-1-84564-801-5
ISSN: 1746-448X (print)
ISSN: 1743-3541 (online)

The texts of the papers in this volume were set
individually by the authors or under their supervision.
Only minor corrections to the text may have been carried
out by the publisher.

Preface

This book contains papers presented at the 6th International Conference on Sustainable Tourism organised in Opatija, Croatia, by the Wessex Institute of Technology, with the collaboration of the Complutense University of Madrid. The Meeting was reconvened in 2014 following the success of the five previous conferences starting in Segovia in 2004, followed by Bologna (2006); Malta (2008); The New Forest home of the Wessex Institute (2010); and A Coruña (2012).

The Sustainable Tourism Conference after ten successful years, is now well established and attracts papers on a wide variety of topics. The material presented in this book as well as those from previous conferences is of interest to the research community as well as to the tourist industry which can find in these volumes, a point of reference for strategic planning and programme development. All the papers published since the first meeting in 2004 are part of the WIT Transactions in Ecology and the Environment and archived in the Wessex Institute's eLibrary (http://library.witpress.com) where they are permanently and easily available to the community. There the wide variety of topics discussed during the meetings can be appreciated. The papers also demonstrate the importance of this conference series in providing invaluable material to study this ever expanding field of human activity.

Tourism, research and development encompassed many different fields of knowledge. The Sustainable Tourism conferences offer a forum to discuss the diverse components of tourism phenomena, ranging from biophysics, to socio economic and cultural aspects, as well as field studies and academic research, stressing as well the entrepreneurial and institutional side of the industry.

During the last decade, the meeting has evolved and reflected the changes in the field and the Conference now tries to address, among other aspects, the need to develop dynamic models that can analyse existing data to predict future trends. In this manner, pathways can be established for different sections of the market involving diverse types of tourism, ranging from the classical "4S" to historical, cultural and ecological tourism.

The common denominator of all tourism modes is the growing availability of leisure time. This is a consequence of the changes that have taken place in the pattern of our society in the last hundred years or so. In 1900 the life expectancy of the world's population was only 35 years in developed countries, now the world population in general has more free time and, at the same time travelling has become cheaper and easier.

This book analyses those as well as other issues presenting new research ideas in the field of tourism, with contributions from different specialists focusing on the visitors and their leisure time.

The Editors are grateful to all authors for their contributions and particularly indebted to the members of the International Scientific Advisory Committee and other colleagues who helped select the papers, thus ensuring the quality of this volume.

The Editors
Opatija, Croatia
2014

Contents

Section 1
Tourism strategies

Do sustainability-experienced travellers prefer a more rational communication of the sustainability of a tourism product?

R. Wehrli, J. Priskin, D. Schaffner, J. Schwarz & J. Stettler
Lucerne University of Applied Sciences and Arts,
Institute of Tourism ITW, Switzerland

Abstract

This study empirically examines, in four countries, which communication style (emotional or rational) is most appropriate for addressing sustainability-experienced travellers. There are only small differences compared to the average tourist. Rational communication elements, which explain the sustainability of the product, become more important for this specific customer group. However, most emotional communication elements are still more important in most countries, indicating that experienced tourists also process sustainability information in a heuristic way.

Keywords: sustainable tourism, communication, marketing, empirical survey, choice experiment, conjoint, experience.

1   Introduction

There are different ways for a destination and other tourism actors to become more sustainable. One possible way to stimulate a destination's sustainable development is to attract people who behave in a more sustainable way (Dolnicar [1]). This will not only decrease the ecological footprint of the destination due to the more ecological behaviour of this customer group but will also deliver an incentive to all actors in the destination to develop more sustainable offers.

Although the general academic literature about green consumerism and pro-sustainability behaviour dates over two decades (Young *et al.* [2], Cherian and Jolly [3]), in a tourism context the field remains fairly new with just a few publications (Han *et al.* [4], Lee *et al.* [5]), Some frameworks from the academic

WIT Transactions on Ecology and The Environment, Vol 187, © 2014 WIT Press
www.witpress.com, ISSN 1743-3541 (on-line)
doi:10.2495/ST140011

literature and some guidelines for the general marketing of sustainable products exist, but there are still major research gaps to empirically explain which way of communication is most effective to influence pro-sustainability consumer choice in tourism. Wehrli *et al.* [6] is one of the first studies to address this research gap, whereby the research finds a general preference "for emotionally laden communication styles for sustainable tourism products."

Dolnicar and Leisch [7] conclude that selective target marketing should be part of sustainable tourism marketing and that those who behave environmentally friendly should be targeted differently. They find empirically that Australians who behave environmentally friendly can be characterised differently with respect to psychographic, behavioural and socio-demographic personal characteristics. However, they do not answer how to communicate with this specific customer segment. Wehrli *et al.* [6] do not look specifically at this market and they do not deliver any insights about the best communication style towards this specific market segment. Other studies which distinguish between environmentally friendly customers and other customers mainly examine socio-demographic differences between the two groups (Fairweather *et al.* [8] and Dolnicar [9]).

There is no empirical research on which type of communication (e.g. emotional or rational communication styles) is best suited for the specific market segment of sustainability aware tourists, as identified in Wehrli *et al.* [10], or even for those who have already booked sustainable tourism products. Therefore, this paper addresses this research gap empirically by providing insights into the following:

a) Do sustainability-experienced travellers prefer a different communication style compared to travellers who have never booked a sustainable tourism product before?

b) Should the textual communication focus more on the rational level for sustainability for experienced travellers in order to increase purchase intention?

c) Does the inclusion of a graph explaining the sustainability of the product increase the purchase intention for this specific customer group?

In this paper tourists who indicate in the survey conducted for the study having already booked a sustainable tourism product are referred to as "sustainability-experienced tourists" from here on.

2   Literature review

Extensive research in consumer behaviour has investigated communication effectiveness. Most prominent are dual-process models explaining the effectiveness of communication on the bases of two strategies of information processing. One strategy is referred to as heuristic (Chaiken, [11], Tversky and Kahnemann [12]) or peripheral (Petty and Cacioppo [13]). Heuristic processing is characterized by an application of simple decision rules or heuristics (e.g. the lower price is a better deal or a green label indicates ecological sustainability). Judgment formation based on heuristic cue information is a relatively effortless and cognitively minimally demanding way of information processing. Relating this reasoning to the effectiveness of emotional appeals we assume that emotional responses function as heuristic cues (Bless *et al.* [14], Pham [15]) inducing heuristic information processing. The other strategy is referred to as systematic (Chaiken [11], Tversky and Kahnemann [12]) or central (Petty and Cacioppo [13]). Systematic processing is marked by a more effortful and cognitively demanding analysis of judgment-relevant information than heuristic processing (Chen and Chaiken [16]). Subsequently, systematic processing is more complex, logical, rational and related to facts (Pacini and Epstein [17], Sloman [18]).

From the family of dual-process frameworks this research uses the heuristic-systematic model (HSM) (Chaiken [19], Chaiken and Stangor [20]) to attempt to explain persuasion in the context of sustainable products. The HSM defines ability and knowledge as central factor to determine when judgments will be mediated by systematic information processing (Chen and Chaiken [16]): people who are expert about a topic tend to use systematic information processing while people with a lack of knowledge about a topic tend to process information relying on heuristic cues (Mackie and Worth [21, 22]). Additionally, Bohner *et al.* [23] found that heuristic effects related to emotional responses tend to be restricted to situations when expertise is low. We assume that these effects also apply in the context on sustainable products: On the one hand, consumers with experience in sustainability will have more ability to process appeals related to sustainability and will tend to use a systematic route of information processing (Mackie and Worth [21, 22]). For those consumers we assume rational appeals to be more important for decision-making. On the other hand, travellers with no experience with sustainable products will exhibit low ability for information processing motivation and are expected to use heuristic cues as a bases for decision-making. Hence, we propose emotional appeals to be more useful. Therefore, we propose the following hypothesis:

Hypothesis 1: For (non-)experienced travellers rational (emotional) texts are more important for decision making.

3   Empirical method

This study consists of two empirical phases: a pre-test experiment and a choice experiment surveying only people who have travelled during the last year. Both surveys were conducted in Germany, Switzerland, UK and USA with a sample size of at least 750 valid and completed responses. The samples of both phases are representative of the population of each country. This section briefly explains the two experiments, while Wehrli *et al.* [6] provide a detailed description

A pre-test experiment was conducted to determine tourists' perceived level of emotionality and rationality of text and image communications. The experiment proposed different pictures and short texts relating to the standard and sustainable characteristics of a beach holiday (e.g. the beach is nearby, local products are served and so on). The sustainable characteristics used in the experiment are the most important elements of a sustainable tourism product as identified in Wehrli *et al.* [10]. The same feature was described three times with different levels of emotionality and rationality in each case. These levels were changed for each case based on insights from linguistic literature, particularly the methods proposed by Demarmels [24]. This method proposes different means to alter communication emotionality by using different verbal and visual language, symbols, punctuation marks, key words, emotional connotations, rhetorical figures or promises of happiness and threats. Each respondent rated the communication elements by means of a Likert scale from 1 to 7 according to emotionality and rationality using items based on the works of different researchers (Holbrook and Batra [25], Mehrabian and Russel [26] and Rosselli *et al.* [27]).

To test communication preferences by potential customers, a choice experiment was conceived with different ways to communicate the features of a fictive holiday product. This product represented a typical mass tourism beach holiday. The choice experiment did not vary the characteristics of the product; instead respondents were shown different versions of the same product's sustainability attributes and general attributes. Respondents had to choose the preferred version from two different versions in each set. A total of six sets were presented to respondents.

The choice experiment attributes were chosen based on results from the pre-test experiment. The elements where the variation is maximal in one dimension (e.g. emotionality) and minimal in the other dimension (e.g. rationality) were selected in order to ensure the result could be explained by the maximal variation in one communication dimension. The following attributes were used:

- Two pictures at different emotional levels.
- Two text elements explaining standard features of the offer at different emotional levels.
- Two text elements explaining the sustainability of the offer at different emotional levels.
- Two text elements explaining the sustainability of the offer at different rational levels.
- A graph visualising the sustainability was included in some sets.

A detailed description of the choice experiment attributes can be found in Wehrli *et al.* [6].

4 Results

4.1 Descriptive statistics

In the sample 11.1% of the respondents had already booked a sustainable tourism product and belong to the sustainability-experienced group. The values range from 6.9% for UK respondents, 7.7% in USA, 13.3% in Germany, to 16.4% of sustainability-experienced tourists in Switzerland.

This group of sustainability-experienced tourists shows some specific socio-demographic characteristics and travel habits. The following differences are statistically significant (see Table 1 for the descriptive statistics and test statistics):

- Sustainability-experienced travellers have better education.
- More men than women belong to the sustainability-experienced traveller group.
- Sustainability-experienced travellers book a package group travel deal more often than single packages deals.
- Sustainability-experienced travellers travel more frequently.

Table 1:   Socio-demographics of sustainability-experienced travellers for the overall sample.

		Sustainability-experienced travellers	Non-sustainability experienced travellers	Significance (between group Chi-Square)
Education	low	4%	10%	$\chi(2) = 12.704$ $p = 0.002$
	middle	36%	36%	
	high	60%	54%	
Sex	female	45%	51%	$\chi(1) = 4.818$ $p = 0.028$
	male	55%	49%	
Type of trip	No package deals – all travel products individually booked.	48%	61%	$\chi(3) = 15.566$ $p = 0.001$
	Single package deal	33%	28%	
	Package group travel deal	14%	6%	
	Another form of package deal	5%	5%	
Travel frequency (per year)	1 Trip	9%	18%	$\chi(7) = 25.974$, $p = 0.001$
	2 Trips	22%	27%	
	3 Trips	20%	18%	
	4 Trips	14%	11%	
	5–6 Trips	17%	14%	
	7–8 Trips	4%	3%	
	9–10 Trips	5%	4%	
	> 10 Trips	10%	6%	

No statistically significant differences are found for the variables age, marital status, having children and income. The average duration of a trip does also not differ significantly.

4.2 Results from the choice experiment: importances and preferences

The results from the choice experiment are presented with a focus on the difference between tourist groups, i.e. those classified as "sustainability-experienced" and those as "non-experienced".

Table 2 shows the importance of each attribute for the two groups separately. The importance measures the relative importance of an attribute on preference changes compared to the other attributes (Hair *et al.* [28]). It is derived by evaluating the level of influence of each attribute on total utility. The difference between the highest and lowest utility of the levels of each attribute has to be divided by the sum of all ranges of all attributes. The calculation of relative importance values on individual levels was completed and averaged using a tool from Sawtooth (Orme [29]).

Table 2: Importance of the attributes.

		Graph	Picture	Standard text emotional	Text sustainability emotional	Text sustainability rational
Germany (n = 754)						
	Experienced	25.20	21.65	17.18	18.34	17.63
	Non-experienced	41.22	19.90	13.84	13.21	11.82
	Significance	0.000	n.s.	0.012	0.000	0.000
Switzerland (n = 751)						
	Experienced	31.94	23.81	14.69	16.69	12.86
	Non-experienced	38.26	22.62	12.86	15.79	10.48
	Significance	0.001	n.s.	n.s.	n.s.	0.005
UK (n = 751)						
	Experienced	31.91	17.78	17.08	15.53	17.70
	Non-experienced	44.07	17.97	12.76	15.94	9.27
	Significance	0.000	n.s.	0.005	n.s.	0.000
USA (n = 750)						
	Experienced	20.99	28.46	19.85	18.56	12.14
	Non-experienced	35.24	24.43	14.95	16.82	8.55
	Significance	0.000	n.s.	0.001	n.s.	0.000

The importance of the rational sustainability communication attribute is significantly higher for sustainability-experienced travellers compared to non-experienced customers in all countries as shown in the last column in Table 2. Nonetheless, it is still not as important as the emotional textual communication of the sustainability related text element and the standard text element. Interestingly, the graph's importance is clearly lower in all countries. There is one main exception regarding the importance of the text elements: In the UK, the rational sustainability communication attribute is ranked as the most important textual element by experienced tourists. Another smaller exception is Germany where the rational element is more important than the standard text element.

Therefore, Hypothesis 1 is not confirmed. Although the importance of rational sustainability communication is higher for sustainability-experienced travellers, emotional elements are still more important in three of the four countries investigated. This implies that emotional appeals have a higher influence on booking intention. Therefore, experienced tourists do no not mainly process information about sustainability systematically as proposed in Hypothesis 1.

In a next step, the preferences are analysed. The preference share shows how often a single level of an attribute was chosen if this specific level of the attribute was included in the choice set. Table 3 shows the results of the between group Chi-square test, testing if the preferences are different in the two sub-groups. Generally, the preferences are the same for experienced and non-experienced tourists and they do not differ from the preferences as shown in Wehrli *et al.* [6]. They find that the respondents prefer an emotional communication of the sustainability, that they are overall indifferent about the emotionality of the communication about standard product features, that there is only a small significant preference for more rational texts in Switzerland, Germany and the USA and that respondent do not show a preference for including a graph explaining the sustainability of the product.

Table 3 shows that the only significant differences between experienced and non-experienced tourists are the preferences about the inclusion of a graph in Germany and USA and about the "none" option in all countries.

The preferences for a graph are different between the two groups in Germany and USA (Table 4). However, the preferences do not show a significant result within the sustainability-experienced tourist group. Therefore, sustainability-experienced travellers in Germany and USA are indifferent about the inclusion of a graph explaining the sustainability of the product compared to the verbal explanation of the same information. However, non-experienced travellers clearly prefer verbal communication.

Table 3: Comparison of preferences.

	Germany (n = 754)	Switzerland (n = 751)	UK (n = 751)	USA (n = 750)
Graph	$p < 0.01$	n.s.	n.s.	$p < 0.01$
Picture	n.s.	n.s.	n.s.	n.s.
Text sustainability emotional	n.s.	n.s.	n.s.	n.s.
Standard text emotional	n.s.	n.s.	n.s.	n.s.
Text sustainability rational	n.s.	n.s.	n.s.	n.s.
None	$p < 0.05$	$p < 0.01$	$p < 0.01$	$p < 0.01$

Table 4: Preferences for a graph in Germany and USA.

Graph	Germany			USA		
	Total	Experienced	Non-Exp.	Total	Experienced	Non-Exp.
Total respondents	754	100	654	750	58	692
No Graph	48.1%	44.4%	48.7%	47.8%	44.5%	48.1%
Graph included	38.2%	45.3%	37.1%	38.4%	48.7%	37.5%
Within Att. Chi-Square	51.626	0.054	61.257	46.51	0.651	54.147
D.F.	1	1	1	1	1	1
Significance	$p < 0.01$	n.s.	$p < 0.01$	$p < 0.01$	n.s.	$p < 0.01$
Between Group Chi-Square	9.857			8.499		
D.F.	1			1		
Significance	$p < 0.01$			$p < 0.01$		

5 Conclusions

By using an empirical approach to differentiate amongst tourists who have already booked a sustainable tourism product (sustainability-experienced travellers) compared to those who have not, this explorative study shows limited differences in preferences for communication styles. Therefore, emotional communication is mostly preferred by both groups. The only difference in group preferences is the inclusion of a graph explaining the product's sustainability. Non-experienced travellers don't prefer such a graph in all four countries examined, whereas sustainability-experienced respondents are indifferent about this feature in Germany and in the USA.

However, some changes in the importance of the attributes of the choice experiment are observed. Generally, the importance for rational textual communication elements about the sustainability is higher and the importance of the graph is much lower for sustainability-experienced tourists compared to non-experienced tourist in all countries. However, emotional communication elements have still higher importances in USA, Switzerland and Germany. This indicates that experienced tourists also process sustainability information in a heuristic way. The only exception is the UK where the rational textual communication element about the sustainability is the most important textual element.

The fact that no large differences are observed amongst the groups investigated could be explained by considering findings from other researchers. For example, Lee and Moscardo [30] empirically investigated how a tourist's environmental knowledge, awareness, attitudes and behavioural intentions changed after the visit of an ecotourism resort. Overall, they found "few significant differences in respondents' environmental awareness, attitudes, and preferences". Such results also suggest that previous experience does not have a large impact on overall perceptions about the broader sustainability topic. Therefore, it may be conceivable that tourists do not process information significantly more systematically in most cases, since their expertise (about sustainable tourism product attributes) has not really augmented. Hence, it may be plausible to conclude that communication needs and requirements might be only slightly different for tourists who can be broadly classified as "sustainability-experienced tourists" in general.

According to the findings of this study the following recommendations can be suggested for the broader tourism industry:

-   At least some parts of textual messages about the sustainability should be written more rationally for sustainability-experienced travellers than for non-experienced customers, because this element seems to have a higher importance in the decision process of experienced travellers. Therefore, additional rational information about the sustainability of the product should be delivered. However, emotional communication of the sustainability is still the most important textual part in most countries (except UK).

-    The graph explaining the sustainability of the offer has still a high influence on the booking decision, but the importance is clearly lower compared to the non-experienced travellers. Additionally, the respondents are indifferent between including a graph and the textual explanation in Germany and the USA. Therefore, the inclusion of a graph does not harm bookings in these countries. It might even increase booking intention if the graph is designed in a less business-like way since we believe that the preferences for a graph could be more positive if the graph is more congruent with enjoying holidays and not with daily business as it was designed in this choice experiment.

This paper generally shows no large main differentiation according to experience. The authors consider that there could be a differentiation about best communication styles according to values and attitudes, and social norms of tourists. However, this study did not include these variables, and it is still not clear if these variables explain actual behaviour (Yoon et al. [31]), since the attitude-behaviour gap has been shown in several studies (Antimova et al. [32], Eijgelaar [33], Hares et al. [34], McKercher et al. [35], Cohen and Higham [36]). One of the reasons that this gap is especially severe in the case of tourism is that tourists even tend to suspend their sustainable attitudes of their everyday life during their holidays (Becken [37], Weaver [38]). The attitude behaviour gap is another limitation of this study since the method used is a method of stated preferences. Therefore, the authors are unsure if the respondents actually bought the product in reality. However, they can at least confirm that some communication styles are more effective from a relative viewpoint.

Furthermore, online surveys are prone to self-selection bias (Dolnicar et al. [39]) and the graph may have been too prominent in the choice experiment applied in this study. Therefore, the authors consider that this might have led to an overestimation of the importance of the graph as the picture and the graph had the same size in order to ensure the readability of the graph in the experiment. Normally, pictures would cover a higher part of the surface of a page in a travel brochure.

References

[1]   Dolnicar, S., Nature-conserving tourists: The need for a broader perspective. *Anatolia,* **17(2)**, pp. 235-256, 2006.

[2]   Young, W., Hwang, K., McDonald, S., & Oates, C., Sustainable consumption: green consumer behaviour when purchasing products. *Sustainable Development,* **18(1)**, pp. 20-31, 2010.

[3]   Cherian, Jacob, & Jolly, Jacob., Green marketing: A study of consumers' attitude towards environment friendly products. *Asian Social Science,* **8(12)**, 2012.

[4]   Han, H., Hsu, L., & Sheu, C., Application of the Theory of Planned Behaviour to green hotel choice: testing the effect of environmental friendly activities. *Tourism Management,* **31**, pp. 325-334, 2010.

[5]   Lee, J., Hsu, L., Han, H., & Kim, Y., Understanding how consumers view green hotels: how a hotel's image can influence behavioural intentions. *Journal of Sustainable Tourism*, **18(7)**, pp. 901-914, 2010.

[6]   Wehrli, R., Demarmels, S., Priskin, J., Schaffner, D., Schwarz, J., Truniger, F. & Stettler, J., Effective communications of sustainable tourism products to guests. *ITW Working Paper*. Lucerne University of Applied Sciences and Arts: Lucerne, 2013.

[7]   Dolnicar, S. & Leisch, F., Selective marketing for environmentally sustainable tourism, *Tourism Management*, **29**, pp. 672-680, 2008.

[8]   Fairweather, J. R., Maslin, C., & Simmons, D. G., Environmental values and response to ecolabels among international visitors to New Zealand. *Journal of Sustainable Tourism*, **13(1)**, pp. 82-98, 2005.

[9]   Dolnicar, S., Insight into sustainable tourists in Austria: Data based a priori segmentation approach. *Journal of Sustainable Tourism*, **12(3)**, pp. 209-218, 2004.

[10]   Wehrli, R., Egli, H., Lutzenberger, M., Pfister, D., Stettler, J., Tourists' understanding of sustainable tourism: An analysis in eight countries. *GSTF Journal on Business Review* **2(2)**, pp. 219-224, 2012.

[11]   Chaiken, S., The heuristic model of persuasion. In M. P. Zanna & J. M. Olson (Eds.), Social influence: The Ontario symposium, Vol. 5., pp. 3-39. Mahwah: Lawrence Erlbaum Associates, N.J, 1987.

[12]   Tversky, A. & Kahnemann, D., Extensional versus intuitive reasoning: The conjunction fallacy in probability judgment. In T. Gilovich & D. Griffin (Eds.), Heuristics and Biases: The Psychology of Intuitive Judgment. pp. 19-48. New York: Cambridge University Press, 2002.

[13]   Petty, R. E., & Cacioppo, J. T., The elaboration likelihood model of persuasion. In L. Berkowitz (Ed.), Advances in experimental social psychology. pp. 123-205. San Diego, CA: Academic Press, 1986.

[14]   Bless, H., Bohner, G., Schwarz, N., & Strack, F., Mood and persuasion: A cognitive response analysis. *Personality and Social Psychology Bulletin,* **16(2)**, pp. 331-345, 1990.

[15]   Pham, M. T., The Logic of Feeling. *Journal of Consumer Psychology,* **14(4)**, pp. 360-369, 2004.

[16]   Chen, S. & Chaiken, S., The heuristic-systematic model in its broader context. In S. Chaiken & Y. Trope (Eds.), Dual-process Theories in Social Psychology. pp. 73-96. New York: Guilford Press, 1999.

[17]   Pacini, R. & Epstein, S., The Relation of Rational and Experiential Information Processing Styles to Personality, Basic Beliefs, and the Ratio-Bias Phenomenon. *Journal of Personality and Social Psychology,* **76(6)**, pp. 972-987, 1999.

[18]   Sloman, S. A. The Empirical Case for Two Systems of Reasoning. *Psychological Bulletin,* **119(1)**, pp. 3-22, 1996.

[19]   Chaiken, S., Heuristic versus systematic information processing and the use of source versus message cues in persuasion. *Journal of Personality & Social Psychology,* **39(5)**, pp. 752-766, 1980.

[20] Chaiken, S. & Stangor, C., Attitude and attitude change. In M. R. Rosenzweig & L. W. Porter (Eds.), *Annual Review of Psychology*. **38**, pp. 575-630, 1987.

[21] Mackie, D. M., & Worth, L. T., Processing deficits and the mediation of positive affect in persuasion. *Journal of Personality and Social Psychology*, **57(1)**, pp. 27-40, 1989.

[22] Mackie, D. M., & Worth, L. T., Feeling good, but not thinking straight: The impact of positive mood on persuasion. In J. P. Forgas (Ed.), *Emotion and Social Judgments. International Series in Experimental Social Psychology*. pp. 201-219. Elmsford, NY: Pergamon Press, 1991.

[23] Bohner, G., Chaiken, S., & Hunyadi, P., The role of mood and message ambiguity in the interplay of heuristic and systematic processing. *European Journal of Social Psychology*, **24(1)**, pp. 207-221, 1994.

[24] Demarmels, S., *Ja. Nein. Schweiz. Schweizer Abstimmungsplakate im 20. Jahrhundert*, Konstanz, UVK, 2009.

[25] Holbrook, M. B. & Batra, R., Assessing the Role of Emotions as Mediators of Consumer Responses to Advertising. *Journal of Consumer Research*, **14,** pp. 404-420, 1987.

[26] Mehrabian, A. & Russel, J. A., The basic emotional impact of environments. *Perceptual and Motor Skills*, **38**, pp. 283-301, 1974.

[27] Rosselli, F., Skelly, J. J. & Mackie, D. M., Processing Rational and Emotional Messages: The Cognitive and Affective Mediation of Persuasion. *Journal of Experimental Social Psychology*, **31**, pp. 163-190, 1995.

[28] Hair, J. F., Anderson, R. E., Tatham, R. L. & Black, W. C., *Multivariate Data Analysis with Readings*, Englewood Cliffs: New Jersey, Prentice Hall, 1995.

[29] Orme, B., *Getting Started with Conjoint Analysis: Strategies for Product Design and Pricing Research*, Research Publishers LLC: Madison, 2010.

[30] Lee, W. H., & Moscardo, G., Understanding the impact of Ecotourism resort experience on tourist's environmental attitudes and behavioural intentions. *Journal of Sustainable Tourism*, **23(6)**, pp. 546-565, 2005.

[31] Yoon, J. I., Kyle, G., J., Van Riper, C. J. & Sutton, S. G., Climate Change and environmentally responsible behavior on the Great Barrier Reef, Australia. *Proceedings of the 2010 Northeastern Recreation Research Symposium*, 2010.

[32] Antimova, R., Nawijin, J. & Peeters, P., The awareness/attitude-gap in sustainable tourism: a theoretical perspective. *Tourism Review*, **67**, pp. 7-16, 2012.

[33] Eijgelaar, E., Voluntary carbon offsets a solution of reducing tourism emissions? Assessment of communication aspects and mitigation potential. *EJTIR*, **11**, pp. 281-296, 2011.

[34] Hares, A., Dickinson, J. & Wilkes, K., Climate change and the air travel decisions of UK tourists. *Journal of Transport Geography*, **18**, pp. 466-473, 2010.

[35] McKercher, B., Prideaux, B., Cheung, C. & Law, R., Achieving voluntary reductions in the carbon footprint of tourism and climate change. *Journal of Sustainable Tourism,* **18**, pp. 297-317, 2010.

[36] Cohen, S. A. & Higham, J. E. S., Eyes wide shut? UK consumer perceptions on avation climate impacts and travel decisions to New Zealand. *Current Issues in Tourism,* **12**, pp. 1-19, 2010.

[37] Becken, S., Tourists' Perception of International Air Travel's Impact on the Global Climate and Potential Climate Change Policies. *Journal of Sustainable Tourism,* **15**, pp. 351-368, 2007.

[38] Weaver, D. B., *Reflections on sustainable tourism and paradigm change,* USA: Routledge, 2008.

[39] Dolnicar, S., Laesser, C. & Matus, K., Online versus Paper, Format Effects in Tourism Surveys. *Journal of Travel Research,* **47**, pp. 295-316, 2009.

Sustaining tourism in South African game farms: the benefits of ownership of restituted land by African communities

M. P. Sebola
Department of Public Administration,
University of Limpopo, South Africa

Abstract

The purpose of this paper is to argue that land restituted for ownership by black communities in South Africa is unable to attract tourists compared to previous private ownership. The South African government introduced land restitution through their land reform policy in order to redistribute land equally to South African communities. Equally, the process as viewed from the critics' perspective; the land reform process portrays an image of a country that is taking over land from ownership of white minority class to ownership by Africans. Ownership of land in the country was racially skewed with 87% of productive land owned by the white people in the country with Africans congested to 13% of infertile and unproductive land. The Land Restitution Act of 1994 was passed to ensure that Africans are beneficiaries of new land allocation through the willing buyer willing seller principle. The ownership of land by Africans (Blacks) is viewed to a particular extent as being responsible for low economic output from game farms as compared to ownership by previous owners. This paper is conceptual and intends to investigate and establish the cause and reasons of low output of game farms through tourism. The purpose of this paper is to propose a useful model that South Africa could adopt for the benefit of new owners who are exclusively black. This paper therefore concludes that a new approach by the government aimed at promoting economic activities of game farmers (black game beneficiaries) is possible through continuous monitoring, mentoring, support and enforcement of good managerial practices of the Communal Property Associations.

Keywords: land reform, land restitution, game farm, tourism, communal property association.

WIT Transactions on Ecology and The Environment, Vol 187, © 2014 WIT Press
www.witpress.com, ISSN 1743-3541 (on-line)
doi:10.2495/ST140021

1   Introduction

The South African government introduced a willing-buyer willing-seller principle to attract white farmers that voluntarily wanted to sell their farms to the government at current market related value. That was a peaceful manner of resolving the land inequality problems in which bought land is returned to the black communities previously removed through past racial legislation. Some farmers sold to the government their game farms as per requirements of the willing buyer willing seller principle. Such farms were given over to the new management of black communities through Communal Property Associations as established by those communities in terms of the requirements of the law. The ownership by new beneficiaries has been to a particular extent responsible for low economic output from such farms as compared to ownership by previous owners. This is a conceptual paper based on literature analysis and it raises the following question: Are there quantifiable benefits generated from restituted lands in South Africa to benefit the government and the local people? In addressing the question posed, this paper will keep its relevance to the following aspects; the land reform process in South Africa, the political Significance of land restitution in South Africa, game farms and tourism in South Africa, Communal Property Associations and Game farm management models, Benefits from restituted farms and possible options for solution.

2   South Africa's land reform and restitution

South Africa's land reform processes follow two processes: The land restitution by which Africans were dispossessed of their land in 1913 and the redistribution of land to deal with hunger and land ownership inequality (African National Congress [1]). The *Land Restitution Act of 1994* in South Africa (which is a focus of this paper) gives the black communities the opportunity to claim back their land lost because of the implementation of the *Native Land Act of 1913* by the previous apartheid regime which caused skewed patterns of land ownership in the country characterising the South African land ownership environment even today. The *Native Land Act of 1913* prohibited Africans (Blacks) from owning land outside the rural reserves which only constituted 13% of the South African land (Bradstock [2], Velente [3], South African Institute of Race Relations [4]). It has been argued that the said 13% was indeed given to Africans based on the geological survey done and confirmed that the portions are indeed infertile and unproductive. The African people then lacked that knowledge of science. And therefore were removed and compensated with areas where no reasonable agricultural or economic activities are likely to take place. The selected productive and fertile land (87%) was therefore reserved for the white minority class so that they can practice productive agriculture and sound economic activities for the country. That is a move which by design aimed to portray Africans as less economically productive citizens against their white counterparts. By design such system meant to subject African people to being job seekers to white commercial farmers and was not to engage in any sound economic activities except for those that will subject their produce to the white commercial farmers. The worst part of the *Native Land Act of 1913* was that even though an African can afford a property but was not allowed to buy a farm from a white man and therefore could not own a property within the 87% demarcated area allocated to white ownership.

For purposes of nation building, reconciliation and peace the African National Congress (ANC) introduced the *Land Restitution Act of 1994* as a peaceful means to achieve land redistribution by striving for equity in property ownership. The willing buyer willing seller principle was a peaceful gesture than the violence and discriminatory manner by which the white minority government took land from the Africans in the past. This principle yielded some goods results in the sense that some farmers voluntarily sold their farms to the government as required, but on the same note most white minority farmers in the country did not respond positively to the gesture as suggested and therefore are said to be delaying the objectives of the Land Restitution Act that a particular percentage of farm ownership by Africans should have been achieved at some stage. According to Metelerkamp [5] and South African History Online [6] the government intended to achieve a 30% land allocation to Africans by 2014, an objective which thus far sound impossible to achieve since it risks a budget shortfall of 72 billion rands (Paul [7]). On the other hand farms that are already owned by African farmers are denoted negative and are said to have been responsible for economic loss in agricultural production of the country. Tourists' intake in game farms is argued to be going down with unsustainable features of profit losses and managerial problems in which restituted farms are either occupied by few families or are completely disserted. Hall [8] argues that most restituted farms are either underutilised or are used for less productive activities such as grazing land. Such activities are subjecting the efforts of the South African land reform into nothing other than an economic loss of agricultural commodities of the land.

3   The political significance of land restitution in South Africa

The issue of land restitution in South Africa is mainly viewed from its political significance other than economics of land redistribution. Brandon [9] showed that from the period 1994–2013 the government of South Africa has spent approximately R25.72 billion. It is known, however, that land was always a central political denominator for African struggle against the white settlers (Kariuki [10]). Land issue in South Africa and other parts of Africa as a whole is still a highly political matter in the country because of the manner by which it was taken from the local people. The politically conscious manner by which the South African government is handling land issue is criticised by both the external communities and the local as a manner that could results in political turmoil in future. Unlike the Zimbabwean arrangements of the Lancaster House Agreement (Lancaster House Agreement [11], Africa All Party Parliamentary Group [12]), in which the British government promised the Zimbabwean government compensation on behalf of its citizens in Zimbabwe, the South

African government on its own promised to take care of the costs of redress for its own people. This was mainly a move to fulfill reconciliation and on the other hand repossessing the land from the white minority in a peaceful and human manner as possible.

Fourie and Schoeman [13] are of the opinion that land restitution of South Africa which cannot be viewed outside the political environment should be seen as a vehicle for socio-economic empowerment for black people than mere settling of claims. The settlement of these claims is however not viewed outside the perspective of political revenge by the previous beneficiaries of the system who accused the present government for implementing apartheid in reverse by taking land from selected race of whites' people. The adopted approach by the South African government of willing buyer willing seller principle is criticised for its humanitarian approach which according to Sangonet [14] is giving former land owners an option of either not selling or selling the farms to the government at exorbitant prices. The South African government is however trying its best to find a reasonable political solution which in turn the African citizen view as being too soft against people who took the land violently from its owners. To a particular extent the South Africans feels that the Zimbabwean- Mugabe route is better in situation like this where the approach is delaying the government to achieve its set objectives. On other hand as England [15] attests is that the land reform process in South Africa is very slow- but those that were given land also are struggling with lack of resources to manage their claimed farms successfully.

It can be argued that the South African government approach to land restitution is more informed by politics of reconciliation than politics of revenge. In trying to resolve land claim as a political problem in South Africa the government tries by all means to satisfy the needs and interests of both the white minority farmers and the African majority who claims that the occupied land by famers rightfully belongs to them. This is shown by the government willingness to pay in financial terms the claiming society than giving them a farm (White [16]) or providing an alternative farm to the claimants other than removing a farmer (Stickler [17]). This means that a political settlement would have been achieved other than removing a farmer from the land he is tilling and producing for the country. It is not clearly known however whether the government would have sustainable resources to buy farms for both the whites and Africans demanding compensation either in the form of money or land or an alternative land. It may seem from the practical South African experience that the government is not coping with either of the available options its sets for the land restitution process. Weideman [18] and Lahiff [19] argue that the land reform of South Africa has completely failed to achieve set objectives by long margins which include inability to achieve targeted percentage before 2014 and the dominance of agriculture by similar commercial farmers(white minority group). It is therefore possible to conclude that the political solution used by the current government in solving land issues is not progressive. The likelihood is that solving land issues by balancing the interests of white farmers and the anticipated aggrieved African farmers on similar scale is derailing the progress of land reform and rendering the countries land reform policies ineffective.

Whether the land reform is meant to achieve a political objective or otherwise the economic considerations are equally also important. Of significance in land acquisition is its ability to sustain the economics of its agriculture. Restituted game farms in South Africa are heavily affected by land claims controversies and therefore threatening their economic potential through tourism that used to sustain them.

4   Game farms and tourism in South Africa

Van der Merwe and Saayman [20] define a game farm as an adequately fenced land, with a variety of game species that can be used for hunting, photographic opportunities, environmental education, meat production, life game sales and which provides infrastructure and superstructures for eco tourists. Game farms are an important part of what is called rural tourism (Viljoen and Tlabela [21]) which unlike other conventional forms of tourism which are not pro-poor in approach. Game farms in South Africa are major contributors to tourism related activities through both hunting and accommodation provision. Game hunting in South Africa plays a significant contribution into the local economy (Langholz and Kerley [22], Saayman et al. [23]) through seasonal employment of game guides and buying of local products by tourists.

The game industry in South Africa rests on three pillars (hunting, game trade and eco-tourism) which are highly driven by trophy and biltong hunting (Cloete et al. [24]). The economic contributions statistics of game farms are that in 2005 trophy hunting generated R417 million, biltong hunting 2.3 billion while life game auctions contributed R93.5 million to game ranchers therefore making game farming in South Africa the most attractive tourism economic related activity. Child et al. [25] indicated that trophy hunting alone generate billions of dollars in South African revenue. And such dollars are significant for the South African economy in a diverse manner.

South Africa because of its rich biodiversity is a preferred tourist destination for nature and eco-tourists (Sebola [26]). According to Carruthers [27] South Africa is the third most bio diverse nation in the globe. With the exclusion of national parks and other government managed tourists attractions in the country, private game farms are said to be very effective in attracting international tourists because they are meant to achieve a maximum profit for their owners and benefit the local communities in a manner that is either direct or indirect. Most private game farms have high class accommodation facilities and effective management structures compared to government managed attractions which do not exists for purposes of profit.

South Africa is reportedly having closer to 9000 private game farms registered and about 6000 which are unregistered or in the process of registration (Cousins et al. [28]; Child et al. [25]) and its economic contributions to tourism is increasing at a larger scale while normal agricultural farming is showing a significant decline in revenue. Smith and Wilson [29] have noted that South Africa have shifted from pastoralism to game farming as early as in the 1980s. This move shows that game farming has always been considered significant for long in South Africa. It is however the same move which has resulted in land dispossessions for local Africans that resulted in land ownership disparity in the country. Most literature on the practice of conservation in South Africa argues that the government forcibly removed the locals from their areas in order to make space for nature conservation reserves without providing alternative means of survival for the dispossessed communities. That has often raised serious political questions like how do you entertain the tourists at the expense of landless South Africans who are barred from the vicinity of their own land? Other than the politics of land dispossessions, game farming is arguably a rising mode of tourism related activity in South Africa. And this rising tourism mode is currently highly affected by the land claims processes which to a particular extent land offered under the restitution legislation are unable to attract tourists because of the lowered standards under the management of Communal Property Associations which shows little interest in further development of the already existing infrastructure.

5   Game farming and land claims

Ironically in South Africa the land claimants targeted only economically active conservation areas, game farms and agricultural lands. This kind of approach in land claims was criticised by minority farm owners who accused the claimants of only wishing to take land that is already economically developed and leaving the less developed farms. The peaceful approach of land claim in South Africa is often likened to the Zimbabwean situation in which the war veterans only attacked and repossessed violently only farms that were well developed with good technologies and machineries. That is the behaviour which thus far has risked the economic stability of Zimbabwe which is a direction the South African people are avoiding at all costs. South Africa is very conscious in dealing with issues that will destabilise the tourism potential of a country. It is acknowledged that historically the country managed to move tourism contribution to the economy from 4% to closer to 10% in post-apartheid South Africa. Manji [30] however argues that the whole behaviour of violent takeover of lands by modern societies has all to do with the realisation that the civil handling of land issue in Africa does not want to see its conclusion therefore violent take over by the dispossessed becomes legitimate. In South Africa very few of the land claimed seems to be sustainably used by the new beneficiaries. Their management are often queried and criticised as contributing to low economic output in comparison to economic performance of the previous owners. One of the few successful cases of land claims and benefits in South Africa is of the Makuleke Community at the Kruger National Park and it differs from other cases in the country (Spenceley [31]) in the sense that the Makuleke land claims achieved wider media coverage and sympathy from many institutions. Other than that the Makuleke Community made a land claim against a national park other than a simple game farm or a non- economic provincial nature reserve in which the management never included the local communities. The Kruger National Park established a Social ecology unit to work in collaboration with the same communities in the 1980s (Spenceley [32]) almost fourteen years before the formalisation of the land claims in the country. This may therefore imply that the Makuleke Community have indeed benefitted from the benefits of conservation at the Kruger National Park long before their successful land claim against the Kruger National Park management. This can therefore be treated as an isolated case of land restitution.

6   Communal Property Associations and game farm management models

Most land claimant's beneficiaries in South Africa prefer the model of managing claimed farms through the Communal Property Association (CPA) model than the Community Trusts (CT). The CPA model is preferred because it is democratic in the sense that it has an established constitution in which the term of office for office bearers may have a prescribed term other than the Community Trusts that will put ownership of land under the trust of a chief. Chieftainship is not significantly trusted since Chiefs often uses the communities' funds for own benefit than the people and that Chiefs are traditionally not supposed to account to their subjects.

There are commonly three partnership models that are used in farm management practice to benefit the dispossessed (Aliber and Maluleke [33]) and at the same time increasing the possibility of the economic productivity of the distributed land. Those are farm worker share equity schemes (in which land redistribution applicants are awarded grants to purchase equity in a going concern and become part of the farm management); strategic partnerships (in which an operating company is created and the community owns half or more of the share and the strategic partnership balance in which the agricultural land operates through a lease agreement wherein the present owner is expected to transfer skills and employ beneficiary communities); and, the out-grower schemes (in which the small-scale farmers are linked to an agro-processor). The adoptions of any of these models are not a problem *per se*, but the unknown nature of these models by the dispossessed beneficiaries could poses economic challenges that the ruling party does not seek to confront. However at small-scales, these models have not only been applied to improve the efficiency of farm land for the dispossessed in South Africa, but have also been attempted in communal nature reserves without significant successes (Sebola [34]). To a larger extent most South African beneficiary communities spent most of their time arguing with their Communal Property Associations (CPA) about which model to adopt and often failing to delegate their representatives to enter into such unknown contracts on their behalf. As a result, acquired land properties end up being unprofitably used. To those beneficiary communities in which the CPA succeeded in entering into contracts with partners to improve the effectiveness of the claimed agricultural land, members of the beneficiary communities have continued to hold negligible knowledge and skills about the activities taking place in their farms. As such the tourism potential of such game farms becomes impossible to operate effectively. Barry [35] also noted that the other causes of conflict in claimed land come to the fore when other beneficiaries considers themselves to be rightful beneficiaries than others. Those ultimately limit the farms ability to sustain its usability to benefit the targeted beneficiaries.

7 Benefits from restituted game farms

The benefit of the South African communities from the land restitution programme is very complex. Up to so far they have been many challenges of disputes among beneficiaries of land claimed. South African Institute of Race Relations [4] noted that the fact that the claimed land is owned by the community than by individual community members is a flaw on its own. It could be argued that a farm can only function effectively if it is owned by an individual than a group. The farm and its property need an individual who can accept a full responsibility of running costs of the farm business. Thus far in communal lands of South Africa meant for either game farming or agricultural farming of any type the communities running the farms are failing to take financial responsibilities of maintaining the farm claimed. That ultimately led to members leaving the given land with dysfunctional facilities which will affect its economic productivity. Dikganga and Muchapondwa [36] argue that a land reform programme is measured by its success in bringing about wealth, consumption and income to the beneficiaries. In the South African situation such a claim might be difficult to make considering the fact that more beneficiaries of such land claims deserted the claimed lands which automatically denounces their membership of the communal land. While land is a rare commodity and a requirement for economic benefits, but restituted game farms in South Africa are not able to make an expected economic benefits to the targeted communities as expected.

The end results of game farm management through CPA's are that only the minority groups within the beneficiary communities knows what is going on in claimed farms. Bennett [37] mentioned that CPA's are supposed to be accountable institutions in local resources management. To a particular extent the CPA's existence as a structure of local resource management often are in conflict with the tribal institutions under which such land claims have been made. That ultimately made the benefits from claimed farm difficult to measure and attests. Chairpersons of CPA's often claim to report the farm activities directly to the Director-General of Land Affairs than to the Community and the Chiefs. The accountability part of the CPA's therefore becomes questionable. Not only is this a problem to the communities concerned, but it is also a problem for the government that has authorised or bought on behalf of the community an economically active game farms which have not lost their productive value. Most farms acquired through the land restitution are dysfunctional and their one time attractive facilities are in a state of dilapidation. There is low tourists intake and therefore their role as tourism destinations are not sustainable anymore. Although communal lands under the CPA's are meant for agricultural purposes than residential (McCusker [38]), there has been a lot of conflict among community members whom others feel they should be for residential settlement while others are arguing for grazing land usage only.

8   Are there available options?

The options between the political and economic route is not easy to take. The land restitution process should move from its political perspective towards economic considerations. Governments of colonial history such as South Africa find it difficult to consider economic issues against political issues. More often than not political considerations supersede the economic considerations. The reality is that people do not eat political talks than economic difficulties facing them on daily basis. It is understandable that land ownership disparity is a serious political concern of governments' administration, but of significance is that economic realities should not be discounted in the process. It is a fact that governments have always disregarded the interests of the local communities against the needs of the tourists, therefore meeting their economic needs and caring less about the satisfaction level of the local communities. Rolston [39] has argued that there should be a balance between tourism interests and those of the community. In this instance the South African government need to balance the political needs of the people on land ownership as against the economic needs of the country to support the same people. Thus far there is a great imbalance of land distribution issues. However not enough, but literature on game farming show that game ranching contributed a lot in the tourism economy through accommodations (lodges), hunting and game auctions (Cloete *et al.* [24]) in the previous years. The economically deteriorating status of some restituted game farms are likely to take the tourism potential of the country down and results in major economic loss for a country. Options are indeed difficult to either retain the unequal ownership of land in the country or to compromise the economic potential of restituted game farms. A recommended solution in this case is that an approach be reconsidered in which restituted game farms can be allocated responsible entrepreneurs who will account to the government on their activities. The government should on regular basis audit the benefits of the restituted farms to the intended beneficiaries in which remedial actions should be taken if they are not measurable.

9   Conclusion

This paper argues that game farms obtained by communities through land restitution in the country are not beneficial to the intended communities. Neither are they beneficial to the South African government in economic terms. Game ranching or rather game farming has a good record of contributing to the tourism economy in many forms which are either direct or indirect. Directly the contributions are through accommodations game hunting and game auctions. Indirect contributions are through employment, buying of local goods by tourists and local filling stations. Of significance also is the contributions top government by means of taxations. Information gathered from literature analysis on the subject of enquiry shows that indeed the game farms obtained through restitution requires a new approach by the South African government in order to benefit either government or the intended beneficiaries or both.

References

[1]   African National Congress. Policy on the Restitution of Land Right. http://www.anc.org.za/show.php?id+228.

[2]   Bradstock, A., Changing Livelihoods and Land Reform: Evidence from the Northern Cape Province of South Africa. *World Development*, 33 (11), 1979-1991, 2005.

[3]   Velente, C., The food (In) Security Impact of Land Redistribution in South Africa: Micro econometric Evidence. *World Development*, 37 (9), 1540-1553, 2009.

[4]   South African Institute of Race Relations (NCP). Restitution of Land Rights Amendment Bill, 1-13, 2013.

[5]   Metelerkamp, L., Land Reform in South Africa: Reflections on Indian Experience. Institute of Sustainability, 1-23, 2011.

[6]   South African History Online. Timeline of Land Dispossession and Restitution in South Africa 1995-2013. http://www.sahistory.org.za.

[7]   Paul, D., Analysis: Land Reform or Restitution, that is the question. Daily Maverick. http://www.dailymaverick.co.za/2011-05-04.

[8]   Hall, R., The Impact of Land Restitution and Land Reform on Livelihoods. School of Government, University of Western Cape, 1-22, 2007.

[9]   Brandon, E., Parliamentary Exhibitions: 'South Africa, our Land – The 1913 Land Act: One Hundred Years On'. Republic of South Africa, Pretoria, 1-11, 2013.

[10]   Karuiki, S., Agrarian Reform, Rural Development and Governance in Africa: A Case of Eastern and Southern Africa. Centre for Policy Studies, 2009.

[11]   Lancaster House Agreement. Southern Rhodesia Constitutional Conference. London, 1-51, 1979.

[12]   Africa All Party Parliamentary Group. Land in Zimbabwe: Past Mistakes, Future Prospects. 1-52, 2009.

[13]   Fourie, D.J. & Schoeman, L., Local Government and Sustainable Post-Settlement Support for Restitution: in Search of Efficient Governance Objectives in Public Administration. *Journal of Public Administration*, 45 (1.1), 145-161, 2010.

[14]   Sangonet. http://www.ngopulse.org/article/land-redistribution-case-land-reform-south-africa.

[15]   England, A., South Africa's Black Farmers Struggle with Land Reform. http://www.ft.com/intl/cms/s/0/efb94b78-5bf2-11e3-00144feabdc0.html.

[16] White, M.J., Land Claims and Restitution in South Africa: The Valuation Perspective. 4th Pacific Rim Real Estate Society Conference, Perth, 1-8, 1998.

[17] Stickler, M.M., Land Restitution in South Africa. World Resources Institution, 1-8, 2012.

[18] Weideman, M., Who Shaped South Africa's Land Reform Policy? *Politikon,* 31 (2), 219-238.

[19] Lahiff, E., Land Reform in South Africa: A Status Report. Programme for Land and Agrarian Studies, 1-42, 2008.

[20] Van der Merwe, P., & Saayman, M., Game Farms as Sustainable Ecotourist Attractions'. *Koedoe,* 48 (2), 2005.

[21] Viljoen, J., & Tlabela, K., Rural Tourism Development in South Africa. Human Science Research Council, Cape Town, 2007.

[22] Langholz, J.A., & Kerley, G.I.H., Combining Conservation and Development on Private Lands: An Assessment of Ecotourism-Based Private Game Reserves in the Eastern Cape. Center for African Ecology, 56, 2006.

[23] Saayman, M., van der Merwe & Rossouw, R., The Impact of Hunting for Biltong Purposes on the SA Economy. *Acta Commercii,* 1-11, 2011.

[24] Cloete, P.C., Taljaard, P.R., & Grove, B., A Comparative Economic Case Study of Switching from Cattle Farming to Game Ranching in the Northern Cape Province. *South African Journal of Wildlife Research,* 37 (1), 71-78, 2007.

[25] Child, B.A., Musengezi, J., Parent, G.D., & Child, G.f.T., The Economics and Institutional Economics of Wildlife on Private Land in Africa. *Pastoralism Journal,* 2 (18), 2012.

[26] Sebola, M.P., Ecotourism in South Africa: Potential, Opportunity and Politics. Journal of Public Administration, 43 (1), 59-71, 2008.

[27] Carruthers, J., "Wilding the Farm or Farming the Wild"? The Evolution of Scientific Game Ranching in South Africa from the 1960s to the Present. Transactions of Royal Society of South Africa, 63 (2), 159-181, 2008.

[28] Cousins, J.A., Sadler, J.P., & Evans, J., Exploring the Role of Private Wildlife Ranching as a Conservation Tool in Soul Africa: Stakeholder Perspectives. Ecology and Society, 13 (2), 1-16.

[29] Smith, N., & Wilson, S.L., Changing Land Use Trends in the Thicket Biome: Pastoralism to Game Farming. Territorial Ecology Research Unit, 38, 1-22, 2002.

[30] Manji, A., Land Reform in the Shadow of the State: the Implementation of New Land Laws in Sub-Saharan Africa. Oxfarm, Addis Ababa, 1-11, 2001.

[31] Spenceley, A., Tourism, local livelihoods, and the Private Sector in South Africa: Case Studies on Growing Role of the Private Sector in Natural Resources Management. Sustainable Livelihoods in Southern Africa. Research Report 8, 1-134, 2003.

[32]   Spenceley, A, 2004. Responsible Nature Based Tourism Planning in South Africa and the Commercialisation of the Kruger National Park, in D Dimitrios (ed), Ecotourism. Learning Thomson Learning, London.

[33]   Aliber M., & Maluleke T., The role of "black capital" in revitalizing land reform in Limpopo, South Africa. *Law, Democracy and Development,* 14: 1-3, 2010.

[34]   Sebola, M.P., Community Prosperity through Local Economic Development: Maleboho Nature Reserve. Tshwane University of Technology, Pretoria, 1-2812007.

[35]   Barry, M., Dysfunctional Communal Property Associations in South Africa: the Elandskloof Case. 1-23, 2009.

[36]   Dikganga, J., & Muchapondwa, E., The Effect of Land Restitution on Poverty Reduction Among the Khomani San "Bushmen". Economic Research Southern Africa. National Treasury, Pretoria. 1-21, 2013.

[37]   Bennett, J.E., Institutions and Governance of Communal Rangelands in South Africa. *African Journal of Range & Forage Science,* 30 (1), 77-83, 2013.

[38]   McCusker, B., The Impact of Membership in Communal Property Association on Livelihoods in the Northern Province, South Africa. *GeoJournal,* 56, 113-122, 2002.

[39]   Rolston, H. Feeding People Versus Saving Nature. In Light A & Rolston H (eds). Environmental Ethics: An Analogy. Blackwell Publishing, Oxford, 2003.

Promoting sustainable tourism in the Pacific Forum Island countries

V. Saverimuttu[1,2] & M. E. Varua[2]
[1]*Australian Institute of Higher Education, Australia*
[2]*School of Business, University of Western Sydney, Australia*

Abstract

Tourism is vital to the sustainability and development of the Pacific Forum Island economies. Australia and New Zealand are major markets for these island nations followed by the US and Japan. The region is prone to tropical cyclones, in most years, typically occurring during the months of November to April. This paper investigates the impact of tourism on economic growth and its contribution to employment in Fiji, Samoa, Tonga and Vanuatu. The paper also examines the impact of income (GDP) growth in visitor origin countries (Australia, New Zealand and the US), the inertial effect on travel destination choice, investment in travel and tourism and extreme weather conditions on tourism receipts in these countries using panel data analysis. In 2012, tourism's contribution to GDP ranged between an estimated 14.2% of GDP (Tonga) and 50.7% (Vanuatu). The contribution to employment ranged between 13.8% (Tonga) and 44.9% (Vanuatu) of total employment. Travel and Tourism investment ranged between 11.1% (Tonga) of total investment and 28.1% (Fiji). The variable for investment in travel and tourism was not significant which was not surprising. The variable for extreme weather was also not significant, suggesting that other factors mitigate the impact of the seasonal cyclones on tourist arrivals. The impact of Australian GDP was significant but negative, implying that Australian tourists preferred to travel elsewhere rather than to Pacific Island destinations when their income increased. The impact of all other variables tested on tourism receipts was significant and positive. The paper concludes with recommendations to improve the long term sustainability of tourism in this region.
Keywords: tourism and economic growth, Pacific Islands, sustainable tourism, extreme weather patterns, tourism strategies.

WIT Transactions on Ecology and The Environment, Vol 187, © 2014 WIT Press
www.witpress.com, ISSN 1743-3541 (on-line)
doi:10.2495/ST140031

1   Introduction

Tourism is of vital importance to island economies, especially for those in the Pacific that lack industry and are dependent on this sector as a source of revenue, foreign currency and employment [1]. The islands in the Pacific are naturally attractive tourist destinations with their 'sun and sand' image and exotic ambience and in recent years travel and tourism forecasts for this region have been extremely favourable. In the Oceania region travel and tourism contributed 10.8% of GDP (total contribution) in 2013 and is expected to rise by 2.9% in 2014 and by 3.2% pa to US$264.8 billion in 2024 [2]. At the same time limited resources, lack of infrastructure and other development constraints, environmental vulnerabilities and the lack of proper plans and procedures hinder the sustainable development of tourism in these economies. Recognising this, the Waiheke Declaration on Sustainable Economic Development, signed in 2011 by the leaders of the Pacific Forum Island countries (FICs), includes a commitment to support growth in the tourism sector [3].

The FIC group consists of 16 self-governing independent states including Australia and New Zealand, the rest being Polynesian and Melanesian island nations in the region of Oceania. New Caledonia and French Polynesia are associate members while Tokelau, Wallis and Futuna, American Samoa, Guam and the Commonwealth of the Northern Marianas along with some international organisations such as the United Nations are Forum observers. The Forum was founded in 1971 with Australia, Cook Islands, Fiji, Nauru, New Zealand, Tonga and Samoa being the founding members. In 1996, the FIC leaders decided that annual meetings of the Forum Economic Ministers would improve regional and subregional co-operation in dealing with issues such as good governance, economic management and the ongoing sharing of experiences in economic reform. In addition this collaboration includes a stocktake and feedback mechanism which allows for the identification of areas where a greater concentration of effort and resources are required [4].

Australia and New Zealand are the major markets for the other FICs in the Oceania region followed by the US and Japan. Thus excluding Australia and New Zealand, the tourism sector contributed approximately 400,000 jobs directly and indirectly in 2012 in the remaining FICs [5]. These FICs rely on Australia and New Zealand for assistance with their development programmes. Among these countries Fiji (US$ 3,908 million in 2012) and Papua New Guinea (US$15,654 million in 2012) are the largest FICs in terms of GDP. In the rest GDP is less than US$1000 million [6]. Tourism is the key sector for income generation and socio-economic development in a number of these FICs and the vulnerability of this sector is worsened by the lack of adequate resources to fund infrastructure development as well as to prepare for the impact of climate change on the sector. The region is also prone to tropical cyclones, in most years, which typically occur during the months of November to April. Thus, these FICs require both strategic and tactical financial and non-financial assistance to ensure the long term viability of their tourism sectors. The South Pacific Tourism Organisation (SPTO) has recently commenced a capacity building programme funded by the European Development Fund (EDF) to sustainably develop the region's tourism sector [3].

This paper investigates the impact of tourism on economic growth and its contribution to employment in Fiji, Samoa, Tonga and Vanuatu. The paper also examines the impact of income (GDP) growth in visitor origin countries (Australia, New Zealand and the US), the inertial effect on travel destination choice, investment in travel and tourism and extreme weather conditions on tourism receipts in these countries using panel data analysis. The paper concludes with recommendations to improve the long term sustainability of tourism in this region.

2   Overview of selected FICs

Fiji and Vanuatu are a part of the Melanesian region while Samoa and Tonga are located in the Polynesian region. These four FICs are selected as a focus of this study partly to represent both regions of the Pacific and partly due to the great disparity in the number of tourists visiting the countries in each region. Comparative data on selected economic and tourism related indicators are reported in the Table 1 below [6–10].

Table 1: Comparative data on selected economic and tourism related indicators.

Countries	Fiji	Samoa	Tonga	Vanuatu
GDP US $ millions – 2012	3908	684	472	787
World ranking	155	181	184	177
Tourist arrivals '000s – 2011	675	121	46	94
Tourism receipts US $ millions – 2011	599.0	134.9	n.a	252.0
US $ millions – 2009	n.a	n.a	16.8	n.a
Rural population '000s	414.8	150.1	79.99	184.4
Urban population '000s	453.6	37.3	24.52	61.2
Total population '000s – 2011	868.4	187.4	104.51	245.6
FDI US$ million	204.3	14.8	10.4	58.1
GDP per capita US $ 2011	$4,325	$3,361	$4,046	$3,252
Tourism sector contribution to GDP				
- direct plus indirect contribution in 2012	35.8%	n.a	14.2%	50.7%
- direct contribution 2010		30%		
Tourism sector contribution to employment				
- direct plus indirect contribution in 2012	32.3%	n.a	13.8%	44.9%
- jobs	108,500	n.a	4,500	30,500
- direct contribution 2010		10%		
- jobs		5400		

2.1 Fiji

Among the 16 FICs excluding Australia and New Zealand, Fiji is the most developed economy even though it has a large subsistence sector. The island is richly endowed with forest, mineral and fish resources. The country's industrial activity is based on an inefficient sugar processing industry, construction, a declining garment industry and tourism. Major foreign currency earners are sugar exports, remittances and the tourism sector even though the coup in 2006 saw a decline in tourist arrivals in 2007. With an uncertain future facing the sugar and garment industries and declining remittances from abroad after the coup, tourism is expected to play a major role in the Fijian economy. Tourists generally travel to Fiji for holiday purposes and in 2012, approximately 51% originated from Australia followed by 16% from New Zealand and 9% from the United States [11–13].

2.2 Samoa

Traditionally the Samoan economy was based on agriculture, limited forestry and overseas remittances. Semi-subsistence agriculture and plantations employ the majority of the labour force and are the source of products processed by the manufacturing sector. After two devastating cyclones in 1990 and 1991 and taro leaf blight in 1995, commercial fishing, small scale manufacturing and tourism were recognised as possible engines of future growth [14–15]. However, tourism has since become especially important for growth, foreign currency and employment following the more recent declines in the fisheries and agriculture industries [8]. The majority of visitors to Samoa originate from the Oceania region with nearly 44% from New Zealand, followed by approximately 24% from Australia and 15% from neighbouring American Samoa. Approximately 6% of the tourists originate from the United States. The majority of the visitors are Samoans now resident abroad mostly in New Zealand visiting relatives [16].

2.3 Tonga

A very narrow agricultural export base and fish account for nearly two thirds of Tonga's exports with a high proportion of food being imported from New Zealand. Foreign currency earners are mainly remittances from Tongans living abroad followed by tourism receipts [9, 12]. In Tonga, Tourisms main attraction is its whale watching industry, an important industry in the Oceania region, and the opportunity to swim with humpback whales. This industry became possible due to a Royal decree which banned the harvesting of whales and has grown to about 19 operators, 9 of which are fully owned by Tongans. The industry has also developed strict guidelines to protect the whales due to concerns about the welfare of the whales [17]. 48% of visitors to Tonga are from New Zealand, followed by 22% from Australia and 13% from the United States [18].

2.4 Vanuatu

With a relatively high dependence on subsistence agriculture, Vanuatu is classified as a least developed country. With negligible mineral deposits, fishing, offshore financial services and tourism are the other industries supporting the economy. Although dependence on tourism is high, development of the sector to a large extent has occurred on Efate, the main island, with outer islands being neglected. Apart from tourism receipts, remittance flows, following the introduction of the Recognized Seasonal Employer Scheme by New Zealand and later the Seasonal Pilot Worker Scheme by Australia, are another important source of foreign currency [19–20]. Nearly 62% of visitors to Vanuatu originate from Australia, followed by 12% from New Zealand and 12% from New Caledonia, mainly Melanesians of Vanuatu origin visiting relatives especially during the months of December and January. Approximately 6% of visitors originate from North America mainly the United States [21].

3   Methodology and analysis of results

Two models are specified for this study. Model 1 estimates the impact of the inertial effect on travel destination choice and income growth in Australia, New Zealand and the United States on tourism receipts in the FICs. The impact of capital expenditure on the tourism sector and extreme weather were initially included but proved to have an insignificant impact and are therefore excluded from Model 1. Model 2 tests the impact of tourism, foreign direct investment (FDI), population and extreme weather on the GDP of the FICs.

The proxy for tourism in Model 2 is derived using the redefined Model 1. All other data are from secondary sources based on government statistics. The period of analysis is from 1996 to 2011. Panel data analysis using $STATA$ is applied to estimate both models. To control for omitted variables that differ between the countries but are constant over time fixed effects regression is used in the analysis. The Im-Pesaran-Shin unit root test, the Breusch-Pagan LM test for contemporaneous correlation and a modified Wald test for group wise heteroskedasticity were conducted to verify the robustness of the models.

3.1 The models

The equations representing the two models are given below and a definition of the variables and the results of the analysis with coefficients, p *values*, and significance levels at 1%, 5% and 10% are displayed in Tables 2 and 3 following equations (1) and (2).

$$lnRect_{i,t} = \beta_i + \beta_2 lnRect_{i,t-1} + \beta_3 lnGDPOz_{i,t-1} \tag{1}$$
$$+ \beta_4 lnGDPNZ_{i,t-1} + \beta_5 lnGDPUS_{i,t-1} + \varepsilon_{i,t}$$

$$OwnGDP_{i,t} = \alpha_i + \alpha_2 \widehat{lnRect}_{i,t} + \alpha_3 FDI_{i,t-1} + \alpha_4 Pop_{i,t} \tag{2}$$
$$+ \alpha_5 CyclOz_{i,t} + \varepsilon_{i,t}$$

Table 2: Results for Equation (1).

Variable Name	Definition	Model 1 $lnRect_t$
$lnRect_{t-1}$	Log of tourism receipts of country i in period $t-1$	0.6458 (0.0000)***
$lnGDPOz_{t-1}$	Log of Australian GDP in period $t-1$	-0.5107 (0.0200)**
$lnGDPNZ_{t-1}$	Log of New Zealand GDP in period $t-1$	0.7013 (0.0000)***
$lnGDPUs_{t-1}$	Log of United States GDP in period $t-1$	0.4807 (0.0230)**
cons	Constant	-11.7685 (0.0030)***

***, **, * significant at 1%, 5% and 10% respectively.

Table 3: Results for Equation (2).

Variable Name	Definition	Model 2 $OwnGDP_t$
$\widehat{lnRect_t}$	Estimated log of tourism receipts of country i in period t	0.0000000011 (0.064)*
FDI_{t-1}	Foreign Direct Investment of country i in period $t-1$	1.9313 (0.0000)***
Pop_t	Population of country i in period t	9620.769 (0.0000)***
$Dcycl2_t$	Extreme weather events (cyclones)	-0.0000000269 (0.5090)**
cons	Constant	-0.000000004 (0.0030)***

***, **, * significant at 1%, 5% and 10% respectively.

3.2 Analysis of results

The results for equation 1 indicate that the impact of the inertial effect of travel in the previous year on tourism receipts in the current year is positive and significant. This inertial effect represented by the auto regressive lagged dependent variable captures return visits based on habit persistence and the 'word of mouth (WOM) effect' spread via 'blogs', both of which are based on prior positive travel experiences as they remove the uncertainty element for returning and new travellers to the region. This variable also captures return visits by former nationals residing abroad who travel to the region to visit family and friends [22]. The majority of tourist travel to the Melanesian FICs originates in Australia, whereas the majority of travel to the Polynesian FICs originates in New Zealand where former Samoan and Tongan citizens now reside.

Purchase decisions relating to travel are usually made in advance of the actual travel date [22]. The results of the lagged GDP representing past income indicate that an increase in Australian income decreases travel to these FICs, whereas for New Zealander and US citizens, an increase in income increases visits to these FICs. As mentioned before the impact of capital expenditure in the tourism sector on tourism receipts is not significant and is probably correct. These FICs do recognise that the sector lacks the infrastructure to support tourism in the areas of transportation and road networks especially in remote areas [5]. In addition the level of private investment, past and present, in the sector does not seem to generate a sufficient number of visitors per annum, especially in Samoa, Tonga and Vanuatu.

The results for equation 2 indicate that tourism has a positive and significant impact on GDP as do the level of FDI in the previous year. The impact of the control variable population as expected is also positive and significant on the GDP of these countries. Extreme weather, represented by years in which severe tropical cyclones occurred in this region, has the right sign, in that a cyclone is expected to affect GDP in equation 2 and tourism receipts in equation 1 negatively, but is not significant in model 2 as well. Thus no conclusion can be reached except that perhaps a better proxy is required to represent extreme weather or since severe cyclones occur generally between November and April in this region using monthly or quarterly data may produce a better result. Gathering consistent and appropriate data is a challenge with respect to these FICs and not always possible. It is also possible that the impact of return visits by former nationals especially in December to visit relatives is sufficient to mitigate the impact of reduced travel due to extreme weather.

4   Climate change and extreme weather in FICs

Although the impact of extreme weather is inconclusive in this study, both the impact of climate change and extreme weather are recognised by the FICs as factors of paramount importance to the strategic and sustainable development of the tourism sector. Tourism is both climate dependent and weather sensitive and these FICs have become increasingly dependent on the sector for their general economic well-being and in some cases survival. Climate characterises a location based on that location's meteorological long term average conditions. Given the climate at a particular point in time weather refers to the state of the atmosphere at that time [22].

Climate variability has been associated by many with the El Niño Southern Oscillation (ENSO). The ENSO and its connection to climate are used by many meteorological agencies to produce monthly weather forecasts. Swings in the Southern Oscillation Index (SOI) are associated with El Niño (sustained negative values of the SOI) and La Niña (sustained positive values of the SOI) events. Generally, tropical cyclones are more frequent during years when La Niña conditions prevail [22, 23]. Based on the prevailing ENSO over the preceding July to September period, the Australian Bureau of Meteorology (BOM) is able to predict, with a fair degree of accuracy, the number of cyclones that are likely to occur in the western region of the South Pacific during the November to April period in the subsequent year. Predictions are less accurate for the eastern region. However in either case the BOM is unable to predict the exact strength and path including whether the cyclone will make landfall [23].

For the islands located in the Oceania region, the potentially serious climate change impact is the rise in sea levels and its possible impact on the coastal population and tourism resorts. Among the four FICs in this study, Fiji and Samoa have been identified as particularly vulnerable to a rise in sea levels [8, 24]. Apart from sea level rise climate change could also destroy coral reefs, beaches and other inland tourism assets. The potentially serious extreme weather event is a severe tropical cyclone which could devastate the population and economy of all four FICs. Cyclones could prevent popular tourist activities such as swimming and snorkelling, cause damage to accommodation and infrastructure resulting in cancellations of travel bookings. Fiji has proven particularly vulnerable experiencing ten cyclones of category 3 or above during the period 1996 to 2011. In comparison Samoa experienced 1, Tonga 2 and Vanuatu 4 cyclones of similar strengths during this period. However, Samoa and Tonga also experienced devastation and flooding due to a Tsunami that occurred in 2009 [23].

5 Strategies for the future and conclusions

It is clear from the preceding discussion that the tourism sector is an important element in sustaining the economies of all four FICs though to varying degrees and for different reasons. Of the four economies Fiji is the most developed and also the largest tourist destination within the Melanesian and Polynesian regions of the South Pacific. In the other three FICs the level of development of the tourism sector is not only similar but concentrated on the main islands with less development in remote regions. All four FICs have progressed beyond the traditional destination management techniques of advertising campaigns and other promotions to well developed and tightly controlled websites with direct and indirect online means of communication and trading. However, the marketing of these destinations requires more than well maintained websites and the ease with which a tourist could purchase hotel accommodation within these FICs.

Currently, the majority of the visitors to these islands are from the Oceania region. Even the tourists on cruise ships that call on these islands are mostly Australian. If these islands are to sustain their tourism sector well into the future they need to look beyond Oceania and returning tourists to attracting new tourists and from other regions. Visitors to these FICs from beyond Oceania are mostly from the US. These FICs could benefit from destination managers who could expand their market capabilities. Further, current source markets may not be sufficient to sustain the sector in these FICs with growing competition for tourist dollars from other parts of the world. China could be an important source market given that Chinese outbound tourists are expected to outstrip the United States by 2023 [2].

The FICs do recognise their limitations with respect to long term sustainability of the sector. The linkages between tourism and transportation and tourism and agriculture specific to each FIC has been considered in terms of improving and extending road networks to facilitate tourism to remote areas and to link agricultural areas to markets. Strengthening the supply chain for tourism consumption products has also been explicitly recognised as an area for policy concern as the exposure of tourists to local produce would support and facilitate export market penetration [3, 20].

On a regional level, co-operation in the co-ordination of aviation expansion needs is seen as critical to tourism growth. The linkage between passenger aviation services and freight capacity for fresh export produce is recognised as crucial to improving the viability of increased airline services within the region. Another area recognised for a regional initiative is the potential for increasing the number of international cruise ship destinations and port calls within the South Pacific. Currently Vanuatu leads the way with 252 port calls in 2013. Fiji had 77 calls while Samoa and Tonga had less than 20 port calls [5, 20]. Destination managers could be employed to create awareness of the possibilities within the region among potential cruise passengers and cruise operators. In addition Government support is required in terms of the infrastructure requirements of such an initiative although these ships have little impact on life in these FICs as the port call is usually limited to a day.

The coastal nature of tourist attractions in these FICs underline the necessity for studying the impact of rising sea levels and extreme weather events on the tourism sector. In Samoa, relocating beach *fales* (a thatched hut) away from the beach is not an option and further they are not insurable [8]. In Fiji, the Mamanuca Islands (low lying atolls) are extremely vulnerable to cyclones and rising sea levels. Equally, the long term viability of the Fijian tourism industry itself which is predominantly linked to marine environments is at risk from these phenomena [24]. A similar scenario exists in Tonga and Vanuatu. Tackling the overall climate change impact has to be a regional initiative given the financial and non-financial resource requirements although applications would require initiatives that are island specific. The identification of indicators, monitoring and measurement requirements is best addressed at regional level. Specific scenario analysis would have to be island specific in order to assess future vulnerabilities and determine adaptation patterns if the sector is to be sustainable in the future. Developing and improving the early warning systems and the sharing of information on extreme weather events is a regional responsibility. Risk management strategies to cope with such events would be island specific.

Promoting sustainable tourism also requires recognising the negatives of tourism growth and its impact on the lives of the people and the economy.

Tourism development must be accepted by the residents as it would undoubtedly change their way of life. Anecdotal evidence as well as literature suggests that many residents of these islands do not want a change in their traditional way of life [25, 14]. Samoa's approach to tourism growth has always been cautious such that it respects the *fa'aSamoa* – the traditional way of life [14]. In Fiji, the life of the people is quite diverse depending on the village and the majority do not want drastic changes [25]. In Tonga, the King determines the way of life, for example, the change from whale hunting to whale watching based on a royal decree [17]. In Vanuatu, much of tourism is concentrated in Efate [20], whereas the rural population who are mostly unaffected outnumber the urban population 3:1 [Table 1]. However, the 2014 Lelepa Declaration [26] makes clear the value placed on the traditional economy and the rights of customary land owners. Unless these sentiments are respected in any planning for increased growth in the sector a long term strategy would be jeopardised.

Other negatives include the loss of cultural and natural assets and prime agricultural land due to infrastructure development to sustain tourism. Negative environmental impacts such as deforestation, crowding, potential pollution and problems with waste disposal and sanitation may also result from poor planning. Addressing these issues would require a long term commitment of financial resources as well as human resource development through training programmes targeting the labour force and educational programmes targeting schools. In addition forums to disseminate information on the impact on the traditional way of life and to assess the reaction of the residents of the affected area are required.

In conclusion, promoting sustainable tourism in FICs would require financial and non-financial resources which are scarce in these countries with competing development needs. As has been recognised by these FICs, regional co-operation and collaboration is vital. The framework already exists in the form of the FIC group which meet annually to address such issues and use their feedback mechanism to assess progress and target areas for additional support and resources. The group includes Australia and New Zealand who have long supported the budgetary and other requirements of their neighbouring island economies. The group also includes international organisations, which fund specific programmes, as observers. Such financial support is vital for strategic decision making to fund major initiatives especially in dealing with the challenge of climate change and exploring different adaptation options for the tourism industry. Funding is also vital for improving the current early warning system and assistance in the event of an extreme weather event. Ensuring the continuance of such support requires a commitment by these FICs of honest assessment and feedback. For the present, if policymakers can identify their core areas of competence and build on it, then they can build up their resilience against short term shocks with tactical decisions which do not require a long term commitment of resources. Strengthening their core areas of competence would also give them the flexibility to then focus more resources on long term sustainability.

References

[1]   Gössling, S., (ed). Tourism and Development in Tropical Islands: Political Ecology Perspectives, Edward Elgar Publishing, 2003.

[2]   Travel & Tourism: Economic Impact Oceania 2014; World Travel & Tourism Council (WTTC), London, UK, www.wttc.org.

[3]   Pacific Plan 2012 Annual Progress Report; Pacific Islands Forum Secretariat, Fiji, www.forumsec.org.

[4]   Pacific Islands Forum Secretariat, Fiji, www.forumsec.org: Accessed 20th February 2014.

[5]   Tourism as a Pillar of Economic Growth; Pacific Islands Forum Secretariat, Fiji, www.forumsec.org.

[6]   GDP ranking 2012. www.data.world.org/data-catalog/GDP-ranking-table: Accessed 20th February 2014.

[7]   Travel & Tourism: Economic Impact Fiji 2013; World Travel & Tourism Council (WTTC), London, UK, www.wttc.org.

[8]   National Tourism Climate Change Adaptation Strategy for Samoa 2012–2017: Samoa Tourism Authority.

[9]   Travel & Tourism: Economic Impact Tonga 2013; World Travel & Tourism Council (WTTC), London, UK, www.wttc.org.

[10]   Travel & Tourism: Economic Impact Vanuatu 2013; World Travel & Tourism Council (WTTC), London, UK, www.wttc.org.

[11]   Prasad, C. P. & Narayan, P. K., Reviving growth in the Fiji islands: are we swimming or sinking? *Pacific Economic Bulletin,* **23(2)**: pp. 5-26, 2008.

[12]   Narayan, P. K., Narayan, S. Prasad, A. & Prasad, B. C., Tourism and economic growth: a panel data analysis for Pacific Island countries. *Tourism Economics,* **16(1)**: pp. 169-183, 2010.

[13]   Fiji Bureau of Statistics, Fiji, www.statsfiji.gov.fj: Accessed 27th February 2014.

[14]   Pearce, D. G., Tourism planning in small tropical islands: methodological considerations and development issues in Samoa. Études caribéennes, 9-10 April–August 2008 http://etudecaribeennes.revues.org.

[15]   Twining-Ward, L. & Butler, R., Implementing STD on a small island: development and use of sustainable tourism development indicators in Samoa. *Journal of Sustainable Tourism,* **10(5)**: pp. 363-387, 2002.

[16]   Samoa Bureau of Statistics. http://www.sbs.gov.ws. Accessed 27th February 2014.

[17]   Kessler, M. & Harcourt, R. Aligning tourist, industry and government expectations: A case study from the swim with the whales industry in Tonga. *Marine Policy,* **34**: pp. 1350-1356, 2010.

[18]   Tonga Department of Statistics. http://www.spc.int/prism/tonga. Accessed 27th February 2014.

[19]   Kumar, R. R., Naidu, V. & Kumar, R., Exploring the nexus between trade, visitor arrivals, remittances and income in the Pacific; a study of Vanuatu. *OECONOMICA,* **7(4)**: 2011.

[20] Cassidy, F. & Brown, L., Determinants of small Pacific island tourism: a Vanuatu study. *Asia Pacific Journal of Tourism Research,* **15(2)**: pp. 143-153, 2010.

[21] Vanuatu National Statistics Office. http://www.vnso.gov.vu. Accessed 27th February 2014.

[22] Saverimuttu, V. & Varua, M. E., Climate variability in the origin countries as a "push" factor on tourist arrivals in the Philippines. Asia Pacific Journal of Tourism Research, 2013. http://dx.doi.org/10.1080/10941665.2013.806940.

[23] Bureau of Meteorology, Australia. http://www.bom.gov.au.

[24] Moreno, A. & Becken, S., A climate change vulnerability assessment methodology for coastal tourism. Journal of Sustainable Tourism, **17(4)**: pp. 473-488, 2009.

[25] Kerstetter, D. & Bricker, K., Exploring Fijian's sense of place after exposure to tourism development. Journal of Sustainable Tourism, **17(6)**: pp. 691-708, 2009.

[26] The Lelepa Declaration 2014, Pacific Islands Report Pacific; Pacific Islands Development Program, East-West Center, March 2014. http://pidp.eastwestcenter.org/pireport/2014/March/03-27-st.htm.

The life cycle of sustainable eco-tourism: a Kazakhstan case study

T. I. Mukhambetov, G. O. Janguttina, U. S. Esaidar,
G. R. Myrzakulova & B. T. Imanbekova
Almaty Technological University, Kazakhstan

Abstract

This article is devoted to some theoretical, methodological and practical aspects of sustainable eco-tourism.

In the theoretical part of the paper it is noted that in the CIS the term "sustainable tourism" is rarely used and the more common term "Ecotourism" is most familiar. This article analyses the similarities and differences between them as well as other close and related "isms" within the meaning of the definitions: "Moral tourism", "Nature tourism", "Green tourism", "Responsible Tourism".

According to the authors, "Sustainable Tourism" is not a kind of tourism. The characteristics of the listed types of tourism all have certain indicators associated with sustainable tourism. From this perspective, we can talk about eco-tourism as a pillar of sustainable tourism.

In the practical part of the paper the authors give a general characterization of tourism in Kazakhstan. It analyses the problems encountered in the formation and development of ecological tourism. Based on a comprehensive analysis it concludes that tourism in Kazakhstan is not developed nor is there the political will to adopt a common organizational approach to the development of sustainable eco-tourism.

In the methodological part of the paper, the authors develop the most important aspect – the "life cycle of the tourism product", particularly its sustainability.

The authors demonstrate its features, allocate life cycle stages and discuss the causes and factors contributing to the rate of aging of the product. One example of eco-tourism in Kazakhstan shows that some Kazakhstan ecotourism products require urgent measures to prolong their life cycle, which will be beneficial to all participants in the tourism industry.

Keywords: tourism in Kazakhstan, sustainable tourism, eco-tourism in Kazakhstan, the life cycle sustainable eco- tourism product.

WIT Transactions on Ecology and The Environment, Vol 187, © 2014 WIT Press
www.witpress.com, ISSN 1743-3541 (on-line)
doi:10.2495/ST140041

1   Introduction

The term "sustainable tourism" in Kazakhstan is rarely used at any level and will not be familiar to most. The State Tourism Development Program uses the term "Eco-tourism", but this is only being developed through the efforts of USAID and several other non-governmental organizations.

However, the question is whether the present state of the industry adequately meets the expectations associated with the terms "ecological tourism" and "sustainable tourism"? What are the differences between these and many other similar ones within the meaning of the terms? Can we assume that sustainable tourism takes place in Kazakhstan? What is the situation and what are the prospects for sustainable tourism in Kazakhstan? Which factors affect the product life cycle of sustainable eco-tourism? At what stage of the life cycle of eco-tourism are tourist products in Kazakhstan? What affects them? These and other questions need to be answered in order to build the future strategy of tourism development and the maintenance of tourist destinations in Kazakhstan.

2   Terminology of sustainable tourism

In Kazakhstan, as well as in the CIS countries as a whole, the term "sustainable tourism" is not appreciated and is almost unknown to most. It is not even used at the government level and would not seem to have a place in other sectors of tourism development.

Also rare, but you can find similar and related terms "Responsible Tourism", "soft tourism", "moral tourism", "Nature tourism" as well as "green tourism". With so many terms, concepts and definitions, often interconnected with each other, it is not surprising that few people understand the differences between them. In the recent past there were clear differences between the different types of tourism, but now the boundaries are becoming increasingly blurred.

In many ways, this can be attributed to the English-language literature, as well as to international organizations, all of which have contributed a number of terms with similar meanings. Each of them gives its own definition of sustainable tourism the differences between which are not always clear even to specialists in the field. Some of the scholars consider them as separate types of tourism, others see them as mutually overlapping concepts or as components of each other.

Mexican economist and ecologist Hector Tsebalass-Laskureyn first coined the term "ecological tourism", and defined it as a journey with responsibility to the environment in relatively undisturbed natural areas to explore and enjoy nature and cultural attractions. Ecotourism, as he says, contributes to the protection of nature, makes a "soft" impact on the environment, and provides for an active socio-economic involvement of local people that enables them to receive the benefits of this activity (Ceballos-Lascurain [1]). This is the classic definition of eco-tourism, although, a scholar such as Matthews [2] identifies seven characteristics of ecotourism.

What is the difference between the terms "Ecotourism" and "Sustainable Tourism"?

Fennell and Dowling [3], when listing standards of ecotourism, include sustainability. Thus, they include sustainability of the eco-tourism as one of its properties.

However, the more common view is that ecotourism is an integral part of sustainable tourism (Sâmbotin et al. [4], Bansal and Kumar [5]).

Indeed, sustainable tourism aims to provide three key target indicators:

- Quality – tourism should have an impact on the quality of life for all members of the tourist process;
- Optimality – exploitation of natural resources should be optimal and ensure their regeneration;
- Balance – distribution of benefits among participants in the tourist process must be fair.

From this perspective, sustainable tourism is not a type of tourism, but a kind of unifying concept that includes different types of tourism that are linked with the use of natural places, parks and protected areas. These qualities have the character of sustainable tourism, when they combine to provide quality and optimal balance. "Eco-tourism" and "Nature tourism" are separate types of tourism. At the same time, terms such as "Responsible Tourism", "soft tourism", "A moral Tourism" and "Green Tourism" are simply different names for these types of tourism. They reflect the various aspects of ecological tourism.

Sustainable tourism is the goal that must be advanced in any kind of tourism, despite the fact that it is rarely achieved. Sustainable tourism does not imply a specific set of events. This is more than an approach that aims to express itself in all sectors of tourism. This is a natural extension of the concept of sustainable development. Sustainable development – the development that meets the needs of the present without disrupting the ability of future generations to meet their own needs (IISD [6]).

The concept of sustainability was first proposed in the report of the World Commission on Environment and Development in 1987, in which it was noted that economic growth and environmental conservation should be carried out in unity. This development satisfies the needs of the present without compromising the ability of future generations to meet their own needs (IISD [6]).

Sustainable tourism implies a much greater social responsibility, fulfillment of obligations in relation to nature, as well as the involvement of local people in all processes related to the management of tourism activities.

World Tourism Organization (WTO [7]), the World Council of Travel and Tourism (WTCC [8]) gave the definition of sustainable tourism. Sustainable tourism development satisfies the needs of present tourists and host regions while protecting and enhancing opportunities for the future. Management of all resources must be exercised so that they meet the economic, social and aesthetic needs, but also protect the cultural integrity, essential ecological processes, and biological diversity and life support systems.

The concept of sustainable tourism is not widely accepted in the CIS countries, mainly because most of these countries are not familiar with the concept, with the result that it is weakly correlated with the management of the raw material economy.

Nevertheless, Kazakhstan in 2012 took over the fashionable concept of "green economy", similar to the ideas of sustainable development. However, this concept as appears to be an independent branch of the economy. It is at least, but is not dominated by, the idea of maximum conservation for future generations and by minimizing damage to nature. Green economy, rather, is based on technological projects of alternative energy and energy efficiency of the economy. It does not focus on environmental pollution in some sectors (e.g. oil), but it is actively developing environmentally friendly technologies in other sectors (energy, water, etc.).

Nevertheless, in our opinion, you can use the term "green tourism", implying not only eco-tourism, but in general any tourism based on the principles of sustainable tourism. This is a kind of adaptation to the political context in which the political coloring becomes more important when the essence and importance of the term "sustainability" is used in all other terms. In this case, the term "Green" ("Green Transportation", "Green Energy", "Green University", "Green House", etc.)

3   Tourism in Kazakhstan

The structure of the flow of Kazakhstan tourism is typical for most of the CIS countries, where outbound tourism is most intensive. Flows of outbound tourism grew and continue to grow over the years. The balance of Kazakhstan tourism is decidedly negative with more than 500 million dollars in favor of outbound tourism in 2012. Kazakhs prefer beach, shopping and visit holidays in Turkey, China, United Arab Emirates, the Kingdom of Thailand and other countries.

In real terms, the share of inbound tourism, however, remains high. In 2012, the share of inbound tourism constituted 31.4% of total tourism revenues, whilst outbound made up 50% and domestic tourism less than 18.6%. The number of foreign nationals who had entered Kazakhstan was 6163 thousand people. However, of these 5542 thousand were citizens of the CIS. In other words – it is a working tourism – people who came to work from Uzbekistan, Kyrgyzstan and other Central Asian republics (Turism [9]).

From the remaining 620 thousand visitors, foreign tourists who entered for private purposes accounted for 80%, and transit travelers for 13%. The remaining 7% was made up of business travel and leisure and recreation, or slightly more than 43 000 people. This is an extremely low figure, indicating that Kazakhstan has not yet become an attractive country for pure tourism. It is not surprising that hotel occupancy in 2012 was only 25%.

Share of GDP is about 2 percent. For comparison, in developed countries this figure reaches 30 percent. Reasons for the low attractiveness of Kazakhstan for many foreign tourists: low country marketing, low attractiveness of tourist objects that do not represent a high cultural and historical value in comparison with world objects, a huge distance to nature reserves, lagging service sector, high prices for services.

In general the country, despite the presence of a government agency to adopt a state program for the development of tourism, still misses a holistic approach to tourism development. This is evident in the unrelated development of different branches of tourism.. The recent trend has been the focus of attention on the development of the state space tourism (Baikonur Cosmodrome), the development of the capital Astana as a center for business tourism. As it happens, time will tell. These initiatives have been many albeit unsuccessful.

At the same time it is accepted that attempts have been made to expand the participation of Kazakhstan in international exhibitions, the opening of tourist information centers at the airport and in the largest city Almaty. However, the city remains environmentally dirty and urban infrastructure is not designed to attract foreign visitors (traffic jams, noise, poor public transport, lack of inscriptions in English, etc.).

In the whole country there are certain prerequisites for the development of ecological tourism that are missing.

In the state are nature reserves and national parks, several thousands of archaeological and historical monuments of different historical and cultural value. The most popular and visited are the natural parks and reserves: Burabai, Bayanaul, Korgalzhyn reserves, Kolsai Lake, Bukhtarma reservoir, Lake Alakol, Charyn Canyon, Ile-Alatau National Park, etc. But many of them, such as the island Araltobe Canyon Zhamanty lake Zhalanashkol, Zhabyktau and many others are almost impossible to visit. These are almost no roads, nearby infrastructure and people's homes.

Among cultural monuments can list the Mausoleum of Khoja Ahmed Yassaui mausoleum Arystan Baba, Otrar.

As already mentioned, in 2003, several international NGOs funded the project implementation of the principles of eco-tourism in Kazakhstan. Since then, to some extent the country began to use the term "Eco-tourism" and undertook certain work. In particular the framework of this project involved the creation of ecosites 15 (Ecotourism [10]).

To call them ecosites is difficult because an ecosite in international practice involves villages where residents take guests under the concept of rural ecotourism. In Kazakhstan – there are about 50 families living in 25 villages in Kazakhstan. The cost of living in these villages is quite high: about $50 per day, which usually includes accommodation, meals and outdoor bathrooms.

The State Program on development of tourism in the Republic of Kazakhstan eco-tourism has been recognized as one of the priority directions for the development of tourism in the country. But, despite the fact that this program was adopted in 2006, Kazakhstan has not formulated unified organizational policies and approaches to the development of ecotourism.

In practice eco-tourism is associated with tourists visiting protected areas and rural areas, the increase in national and international flows of tourists and the associated development of tourism infrastructure in these areas. However, in fact, sustained eco-tourism – it is not mass tourism, and it is not intended to support large flows of tourists to natural areas. In this sense, it is an alternative to this approach. It is aimed at the preservation of nature while offering the benefits of tourism to the local population (Ni *et al.* [11]).

4 The life cycle of sustainable eco-tourism product

The concept of life cycle applies to the tourism product as well as to any commercial product. Plog [12] identified three kinds of tourists (allocentric, midcentric and psychocentric) whose psychology and preferences conditioned the rise and fall of destinations. However, the most widely accepted and discussed model was proposed in 1980 by Butler which represented an adaptation of the life cycle model to the destination context. In the longitudinal analysis, changes in tourist destinations have been considered as elements of the different stages they pass through in time. The life cycle model (Butler [13]) proposed a hypothetical evolution of a tourist area, and suggested that destinations pass through six stages (Exploration, Involvement, Development, Consolidation, Stagnation, Decline and Rejuvenation)

Using the category of "The life cycle sustainable eco-tourism product" is particularly important. The fact is that the meaning of sustainable tourism is to cause minimum damage to nature and to preserve it for future generations. In other words, this means that the priority of a sustainable tourism product is to have a long life cycle, and the actual length of the product life cycle is the criterion of the principles and objectives of a sustainable ecological tourism product.

Sustainable tourism in contrast to the usual eco-tourism product has its own peculiarities.

The World Tourism Organization has identified the objectives of ecotourism:

1. Ecotourism should assist in the protection and conservation.
2. Ecotourism should help create jobs, and in a way – additional income for local communities.
3. Ecotourism should help to increase knowledge and awareness about the local culture.
4. The aim of eco-tourism is to teach tourists. That is, sustainable tourism should provide educational influence on tourist increase its awareness of sustainable development issues and promote sustainable tourism practices (WTO [7]).

We would add the following features.

1. Sustainable tourism implies the maximum use of "green technologies" in its process ("green energy", "green food", "green home", etc.).
2. Sustainable tourism as opposed to mass tourism, is largely a personalized tourism aimed at promoting ecology and conservation.

3. Sustainable tourism requires conscious participation of all stakeholders, as well as strong political leadership to ensure wide participation and consensus (Hall [14]).
4. Sustainable tourism requires continuous monitoring of the human impact on nature presenting the necessary preventative and/or corrective measures whenever necessary (Kiper [15]).

These and other features are making adjustments to the understanding of the life cycle of the tourism product.

Violation of these features and the rules leads to a drop in eco-tourism product life cycle. Distortion occurs when the idea of sustainable tourism transforms into the usual tourist product of mass consumption.

5 Problems of sustainable eco-tourism in Kazakhstan and maintaining its life cycle

As we mentioned above, the concept of sustainable tourism is not widespread in Kazakhstan. Eco-tourism is largely related to sustainable tourism but is also not the dominant type of tourism in Kazakhstan.

Tour operators in Kazakhstan have recently started to use the prefix (brand) "eco", to attract visitors, as it significantly increases the price of the tour.

Completion of the mentioned project for the development of ecological tourism in Kazakhstan has also reduced the development of the principles of ecotourism. Thus, curtailment eco-tourism, in fact, led to a rapid reduction in their life cycle. What difficulties and obstacles exist to prevent the implementation of the principles of sustainable tourism and the support life cycle for sustainable eco-tourism in Kazakhstan?

Minor amounts of unique natural objects led to the fact that, in practice, ecological tours were established on the basis of existing tours and routes of mass tourism. It is very difficult to follow the principles of sustainable tourism, where the mass tourist routes pass. In such cases, tourists who came to enjoy wildlife, see foot-worn paths and traces of mass or, as it is called in Russian, "wild" tourists in the form of numerous hearths (remains of the bonfires), mountains of garbage etc.

All available routes in Kazakhstan were developed in the Soviet era. One of the authors of this article went on many of them in the early 90s. At that time they were in a more natural state due to the fact that the numbers of people who went on them were much less than is the case today.

Ecosites were placed in the same villages where through which the mass tourist passes. Improving the living standards of the local population leads to their turning into the domestic "wild" tourist, traveling by the car through the same sites, which are trying to develop eco-tourism. Self-organized domestic tourists in cars usually drive up close to objects of tourism. Basically, the vehicle can reach most of them. They come with their families and friends, bring with them a huge amount of food, arrange bonfires, spread litter and sing songs.

In this form you can see the main tourist destinations, which are in protected areas and parks: Turgen and Turgen waterfalls, Canon Charyn, Kolsai Lake, Lake Alakol, Bayanaul, State national natural park "Kokshetau" Tamgali and Tambaly and Tas. Kazakhstan has a short beach holiday and swimming season which is why wild "outdoor recreation" is one of the most common forms of spending free time. It has no relation to eco-tourism, but is practiced on the territory of ecological tourism.

It is implemented where the principal beneficiaries of eco-tourism are the locals? The fact is that the residents of the villages located near the natural parks and protected sites receive more income from the mass tourist than from the ecological rare guest and therefore cannot wait for the latter. The mass tourist is more profitable and can be a major source of income for the villager. In this case, locals have also contributed to the increased pressure on nature together with the "wild tourist."

One of the reasons for low ecological orientation of tourism is the weak activity of the Government to promote the ideas of ecological tourism. Officials perceive psychologically sustainable and eco-tourism as a costly and troublesome initiative.

No indicative planning and monitoring of the development of ecological tourism. Statistics and records of tourism is one of the main problems in the development of tourism. Thus, according to official numbers domestic tourism in 2012 was covered by 201 thousand people [9]. But these numbers are highly questionable, as domestic tourism has the character of weekend tours and "wild tourism". Wild tourists are weakly identifiable and can be considered only based on the number of tickets sold at the entrance to the natural park or ecological reserve.

However, there are places where turnpikes are subject to corruption and unaccounted cash, and therefore no reliability can be placed on their accounting of who came to visit. In fact, according to our estimates, the number of domestic tourists is not less than 2 million people a year. Naturally, this mass tourism sector significantly exceeds the number of eco-tourists, the number of which is not known to anyone. Local residents in these conditions will always be focused on the "wild" mass tourists, reducing even more the life cycle of sustainable tourism.

In the places of eco-tourism "green technologies" such as solar cells, biological water purification, etc. are absent .The cottages and houses are built close to the objects (e.g. Kolsai Lake), and electricity and electric poles surround every house and cottage. Can accommodation in yurts (ethnic house of felts), be considered as eco-tourism if it is located next to modern cottage homes?

The state does not pay enough attention to the development of ecotourism and solving its problems.

These factors significantly reduce the life cycle of sustainable tourism product. This product will always lose mass tourist product. Since the beginning of its launch such a product will quickly collapse and interest in it will decline on all sides of the tourist process. Consumer (tourist) will not get satisfaction, a local resident will be oriented to the mass tourist and nature will continue to be polluted. Eventually the product will close.

In Kazakhstan, we are fond of saying that there is a huge potential for tourism development. It is difficult to agree with this when even the existing tourism facilities are not used as efficiently as possible.

As we have shown, there are many problems in the field of tourism, especially eco-tourism. As a result, there is no optimal resource consumption, which violates the principle of sustainable tourism. Natural parks are choking on the influx of informal local tourists, their litter and noise. It is hardly possible to talk about biodiversity in such cases. For example, at the entrance to the reserve of Bayanaul standing sculptures of birds can be seen along the road. Eagles, swallows and larks once lived here flying freely in the sky. But since the 80s there are none. What influenced their disappearance: radiation from a nearby Semipalatinsk nuclear test site, or noise from "wild" tourists coming to the bosom of nature to relax for the weekend is difficult to judge. But now there are only flying crows and sparrows.

Disappointment also engulfs one when visiting places of rock inscriptions such as Tamgaly Tas, when one sees see inscriptions of modern people "Here was Aydin" adjacent to the drawings of ancient people.

6   Fields of activities to increase the life cycle of sustainable tourism

The Government of the Republic of Kazakhstan in 2013 discussed the concept of tourism industry development until 2020 but this is still not accepted. As far as we know, insufficient attention is once again paid to sustainable tourism, although the concept of regional clusters is highlighted.

In accordance with this concept of an eco-tourism zone in Eastern Kazakhstan, is planned with the development of the Katonkaragay zone and the West Altai Mountains. Almaty and Almaty region will ensure the development of skiing and urban tourism. On the territory of South Kazakhstan region, Kyzylorda and Zhambyl regions planned to create cultural tourism. West Kazakhstan becomes a zone of beach tourism to the city center that Kenderli on the beach in the city of Aktau and adventure tourism.

Such a concept of the cluster approach is more balanced. But it also has certain disadvantages.

Show the main ways to increase the life cycle of sustainable tourism product on the example of Kazakhstan.

To develop eco-tourism in the cluster basis is not enough of the right approach. Sustainable tourism – is not the kind of tourism, like the beach or cultural and historical tourism. This kind of philosophy for tourism pays careful attention to any object, including objects like the beach, historical or any other kind of tourism. Therefore, a regional approach to its development is not applicable. Otherwise, such an approach would be to store objects of tourism in this region and in other regions of ruin. Thus, a sustainable approach should be defined in the Concept as a political statement, as a general approach to the development of tourism in general.

Eco-tourism will benefit if the domestic tourist goes to the principles and rules of eco-tourism. And only when the environment is restored and all routes will be audited, classified into categories of tourism and there are special routes and ecotours. These ecotourism routes must be protected from environmental patrol mass tourism and based on the principles of sustainable tourism, best avoided.

For classification and identification of environmental routes in all regions of Kazakhstan, you must first calculate the potential capacity for sustainable tourism.

Middleton and Hawkins give the definition of tourist capacity of tourism as the level of human activity, which can be implemented on the site without harming the area without affecting the local community, and the quality does not deteriorate stay visitors (Middleton and Hawkins [16]).

UNEP proposed the following definition of tourism capacity as the maximum number of people who can visit the destination at the same time, without causing destruction of the physical, economic and socio-cultural environment and an unacceptable decrease in the quality of visitor satisfaction (UNEP [17]).

According to our calculations, the total capacity of ecological routes of Kazakhstan is approximately 50,000 visits per year. Increase in load will reduce the life cycle of sustainable tourism products. In fact, these routes are currently experiencing at least 10 times greater. This means that ecological routes of Kazakhstan are in a state of decay, and they will not grow, as they will become definitively a product of mass tourism.

We should carry out certification and Ecological Monitoring of routes and expose the annual assessment of the negative impact of tourism on local resources such as energy, fauna, flora, land, water. Environmental labeling will identify routes and amount of state financial assistance to eco-tours.

7 Conclusions

Currently, in terms of sustainable tourism uncertainty persists. Their analysis allowed us to determine the stability of the resulting quality as the final, which should seek forms of tourism such as "sustainable tourism", "eco-tourism". From this perspective, the concept of eco-tourism in the sustainable tourism is preferable to determine how sustainable eco-tourism is.

Analysis of the development of sustainable tourism in Kazakhstan showed that international inbound tourism in the country has a weak pace of development. Eco-tourism has a number of problems associated with the lack of attention the government gives to this type of tourism, a violation of the basic principles of ecotourism. As a result, product life cycle is short of eco-tourism, and this type of tourism is on the stage of rapid decline.

Dedicated reasons for the reduction of product life cycle eco-tourism should be allowed to make recommendations that will contribute to the revival of ecological tourism in Kazakhstan. Among them: strengthen state regulation, to introduce eco patrol, inspection and certification of tourist routes ecological routes, enter state support ecotourism monitoring using key indicators, etc.

References

[1]   Ceballos-Lascurain H. Introduction: Ecotourism as a Worldwide Phenomenon. In Ecotourism: A Guide for Planners and Managers (K. Lindberg, D. Hawkins, Eds.). The Ecotourism Society, Alexandria, Va, USA: 1-3, 1993.

[2]   Matthews E. J, Ecotourism: Are Current Practices Delivering Desired Outcomes? A comparative case study analysis Major Paper submitted to the Faculty of the Virginia Polytechnic Institute and State University in partial fulfilment of the requirements for the degree of Master of Urban and Regional Planning in Urban Affairs and Planning. 106, 2002.

[3]   Fennell D. A, Dowling R. K, Ecotourism Policy and Planning CABI Publishing: Oxon and Cambridge, 2003.

[4]   Sâmbotin D, Sâmbotin A, Pătrăşcoiu M, Coroian A, Mercel I. I, Ecoturismul – Model de Valorificare Durabilă a Resurselor Turistice, Lucrări Ştiinţifice, Seria I, Vol. XIII (4). 2011.

[5]   Bansal S. P, Kumar J, Ecotourism for Community Development: A Stakeholder's Perspective in Great Himalayan National Park. International Journal of Social Ecology and Sustainable Development, 2(2), 31-40. 2011.

[6]   IISD, What is Sustainable Development? International Institute for Sustainable Development, IISD, 2012.

[7]   WTO, http://www.world-tourism.org

[8]   WTTC, http://www.wttc.org

[9]   Turism Kazakhstana 2008–2012. Agentstvo Respubliki Kazakhstan po statistike, 2013.

[10]   Ecotourism, http://www.eco-tourism.kz

[11]   Ni V., Mirhashimov I., Klimov E., Tonkobayeva A. Rukovodstvo po razvitiyu ecologicheskogo turisma v Kazakhstane. Almaty, 2009.

[12]   Plog S.C. Why destinations areas rise and fall in popularity Cornell Hotel and Restaurant Association Quarterly, 13, 6-13, 1973.

[13]   Butler, R.W. The concept of the tourist area life-cycle of evolution: implications for management of resources. Canadian Geographer, 24 (1), 5-12, 1980.

[14]   Hall C.M., Tourism Planning: Policies, Processes and Relationships. nd Edn., Pearson/Prentice Hall, Harlow, England, New York, 2008.

[15]   Kiper T. Role of Ecotourism in Sustainable Development, in "Advances in Landscape Architecture". Ed. by Murat Özyavuz, Intech. 2013.

[16]   Middleton V.C., Hawkins, R. Sustainable Tourism: a marketing perspective Butterworth-Heinemann, 1998.

[17]   United Nations Environment Program Eco-labels in the tourism industry. UNEP Industry and Environment, Paris, 1998.

Subjective well-being and personality: implications for wellness tourism

I. G. Malkina-Pykh & Y. A. Pykh
Research Center for Interdisciplinary Environmental Cooperation,
Russian Academy of Sciences (INENCO RAS), Russia

Abstract

The aims of this study are to demonstrate that 1) personality differences can be considered as the mechanisms underlying differences in subjective well-being and 2) rhythmic movement therapy (RMT) can be regarded as an effective tool for increasing subjective well-being (SWB) in the wellness tourism context. The proposed operationalisation of SWB includes five domains and several psychological constructs that are hypothesised to be components of a mental map, underlying SWB. A total of 213 subjects were recruited among those searching for psychological counselling and assessed with the appropriate questionnaires. Two groups were formed in accordance with their SWB level: group 1 – (very low, low and medium SWB levels) – 96 subjects, 75 females, 21 males, mean age 36, 3 ± 11, 0 years) and group 2 – (high and very high SWB levels) – 117 subjects, 96 females, 21 males, mean age 36, 8 ± 8, 68 years). ANOVA analyses with the SWB group as a factor revealed significant differences in all psychological variables in two groups except for personal standards. ANOVA analyses with gender as a factor revealed no differences in psychological variables except for body image dissatisfaction. The theoretical background for RMT as an effective part of a wellness service was provided. Our research provides evidence that thinking styles (mental models) may significantly influence SWB and any program used for increasing SWB must include a mental healing service.
Keywords: subjective well-being, leisure/vacation satisfaction, personality, rhythmic movement therapy, wellness tourism.

1 Introduction

1.1 Definition of subjective well-being

Subjective well-being (SWB) refers to a person's declared well-being and is based on an answer to either a single question or a group of questions about his/her subjectively perceived satisfaction with life or happiness. SWB is defined as a multidimensional construct, consisted of three major components – satisfaction with life (LS), positive affect (PA), and negative affect (NA) that represent an ongoing state of psychological wellness [1]. More recently, satisfaction in specific life domains (henceforth domain satisfaction (DS), e.g. satisfaction with health) was included in the definition of SWB [2]. Life satisfaction and domain satisfaction are considered cognitive components because they are based on evaluative beliefs (attitudes) about one's life, positive affect and negative affect assess the affective component of SWB [1, 2].

Two main theoretical traditions have contributed to the understanding of SWB. A 'bottom up' perspective explained the SWB of individuals by contextual factors and presented it as a linear combination of DS variables. 'Top-down' model proposed by Diener [1] was based on the idea that satisfaction might be determined more by personality characteristics, such as temperament, social comparison, the goal-achievement gap and adaptation, than situational circumstances. However, numerous studies have examined the possibility that LS-DS correlations are due to the common influence of personality traits (e.g. [3]).

1.2 Subjective well-being and personality

The five-factor model of personality (Big Five) is the most widely used in SWB studies and certainly provides results about important personality dimensions. However, it is just as certain that there are other personality characteristics not embodied by the big five that are just as worthy of study. To date, a great deal has been learned about the personality traits, values, goals, and social behaviours and cognitions of happy individuals compared to their less happy counterparts (e.g. [4] for review).

It is necessary to stress that overwhelming proportion of the studies on the associations between SWB and personality are conducted in the framework of 'top-down' approach (see [4] for review). The studies of the influence of personality variables on DS are rather rare and leisure/vacation satisfaction is not the exception [5, 6].

1.3 The origin of subjective well-being

Both bottom-up and top-down theoretical approaches, however, do not explain how personality influences SWB or any of its domains. One possible way of better constructing these theories is by linking them to individual mental maps (models). Mental maps are those core beliefs that may explain how individuals select and process information in interpreting life events, and may account for individual differences in these interpretations (e.g. [7]).

Some kind of mental map was used in the model of SWB homeostasis proposed by Cummins *et al.* [8]. This important theoretical model postulates that SWB fluctuates around a stable set point that is determined by heritable factors such as personality. The homeostasis model couples a primary genetic capacity (neuroticism, extraversion and positive and negative affect) with a secondary buffering system (the cognitive aspects of control, self-esteem, and optimism).

Recent findings in neuroscience and developmental psychology propose some possible explanations of the sources of these thought processes (mental models). Attachment theory explains how children form mental representations of relationships based on their interactions with, and adaptation to, their care-giving environment [9]. Described as internal working models, these cognitive/affective representations are encoded and stored as implicit (unconscious) procedural memories and help organize affect and social experience and shape not only current but future interpersonal relationships [10].

1.4 Stability of subjective well-being

Recent research suggests showed that set point theory overstates the stability of happiness and it can, to some degree, be changed [11]. Findings from neuroscience reveal that the brain remains open to new experiences from the environment during the lifespan. This process was called "brain plasticity" or "neuroplasticity" and involves not only the creation of new synaptic connections among neurons but also the growth of new neurons [12]. A wide variety of approaches that have been developed to increase well-being are based on positive psychology concept (see [13] for review).

1.5 Benefits of traditional tourism for subjective well-being

It is supposed that holiday trips, vacation as a special type of leisure, pleasant activity potentially add to individuals' happiness [14]. In tourism, a number of scholars [15, 16] have examined the benefits of travel based on the bottom-up spillover theory. Neal *et al.* [15] undertook survey research of tourist satisfaction of travel services and trip experiences and found that tourist's satisfaction of their holiday experiences was related to their life satisfaction scores, which adds some weight to the role of personality traits to understanding links between tourism participation and measures of QOL. Sirgy *et al.* [16] investigate how positive and negative trip experiences affect overall well-being. Their model illustrates the connections between trip experiences, satisfaction with life domains, and overall satisfaction with life.

More recently several meta-analysis of literature were provided to assess the tourism benefits for quality of life and well-being (e.g. [17]). The main results of these meta-analyses revealed the positive effects of vacationing on perceived quality of life and happiness. However, it has also been found that vacation effects might last for only a few days, two to three weeks, or no more than one month [18].

It is important to note here that studies mentioned above were examining the benefits of traditional tourism. If we remember about strong influence of personality (mental models) on subjective well-being and happiness, then the obtained results about the absence of post-trip effect are not surprising. The traditional tourism doesn't aim to influence mental models (personality) of a person. It is simply not that case. We found few studies investigating the influence of personality on leisure satisfaction (e.g. [19, 20]) and/or vacation satisfaction [5, 21], but not vice versa.

1.6 Wellness tourism

However, certain types of trips are aimed at relaxation of mind and body, such as wellness trips (e.g. [6]). These types of trips may be more beneficial to an individual's sense of well-being compared to other types of trips. Health tourism, with a focus on good health, general wellbeing and its pursuit, is not a new phenomenon. Health-enhancing practices date back to ancient times (see [22] for detailed overview).

The concept of wellness includes domains such as physical, mental and spiritual health, self-responsibility, social harmony, environmental sensitivity, intellectual development, emotional well-being, and occupational satisfaction [23]. Wellness tourism refers to trips aiming at a state of health featuring the harmony of the body, mind and spirit, self-responsibility, physical fitness, beauty care, healthy nutrition, relaxation, meditation, mental activity, education, environmental sensitivity and social contacts as fundamental elements. These benefits can be enhanced significantly if people engage in health or wellness tourism specifically. That is to say, people travel with the explicit aim or principle motivation of improving their physical and mental condition [24]. Wellness tourism brings with it many new, potentially loaded responsibilities, not just for the normal touristic concerns of transport, accommodation and restaurant standards, but perhaps also for the care of the psyche.

1.7 Benefits of wellness tourism for subjective well-being

Although many statements on holistic nature of wellness tourism are declared, the real situation is drastically different. We provided the literature review of the existing wellness services and products and analysed which of them were aimed to manage or improve subjective well-being or wellness. The report of "Wellness Tourism Worldwide" indicates that the most popular wellness tourism services are: beauty treatments; sport and fitness services; leisure and recreational spas, and spa and wellness resorts [25]. Another report on wellness services and products worldwide [22] indicated the following wellness services and products: massage; acupuncture; naturopathy; Ayurveda; meditation; biofeedback; yoga; qigong; deep breathing exercises; guided imagery. Thus it becomes evident that this field, however, is dominated by the traditional biomedical view of health with minimal consideration for positive health and well-being conceptualisations [26].

While there are some studies that focus on the relationship between wellness tourism and well-being or health outcomes, most of those studies concentrate on the *physical* wellness dimension [26]. This is because the medical effectiveness of wellness tourism on physical symptoms has played an important role in destinations where *spa cure* has a long-standing tradition.

We found only one exception – over 500 wellness retreat centres' data were collated and reviewed in the study [27]. Content analysis of the type of treatments, programs and product offering at retreat centres indicates that a unique product of personal-development/counselling/coaching/confidence-building, along with other personal development are offered at a retreat that is different to many others in the wellness tourism sector.

1.8 Implications of personality for wellness tourism

Filep [28] specifically recommends the application of positive psychology theories and constructs to the tourism field, which would offer a more balanced view of tourism influences on well-being. Similarly, Pearce [14] has recently argued that tourism researchers and positive psychologists would benefit substantially by interconnecting their knowledge and ideas.

The spa experience is designed to be a healing transformation of the mind, body and soul. Whether in a day, resort or wellness spa, the mental healing service can truly benefit those in need of a mind makeover. And, presented correctly, it can be a new market niche and cash stream for the spa. The object is to promote it as a value-added service and part of the holistic experience. Offering mind analysis and healing techniques as part of spa's menu list broadens the potential for true healing to take place. It is a holistic mind, body, soul approach that fosters the promise for an unforgettable experience.

In addition to positive psychology one more promising holistic approach is body-oriented therapy. The interest in body-oriented approaches for increasing subjective well-being has been growing continuously during the past years. Within the embodiment concept the body is linked directly to thought and subsequently to understanding, and that cognitive processes are intrinsically connected to the body [29].

In the present study we argue that the approach of rhythmic movement therapy (RMT) for increasing subjective well-being [30, 31] can be regarded as highly effective in wellness tourism context. RMT, as well as many other body-centered psychotherapies, view the body as part and parcel of the 'mental' processes that govern the flexibility and range of our response patterns [32]. It means that body literally holds and maintains implicit cognitive, emotional, and perception material that shapes and constrains how we act and that access to and transformation of this material is necessary for increased flexibility and choice in one's life situations.

RMT is a model of psychological intervention that is philosophically and theoretically rooted in body-oriented psychotherapy, dance movement psychotherapy, and rhythmic gymnastics (aerobics) [30, 31]. The therapeutic work in RMT includes two main components: (1) diagnostic system of core personal problems corresponding with various characters and body types and

(2) rhythmic movement as a medium of change. RMT proposes theory and techniques that allow individuals access deep implicit material and transform related internalized emotional schema (core beliefs). The findings of the previous studies revealed the effectiveness of RMT for the treatment of disordered eating behaviours and obesity [30] and alexithymia [31] and for increasing SWB [33].

The paper unfolds as follows: at first we propose our operationalisation of SWB. It is supposed that the SWB of participants is a multidimensional variable that is composed of evaluations about different domains of satisfaction with life in a bottom-up or component-based approach, where participants appraise in a cognitive and affective way how they experience their lives. Our operationalisation of SWB includes five domains: material, health, work, leisure and recreation and personal competence.

Furthermore, our operationalisation of overall SWB (evaluated in domains) includes dimensions of several psychological constructs that are hypothesised to be components of mental map, underlying SWB, namely level of self-actualisation, sociotropy, perfectionism, locus of control, body dissatisfaction, neuroticism, and alexithymia [4].

The aims of this study are to demonstrate that 1) personality differences can be considered as the mechanisms underlying differences in subjective well-being and 2) rhythmic movement therapy (RMT) can be regarded as effective tool for increasing of SWB level in wellness tourism context.

2 Method

2.1 Participants

The study was conducted in the framework of Mental Health Management Program organised in the "Human Ecology" department of the Research Center for Interdisciplinary Environmental Cooperation of Russian Academy of Sciences, St. Petersburg, Russia.

At the baseline, a total of 213 subjects were recruited among those searching for counselling (psychotherapy) regarding various non-clinical psychological problems: e.g. low self-esteem, family problems, workplace bullying, etc. No any medical disorders or clinical complaints (e.g. diabetes mellitus, rheumatoid arthritis, pulmonary disease, depression, panic attack, etc.) were claimed by the participants. Demographic items included age and gender, which were assessed with single questions. The participants were aged between 18 and 65 years old, mean age was 36.6 ± 9.8 years, 42 (20%) were males and 171 (80%) were females.

The study was approved by the Ethics Committee of I.I. Mechnikov North-West State Medical University, St. Petersburg, Russia, and was performed in accordance with the ethical standards laid down in the 1964 Declaration of Helsinki. All participants signed informed consent form before participating in the study.

2.2 Measures

Subjects were assessed with the measures listed below. Russian-validated translations of all measures were used.

SWB was measured using *Integral Index of Social Well-being* (IISW) [34]. The test includes 20 items based on a three-point Likert scale and covers five domains of SWB: work, material well-being, health, leisure/recreation and personal competence. Examples of IISW items include 'How satisfied are you with your job?' etc. Two questions reflect the Leisure and Vacation domain: "How satisfied are you with the amount of leisure in your life?" and "How satisfied are you with the length, frequency and quality of vacations you have?" The responses are tabulated as follows: 1 = 'not satisfied'; 2 = 'don't know (not of interest)'; 3 = 'satisfied'. Higher scores show higher level of SWB, maximum score is 60.0. The IISW has demonstrated strong internal consistency and test-retest reliability (0.67). In the experimental sample, the IISW items generated alpha coefficients of 0.87 [34].

The *Personal Orientation Inventory* (POI) [35]. In the present study, only the main scales were used because Shostrom [35] recommended that the Time Competence (*Tc*) and Inner-Directed (*I*) scales may be used when a quick estimate of examinees' levels of self-actualization is desired.

General Locus of Control Scale of the *Locus of Control Inventory* (LOC) was used to measure locus of control because it uses all the items in the LOC and is the only LOC scale that does not have overlapping items [36].

The Neuroticism (N) Scale was selected from the *Eysenck Personality Inventory* (EPI [37]) to measure the traits of extraversion–introversion and neuroticism. Scores range from -12 to 12.

Alexithymia was investigated using the *Toronto Alexithymia Scale-26* (TAS-26) [38]. The TAS-26 is a 26-item self-report measure of alexithymia with a three-factor structure theoretically congruent with the alexithymia construct. A cut-off score of 62 was used to define alexithymia as recommended.

Body Image Test [39] was used to investigate body image dissatisfaction. Participants answered how often they felt uncomfortable about their appearance in different situations. The test includes 20 items, which are answered based on a four-point Likert scale. Higher scores show greater body image dissatisfaction.

Personal Perfectionism Scale (PPS) includes three subscales from the Multidimensional Perfectionism Scale by Frost *et al.* [40]: 'Personal Standards', 'Concern over Mistakes' and 'Doubts about Action' and 'Concern over Mistakes' and 'Doubts about Actions' subscales were combined into one scale. Thus, PPS includes 20 items, which are answered based on a seven-point Likert scale. The reliability and validity of the Russian version of the PPS were described in our previous study [30].

Sociotropy Scale of *Personal Style Inventory* (PSI [41]) was used to assess the constructs of sociotropy. The PSI Sociotropy Scale consists of 24 items which are rated on a six-point Likert scale. Higher scores show greater chance of sociotropy.

Participants were given approximately 1 hour to complete the scales described above.

2.3 Statistical analysis

Statistical analyses of the obtained data were carried out using SPSS 16.0 for Windows. Prior to completing analyses, all the obtained data were checked for normality (Kolmogorov–Smirnov test), homogeneity of variances (Levene's test), sphericity (Mauchly's test of sphericity) and equality of the covariance matrixes across groups (Box's M-test). Bivariate, two-tailed correlations were used to investigate the strength of the associations between leisure/vacation satisfaction and overall subjective well-being. A one-way ANOVA was used for between-group comparisons.

After assessment all subjects of experimental group were divided into two groups in accordance with their SWB level: group 1 – (20–40 IISW scores mean very low, low and medium SWB levels) – 96 subjects, 75 females, 21 males, mean age 36, 3 ± 11, 0 years) and group 2 – (41–60 scores of IISW mean high and very high SWB levels) – 117 subjects, 96 females, 21 males, mean age 36, 8 ± 8, 68 years. Two types of ANOVA analyses were provided: with SWB group as a factor and with gender as a factor.

3 Results

Leisure/vacation satisfaction was significantly positively associated with overall subjective well-being ($r = 0.597$, $p < 0.01$).

Table 1: Table assessment scores in groups 1 and 2.

Psychological variables, IISW and Leisure/Vacation Satisfaction	Group 1 N = 96 M (SD)	Group 2 N = 117 M (SD)	ANOVA F(1,212)	p
Integral index of social well-being	38.8(3.7)	50.3(3.9)	473.2	< 0.001
Time competence	7.1(3.2)	8.8(2.8)	18.7	< 0.001
Inner-directedness	41.5(10.2)	49.6(9.5)	35.9	< 0.001
Sociotropy	92.3(16.0)	80.5(17.3)	26.3	< 0.001
Personal standards	21.7(5.5)	20.9(4.6)	1.5	0.224
Concern over mistakes/ doubts about actions	37.5(10.2)	28.3(8.6)	51.1	< 0.001
General locus of control	4.6(1.7)	6.2(1.6)	50.6	< 0.001
Body image dissatisfaction	20.3(12.2)	15.2(11.7)	9.6	0.002
Neuroticism	3.5(4.7)	0.33(4.6)	25.9	< 0.001
Alexithymia	66.3(12.1)	58.5(11.2)	23.9	< 0.001
Leisure/vacation satisfaction	3.0(1.1)	4.6(1.5)	73.6	< 0.001

After the groups 1 and 2 were formed, the results of one-way ANOVA with group as a factor in entire sample indicated no differences in SWB level due to age ($F(1,212) = 0.14$, $p = 0.71$) or gender ($F(1,212) = 0.51$, $p = 0.48$). The

ANOVAs demonstrated that subjects of group 1 compared with the subjects of group 2 have significantly different levels of SWB as well as of all other personality variables, except for "Personal standards" (Table 1). 0

The results of ANOVA with gender as a factor didn't indicate any significant differences between males and females in all variables under study ($p > 0.05$) except for body image dissatisfaction. The scores of this variable in female group are equal 19.4 ± 12.3, in male group $- 9.9 \pm 7.9$, $F (1,212) = 22.4$, $p < 0.001$.

4 Discussions

Our result of the significant association of SWB with several personality variables is consistent with many other results. Results of several studies revealed the significant associations between SWB and neuroticism, high self-directedness and time competence, external locus of control, low levels of alexithymia, body image dissatisfaction, sociotropy and perfectionism (see [4] for review). Thus, we suppose that our specific operationalisation of SWB construct has merit. Our research provides evidence that thinking styles (mental models) may significantly influence SWB. Their role is not directly included by existing psychological theories of subjective well-being. This particular result provides at least partial explanation how personality may be linked to SWB.

Another purpose of this study was to explain the potential efficacy of RMT intervention for increasing SWB as a part of wellness service. Body-oriented psychotherapies for increasing SWB are rather rare. Nevertheless, our findings of RMT effectiveness are generally consistent with the results of several other studies in the field. RMT relies on body-based mindfulness as a primary tool to explore the implicit beliefs that organize life experiences and to address the attachment injuries that shape our emotional realities. Mirror neuron research has pointed toward a strong neuronal connection between one's own motor experience and intersubjective and empathic processes [42]. Our results on differences in body-image dissatisfaction between males and females give additional basis for importance of body-oriented approaches in holistic wellness healing. The findings of the previous studies revealed the effectiveness of RMT for the treatment of disordered eating behaviours and obesity [30] and alexithymia [31] and for increasing SWB [33].

The study limitations highlight the need for future research in this area of SWB. One limitation of our research is that we only provide a partial explanation for the influence of thought processes (personality) on SWB. The second limitation is that we provide only theoretical background for RMT as effective service in wellness tourism context. The further experimental studies are needed.

5 Conclusions

In general, individual differences play an important role in determining the manner in which people react on life circumstances and then play out in turn in the SWB that is experienced. Our research provides evidence that thinking styles (mental models) may significantly influence SWB and any program for its increasing must include mental healing service. Theoretical background provided for RMT as effective part of wellness service can be regarded as a good starting point for further studies in this field.

References

[1] Diener, E. Subjective well-being. *Psychological Bulletin*, **95**, pp. 542–575, 1984.

[2] Diener, E., Suh, E.M., Lucas, R.E. & Smith, H.L. Subjective well-being: Three decades of progress. *Psychological Bulletin*, **125**, pp. 276–302, 1999.

[3] Schimmack, U., Diener, E. Oishi, S. Life-satisfaction is a momentary judgment and a stable personality characteristic: The use of chronically accessible and stable sources. *Journal of Personality*, **70(3)**, pp. 345–384, 2002.

[4] Malkina-Pykh, I.G. & Pykh, Yu. A. *The Method of Response Function in Psychology and Sociology*. Southampton, Boston: WIT Press, 2013.

[5] Dolnicar, S., Yanamandram, V. & Cliff, K. The contribution of vacations to quality of life. *Annals of Tourism Research*, **39 (1)**, pp. 59–83, 2012.

[6] Nawijn, J. *Leisure Travel and Happiness. An Empirical Study into the Effect of Holiday Trips on Individuals' Subjective Wellbeing.* Dissertation Erasmus University Rotterdam, 2012.

[7] Erez, A., Johnson, D.E. & Judge, T.A. Self-deception as a mediator of the relationship between dispositions and subjective well-being. *Personality and Individual Differences*, **19(5)**, pp. 597–612, 1995.

[8] Cummins, R.A., Gullone, E. & Lau, A. L. D. A model of subjective well-being homeostasis: The role of personality. In: E. Gullone & R.A. Cummins (Eds.), *The Universality of Subjective Wellbeing Indicators: Social Indicators Research Series*. Dordrecht: Kluwer, pp. 7–46, 2002.

[9] Bowlby, J. *Attachment and Loss. I: Attachment.* New York: Basic Books, 1969.

[10] Schore, A.N. The neurobiology of attachment and early personality organization. *Journal of Prenatal and Perinatal Psychology and Health*, **16(3)**, pp. 249–263, 2002.

[11] Diener, E., Lucas, R.E. & Scollon, C. Beyond the hedonic treadmill: Revising the adaptation theory of well-being. *American Psychologist*, **61**, pp. 305–314, 2006.

[12] Barbas, H. Anatomic basis of cognitive-emotional interactions in the primate prefrontal cortex. *Neuroscience and Biobehavioral Reviews*, **19**, pp. 499–510, 1995.

[13] Sin, N.L. & Lyubomirsky, S. Enhancing well-being and alleviating depressive symptoms with positive psychology interventions: A practice-friendly meta-analysis. *Journal of Clinical Psychology*, **65**, pp. 467–487, 2009.

[14] Pearce, P.L. The relationship between positive psychology and tourist behavior studies. *Tourism Analysis*, **14(1)**, pp. 37–48, 2008.

[15] Neal, J., Sirgy, M. & Uysal, M. The role of satisfaction with leisure travel/tourism services and expenditure in satisfaction with leisure life and overall life. *Journal of Business Research,* **44**, pp. 153–163, 1999.

[16] Sirgy, M.J., Kruger, P.S., Lee, D.-J. & Grace B. Yu. How does a travel trip affect tourists' life satisfaction? *Journal of Travel Research,* **50(3)**, pp. 261–75, 2011.

[17] Chen, C.-C. & Petrick, J.F. Health and wellness benefits of travel experiences: A literature review. *Journal of Travel Research,* **52(6)**, pp. 709–719, 2013.

[18] Nawijn, J. Determinants of daily happiness on vacation. *Journal of Travel Research,* **50(5)**, pp. 559–566, 2011.

[19] Kovacs, A. *The Leisure Personality: Relationships between Personality, Leisure Satisfaction, and Life Satisfaction.* PhD Thesis, Indiana University. School of Health, Physical Education, and Recreation, 2007.

[20] Moghadam, M.B. Exploring relationship of personality's models and constructs of leisure. *Middle-East Journal of Scientific Research,* **8(2)**, pp. 530–535, 2011.

[21] Reisinger, Y. & Mavondo, F. Modeling psychographic profiles: A study of the U.S. and Australian student travel market. *Journal of Hospitality & Tourism Research,* **28(1)**, pp. 44–65, 2004.

[22] Global Spa Summit, *Spas and the Global Wellness Market: Synergies and Opportunities,* prepared by SRI International, May 2010.

[23] Mueller, H. & Kaufmann, E. (2001). Wellness tourism: Market Analysis of a special health tourism segment and implications for the hotel industry. *Journal of Vacation Marketing,* **7(1)**, pp. 5–17, 2001.

[24] Smith, M., & Puckzo, L. (Eds.). *Health and Wellness Tourism.* Oxford: Butterworth-Heinemann, 2008.

[25] The *4WR: Wellness for Whom, Where and What? Wellness Travel 2020 Full Report* is prepared for Wellness Tourism Worldwide by Xellum Ltd. (Hungary) with the support from Global Spa and Wellness (USA), 2011.

[26] Voigt, C. *Understanding Wellness Tourism: An Analysis of Benefits Sought, Health ‑ Promoting Behaviours and Positive Psychological Well ‑ Being.* PhD Thesis. University of South Australia, 2010.

[27] Kelly, C. Analysing wellness tourism provision. A retreat operators' study. *Journal of Hospitality and Tourism Management,* **17**, pp. 108–116, 2010.

[28] Filep, S. *"Flow", sightseeing, satisfaction and personal development: Exploring relationships via positive psychology.* Paper presented at the CAUTHE 2007: Tourism: Past Achievements, Future Challenges, 2007.

[29] Koch, S. & Fuchs, T. Embodied arts therapies. *The Arts in Psychotherapy,* **38(4)**, 276–280, 2011.

[30] Malkina-Pykh, I.G. Effectiveness of rhythmic movement therapy for disordered eating behaviours and obesity. *The Spanish Journal of Psychology,* **15**, pp. 1371–1387, 2012.

[31] Malkina-Pykh, I.G. Effectiveness of rhythmic movement therapy: Case study of alexithymia. *Body Movement and Dance in Psychotherapy,* **8**, pp. 141–159, 2013.

[32]   Mowrer, J. Accessing implicit material through body sensations: The body tension sequence. *Hakomi Forum*, **19-20-21**, 2008.

[33]   Malkina-Pykh, I.G. Effectiveness of rhythmic movement therapy: Case study subjective well-being. Body Movement and Dance in Psychotherapy, 2014, under review.

[34]   Panina, N. & Golovakha, E. *Tendencies in the Development of Ukrainian Society (1994–1998), Sociological Indicators.* Kyiv: Institute of Sociology, 2001.

[35]   Shostrom, E. *Personal Orientation Inventory: Manual.* San Diego: Edits, 1974.

[36]   Rean, A.A. *Handbook of personality assessment.* Saint-Petersburg: Saint-Petersburg University Press, 2001.

[37]   Eysenck, H.J. & Eysenck, S.B.G. *Manual of the Eysenck Personality Inventory.* London: University of London Press, 1963.

[38]   Taylor, G.J., Ryan, D.P. & Bagby, R.M. Toward the development of a new self-report alexithymia scale. *Psychotherapy and Psychosomatics*, **44**, pp. 191–199, 1985.

[39]   Jade, D. (2002). How good is your body image? http://www2.netdoctor.co.uk/testyourself/facts/body_image.asp. Accessed 20 February 2012.

[40]   Frost, R.O., Marten, P., Lahart, C. & Rosenblate, R. The dimensions of perfectionism. *Cognitive Therapy and Research*, **14**, pp. 449–468, 1990.

[41]   Robins, C.J., Ladd, J., Welkowitz, J., Blaney, P.H., Diaz, R. & Kutcher, G. The Personal Style Inventory: Preliminary validation studies of new measures of sociotropy and autonomy. *Journal of Psychopathology and Behavior Assessment*, **16**, pp. 277–300, 1994.

[42]   Gallese V. The roots of empathy: the shared manifold hypothesis and the neural basis of intersubjectivity. *Psychopathology*, **36**, pp. 171–180, 2003.

Section 2
Planning and development

Positive tourism precinct outcomes in developing countries

R. Moore
Anglia Ruskin University Chelmsford and Cambridge, UK

Abstract

Overriding goals and aims of improved and ongoing ecological performance arise when implementing 'sustainability' throughout the delivery process. This is seen where innovative organizations want their tourism developments to become accredited iconic master planned facilities. In a developing country using assessed world best practice planning, design, construction and operational principles has distinct advantages. An integrative process methodology leads to projects becoming great places to visit, to stay and to work. Adopting integrated economic and holistic approaches can result in decisions that provide long and short stay residents with healthy lifestyles and improved quality of life opportunities. These outcomes are closely linked to improvements in the built and natural environment so that it delivers for example privacy and quiet along with opportunities for safe and possible inspiring interaction with others. Also protection and regeneration of large areas of existing landscape encourages respect for the surrounding ecology and bio-diversity. As well they encourage equitable economic opportunities and growth. However reward and recognition go hand in hand with the approach. This paper reports on the use of an assessment framework tool engaged on several projects in China and Vietnam. The tool known as the EarthCheck Precinct Planning and Design Standard (PPDS) gave consideration to a perception that where positive development principles are being applied to mixed-use precincts there needs to be a means by which the outcomes of drivers can be assessed, benchmarked and certified as industry best practice for improved and on-going ecological performance betterment. The standard supports full integration of total development processes which aids delivery of balanced triple bottom line agendas.
Keywords: positive development, assessment, tool, reward and recognition.

WIT Transactions on Ecology and The Environment, Vol 187, © 2014 WIT Press
www.witpress.com, ISSN 1743-3541 (on-line)
doi:10.2495/ST140061

1 Introduction and primary findings

The aim of this paper is to report on the continuing diffusion of an international accreditation precinct and planning design standard **(PPDS)** into the travel and tourism industry. This latest phase involves the commercial usage of the standard which provides essential information for developers, planners and designers involved in a total development delivery process. The associated assessment reporting elaborates on the provision of a more rigorous and meaningful mechanisms of 'Sustainability Assessment' which is now a major goal [1]. This is primarily done by offering support through Key Performance Areas **(KPA)** and Sector Benchmarking Indicators **(SBI)** and actual measures. Described here is the linking of these to the crucial decision-making stages of a projects master planning and design with PPDS (see Figure 1), which is principally a framework management tool [2].

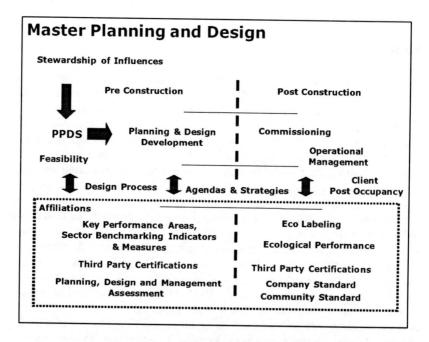

Figure 1:   Framework management tool.

The resultant analysis of a number of schemes in two developing countries in the Australasia region (China and Vietnam) is being used to further establish the sagacity of process engagement with precinct development particularly those with travel and tourism infrastructure. It also provides additional evaluation of model use in assessing the sustainability of mixed use undertakings that is consistent with independent international third party methodologies of sustainable development accreditation. This is needed for there to be supplementary refinement of the integrated framework model and associated tools for a developing country. The aim is to better meet the needs of developers and independent external accreditation as the standard is more widely diffused into other international regions and markets.

Achieving ecological performance improvements on medium to large mixed use precincts is a significant outcome for any developer and associated stakeholders. It offers opportunities to mitigate or reduce environmental and social impacts, improve bio diversity, ensure economic viability and increase returns on capital. These gains are as important for a developing country as for a developed one. The research shows that accredited triple bottom line outcomes are possible in the developing world without significant compromise of sustainability principles. In fact it is conceivable that in some places and with an innovative and committed developer it will be easier than in more established regions and markets due to fewer regulatory and institutional barriers.

These assertions are made because the integrated standard provides organisations with planning and design frameworks, environmental and ecological mitigation measures, energy and water models, social and economic commitment guidelines and checklists. Much of the content of the tool evolving from a data base of other projects firmly aligned to and collecting information from facilities being built and operating in developing countries. This enables the assessment of the developments and their operations in terms of outcomes and overall enhancement of total ecological or 'triple bottom line' performance to be firmly placed geographically and virtually site specific.

Further for schemes to achieve an Industry Best Practice level they need to establish a set of 'Environmentally Sustainable Development' (ESD) related goals to assist in aligning development outcomes with ethical and socially responsible business principles. Many of these match those found in newly aspirational development documents created in developing countries, not least China and Vietnam. Much of the content is inspired by UN declarations and national visions [3]. The translation into policy and strategy is often very succinct, localised and pragmatic because of existing infrastructure limitations i.e. water and energy supply. Due in part because resultant legislative directives and regulations often benefit from understandings gained from reviewing more mature regulatory systems. These developed structures have had to make significant changes to accommodate growing calls for more targets driven sustainable development. The two countries have reflected this demand in their statutory processes but benefit from considerable retrospection. They also show a considerable willingness to engage with wide ranging international expertise that offers innovative integrated management and technical methodologies based on whole system process approaches.

2   Research methodology and context

The research reported on in this paper is facilitated by investigations into the management, planning and design processes of a number of medium to large mixed use precincts. The ensuing analysis of these actual in-time case studies provide insights into how major developments come to life, evolve and are undertaken. They are part of larger number of case studies providing an evidentiary base used for determining comparative outcomes. Use of multiple case studies generates a cross case analysis which is both descriptive and covers explanatory topics as recommended by [4]. This option recognizes that each of these developments has its own context and perspective. The large number accommodates and overcomes the uniqueness and artificial conditions surrounding case studies. In doing so they are able to provide a means to access highly pertinent information and understanding of real life phenomenon.

Case studies predominantly provide qualitative data but are still able to use quantitative input to add to an overall picture of outcomes [5, 6]. Qualitative findings come into their own [7] when evaluating and developing the knowledge of how things worked on these case studies. From the lessons recorded it is possible that the observations on actual implementation of processes aid future precinct developments. This is due to these amplifications of good practice being formulated into amendment of this pragmatic framework model and tool which is already in use within the tourism development industry.

The actual case studies are mixed use precincts with an extensive mix of travel and tourism infrastructure and facilities. Their importance is not only scale but also the implementation timescales involved. All are underway and at various stages of the development process. On one of the projects major facilities (i.e. hotel, golf course, structural landscaping) have been completed and tourist occupancy is now underway.

Information flowing from the schemes is underwritten by the clients' own development teams. The projects were also targeted at several crucial areas of what have become major considerations for any sustainability agenda. They are 'Quality of Life' and ecological enhancement of a development and its surrounds. A further dynamic is that they are subject to the PPDS assessment and certification process. This provides a comparative assessment of employing a specific tool in different countries, geographical locations and demography and within dissimilar regulatory systems. Further they have important similarities despite variances in location, scale, nature and mix. These disparate features are not uncommon occurrences given the growth of tourism.

All of the case studies underwent an extensive independent third party assessment that utilised a significant number of practices. These include site visits, workshops, interviews and an array of investigative methods such as spreadsheets and checklists. The approaches aim at achieving transparent and relevant measurement of sustainability. Other measured factors have more to do with timescales and deliberate environmental, social and economic policies.

Crucially the major commonality aspects are as follows:

- *A Client/Developer was the promoter of development;*
- *They all were facilitated by a Development Director/Manager;*
- *All were subject to an integrated master plan approach;*
- *An integrated planning, design and construction management team was in place;*
- *A sustainability agenda was being pursued;*
- *Most underwent a third party assessment and certification process outside of normal statutory requirements.*

Data requirements to facilitate a PPDS appraisal are extensive and as with any proactive assessment tool the process is evidence hungry [8]. This facet of assessing a project is met by the client/developer's project planning and design team following directions from an independent accreditation assessor. The details supplied are used to corroborate and measure where practical predicted total development outcomes. They also inform expert judgements made regarding evaluation of predicted consequences and possible impacts against the suite of PPDS KPA's, indicators and measures. The initial overviews are provided by the project developer through a specific pre-qualification questionnaire that determines if the scheme is suitable for accreditation.

On acceptance into the PPDS process an assessment of the mixed-use precinct using PPDS KPA's, benchmarking indicators and measures takes place. To support expert opinion data/spread sheets are used to evaluate and determine how predicted values compare with industry best practice or norms. This comparative study route uses data collected over 10 years from similar resort operations around the Australasian and Caribbean regions [9]. It is in many cases location and geographical specific. The resultant matrix and in-depth reports are scheme discrete and provide the scored KPA best practice or industry norm outcomes of the assessor's findings. The resultant score identifies if the scheme has achieved industry best practice.

3 PPDS: a framework model and tool for accreditation

The accreditation procedure is formulated to be used from project inception and early planning and design stages of a development. It can also assess construction along with operational strategies and actual sequential activity. In essence it is a management framework for delivering sustainability agendas on developments. These should be integrated into the master plan as early as possible. This interjection allows for early detection, mitigation and/or enhancement of aspects of the total process which may impact on a schemes positive development [10]. It is not a rating tool but rather a continuing improvement journey map which allows the client-developer to respond to the uniqueness of the project's geographical and demographic location and socio-economic profile [11].

The assessment methodology employed by the PPDS process is based on quantitative and qualitative modelling and continued evolution via testing and amendment where appropriate of relevant KPA's, indicators and associated measures. This is done by concurrent in-depth evaluation of the management, planning and design processes employed on other assessed and accredited developments. Many of these as previously noted have similar geographical location, adjacency and development profiles. PPDS identifies impacts and then evaluates how the project teams responded to the challenges resulting from seeking ecological progression. Whilst the standard primarily gives regard to projected precinct planning and design outcomes it also reviews certain facets of the interrelated construction and operational phases. This overview mainly regards the use of policy and implementation strategies that may mitigate or reduce actual impacts. It also considers possibilities regarding evolving community outcomes. This is a critical area because ensuing equitable social and economic results may mean the differences between long term precinct success and failure [11].

Crucially for verification it is sometimes possible to assess these later stages as areas of construction and structural infrastructure work on some projects has started, is underway or fully completed. Further as stated earlier on some precincts occupation by tourists and resort workers of facilities has started. This is not uncommon particularly regarding enabling and off-site works on large mixed use precincts or projects that involve existing facilities scheduled for possible renovation and refurbishment.

4   Basis for assessment

PPDS assessment of sustainability engages ten KPAs for evaluation of a project's progress towards improved ecological performance. The process consists of two stages; assessment and certification. Only master planned precincts providing measurable evidence during appraisal of their sustainability agenda directed at achieving sustainable development attain certification. The review focuses on sustainable development contexts, KPA's, benchmarking indicators and measures. All are used to evaluate the predicted outcomes of a project.

The primary context and related KPAs are:
- *Master plans and design details;*
- *Building location and siting;*
- *Energy efficiency;*
- *Water management;*
- *Waste management;*
- *Resource conservation (materials);*
- *Chemical use;*
- *Wastewater management;*
- *Stormwater management;*
- *Social commitment;*
- *Economic commitment.*

The preceding is applied to appraise projects including any associated infrastructure and is considered for all phases of development including planning, design, construction and operation. To help assess sustainable construction management and occupational operation commitment a number of critical documents are required to be prepared at the planning and design phase. These will need to be submitted for assessment and may include the Master Plan, Building and Infrastructure Designs, Environmental Sustainable Design (ESD) statements and Design and Landscaping Codes. Also required will be Biodiversity and Ecology Reports, Environmental Impact Assessments (EIA), Energy and Waste Management Policies and Social and Economic Commitment Strategies.

Efficient planning and design allows early identification of constraints and opportunities, streamlining delivery progression, leading to sustainable outcomes while achieving the project objectives. PPDS supports the project's multi-disciplinary development team, manage the process. As with any new model or tool training for key members of the developer's organization or development team along with the possible engagement of an existing proficient consultant can further streamline procedures and enhance the outcomes for the precinct.

However as PPDS is based on actual case studies and reflects pragmatic project management approaches which are readily recognizable to most development managers this is not essential. Whilst this may be a potential cost saving a robust system of details and data collection must be created if the information demands of the standard are to be fully met. This feature is not uncommon to all the potential models and tools now available to the industry [12]. Evidence suggests that because PPDS is a framework process approach employed at planning and design phase the flow of data needed for assessment logically reflects the development team's usual information delivery programme.

As indicated the assessment is carried out using ccomparisons with international industry best practice which responds to the location and site specific restraints. Whilst these can include national, regional and district limitations only agreed partial recognition is given to possible accommodations for example issues linked to a developing country's supply chain capabilities.

This is a justifiable approach given that many schemes are instigated by national government development policies and international companies. Both of which often use sustainable development visages as prerequisites for environmental, social and cultural and economic development. The standard responds to these demands by using enhanced actual development project profiles and data. This offers a more rigorous framework for the protection or enhancement of environmental areas such as waterways and natural site features and social and cultural integration planning. It also provides more practical and tested means for reducing energy and water use along with greenhouse gas production. The resultant economic factors provide long term reductions of project operational and maintenance costs which can lead to improved project viability and financial success.

5 Case study precincts features, goals and key performance areas (KPA)

The following provides an insight into features of the assessed developments profiles and KPA's used by the Assessor when considering precinct sustainability. These translate into an ecological continuing improvement analysis which provides an overview of the general criteria, specific issues and major initiatives for medium to large mixed use precincts. Of crucial importance is precinct locality which often drives the nature of the master planned travel and tourism facility. The varied case studied schemes where a large integrated coastal resort located on Vietnam's South Central Coast, a mountain side medium hotel and villa project in southwest China and a large inland mixed use precinct in Eastern China.

Two of the schemes were underway and leant themselves to construction and occupancy interrogation. The final scheme which is an edge of city location is a major undertaking with a possible 7 to 10 year delivery programme. The development sites varied in topographical features, geographical conditions, and site areas, mix of facilities, accommodation type and tenure, low to high rise buildings, structural landscaping and infrastructure. All adjoined major environmental features i.e. coastal sand dunes, mountain ranges and extensive canals. Historical situates featured extensively with the precincts being in close proximity of several National Parks and UNESCO World Heritage Sites. All the locations were accessible via international airports though subject to transfer times of up to an hour in duration. The primary access road infrastructure outside of the project sites were the responsibility of provincial governments. The significance of the sites had generated major road and bridge building. Whilst the construction of this infrastructure was outside of the immediate project areas ecological impacts were considered in the assessments.

Individual precinct locations meant a variety of climatic conditions. These varied from a tropical zone known for weather extremes such as typhoons with violent winds and rain to a cooler and more temperate inland zone. The variations determined that each scheme had to have different approaches regarding comfort control and associated energy and water conservation programmes. The precincts offered a mix of 1 to 3 bedroom coastal, mountain, rural and urban villas, spa and canal detached individual residences, various 1 and 2 bedroom hotel/guest rooms and studios. These variable tenures are mainly formed in clusters of housing around a variety of facilities that include golf courses and associated maintenance stores and workshops, meeting, incentives, convention and exhibition (MICE) facilities, shops, ancillary infrastructure including, roads, as well as water and waste treatment plants. Once completed, the resorts are planned to accommodate approximately 20,000 guests and 8,000 staff/workers at any one time.

Originally secondary forestry and cultivated vegetation blanketed most of the sites. Some of the land areas were previously utilized mainly for agriculture or extraction i.e. titanium mining, making them all brownfield developments due to previous usage. Interestingly the overriding goal of improved and ongoing ecological performance arose from the client-developer seeking to implement 'sustainability' throughout the delivery process. The primary driver was for the precincts to become iconic master planned facilities in a developing country using world best practice urban planning and design principles. This it is believed leads to them becoming great places to visit, to stay and to work.

Adopting integrated development approaches resulted in decisions that provided the precincts long and short stay residents with a possible healthy lifestyle and improved quality of life. These outcomes were closely linked to improving the environments so that they deliver both privacy and quiet along with opportunities for safe and possible inspiring interaction with others. The proposed protection and regeneration of large areas of existing landscape on all the precincts should also encourage respect for the surrounding environment and its bio-diversity.

6 Sustainability: a master planning approach

On these types of mixed-use precincts it is important to find an inclusive design progression, which prioritizes sustainability and eventually improved ecological performance. This approach increases the probability that sustainable outcomes are achieved. The major impacts on sustainable master planning are underlying principles set by and found in the planning and design documentation. These include the initial influences on the precinct's sustainability direction and reflect the client-developer's overview of the primary project aims and objectives.

The development teams involved had ensured that the siting of precinct buildings and associated infrastructure mitigated negative impacts on the remaining natural environment and helped in the creation of positive ecological performance improvements particularly in biodiversity. Also they are committed to reducing the environmental impacts i.e. noise and air quality loss during building activities on site through appropriate management during construction (a crucial undertaking as parts of the resort are operational). This is being achieved by encouraging the selection of contractors and subcontractors with sufficient experience to implement 'green' design and to include sustainable construction in the contractual agreement.

Whilst there are far too many initiatives to note in this paper the following conjoined principles and commitments are common to all the schemes. They included the desire to create a genuine non-gated master planned facilities using world's best practice urban planning principles. To use 'Triple Bottom Line' approaches linked to Agenda 21 sustainability principles creating precincts where guests and workers will visit and work in safety. Importantly there are collaborative processes for the management of high value conservation land areas with the local community and authorities featured. This it is believed will bring equitable social and economic advancements to a developing country, local regions and adjoining villages.

Further goals, aims and objectives flowing from the integrated development team proposals included the protection of natural attributes, character and open space roles. This was achieved by using a low residential/other building land use density on selectively cleared land. Linked to this is the dedication of extensive conservation areas and open spaces along with appropriate land management regimes that meet the conservation requirements of native plants and animals. These will mean an absorbing of impacts that might place pressure on the schemes by sensitive planning and design, innovative technical solutions and operational management by-laws. Further all the precincts provide new nodal points for equitable visitor tenure and staff employment in the adjoining regions and contributing to better opportunities for ecological outcomes interpretation and education of visitors and workers.

In responding to these influences the developments benefit from a developer providing involvement at the highest level of an organisation matched by a long term commitment to the resort precinct and facilities. Clear economic, social and environmentally sustainable goals and vision integrated into the development brief with planning and design given a key development role. This means that the already noted triple bottom line principles implicit throughout the employed processes driven by a corporate culture and dedicated to creating socio economic development aligned with responsible tourism can be achieved.

7 Evaluation lessons, conclusion and recommendation

The precincts have been assessed using an indicator benchmarking evaluation based on measures that reflect accepted good sustainable practice. Achieving on average 45 'Industry Best Practice' outcomes from the potential 50 measures noted in the PPDS assessment matrix places them at the forefront of sustainable medium to large mixed-use resort development. The remaining measures certified as industry baseline or not being measurable is an outcome commonly found on all assessments. They normally involve land disturbance ratios, energy co generation and green materials reuse. These do not lend themselves readily to improved performance outcomes due to many developing countries land availability, construction industry supply chains or regional energy provision infrastructure.

The developer for the assessed precincts is committed to ecological performance improvement. Accordingly most of the KPA's, benchmarks and measures will be revisited and benchmarked regarding operational performance improvement under an aligned EarthCheck Company Standard which has a requirement for yearly recertification. The innovative organisation challenged 'business as usual' process norms whilst recognizing that sustainable agendas require considerable inputs when developing complex mixed-use precincts. The precincts achieved high ratings due in part to the implementation of an innovative delivery strategy and long term commitments to the projects. This willingness to put forward a sustainable agenda of its own making, results in a more effective development process. It also indicates recognition of the need for continuing involvement as many sustainable inputs and their impacts take place over time and may come about by adjustment to aspects of the development. The phenomenon will most likely be seen in the critical social and economic areas.

The power of specifically developed ecological performance strategies are seen throughout the precincts planning and design development. For example the social commitment guidelines seeking to create the equitable capital necessary to aid in the process of building a strong convergent visitor and worker ethos at the precinct. As important, are the management protocols and architectural and landscape guidelines. These ensure compliance throughout the development process regarding use, delivery and quality of all buildings and related infrastructure. The enshrining of documents and the commitment of a dedicated planning and design team and consultants to aid operational users will maintain an important link between developer, consultants, the building team, owners, visitors and staff along with other stakeholders.

The developer has responded to a growing demand for improved ecological performance on travel and tourism facilities. If this call is to be managed in a sustainable manner then it is without doubt that developments must be measured in terms of impacts and eventual ongoing operation. Without the ensuing data, critical planning and design decisions cannot be made with any certainty of success. By challenging the norms of precinct delivery and opening their planning and design to the scrutiny of PPDS the developer indicated a willingness to reduce if not mitigate entirely the impacts of development. These actions and others measured and noted at the p suggest that for those who wish to undertake innovative, responsible and committed approaches on their projects, there must be recognition given to the merits of an open mind in their approaches in seeking and achieving sustainable outcomes.

References

[1]   Berardi U, 2011: *Beyond Sustainability Assessment Systems: Upgrading Topics by Enlarging the Scale of Assessment,* International Journal of Sustainable Building Technology and Urban Development www.tandfonline.com (Accessed March 2012)

[2]   Moore R, Hyde R and Kavanagh L, 2010: *Planning, Designing and Managing Better Precincts,* Sustainable Tourism - Issues, Debates and Challenges Conference Paper Crete and Santorini Greece

[3]   Vietnam Agenda 21 Office, 2008: *Sustainable Development Implementation in Vietnam,* Hanoi Vietnam

[4]   Yin R, 2003: *Case Study Research - Design and Methods*, (4th Edition) Applied Social Research Method Series Vol. 5 Sage Publications California USA

[5]   Gill J and Johnson P, 2010: *Research Methods for Managers 4th Edition,* Sage London UK

[6]   Swanborn P, 2010: *Case Study Research – What, Why and How?* Sage London UK

[7]   Silverman D, 2011: *Qualitative Research 3rd Edition,* Sage London UK

[8]   Bell S and Morse S, 2010: *Sustainability Indicators Measuring the Immeasurable?* Earthscan London UK

[9]   EC3 EarthCheck 2013: *www.earthcheck.org*

[10]   Brikeland J, 2008: Positive Development, Earthscan London UK

[11]   Moore R, 2011: *A Process Framework for Mixed Use Precincts* RICS COBRA Conference Paper Salford University UK

[12]   Cooper I and Symes M. Editors 2009: *Sustainable Urban Development Volume 4 Changing Professional Practice,* Routledge London UK

Developing a more effective regional planning framework in Egypt: the case of ecotourism

E. H. Kenawy[1] & D. Shaw[2]
[1]*Faculty of Urban and Regional Planning, Cairo University, Egypt*
[2]*Department of Geography and Planning, University of Liverpool, UK*

Abstract

In Egypt, rational regional development plans are drawn up, but nobody puts them into practice. They end up gathering dust on the shelves. The main flaws in the current plan-making process are centred on the government's centrality and monopoly in decision-making; fragmentation between government agencies leading to multiple and often conflicting spatial plans for the same location; and an absence of negotiations between various stakeholders. These problems can be clearly demonstrated with reference to ecotourism planning. Such plans are being developed in highly sensitive regions, both environmentally and culturally, and there is a wide spectrum of stakeholders who are affected and influenced by any ecotourism development. Ecotourism development planning is a complex issue to the extent that it is beyond the capacity of any one stakeholder acting alone to resolve. The collaborative approach is an appropriate one, building consensus between the stakeholders, and developing solutions that are acceptable to all. By focusing on two case studies, the Fayoum and New Valley regions, and critiquing existing experiences of ecotourism regional planning, a collaborative ecotourism planning framework will be developed.
Keywords: planning process, collaborative approach, ecotourism, stakeholders, Egypt.

1 Introduction

During the last three decades, particularly after the spatial planning law was issued in 1982, spatial development plans have been produced but rarely implemented. Hundreds of thousands of dollars (from the national budget or international grants) have been spent in developing these plans but they gather

WIT Transactions on Ecology and The Environment, Vol 187, © 2014 WIT Press
www.witpress.com, ISSN 1743-3541 (on-line)
doi:10.2495/ST140071

dust on the shelves of the national agencies or local governments without improving local economic or environmental well-being. An informal survey, conducted by the authors, with nine key Egyptian development planning experts found that inadequacy of planning process was the major factor impeding the implementation of the plans. The current process and practice is centred on national government centrality and monopoly in decision-making and does not involve relevant regional and local stakeholders nor deal with their conflicts.

Moreover, the fragmentation between national government Departments and Agencies combined with competition for the same resources [1] leads to multiple and frequent plans being prepared for the same location under different names. This then leads to incongruous and incompatible proposals for land use, a failure to make decisions about development the loss of potential economic benefits and environmental quality. These plans are produced to a high technical standard by consultants, they do rarely meet the interests of relevant stakeholders and nobody puts them into practice. Without a system to facilitate negotiation and a building of consensus between the stakeholders, this failure cannot be addressed. But in addition the stakeholders also resist the implementation of the plans [2]. According to Kamarudin [3], one way to overcome these problems may be by promoting communication and collaboration within and between institutions, as well as broadening stakeholders' participation during the planning process. The collaborative planning approach (CPA) is exalted as one of the best methods to address this fragmented and highly centralised decision making [4] particularly in developing countries such as Egypt. It can resolve the conflicts between stakeholders and produce more shared and equitable solutions. However, the major contribution of CPA is that it improves the legitimacy and quality of decision-making, as well as building integration among and between governmental and non-governmental stakeholders [5].

Egyptian ecotourism development (ED) is used as a case study for several reasons: i) such plans are being developed in highly sensitive regions, both environmentally and culturally, and there is a wide spectrum of stakeholders who are affected and influenced by any ecotourism development [6]; ii) ED planning is a complex issue; no single actor has all the knowledge and information required to resolve an issue; iii) ED is seen as being important for Egypt in mitigating the issues of mass-tourism strategies which have led to Egyptian tourism products being perceived as low-price and low-quality [7]; iv) well planned and implemented ED could maximise the benefits from the Environmental Sensitive Areas which represent more than 17% of the country's total area [8]; and v) ED also provides opportunities to expand the Egyptian share of the global tourism market [9].

This paper aims to design a practical framework for operationalising a CPA in regional planning using ED as a case study. In order to achieve this aim, the first part of the paper establishes a conceptual framework for successful ED planning based upon an analytical review of the literature relevant. Two ED planning process case studies are then evaluated in the second part of the paper. The paper concludes by developing a practical collaborative ecotourism planning (CEP) framework by comparing the theoretical approach with practice.

2 Developing a conceptual framework

2.1 Collaborative planning approach

CP is a relatively recent approach, which emerged in the 1990s as a response to the deficits in traditional planning approaches which revolved around the central role of an expert. The key deficit of the traditional process was its inability for the experts to harmonise inter-stakeholder conflicts [2]. CP is a collective process for resolving conflicts and advancing a shared vision involving a wide range of stakeholders working together through face-to-face dialogue [10]. Furthermore, CP should be horizontally and vertically structured. The process should include all stakeholders at different levels of governance who have a stake in the issue [11] to produce a better plan and increase the likelihood of successful implementation because of stakeholder buy-in [12]. CP deals with development potentials in a holistic and multi-disciplinary manner to try to achieve 'win-win' solutions. It ensures that stakeholders are involved not only at the beginning but throughout the whole process and have a voice in both framing the problem and in shaping solutions [11]. According to Gray [13] and others (i.e. [10]), the incentives for using CP are: the increasing pressures on the environment and local communities, shrinking the state's abilities to solve social problems, and blurring the boundaries between the public, private and community sectors, particular at the local scale. Although CP is time-consuming, delays the process and reduces plan efficiency, it has been widely recognised as an essential ingredient in the development planning process for two main reasons: i) CP devolves the power from governmental institutions by providing stakeholders with specific responsibilities both during the planning and implementation processes [14]; and ii) it provides educational opportunities for improving stakeholder skills in dealing with planning issues [15].

2.2 Ecotourism context

Ecotourism is a sub-set of the sustainable tourism field. It primarily includes natural, rural and cultural tourism elements that are consistent with environmental, social and community values. Additionally, ecotourism is often considered to be a potential strategy for promoting a combination of visitor/tourist satisfaction, local benefits, and proactive conservation of local natural and cultural resources [16]. ED has been depicted as a system that promotes the organic interrelationships [14] between three subsystems: ecotourism (services, activities and infrastructure), natural and cultural diversity, and local communities [17]. Furthermore, there are several stakeholders who are affected and influenced by the ecotourism system, e.g., public sector, private sector and local people. Ensuring balanced relationships between ecotourism system components during the development requires effective collaboration among the relevant stakeholders within the process. This balance is very unlikely to occur without the stakeholders committing to and implementing the development plan.

2.3 The conceptual framework

Because stakeholder involvement is viewed as an essential component in the CP process, the success of the process can be measured by the degree of their involvement their influence on the decision making, and the development of a shared vision that reflects their interests. So there are three main questions to be considered within the process. Who should be involved? When should they be involved? How should they be involved? [4]. The first question is concerned with identifying who are interested in, and influenced by, the issues. The network is one of the main means of ensuring continuous interactive communication and negotiations between the stakeholders as well as facilitating mutual learning and development skills between them [18]. This network promotes and supports bridge building between the various stakeholders. Identifying and analysing the stakeholders during network building phase has been felt by experienced conveners to have a critical roles in managing relations and building consensus through the CP process [19]. The second question concerns the stakeholder involvement during the process and is concerned with which phase and level of involvement takes place based on Arnstein's ladder of participation [20]. The stakeholders should be fully integrated throughout the planning process from informing level to decision making, implementation and monitoring process [4]. Further, stakeholders should be chosen to participate in the different levels relative to their influence and interests in order to reduce the complexity and gain more control and efficiency. The question of how to involve them is largely concerned with the engagement techniques: effective stakeholder engagement requires a combination of appropriate methods at each step of the planning process for a more pro-active exchange of information and views [21]. These methods should be varied to motivate the specifically targeted stakeholders. Frequently used traditional methods may for example, exclude people uncomfortable with meetings [22].

Further to this, a preparation stage is required to educate stakeholders about key principles of ecotourism development and provide them with helpful information about their engagement [23]. Additionally, due to past promises often going unmet, as well as corruption within the controlling bureaucracy in stakeholders, particularly in developing countries need to be encouraged and motivated to engage with the process [14]. Therefore, a successful CP process should be concerned with the appropriate motivation strategies for each stakeholder group to help ensure their participation during the process. The process and outcomes of the CP need to be constantly evaluated to determine whether the stakeholder inputs have been successful in accomplishing their objectives and systematically adjusted during the process to improve outcomes [24].

Consequently, the analysis of the ecotourism initiative based on the conceptual framework contains four main elements, as Figure 1 shows: a) an investigation of the stakeholder network building process; b) an examination of the stakeholder engagement during the planning process; c) an evaluation of the process and its outcomes; and d) an identification of the barriers to stakeholder involvement and collaboration.

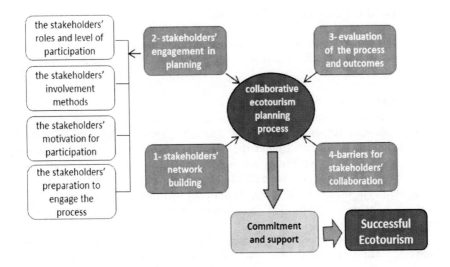

Figure 1: The conceptual framework.

3 Methodology

A case study approach was adopted to examine whether conceptual framework could be applied in practice. Evidence from the case studies were drawn from a critical documentary review of two Egyptian ecotourism planning initiatives, combined with semi-structured interviews with fifty ecotourism experts and stakeholders.

4 Evaluating the Egyptian ecotourism planning initiatives

The establishment of ecotourism development plans was first initiated in Egypt in 1991, but it did not adapt ecotourism as a new strategy for tourism development until 2002. This was after the World Ecotourism Summit recommendations which obligated all participating countries (including Egypt) to formulate national, regional and local ecotourism development strategies. Egypt has since developed dozens of initiatives for ecotourism planning in environmentally vulnerable regions.

This paper has chosen the two most recent projects as cases studies for this research: Fayoum Ecotourism Development Plan 2005–2015 (FEDP) was prepared in 2008 and Ecotourism for Sustainable Development in the New Valley Governorate (ESDNVG) was prepared in 2012. Both are located in the western desert, which includes nature, culture and heritage-based activities which provide a unique personal experience for ecotourists.

4.1 Evaluating FEDP and ESDNVG initiatives

This part aims to evaluate the initiatives through the lens of the conceptual framework to identify gaps in the planning process and the obstacles in applying the CEP in Egypt.

4.1.1 Stakeholder network building

In both initiatives, multi-actor conveners including three representatives of the regional tourism authority, the funder and the planning team [25] identified the stakeholders required to build the network. Both convener teams had the power and legitimacy to bring stakeholders to the table, derived from long experience and because they were independent experts and not representatives of the government office, as Getz and Jamal [26] had observed there was a great deal of stakeholder mistrust of the government because of previous negative experiences.

The stakeholder networks were composed of two sub-networks: an internal network, which included the relevant actors located within the project boundaries; and an external network, which was considered complementary, and includes stakeholders from the outside the local region, such as national and global actors [27].

Identifying the internal stakeholders; in both initiatives this process began by identifying the list of the relevant stakeholder groups then requesting a nominated representative from each group. The list of stakeholder groups for each initiative was slightly different and significant groups were missing from both lists. Hence, one interviewee remarked that *"the lists for both initiatives excluded some important and relevant agencies such as the General Organization for Physical Planning, which prepares several future plans and has an up-to-date database for the key infrastructure in each location"*. Similarly, the local planning offices in the separate Governorates and relevant city municipal administrations were not included even though these bodies were in theory in charge of implementing the plans.

In relation to the stakeholder identification techniques used for each list, there were also slight differences. In the FEDP, the conveners and planning team identified the list of stakeholders based on reviewing the documents of previous tourism plans and their long experience in the Fayoum. The ESDNVG initiative established an initial meeting with the main readily identified partners of ecotourism development such as New Valley Tourism Authority and the Governorate to define other possible relevant actors of ecotourism development by using a snowball technique.

With regards to nominating the specific representatives from each stakeholder group, representatives from the public sector bodies in both initiatives were nominated exclusively by the chief of each agency without any input from the conveners because they were not familiar with the detailed administrative structure of each agency nor the skills and knowledge of employees at each level. Furthermore any interference by the convenors in this process would be considered by the agency chiefs as an intervention in their internal affairs and then they would refuse to participate in the process. Therefore, often their nominated representatives had little or no knowledge about ecotourism development and their participation through the process was not effective because they had no decision making authority and were only observers.

Local community representatives in FEDP were identified following intensive field investigations with the craft producers which led to nominations via informal interviews and face-to-face discussions. But not all community groups in the Fayoum region, particularly those adjacent to the main areas with ecotourism potential were included in this process. In the ESDNVG the local community delegates were nominated using a snowball technique starting with the most famous and main artisans drawn from the NV communities.

Although the private sector will be critical to an effective ecotourism planning and implementing process, because of their long experience in the tourism market and their understanding and promotion of potential business opportunities which will attract their investment, it is interest to not how in practice their involvement in the planning process was very limited. In the FEDP, only a few ecolodge owners were invited as representatives of the private sector [28]. The ESDNVG also only invited a few representatives from hoteliers, small entrepreneurs and local guides [25]. A much fuller and worthwhile contribution of the private sector in the process could have been better facilitated by the Egyptian Tourism Federation (ETF) because it has a solid database and excellent relations with key persons from the tourism industry bodies.

NGOs involvement in both initiatives was very limited and not effective for two reasons: i) the majority of NGOs in Egypt are primarily interested in providing social services for needy people. There are few qualified and experienced NGOs working in the fields of ecotourism or environmental planning; and ii) there is no culture in Egypt which promotes the organisation, evaluation and development of NGOs working in the fields of the natural, cultural and tourism, contexts and thereby complementing the role of the state.

Analysing the internal stakeholders; Due to the wide range of stakeholders who are potentially interested in regional ecotourism development, an analysis of all the key stakeholders is a crucial step in building the network to categorise and define their role during the planning process, as well as identifying gaps in stakeholder so that a balance between underrepresented and overrepresented stakeholders can be achieved [21]. However neither initiative followed any known analysis techniques to achieve this balance. The conveners and planning team classified the stakeholders based on either the level of positions (top executive, first line of decision makers and regional/local executive employees) or sector (public, private, local community and NGOs) [25]. They were all considered as having the same degree of importance, although each stakeholder had a variety of different interests, influences and power for planning issues.

In both FEDP and ESDNVG projects, stakeholders were managed throughout the majority of the project activities as separate but essentially a homogenous (i.e. coming from similar backgrounds, culture and positions) groups [25]. Any success in the negotiation between these groups was based mainly on the convener bringing different stakeholder views together. Consequently, the classification method used in both initiatives could be considered as the first step in building a consensus between the stakeholders, but these groups really needed to be brought together in order to that true collaboration and a real mitigation of the conflicts of interests could be achieved as the foundation for building joint commitment for implementation.

The external stakeholder networks; these networks are just as important for a successful planning process as internal ones. Their support for ecotourism development can assume various forms depending on the type of organisation involved such as co-financing, major experience, political influence, training and media, etc. [27]. However, neither initiative really included any external actors, whether global or national, except ETF (which is an example of a national NGO), during the FEDP process. However in this case the convener did not define those aspects that the ETF could contribute too or support. As one of the interviewees remarked *"there are a huge number of international governmental and non-governmental organisations who are interested in assisting development in Egypt whether from a technical or financial perspective such UNDP, UNTWO and UNESCO, etc. However, they were not invited to participate in any of the initiatives"*.

Dialogue between stakeholder group representatives (SGRs) and their parent bodies; Dialogue between SGRs and their parent bodies during the planning process is very important if the outcomes of the planning are to be accepted and not ignored or disregarded in the future [13]. These dialogues within each of the ecotourism initiatives varied from one stakeholder group to another. In the FEDP, the dialogues between the governmental authorities and their SGRs were not good. The normal communication technique was written summary reports from the SGRs to their managers after each meeting held had been completed. But there was a lack of feedback and no guidance given to the SGRs in terms of what, if anything they should say as part of future negotiations. However, with the private sector agencies during the FEDP process dialogue between the SGRs and the organisations they represented were more pro-active. There was feedback and guidance given after each meeting so that the representatives could negotiate throughout the process to best represent the interests of that particular. For those individuals invited to represent the interests of local people, handicraft groups or NGOs the individuals offered only their own opinions without engaging in dialogue with other members of the group [28].

In relation to the ESDNVG there was limited consultation of SGRs and the constituencies that they were supposed to represent. For example, the majority of the governmental representatives were not accountable because they were the appointed chairmen of the regional or local offices. They rarely reported back to or consulted with the bodies they were supposed to represent. Furthermore, there was no dialogue within the other stakeholder groups (private sector, local community, and NGOs) during the process [25].

4.1.2 Stakeholders' engagement with the planning process

Stakeholders roles and their level of participation throughout the planning process; Stakeholders participation in both initiatives can be seen as tokenism, at least judged against Arnstein's [20] ladder of participation. It was confined to three levels only, namely: informing, consultation and co-producing.

i) Informing means sharing the information in two directions between stakeholders and planning team. The first direction was informing, telling the stakeholders about the planning activities but without giving them any chance to provide feedback [21]. Only ESDNVG produced six-monthly newsletters to help inform the stakeholders. However these were of extremely limited value because they were written in English and not accessible to the key audiences because either they were illiterate or could not speak English. The second direction of informing was getting information from the stakeholders. This was a good opportunity for contacting local communities which were intended to provide the main source of local information. FEDP used informal interviews and intensive field investigation to identify the constraints and potentials for ecotourism development in the Fayoum [28]. Similarly, for ESDNVG the planning team conducted a field survey throughout the study areas. However, the stakeholders were involved only in completing what was identified as being missing data.

ii) The second level of engagement was consultation. Its role was to widen stakeholder participation through an involvement of key legitimate stakeholders who had been left outside the formal stakeholder network. However these consultation events in FEDP did not increase the stakeholder participation because the majority of the attendees at these consultation activities were already participating in the process. In ESDNVG, no formal consultation meetings were held although the convener tried to use a questionnaire to get feedback from the stakeholders beyond the network. But this proved an unsuccessful technique to explore their views.

iii) The third approach to participation was co-production the method whereby stakeholders, decision makers and planners could jointly agree on adequate solutions [21]. However, in both initiatives the majority of stakeholders never participated in such activities. In FEDP, the middle governmental employees shared the production of the final plan with the planning team without inviting other stakeholder groups. In ESDNVG, the outcomes were produced in a different way. The stakeholders' role in this stage was just as an advisor for the planning groups. The planning team, then simply produced the final plan without returning to the stakeholders to gain their views on the proposed outcomes.

With regards to stakeholder roles during the planning process, there was no clear role for them during either initiative, except for the focal actors of the government agencies such as the Tourism Development Authority.

Stakeholder involvement methods; in both cases the main methods of stakeholder engagement focused on informing and training the stakeholders rather than actively involving them so that they had an input into decision-making. Hence one of the interviewees claimed that *"informing or education techniques could not alone fulfil the requirements of a collaborative approach for ecotourism planning"*. In relation to the appropriateness and sufficiency of the method at each phase of the process the following observations can be made:

i) The diagnosis phase consisted of two methods, face-to-face interview and a survey, which might be appropriate for single or small scale traditional communities but were not sufficient for large-scale developments with geographically dispersed stakeholders such as the FEDP and the ESDNVG. A second involvement method was public meeting designed to introduce both initiatives to interested stakeholders. These took place but were largely tokenistic because too little information was passed to the stakeholders because of the large number of attendees and the very limited time devoted to respond to various stakeholder concerns.

ii) The analysis phase also involved two main techniques: The ESDNVG initiative provided a good example of using workshops to involve the stakeholders during the analysis phase. But in FEDP they faced drawbacks because of the large number of attendees. This meant that not all of the participants were given sufficient time to provide their input into the discussion [28]. Secondly, a questionnaire could be used, but this only happened in ESDNVG. But in practice this was not an appropriate technique to gain meaningful input during the analysis phase [25] because the respondents answers were very brief and careless.

iii) The development phase included three different involvement events. In ESDNVG, a best practice exchange between the stakeholders from the Fayoum and the NVG was an appropriate and effective educating event. But in both initiatives, the workshops suffered from the same drawbacks mentioned earlier regarding feedback and a two way rather than a one way direction of information (from the convenor to the stakeholders). Also, one public meeting was not sufficient for large-scale development with geographically dispersed stakeholders. As a result participant feedback was very limited because the majority of them did not know anything about the initiative before.

Furthermore there were other key deficiencies that affected the effectiveness of the meetings such as: i) the time of the meetings was inappropriate for the stakeholders as they took place during work time meaning that many could not get time off work and subsequently attend; ii) the structure of the meeting were organised in such a way that they did not give the stakeholders enough time to provide their inputs; and iii) there was a lack of follow-up so that the stakeholders were kept informed of meeting outcomes.

Stakeholder motivation to be involved in the process; ESDNVG was the only initiative that used two different motivation techniques: fiscal incentives to the local communities and providing the private sector with access to the database of NVG ecotourism resources [25]. However, neither approach was really sufficient. The fiscal incentive was proved equally to all those that attended and was not linked to their inputs into the process. Furthermore the money was not really appropriate for the community leaders. Providing real legitimacy for them to engage or psychological motivations were needed more than money. In relation to making the database available to the private sector was insufficient because it came too late in the process– two years after the project had commenced.

The stakeholders preparedness for engagement; in Egypt, ecotourism development characteristics are not well known, and many of the stakeholders were not really qualified to participate in the planning process nor were they prepare before their engagement in the planning process began. Most of preparation events in both initiatives focused on raising awareness amongst stakeholders about running ecotourism activities, moreover such activities usually took too late within both initiatives being located at the middle or at the end of the process [25]. Likewise, the local communities of both initiatives are predominantly traditional and indigenous and they needed significant efforts to raise their awareness about ecotourism and determine their roles during the process. However, none of the initiatives really provided enough attention for these participants.

4.1.3 The evaluation procedures

Evaluation was one of the weakest parts of the planning process in both initiatives. Any evaluation of previous ecotourism initiatives to identify any potential lessons and within both of the initiatives described here reflection on either the process or outcomes both initiatives were very limited at best.

4.1.4 Barriers to stakeholder involvement and collaboration

In addition to the aforementioned deficiencies already described in previous sections, there were some barriers associated with the governmental and non-governmental stakeholders that create hurdles to their effective participation and collaboration. Understanding and anticipating these barriers should be significant for promoting more effective stakeholder involvement during the planning process.

Deficiencies in the government; there are a number of challenges facing governmental engagement which includes: i) centralisation in the system public administration; ii) a lack of coordination between the governmental authorities and the coordinating bodies do not have a legal mandate to harmonise intergovernmental conflicts; iii) a lack of information which is furthermore scattered across many government agencies. They often collect data separately leading to duplication of effort; iv) a lack of financial resources to initiate or support the planning process for ecotourism development. As the international funding for both of these (and other) initiatives was for the planning process only, the processes stopped once the funding ended; v) the lack of capacity within the staff of governmental bodies whether at central, regional and local levels; and vi) the lack of an appropriate legal framework; due to the ecotourism areas being located under the jurisdiction of several agencies they are governed by various legislations.

Deficiencies in the local communities and other stakeholders; these include: i) a lack of trust in the government as a result of negative experiences and previous unmet promises; ii) a lack of awareness about the importance of ecotourism development and the benefits of their participation; and iii) wide-spread illiteracy and low standard of living, so the major concerns from these stakeholders are their daily needs and providing the basic public services rather than future prospects.

5   The practical framework for CEP

Based on this analysis we suggest a new framework which adds two phases (1 and 4) to Gray's [13] CP model. There are a number of considerations that should be acknowledged during developing a CEP framework. These include: ii) harmonising and maintaining close links between the stakeholders through a good network and maintain relationships as well as regular dialogue between the SGRs and their agencies; ii) organising the process through an agenda reflecting all the stakeholder views; and iii) an experienced and neutral convener who will be significant in applying and achieving the overall objectives of the CEP framework. The CEP framework will include five inter-connected stages. There need to be overlapping and iterative links between them.

1. *The initiation phase* has been proposed to overcome several barriers such as the fragmentation between the stakeholders, lack of awareness and trying to overcome the negative response of stakeholders regarding their participation. This phase includes: i) building the internal and external stakeholders' network and, breaking the ice and starting to build the relations between them; ii) preparing the stakeholders for participation in the process; iii) evaluating previous similar experiences; and iv) trying to be clear about a specification of the end products (tangible and intangible outcomes) of the initiative.

2. *Problem setting* seeks to identify, understand, and then crystallise the issue after face-to-face dialogue. The main activities will be: i) ensuring common problem definition; ii) building commitment to collaboration; and iii) identifying the resources to ensure that these are sufficient to ensure the required negotiation activities can be completed [19].

3. *Direction setting* seeks to advance a shared direction for the future through: i) organising the procedures through establishing ground rules and agenda setting; ii) promoting joint information searches; iii) exploring options and reaching agreements; and iv) advocating a dispersion of power.

4. *The promotion phase* will be preparing for implementation. In this stage attempts need to be made to mitigate potential implementation challenges such lack of financial resources, inadequate products for the ecotourism market and reconciling conflicting responsibilities between stakeholders. The promotion group will be composed of primary and high-ranking actors to try and assist in mitigating these problems during the implementation phase. The main activities will be: i) evaluating the initial outcomes; ii) assigning financial resources for implementation; iii) marketing the outcomes to test their adequacy; and iv) raising awareness among the stakeholders of the implementation needs.

5. *The implementation phase* is to put the shared planning agreements into practical actions [26]. The main activities will be: i) phasing the final product; ii) defining the monitoring the implementation mechanisms; iii)

selecting a suitable structure for institutionalising the implementation process; iv) harmonising the conflict between the public agencies in terms of their land jurisdiction and responsibilities; and v) building external support.

6 Conclusions and future research

This paper has identified the importance of CPA for enhancing planning and implementation in Egypt with particular reference to ecotourism planning. It proposes a conceptual framework and has identified four elements for analysing and evaluating stakeholder involvement. Drawing on the evidence from two ecotourism planning case studies gaps in the current planning processes, as well as the barriers which have hindered the efficiency of stakeholder participation have been identified. The analysis of the two initiatives revealed that ESDNVG performed slightly better than the FEDP, although both initiatives performed similarly on the building of stakeholder network. However, there were very few differences in practice including stakeholder roles during the different stages of the process, the involvement methods, stakeholder preparedness and their motivation for engagement.

Finally, a practical framework for CEP can suggested as the basis for further research in operationalising a CPA for ecotourism planning and development. It can be used as a framework for filling in the identified gaps in the process. But how some of the barriers can be pragmatically overcome need to be addressed through further research. Additionally since the research was undertaken Egypt was and continues to be afflicted by political instability and what impact this has on tourism development more generally and ecotourism in particular and stakeholders willingness to become involved in future orientated planning strategies is uncertain. Once stability returns further research will help complement this paper to enhance the implementation of plans in Egypt in particular and developing countries more generally.

References

[1] Loughlin, J. and M. Nada, Do we Need To Rethink Egypt's Territorial Governance and Planning for Economic Development? in the Strategic National Development Support project, UN-Habitat, Ministry of Housing & Utilities and Urban Development and Ministry of Local Development. p. 167, 2012.

[2] Bonilla, J.C., Participatory Planning for Sustainable Cruise Ship Tourism in Mesoamerican Reef Destinations, in Second International Conference on Responsible Tourism in Destinations: Kerala, India, 2008.

[3] Kamarudin, K.H., Local stakeholders participation in developing sustainable community based rural tourism (CBRT): the case of three villages in the East Coast of Malaysia, in International Conference on Tourism Development, University Sains Malaysia Penang: G. Hotel Penang,Malaysia, 2013.

[4]   Monjardin, L., A collaborative approach to water allocation in a coastal zone of Mexico, in Civic Design Department, University of Liverpool, 2004.

[5]   Jarvis, R., Collaboration as a strategy for developing cross-cutting policy themes: Sustainable Development in the Wales Spatial Plan, in Department of Civic Design, University of Liverpool, 2007.

[6]   Preskill, H. and N. Jones, A Practical Guide for Engaging Stakeholders in Developing Evaluation Questions, in Evaluation series, Robert Wood Johnson Foundation: Princeton, USA, 2009.

[7]   Chemonics, Destination management framework – enhancing the competitiveness of the South Red Sea of Egypt, in Egypt LIFE Red Sea Project, Chemonics International Inc, 2006.

[8]   Ibrahim, M., Protected Areas in Egypt. Second ed, MSEA: EEAA, 2011.

[9]   WEF, The Travel & Tourism Competitiveness Report B.T. Jennifer, Chiesa, Editor, World Economic Forum: Geneva, Switzerland, 2011.

[10]   Kim, J.S., A collabrative partnership approach to integrated waterside revitalisation: the experience of the Mersey Basin Campaign, North West of England, in Civic Design Department, University of Liverpool, 2002.

[11]   Godwin, D.V., Collaboration as a Tool for Creating Sustainable Natural Resource Based Economies in Rural Areas, in Urban and Regional Planning, Virginia Polytechnic Institute and State University, 1999.

[12]   Albert, K., T. Gunton, and J.C. Day. Achieving Effective Implementation: An Evaluation of a Collaborative Land Use Planning Process. 2003 01/12/2003 12/08/2013]; Available from:
http://www.thefreelibrary.com/Achieving effective implementation: an evaluation of a collaborative...-a0114604591.

[13]   Gray, B., collaborating finding common ground for multiparty problems. First ed, San Francisco, USA: Jossey-Bass Inc, 1989.

[14]   Araujo, L.M.d., Stakeholder Participation in Regional Tourism Planning: Brazil's Costa Dourada Project, Sheffield Hallam University: Sheffield, Uk. p. 375, 2000.

[15]   Lima, I.B.d., The Micro Geopolitics of Ecotourism Competing Discourses and Collaboration in New Zealand and Brazil, in Department of Geography, Tourism and Environmental Planning, The University of Waikato, Hamilton, New Zealand, 2008.

[16]   Wood, M.E., Ecotourism: Principles, Practices & Policies for Sustainability: United Nations Publication. p. 32, 2002.

[17]   Ross and Wall, Ecotourism: towards congruence between theory and practice. Tourism Management, 20(1): p. 123-132, 1999.

[18]   Morton, C., Evaluating collaborative planning: a case study of the Morice land and resource management plan, in School of Resource and Environmental Management 2009, Simon Fraser University.

[19]   Jamal, T. and A. Stronza, Collaboration theory and tourism practice in protected areas: stakeholders, structuring and sustainability. Journal of Sustainable Tourism, 17(2): p. 169-189, 2009.

[20] Arnstein, S., A ladder of citizen participation. Journal of the American Institute of Planning, 1969. **35(4)**: p. 216-224.
[21] Taschner, S. and M. Fiedler, Stakeholder Involvement Handbook, in Attaining Energy Efficient Mobility in an Ageing Society, 2009.
[22] MDNR, A User's Guide to Watershed Planning in Maryland, Maryland Department of Natural Resources Watershed Services: Center for Watershed Protection, 2005.
[23] Cameron, J. and A. Johnson, Evaluation for development. Australian Planner, **41(1)**: p. 49-55, 2004.
[24] Kelly, C., S. Essex, and G. Glegg, Reflective practice for marine planning: A case study of marine nature-based tourism partnerships. Marine Policy, **36(3)**: p. 769-781, 2012.
[25] CISS and EDG, Ecotourism for sustainable development in the New Valley Governorate, CISS & Environmental Design Group: Egypt, 2012.
[26] Getz, D.J., Jamal T.B., The Environment-Community Symbiosis: A Case for Collaborative Tourism Planning. Journal of Sustainable Tourism, **2(3)**: p. 21, 1994.
[27] GIZ, capacity works, The Management Model for sustainable development, GIZ: German, 2011.
[28] CISS and EDG, Fayoum ecotourism development plan 2005-2015, Cooperation International South-South & EDG: Egypt, 2008.

VV-TOMM: capacity building in remote tourism territories through the first European transnational application of the Tourism Optimization Management Model

A. Jiricka, B. Salak, A. Arnberger, R. Eder & U. Pröbstl-Haider
University of Natural Resources and Life Sciences, Austria

Abstract

Management concepts for sustainable tourism development tackle the challenges of preventing the use of natural, socio-cultural and economic resources from turning into the abuse of such resources. Their major aim is keeping the balance between visitor numbers and the welfare of the local environment and population. In 1997, a new approach was elaborated – the Tourism Optimization Management Model, called TOMM for short. In contrast to other management approaches, TOMM acts as a motivator to achieve results which will be appreciated by all tourism actors. Rather than focusing on limits, it strives towards a process of mobilisation and identity building. Within a three-year transnational research project – focused on remote areas under transition to a strategic development of tourism – TOMM was first applied in a transnational European context. This paper analyses the potential and flexibility of the TOMM framework under special preconditions: all study areas were either just beginning tourism activities or were re-establishing their tourism businesses. The transnational application in this paper examines the ability of the TOMM-process to introduce a 'strategic' sustainable tourism management concept under difficult conditions, such as low tourism budgets, missing tourism data, heterogeneous stakeholder structures or lack of commitment by stakeholders. Findings of this international comparison demonstrate the potential of the TOMM-framework to encourage a learning process about successful and sustainable destination development, and about the need to monitor multi-dimensional data in order to survey and adapt the tourism strategy if needed.
Keywords: tourism monitoring, destination management, stakeholder involvement.

WIT Transactions on Ecology and The Environment, Vol 187, © 2014 WIT Press
www.witpress.com, ISSN 1743-3541 (on-line)
doi:10.2495/ST140081

1 Introduction

Keeping the balance between the multiple influences of visitors and the welfare of the local environment and population is the major aim of numerous tourism management concepts elaborated over the last thirty years. In order to define an approach which is based more on motivation and common values rather than on thresholds and limits, a new approach was elaborated – the Tourism Optimization Management Model (called TOMM for short). *"The vision of TOMM is to be a centre of excellence and inspirational leader in destination management"* [2]. Methodological comparisons classify TOMM as the most collaborative and transparent framework, compared to other visitor management concepts [3].

Within a transnational research project, called Vital Villages (VV), the successful application of the Australian framework was tested for different sites with various conditions. The developed TOMM-adaptation was named the VV-TOMM model after the project acronym. In contrast to the Australian situation, VV-TOMM was developed for remote destinations with unexploited tourism potential in the European context. Such remote areas, with little or no tourism development and a strong need for a strategic development concept, are a useful testing ground for sustainable tourism development.

This paper analyses the potential and flexibility of the TOMM framework under specific conditions:

1. Remote areas just beginning tourism activities or re-establishing their tourism business
2. Lack of management structures in several case study areas, determined by an analysis of governance structures (prior to the TOMM application)
3. Partial or near complete lack of monitoring systems, data availability and indicator usage, due to low awareness of the need to elaborate such systems

The transnational application in this paper examines the ability of the TOMM-process to:

- introduce a strategic tourism management system under difficult conditions, such as low tourism budgets, heterogeneous stakeholder structures, lack of commitment by stakeholders etc.,
- start an awareness-raising process for coordinated and structured development,
- encourage stakeholder interaction,
- learn from the process itself about successful destination development and the positioning of new attractions.

2 Background

2.1 Sustainable tourism through visitor management concepts

Management concepts for sustainable tourism development tackle the challenges of preventing use of natural, socio-cultural and economic resources from turning into abuse of the same. Their major aim is keeping the balance between visitor numbers and the welfare of the local environment and population. For the last 30 years, several frameworks have been developed by different organisations, mostly US or Canadian Park or Forest Services, and have been tested in their respective settings. These frameworks partly rely on the concept of carrying capacity. Examples of such visitor management concepts are the Recreation Opportunity Spectrum (ROS), Visitor Impact Management (VIM), Limits of Acceptable Change (LAC), and the Visitor Experience and Resource Protection (VERP) [4–7]. In Canada, the Visitor Activity Management Process (VAMP) was developed for the Canadian Park Service, but Canada also applies ROS and LAC processes. Most of these frameworks were developed more than 30 years ago. While these frameworks are very common in the US, few applications exist in Europe [8] and Asia.

Several of the frameworks mentioned above primarily aim at identifying goals and limits. The framework of the Tourism Optimization Management Model (TOMM) originated in Australia and followed a different approach [1, 3]. In contrast to other approaches, TOMM acts as a motivator to achieve results which will be appreciated by all tourism actors [9]. Rather than focusing on limits, it strives towards a process of mobilisation and identity building.

TOMM was developed for a "tourism icon destination" where the local people realised the necessity to preserve their natural resources to maintain the attractiveness of their destination. *"The people of Kangaroo Island see prosperity in tourism, but they know that what they have is a unique resource that must be managed carefully if it is not to be destroyed. They are working hard to find the delicate balance between development and conservation"* [2]. The idea was to build on these common values and to formulate together the desired tourism-related conditions along which all future processes would be oriented.

Ideally, increased tourism activities should be based on detailed information about their impacts. As a consequence, the idea of a management and response system was born. The process was fundamentally led by key government agencies and community groups *"to develop a unified strategic direction to address the changes being ushered in by tourism"* [2].

TOMM is a framework that involves a learning process for all stakeholders involved. Based on a continuous stream of information, the idea was to create awareness through an increase of knowledge about coherences between tourism activities and their impact on several different dimensions. It inspires people to contribute to a common achievement of visions. Following this approach, TOMM tries to minimise conflicts by creating mutually shared desired conditions [10]. TOMM is further characterised by a strong orientation towards future benefits and emerging issues [11]. Its main intentions are not only to monitor tourism activities but also to facilitate the decision making process, in order to make better, more sustainable decisions [12].

TOMM integrates more aspects than just the environmental and market components [9]. Thereby, it acknowledges the dependence of the tourism industry on the quality of the visitor experience and the condition of the natural, cultural and social resources, and emphasises this during the long-term monitoring process [1].

2.2 The TOMM-process

TOMM follows a three-step approach, described in the following studies [1, 2, 13].

In phase one, the destination gains a deeper understanding of the options and alternatives related to tourism development. The individual stakeholders have a commonly based understanding of the desired future development. This shared awareness of their own resources, and the visualisation of visions and strengths, is a fundamental and essential factor for successful results.

The second phase refines the output of phase one. The vision is broken down into desired conditions, which address the diverse components of a tourism product:

- environment
- regional economy
- marketing
- experience at the destination
- socio-cultural aspects

To identify and measure achievements regarding the desired conditions, indicators are selected. Indicators are defined according to the needs and special requirements of the destination [14]. These indicators are adapted by collaborative planning and broad stakeholder involvement. Afterwards, "acceptable ranges" are determined, based on participatory agreement. These ranges guide the destination on its way to achieving optimal desired conditions – a steady improvement provided. Consequently, the destination stakeholders survey 'the performance of each indicator and identify any need for action.

These ranges can be adapted after each monitoring period, which is part of the third phase. In case the acceptable ranges of the indicators cannot be reached, which is revealed in a monitoring and response phase, management response options have to be found. The identification of cause–effect relationships is essential.

As the main output of phase three, destinations can compare their 'performance' with benchmarks identified in phase one and the ranges set in the implementation phase. As a result of the information gained, it is then determined whether and in which category adaptation or modification is required, and which management actions need to be defined, have proven to be successful, or need amendment.

3 Design for VV-TOMM

The European application of TOMM was part of a transnational research project with eight case study areas in seven countries, including Austria, Germany, Italy, Czech Republic, Slovenia and Poland. Within the scope of the Interreg Central Europe project "Listen to the voice of villages", sustainable tourism development was the major goal. The emphasis was set on niche tourism products suited to the cultural background and natural highlights of the case study areas [15].

The following criteria were used for the selection of the case study areas:

- Remoteness of the area
- Start-up of tourism initiatives or re-establishing of tourism development
- Low level of organisational structure of tourism management in the destination compared to other 'established' destinations

As all study areas were either just beginning or re-establishing their tourism business, it was possible to implement an approach towards sustainable development in all case studies. The LISTEN areas were far from reaching limits and in many cases possess precious cultural heritage or natural assets, or both. In some of the pilot areas, traditional housing as well as ancient language and customs – hence the socio-cultural values – are a major topic, whereas others profit primarily from valuable cultural landscapes and/or protected areas.

Within the research project the authors were, on the one hand, involved in the process as experts together with the University of Trento Economic department. In addition to this, the University of Natural Resources and Life Sciences Vienna (BOKU) was also responsible for the implementation process of TOMM in an Austrian case study area in southern Burgenland.

The following table (Table 1) presents relevant elements of the TOMM process which are subject to the analysis.

Table 1: Elements of the TOMM process subject to this study.

TOMM-levels	Relevant aspects
Identification of desired conditions and common values	Destination perspectives, recognition of the added value of sustainable development, collaboration of tourism players and resources
Indicator compilation	Following long-term needs/perspectives, based on common agreement, selected by all stakeholders
Data-collection for monitoring	Linkage to existing data-systems, resources for regular updates, personnel and financial effort
Continuation of VV-TOMM after the international project-lifetime	
Interest for long-term monitoring system, Adoption of management measures	Set-up of a strategic tourism management structure, valid after the project lifetime; formulation of reactive management measures according to monitoring results

The application of TOMM in this specific context was conceptualised to answer the following research questions and hypotheses:

- TOMM encourages awareness in a destination for strategic tourism development at different levels of tourism management, and initiates a learning process,

- TOMM is explicitly suitable for areas with beginning or re-establishing tourism development, since it provides orientation, transparency and opportunities for collaboration. It does not address limits, which tourism stakeholders often perceive as discouraging,
- External knowledge is needed to elaborate TOMM, in particular in areas with beginning or re-establishing tourism initiatives.

Our transnational case study approach allowed the influence of TOMM on a collective learning process to be reflected at two levels:

1. on the transnational project level – which mainly addressed the responsible partners of the project in the eight participating countries. They were composed of representatives of regional development organisations as well as of DMOs,

2. on the regional application level – which comprises a larger group of stakeholders. In this context the before mentioned group (under 1) had a crucial role in knowledge transfer.

4 Results

4.1 Formulation of relevant desired conditions and selection of indicators

According to the original KI-TOMM framework [1], the major topics were elaborated under the five categories environment, socio-cultural aspects, marketing, visitor experience and regional economy. The identification of desired conditions was derived in a participatory manner from an analysis of the pilot areas and their development aims and needs.

Given the heterogeneous planning /starting conditions at the different case study areas, support was needed to identify the main topics relevant for remote areas under transition to sustainable tourism development. The BOKU University introduced TOMM and provided expert advice for the identification of core tourism management topics and the identification of desired conditions for the study areas. As the project partners in the pilot areas had different professional backgrounds (economic, ecological or planning), it was difficult for them to identify suitable indicators for all categories by themselves. With the support of the 'expert steering committee', however, they had a sound base for selecting their topics and amplifying or modifying the desired conditions and indicators to their needs.

The expert committee provided the LISTEN partner areas with a VV-indicator table, which included options for relevant desired conditions, a set of indicators specific to the desired conditions and a specification of information required to measure these indicators based on international studies and guidelines [9, 16, 17]. The chart of possible indicators, provided as an example, gave the regions the opportunity to consider data and indicators they already compiled or had in use. At this step, all of the regions' stakeholders were involved. After initial feedback on the indicators chosen in the regions by the local and regional stakeholders, a meeting took place to discuss the selection results. The expert team gave recommendations on which additional indicators could also be relevant. The results of the second indicator selection phase, in comparison to the first phase before the feedback round, are presented in Figure 1.

This figure shows the benefits of expert induced feedback loops in a cooperative planning design. Before the feedback rounds, the future benefits of an indicator-based evaluation of tourism performance were critically discussed among the partners. They argued that data collection would be too difficult for at least several indicators. Thus, the number of sustainability indicators they had selected was partially quite low. Particularly the environmental indicators were scarcely chosen. Similarities to the original application can be observed, where environmental indicators were considered to be rather weak [11]. This could be a result of the holistic focus on five dimensions, compared to other frameworks that focus more exclusively on ecological impacts. Information on 'creative data compilation', easy access to data and involvement of potentially relevant stakeholders was added by the experts, which lead to a re-consideration of the initial selection.

The second phase of indicator selection reflects the regions' understanding of a need to apply sustainability indicators, especially for long-term monitoring. The question and answer forum – a place where all project partners could ask general and specific questions concerning the implementation phase of VV-TOMM and their specific pilot projects – tried to clarify uncertainties, but also revealed the necessity to apply the indicators regularly and to monitor their performance. Consequently, both efforts (costs) and benefits were evident. These changes in the partners' perception of the VV-TOMM model are reflected in a more diverse indicator selection, with a better balance between the categories in the second phase.

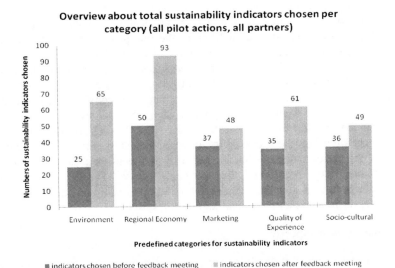

Figure 1: Overview of the indicator selection process.

The average number of indicators chosen per case study (in context to a new orientation of their tourism strategy through a project "pilot action") area was 23 (out of 50 indicators elaborated by the experts, together with the stakeholders represented in the project, as a basis for selection). Half of the pilot partners selected a rather broad spectrum of indicators and reached an average of over 31 indicators per partner. The other half was more conservative in their selection process. The average number of indicators chosen among these partners was around 11 indicators per partner. It showed that some partners were more hesitant in choosing indicators than others.

This can be explained by:

1. a delayed progress of introducing VV-TOMM to their respective case study areas (e.g. if they had difficulties in mobilising the local stakeholders which were not part of the project from the beginning),
2. a general low availability of data and awareness for monitoring in their regions.

4.2 Data collection

Some case study areas were characterised by very active and strong tourism management and/or regional development organisations, such as the Trentino SPA in Italy and the Landkreis Forchheim in Germany. Others had no data on regional tourism development. Overall, the availability of data was the major hindering aspect to an immediate commitment to carry out TOMM for some partners when they were in contact with their local stakeholders. This confirms findings of Australian research. Moore *et al.* [13] consider the TOMM framework more difficult to apply than other frameworks, like ROS and LAC, because of its complexity. Brown *et al.* [11] also state that TOMM *"needs large amounts of information und many resources for data management and manipulations"*. In contrast to the Australian example, which is a precisely defined island situation, the delimitation of the European study areas, and thus also the extent of data compilation, were not as clearly defined in all cases.

Only once 'creative data collection' approaches, as well as opportunities for obliging stakeholders (Federal County, tourism operators etc.) to provide data, were demonstrated, could the project partners be convinced to use the TOMM-model. To facilitate the process, the experts provided help and additional information on the indicator chart. After two VV-TOMM meetings, all partners agreed on the necessity to introduce indicators and to collect data or evaluate the performance of indicators already in use in their case study areas. Furthermore, they recognised the potential of VV-TOMM. It provided opportunities to work together with stakeholders and institutions to collect data, and it established long-term efficient monitoring systems.

4.3 Long-term perspective

Project partners went through an awareness raising process concerning the necessity of data collection and monitoring of tourism development processes in the long term. Before the start of the project, only few of them recognised the benefits of surveying tourism concepts and formulating management actions. The orientation of TOMM towards desired conditions without talking about limits helped to increase acceptance of the concept.

During the meetings, the benefits were compared to the additional costs. Best practice examples demonstrated the value of monitoring development processes, especially in areas with little or no tourism activity to that point. In this context, the application for support and funding by administrations and higher level tourism organisations were addressed in particular. The tourism regions realised the advantage of monitoring data to justify success, and the need to present a strategic concept with a long-term perspective.

5 Discussion

In the context of VV-TOMM, which referred to areas with beginning or barely developed tourism activities, this framework proved to be an excellent guide for establishing and improving tourism actions at first hand. Difficulties became visible later on in the process, which confirm criticism mentioned in previous studies.

For most of the VV-TOMM case study areas, the evaluation of common values and the definition of a strategic positioning, as provided in phase one, was essential, since they were at a starting phase of stronger tourism development and had to identify a new, appropriate niche market. Many of the project partners had not profoundly analysed their niche market and target groups before this project. During the selection process of desired conditions and indicators, tourism stakeholders faced international comparison and encountered good practice examples. VV-TOMM served as a 'catalyst' in raising questions and discussing visions and development options. For case study areas with existing tourism management structures, the second phase of TOMM was of special relevance. Only a minority of responsible stakeholders had recognised the need for broad, multi-dimensional monitoring of their performance before the project. Data compilation in several case study areas was limited by a lack of resources in terms of staff and budget. The inefficiency of tourism development without monitoring only became evident through the discussion process, especially for inexperienced, small tourism businesses and stakeholders. Furthermore, they learned of the existence of un-used data sources and additional inexpensive ways of collecting data. TOMM was a suitable framework in this context, since it strengthens dialogue with and between the stakeholders.

Problems, such as those mentioned before, are very typical for remote areas with little experience in tourism planning and management, and were exacerbated by the high demand for data and for effective response to indicators [11, 13]. It became clear that, under these conditions, strong expert advice is needed to keep the process going. Within the transnational cooperation, only phase one and two of the TOMM process could be approached. With regard to the complexity of the monitoring system and the very low budget resources in some of the case study areas, the continuation of VV-TOMM is at risk. Changes of personal responsibilities and the lack of a coordinator in some areas after the project lifetime pose a particular challenge, since the effective implementation of management actions has been slow even in the original application on Kangaroo Island [1].

6 Conclusion

Findings of the international comparison demonstrate the potential of the TOMM-framework to encourage a learning process about successful and sustainable destination development, and about the need to monitor data of several dimensions in order to survey and adapt the tourism strategy if needed. In Eastern European partner regions, in particular, an awareness-raising process towards a coordinated and structured development of tourism was initiated, which helped tourism stakeholders at a local level to communicate the need for data compilation and monitoring procedures to the responsible higher levels (authorities/ politics).

On the other hand, the European application identified limitations regarding the idea of the implementation, which is primarily driven by local stakeholders. It became evident that at certain steps (e.g. selection of indicators, definition of desired conditions) expert knowledge is explicitly needed as support – in particular in remote areas with starting or re-establishing tourism initiatives.

Acknowledgements

We thank all our project partners for their collaboration in the research process of introducing VV-TOMM. Special thanks are due to our local partners in Burgenland, in particular the regional and national development/tourism authorities.

References

[1]   Manidis Roberts Consultants, *Developing a Tourism Optimisation Management Model (TOMM)*. Surrey Hills, N.S.W.: Manidis Roberts Consultants, 1997.

[2]   Miller, G., Twining-Ward, L., *Monitoring for a sustainable tourism transition. The Challenge of Developing and Using Indicators*. CABI Publishing: Wallingford, UK, 2005.

[3]   Newsome, D, Moore, S. and Dowling, R., *Natural Area Tourism: Ecology, Impacts and Management, Second Edition*. Channel View Publications, Buffalo, NY, 2013.

[4]   Clark, R. & Stankey, G., The Recreation Opportunity Spectrum: A Framework for Planning, Management, and Research. *USDA Forest Service* Genereal Technical Report, PNW-98, 1979.

[5]   Graefe, A.R., Kuss, F.R., & Vaske, J.J., *Visitor impact management: The planning framework*. National Parks and Conservation Association, Washington DC, 1990.

[6]   Stankey, G.H., Cole, D.N., Lucas, R.C., Petersen, M.E., Frissel, S.S., The limits of acceptable change (LAC) system for wilderness planning, *USDA Forest Service*, General Technical Report, INT-176, Ogden 1985.

[7]   National Park Service, *VERP: Visitor Experience and Resource Protection framework*. US Department of Interior, National Park Service Denver, Service Center: Denver, 1997.

[8]   Burns, R. C., Arnberger, A., von Ruschkowski, E., Social Carrying Capacity Challenges in Parks, Forests, and Protected Areas: An Examination of Transatlantic Methodologies and Practices. *International Journal for Sociology*, **40(3)**, pp. 30-50, 2010.

[9]   Tourism Optimisation Management Model, *KI TOMM Strategic Plan Kangaroo Island 2010-2013*, 2010.

[10] Mac Kay, K., *Developing Community Tourism in Uganda*, The Tourism Optimization Management Model, Workshop Report On Community Tourism Development Framework in Uganda June 21st, 2007.

[11] Brown G., Koth B., Kreag G., Weber D., *Managing Australia's protected areas, a review of visitor management models, frameworks and processes*, Sustainable Tourism CRC: Gold Coast, Qld, 2006.

[12] Brown, G. and Weber, D., Using public participation GIS (PPGIS) on the Geoweb to monitor tourism development preferences. *Journal of Sustainable Tourism*, **1**, pp. 1-20, 2012.

[13] Moore, S., Smith, A. J., Newsome, D.N., Environmental Performance Reporting for Natural Area Tourism: Contributions by Visitor Impact Management Frameworks and their indicators. *Journal of Sustainable Tourism*, **11/4**, pp. 348-375, 2003.

[14] Twining-Ward, L., and Butler R., Implementing STD on a Small Island: Development and Use of Sustainable Tourism Development Indicators in Samoa, *Journal of Sustainable Tourism*, **10/5**, 2002.

[15] Jiricka, A., Salak, B., Pröbstl, U., Arnberger, A., Eder, R., *WP3 – Research and Analysis Final Report part II VVTOMM–the Tourism Optimization Management Model for the needs of marginal areas Managing and steering sustainable tourism development processes, Integration report*. European Commission (ERDF), Bruxelles, 2011.

[16] Choi H.C. and Sirakayab, E., *Sustainability indicators for managing community tourism*, Tourism Management **27**, pp. 1274-1289, 2006.

[17] Manning, E.W., Clifford, G., Dougherty, D. and Ernst, M., *What tourism managers need to know: a practical guide to the development and use of indicators of sustainable tourism*. World Tourism Organization: Madrid, Spain, 1996.

Portscape tourism in Japan: diversified and sustainable port space function

H. Kato
Graduate School of International Media,
Communication and Tourism Studies, Hokkaido University, Japan

Abstract

Portscape tourism in typical Japanese urban ports was analysed to reveal what kinds of resources were used for sustainable tourism in port spaces. According to the government policy so-called "Port Renaissance 21", ports should diversify port functions by introducing life-related roles as well as duties for cargo distribution and industrial base into port spaces. 5 ports of different types were selected as case studies to identify tourist attractions and resources in depth, and all of them were visited on site. This study reveals that in many ports the number of people who visit them as tourists exceeds the number of passengers who use them as traffic nodes. This study confirms that each case study utilises its own local resources as tourist attractions which include a) viewing spots on sea, b) drifting sea ice in port space, and c) a sea forest converted from a waste disposal site. Collaboration between each local port residents and people who live outside the regions is a key factor to gain ground in finding, preserving and using local resources as tourist attractions. The results show that many Japanese ports have been diversifying their functions to fulfil their regional expectations by using local resources, except that they wait to be fully exploited for sustainable port tourism.
Keywords: local resource, tourist attractions, Port Renaissance 21, heritage, viewing spot, breakwater, drifting sea ice, life-related, case study, waterfront.

1   Introduction

Portscape is defined in this paper as the overall visual impression of the built environment and nature scenery at ports. Ports and harbours have long been playing a vital role as venues for goods exchange because Japan is an

 WIT Transactions on Ecology and The Environment, Vol 187, © 2014 WIT Press
www.witpress.com, ISSN 1743-3541 (on-line)
doi:10.2495/ST140091

archipelagic nation, and most people have been living or working in the port cities. Since the Meiji Restoration (1868), ports and harbours in Japan have been economic engines to promote regional economic development by developing industrial areas along the coast. It is worthy to note that about one quarter of Japanese coastline is under port jurisdiction [1].

Having gone through a period of remarkable economic growth, people started feeling that quality of life should be given more priority [2]. In 1985, Ports and Harbours Bureau of the Ministry of Transport announced a long-range port and harbour improvement policy "Ports and Harbours for the 21st Century". In this policy, "life-related function", which is defined in this study as port-based function to provide visitors with access to the ports, amenity and enjoyment at waterfront, was officially authorised as one of the basic port functions.

Based on this new policy, port planning works aiming at creation of lively atmosphere at inner harbours were implemented for many ports nationwide. "Port Renaissance 21" is a planning effort to introduce the life-related function to principal ports in Japan. This type of planning efforts has been made for a total of 59 port districts nationwide from 1985–1990 only.

Preceding studies state that 7 functional facilities such as commercial/service, business, passenger terminal, international/regional interchange, culture, amenity, marine recreation are introduced in many waterfronts [3]. The preceding studies contributed to show general information that life-related function and facilities were introduced into many ports and harbours in Japan. Little specific information, however, was given on what kinds of tourist resources, in particular, what kinds of local resources were utilised in each redevelopment projects at inner harbours. In my study local resources are defined as cultural or natural resources which exist in the study region and can be used for tourism promotion. Information on local resources is vital because tourism can generate only when differences exist between subjects and objects of tourist.

The purposes of this paper are following threefold:

(1)   to make clear characteristics of port tourism;
(2)   to identify the kinds and features of tourist resources and local resources which support portscape tourism;
(3)   to examine sustainability of portscape tourism and its requirements.

The results reveal that many Japanese ports have been diversifying their functions to fulfil regional expectations by using local resources, but that they wait to be fully exploited for sustainable port space function.

2   The history of port development in Japan

The Edo Shogunate signed the Japan-US Treaty of Amity and Commerce, and accordingly opened 3 ports of Nagasaki, Hakodate, and Yokohama in 1859 when systematic seclusion policy terminated. A new political system was started in 1868 with the Emperor at the helm of the nation. In the early 1900s, ports in Japan strived for transforming from light industry-lead ports to heavy industry-dominated ports following the government's industry policy. Coastal industrial zone concept was proposed and implemented by business people at this stage of time.

The Port and Harbour Law was enacted in 1950, after the end of World War II. This legislation was a dramatic change concerning the construction, improvement, management, and operation of ports and harbours in Japan. This law clearly stated that ports were to be managed by port management bodies, which could be established by local government entities, not the national government.

Immediately after the war, Japan's economy began to recover. Japan's economic growth was led by mainly heavy and chemical industries. Ports were rapidly expanding terminals to cope with dramatic increases in cargos (fig. 1). These highly mechanized terminals were of such a huge scale that they had to be developed in segregated port areas away from city areas and peoples as a whole.

'Inner harbour' areas are used to be not only central places of the port but also birthplaces of most cities. Ports also started dividing their spatial structure into two parts: developing outer harbour areas for large-scale terminals and leaving obsolete and idle inner harbour areas. The rapid process of port modernization brought about serious disconnections, spatially and functionally, between ports and cities. In addition, people started feeling that more priority should be given to the quality of life rather than abundance of materials (Inoue [2], Murata and Kato [4]).

In 1985, a national port policy "Ports and Harbours for the 21st Century" was formulated by the Ministry of Transport. In this new policy, ports are seen as a comprehensive space where three basic functions are combined: distribution, industrial, and life-related functions (fig. 2). This policy stressed a need to revitalize the inner harbours with a view to providing more amenities and a better quality of life to people. Port management bodies conducted 'Port Renaissance 21', 59 port districts nationwide during 1985–1990.

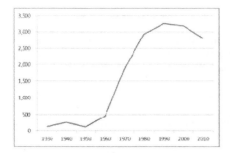

Figure 1:   Port throughput. (Source: Annual Port Statistics.)

Figure 2:   Main port functions.

3 Case studies

3.1 Methodology

The following 5 port districts are carefully chosen as case study ports to be analysed. These ports should represent a variety of port types throughout Japan, and were selected among Port Renaissance 21 ports and other ports which have been actively engaged in creating "life-related function" in their ports [5]. Population size of hinterland city, geographical location, characteristics of port activities as well as degree of touristic activities is taken into considerations:

Yokohama:	metropolis, central Japan, international, industrial;
Tokyo:	metropolis, central Japan, international and domestic, container;
Aomori:	medium size city, northern Japan, ferry port;
Kagoshima:	medium size city, southern Japan, interisland shipping;
Mombetsu:	small size city, northern Japan, fishery activities.

Figure 3 shows the locations of these 5 case study ports.

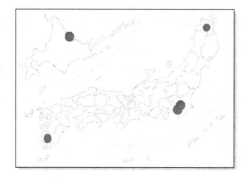

Figure 3: Location of the case study ports.

Table 1 shows both port activity indices and socioeconomic indices of hinterland cities. I visited these case study ports on site and confirmed the present situations of port facilities and their utilisation.

3.1.1 Case study: The Port of Yokohama

3.1.1.1 Outline of the Port of Yokohama Yokohama is situated 30–40km away from Tokyo and is the 2nd largest city in Japan, only after Tokyo. More than 3.6 million people live presently in the port city. Before the port was developed about 150 years ago, Yokohama was an isolated fishery hamlet where less than 100 houses were found (Horiguchi [6]).

The Port of Yokohama has been a leading port throughout the modernised age in Japan. The port handles a total of 121 million tons of cargo in 2011, and has been one of the leading international container ports. More than 3 million TEUs were registered in 2012. Port of Yokohama has also been No. 1 in cruising

Table 1:   Socioeconomic indices of 5 case study ports.

	(1)Throughput (ton)	(2)Population (person)	(3)Passenger at port (person)	(4)Port Visitor (person)	(5)Cruiseship (calls in 2012)	(6)Access (km)	(7)Site visit by KATO
Yokohama	121,326,484	3,605,951	91,175	10,000,000	142	0.9	17Aug2013
Tokyo	73,903,748	8,476,919	1,517,014	9,000,000	28	7.2	03Nov2013
Aomori	2,889,154	306,263	315,662	1,160,000	11	1.7	08Sep2013
Kagoshima	6,137,963	601,790	6,253,783	2,000,000	34	0.7	26Nov2012
Mombetsu	274,428	25,248	61,934	36,000	0	2.7	31May2013

Remarks;

(1) Port statistical yearbook 2011, Ministry of Land, Infrastructure, Transport and Tourism, Japanese government

(2) Ministry of Internal Affairs and Communications, Japanese government, Tokyo denotes central districts only.

(3) Port statistical yearbook 2011, Ministry of Land, Infrastructure, Transport and Tourism, Japanese government.

(4) The Ports and Harbours Association of Japan.

(5) Published from each municipality, figure in 2010

(6) Direct distance between port and city hall, measured based on Google Earth

(7) Dates surveyed by author

activities in Japan, and 142 cruise ship calls were recorded in 2012. More than 90,000 passengers embarked/disembarked at the port in 2011. In addition, coastal area has been extensively reclaimed after the World War II for use of heavy industries such as petroleum, chemical, steel and shipbuilding.

3.1.1.2 Zou-no-hana   Kanagawa was specified as one the five open ports by the Japan-US Treaty of Amity and Commerce in 1858. The Port of Yokohama was opened in 1859 because Yokohama was a part of Kanagawa.

For opening of the port, 2 jetties were built near the present day Osambashi, which now accommodates international cruise vessels. In 1867 eastern jetty was extended and curved like a bow to prevent waves for cargo loading/unloading at the jetty. Because of this shape, the jetty is called Zou-no-hana (elephant nose in Japanese). Since the jetties were too shallow to all ships to dock, lighters were used to transport cargos between the oceangoing ships and the jetties [7].

3.1.1.3 Zou-no-hana Park   Originally Zou-no-hana jetties were used for loading points for lighters as mentioned above. The jetties were crowded with export and import cargoes, and stevedoring people and merchants were busy on the jetties (fig. 4). After steel made wharf was built to the east of the Zou-no-hana jetty and another wharf was built on newly reclaimed land to the west of the jetty, the Zou-no-hana jetty lost roles as the main player at the port of Yokohama, and used as berthing facility and basin for shallow draft barges.

Zou-no-hana was severely damaged and then subsequently rebuilt after the Great Kanto Earthquake in 1923. The Eastern Zou-no-hana Jetty gradually changed its shape age by age, and present one is based on the rebuilt shape after the Great Kanto Earthquake.

Zou-no-hana was opened to the public as a waterfront park on 2nd June 2009 after the 150 years since the opening of the port of Yokohama. Zou-no-hana, where the port and city of Yokohama was born, transformed itself from where at one time being busy for cargo handling to where being public green space filled with open atmosphere. A total of more than 10 million people visited the redevelopment zone in the port of Yokohama annually (Figure 4(b)).

The life span of port facilities is long and their functions change occasionally. It is important to look at facilities and their environment carefully to decide what is the most suitable utilization for them.

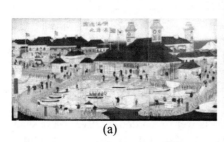 

(a)   (b)

Figure 4:   (a) Zou-no-hana in 1868; (b) Zou-no-hana in 2013 (courtesy of Yokohama Archives of History).

3.1.2 Case study: Port of Tokyo

3.1.2.1 Outline of the Port of Tokyo The Port of Tokyo has been servicing for the capital of Japan for more than 400 years. Presently Tokyo plays as one of the information centres for global economy. As of 2011 about 8.5 million people live in the 23 Special-ward areas only.

The port of Tokyo is situated at the innermost part of Tokyo Bay, and a marine area of 5,194 ha and a land area of 1,033 ha are designated as the port area and the waterfront zone of the port of Tokyo, respectively. Regarding containers, a total of 4,751,643 TEUs was registered in 2012, i.e., by far the No. 1 container port in Japan. Number of passengers embarking/disembarking at the port of Tokyo is about 1.5 million, and 28 cruise ship calls are recorded in 2012.

3.1.2.2 Waste management Socioeconomic activities of Tokyo metropolis urge the port of Tokyo to bear a part of city functions in addition to the primary port logistic function (Shimizu [8]). Table 2 shows the historical change of waste dumping sites in the port of Tokyo. A total of 761 ha of port area (marine area) at seven locations of the port have been reclaimed for waste dumping sites since 1927, and a total of 101 million tons of waste have been dumped into them (fig. 5(a)).

3.1.2.3 Sea Forest The Inner Central Breakwater Reclamation Area has been reclaimed with 12,300,000 tons of waste generated in the 23 Special-ward areas during 1973–1987, and size of the area is approximately 88 ha, forming a hill with about 30 meter high above the sea level.

Table 2:   Historical change of dumping sites in the Port of Tokyo.

Site	Area		Beginning	Completed	Waste (Ton)
	Total Area (m2)	Reclaimed Area (m2)			
No. 8 Reclamation	502,000	364,000	1927	Dec. 1962	3,705,895
No. 14 Reclamation	457,860	450,810	Dec. 1957	Mar. 1967	10,336,246
No. 15 Reclamation	808,260	711,907	Nov. 1965	Nov. 1973	18,438,658
Inner Central Breakwater	1,060,000	780,000	Dec. 1973	Mar. 1987	12,300,000
Outer Central Breakwater	N.A	1,990,000	1977	2011	52,100,000
Off Haneda Airport	N.A	124,000	1984	1991	1,680,000
New Sea Surface Deposit	N.A	3,190,000	1998	-	2,700,000

Source: Shimizu (1992) for No.8 Reclamation ~ Inner Central Breakwater
http://www.kankyo.metro.tokyo.jp for Outer Central Breakwater ~ New Sea Surface Deposit

"Sea Forest" is a name of the 30-year project to create a clean and green park on the Inner Central Breakwater Reclamation Area. "Sea Forest" aims at inheriting green and natural sea environment to next generations. Sea Forest fundraising campaign started to raise funds for tree planting activities, and planting seedlings at the site commenced in 2007. The project is targeting realisation of recyclable resources (fig. 5(b)) [9].

Tokyo Metropolitan Government expects that the large scale green wood which is afloat the port of Tokyo becomes a landmark of the national capital and constitutes one of the new resources for tourism in Tokyo. Actually this location is a good viewing spot to enjoy panoramic view of Tokyo waterfront including Sky Tree (World highest tower) and the Haneda airport. More than 9 million people visit the waterfront parks in the port of Tokyo annually.

(a)   (b)

Figure 5:   (a) Waste disposal site in c. 1994; (b) Sea Forest project (source: Tokyo Metropolitan Government web site).

3.1.3 Case study: the Port of Aomori

3.1.3.1 Outline of the Port of Aomori The Port of Aomori lies at the northernmost part of the Honshu, the largest island in Japan and designated as one of the major ports in Japan. Aomori City is the prefectural capital with a population of 306,263 in 2010. Nearly 3 million tons of cargos except ferry cargo are loaded/unloaded at the port in 2011. Some 300,000 passengers embarked/disembarked in the same year.

The port of Aomori stands at the opposite side of Tsugaru Straits to the port of Hakodate. Seikan ferry had been plying between the ports of Aomori and Hakodate. Passengers and cargoes used to move between the 2 ports in cabins or wagons aboard the Seikan railway ferry. During the peak period, 8,553,033 tons of cargo and 4,985,695 passengers were recorded at the port of Aomori.

Operation of the Seikan ferry was ceased in 1988 when the world longest Seikan tunnel with 53.85 km in length was completed. Trains were able to run 1,000 meter below the sea bed between Aomori and Hakodate. The port of Aomori is no more a railway ferry terminal, but still functions as car ferry terminal although number of passengers dropped significantly.

3.1.3.2 Revitalisation of the waterfront Since the railway ferry terminal is adjacent to the urban centre, revitalization of the obsolete district was a must for the regional economy. First step to revitalise this district was to build a symbolic waterfront building called ASPAM (Aomori Sightseeing Products Mansion) which is 76 meter high and houses a variety of offices and shops including a theatre, information booth, conference facilities, and an observatory. More than 1 million tourists and citizens visit the ASPAM annually.

One of the railway ferries are permanently moored along a quay as a memorial ship museum, and a waterfront park with 4.6 ha in area and a 3m-wide promenade were developed near ASPAM. A museum for local culture and festival is also opened together with commercial facilities for tourist's convenience. Recent efforts by the public sector are to develop a viewing spot on the sea (Muramoto [10]).

3.1.3.3 Promenading breakwater A promenading breakwater was developed in the port of Aomori and opened to the public in April 2004. This breakwater is 310 meter in length and people can enjoy walking and jogging on the breakwater. Surface of the breakwater are made of wood or natural stones, and benches and observation decks are provided at the central parts on the breakwater. At the head of the breakwater, a corn-shaped white lighthouse is installed (fig. 6(a) and (b)).

A local resident gave the following comment: "Visiting citizens and tourists are usually surprised to know that views from the promenading breakwater are so good. Views from the sea are so fresh for people because we have little chance to enjoy views of towns and mountains from the sea while we had ample chances aboard the railway ferries when they ran" [11].

3.1.4 Case study: the Port of Kagoshima

3.1.4.1 Outline of the Port of Kagoshima The Port of Kagoshima is housed in the prefectural capital of Kagoshima City with population of 601,790 in 2010. The port handled more than 6 million tons of cargoes, and chemical products are main commodities.

(a)

(b)

Figure 6:   (a) View from ASPAM observatory; (b) Promenading breakwater.

The Port of Kagoshima has been a maritime traffic hub for surrounding regions and islands. In addition, ferry services between the Honko-district and the port of Sakurajma have been provided. The latter is only 3.5 km away from the former, and ferry boats can transport cars and passengers by 15 minutes. The ferry has been servicing for 24 hours, and more than 6 million passengers use the ferries annually.

3.1.4.2 Old stone breakwaters In 1602 the Shimazu clan moved their residence to Tsurumaru Castle, which was built close to seashore. Area on the Kagoshima castle town was gradually expanded by reclaiming shore land. According to an old illustration drawn in 1843, several breakwaters and dikes had already been built to protect the castle town from high waves (fig. 7(a)).

Some of these stone breakwaters were demolished due to port expansion works or natural disasters by early or middle of the 20th century. According to records, Nabeya gangi (gangi means quay in old Japanese), which was built in c. 1780, was the oldest among them. It is pointed out that construction of the stone breakwaters and quays at Kagoshima was the largest port construction works during the Edo period because these old port facilities were about 14–15m deep. Even compared with other nations, the Kagoshima's port construction works is the world largest class at that time (Shimazaki [12]).

3.1.4.3 Original port plan As rapid economic growth continued during the 1960s and 1980s, the port of Kagoshima needed more space for cargo handling. Prefectural government formulated a long-term development plan of the port of Kagoshima in 1982. The new plan aimed at strengthening cargo handling function.

Only Shin-hashi and Iccho-daida breakwaters remained when the World War II ended, but the new port plan could not avoid negative impact to the historical port facilities. The Shin-hashi breakwater had to be partially cut off to create a new channel and the Iccho-daida breakwater was supposed to be reclaimed to create a land area. According to the new port plan, only top of the stone breakwaters will be visible on the reclaimed area.

Kagoshima Junior Chamber of Commerce expected that redevelopment of the Honko district could revitalise the local economy, and held Waterfront Festival in 1988 to attract people to waterfront. Tens-thousand citizens gathered at the waterfront and enjoyed fresh views and atmosphere at the waterfront. This festival initiated citizen's awareness about the waterfront and port.

3.1.4.4 Revised port plan The Shin-hashi breakwater had been covered with concrete to maintain structural strength. Therefore people considered that aesthetical value of this old port facility was little although historical value maintained. The port management body in 1993 uncovered the concrete in trial and found that surface of stone-made breakwater appeared complete and unhurt (Saito [13]).

The long-term port plan was revised so that surfaces of both the Shin-hashi breakwater and Iccho-daiba breakwater could be seen on sea from town side. Now Kagoshima's port heritage is easily shared by citizens and visitors who come to the Honko-district (fig. 7(b)).

The historical stone breakwater is a nucleus of local resources for port tourism. An aquarium and wooden promenades were built along the old stone breakwaters. More than 2 million people are visiting the inner harbour for shopping, eating and relaxing. People enjoy views of ferries passing nearby.

(a)   (b)

Figure 7:   (a) Kagoshima castle town (1843); (b) Iccho-daiba (2012). (Source: NPO Yume Minato Kagoshima.)

3.1.5 Case study: the Port of Mombetsu

3.1.5.1 Outline of the Port of Mombetsu Mombetsu is located at lat. 44° N, which is far south of London (lat. 51° N). Mombetsu sits on the almost centre of the Okhotsk coast which is the southern limit of drifting sea ice observation. During a harsh winter it comes ashore.

The port was designated as an important port in 1975 and as an open port in 1980. The port has been functioning mainly as a base for fishing activities as well as cargo transport for hinterland. A total of 61,934 passengers embarked /disembarked at the port in 2011.

3.1.5.2 International city for drifting sea ice research Mombetsu city has a population of about 30,000, and fishing has been a main industry for the city economy. Drifting sea ice comes ashore every January or February from the northern Sea of Okhotsk. Boats have to be lifted to land, and the city's marine activities are stopped and locked completely. The drifting sea ice has been considered and treated as a nuisance.

Leaders of the city realized that living together with drifting sea ice is a healthy choice and that drifting sea ice itself should be treated as one of the resources which the city exploits. In 1990 the city set up a long-term plan to aim at "International city for drifting sea ice research." Even before the City's long term plan, Hokkaido University had established a research facility on drifting sea ice at Mombetsu City, and a private shipbuilding company carried out field experiments on ice pressure and development of an ice breaker vessel (Archimedean screw-type) for tourists. International symposium on the Sea of Okhotsk and drifting sea ice was held in 1986 in Mombetsu. This annual symposiums have been collaborative works among academy, administration and civic volunteer groups.

3.1.5.3 Okhotsk Tower and promenading breakwater Okhotsk Tower was built in 1996 to serve as an academic research centre on drifting sea ice studies at 40 meter off the head of No. 3 breakwater. The tower is 38.5 meter high above the sea level and 7.5 meter low below the sea level. Total floor area is 2,344 m^2. The tower is composed of 3 floors above the sea level and an additional underwater observatory, which is the world's 1st underwater observatory in the ice sea. The tower has another function, i.e., to promote tourism in the Okhotsk region, particularly in the city of Mombetsu. Citizens and tourists can look at ecologies under iced sea during winter (Saeki [14]).

No. 3 breakwater is 515 meter long and 12.5 meter wide, and is designed as a promenade on sea with triple deck structure. The 50 meter section of head of the breakwater is widen to 30 meter and is connected to the Okhotsk Tower. People can walk on the top of the breakwater and get into the tower where panoramic views are provided on the upper floor. Both tower and breakwater became popular viewing spots for drifting sea ice on the Sea of Okhotsk.

More than 160,000 visitors were admitted at the Okhotsk Tower in the 1st year of opening. Figs 8(a) and (b) show the Okhotsk Tower, breakwater and ice breaker.

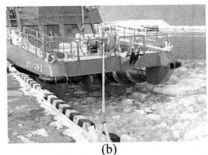

(a)   (b)

Figure 8:   (a) Okhotsk Tower and breakwater; (b) Ice breaker vessel (source: [15]).

4   Conclusion

Conclusions derived from this study can be summarised as follows

(1) Ports have been regarded as traffic nodes for tourists who embark/disembark at ports and depart for their destinations. In tourism ports also play a role as tourist attractions. This study reveals that in many ports the number of people who visit them as tourists exceeds the number of passengers who use them as traffic nodes.

(2) This study suggested that ports are attracting tourists using local resources. Port heritage, large open spaces in the port, good location for enjoying the portscape, and natural resources are identified as local resources for port tourism in the case studies.

▶ Port facilities have potentially multiple functions, and transform from one to another, reflecting needs of hinterland for a long run.

▶ Vastness of port space is potential resources for port tourism. Underwater space was used as waste disposal site, then changes to a tourist landmark.

▶ A breakwater head is a superb viewing spot on sea where people can enjoy a port view, a townscape and a mountain range.

▶ Historical stone breakwater appeared unhurt when capped concrete was uncovered. Citizens awareness helped preserve and create their heritage.

▶ Drifting sea ice, which had been nuisance, became tourist attractions along the Sea of Okhotsk. Recognition of locality creates tourist value.

(3) In general local resources are being utilised effectively to promote port tourism in many case studies. On the other hand, however, it is difficult by nature for local residents to be awakened to the importance of the local resources. Therefore, collaboration is necessary between local residents and people who live outside the regions for sustainable port tourism.

4.1 Suggested further studies

It is suggested that further studies should be applied by other countries, climate, culture, and types of port functions such as river ports and canal ports. Related papers will surely contribute to the portscape tourism and sustainable port space function.

The study reveals that many ports have been expanding their functions to fulfil regional expectations by using local resources, however they are yet to be exploited for other sustainable port space functions in Japan.

References

[1]   The ports and harbours association of Japan, ed., Japanese ports in figures (in Japanese), The ports and harbours association of Japan, pp. 200-201, 2013.

[2]   Inoue, S., Basic framework for integrated port space planning (in Japanese), Doctoral dissertation, 1992.

[3]   The ports and harbours association of Japan, ed., History of Japanese ports and harbours (in Japanese), Seizando-shoten publishing co. Ltd., 2007.

[4]   Murata, T. & Kato, H., The history of port development and its future extension, Japan technical session, 27th International navigation congress, 1990.

[5]   Waterfront revitalization research center, Japan, A synopsis yearbook of waterfront revitalization studies (in Japanese), Waterfront revitalization research center, Japan, 1990–96.

[6]   Horiguchi, T., Port of Yokohama – from birth to today (in Japanese), Journal of the Japan society of civil engineers, 57 (4), pp. 97-104, 1972.

[7]   Planning and Coordination Bureau, the City of Yokohama, Development process of port city Yokohama (in Japanese), pp. 015- 035, 1981.

[8]   Shimizu, K., Development of port of Tokyo and its history (in Japanese), The association for the geological collaboration in Japan, No. 28, pp. 11-18, 1997.

[9]   Umi-no-mori (Sea Forest), Tokyo metropolitan government, Bureau of port and harbor, Marine parks section web site, retrieved 08 November 2013 from http://www.uminomori.metro.tokyo.jp/index_e.html

[10]   Muramoto, S., Aomori port: rediscovery of my home town port (in Japanese), Port and harbour, 87(12), pp. 54-56, 2010.

[11]   Japan dredging and reclamation engineering association, Aomori port (in Japanese), Marine voice 21, retrieved 26 December 2013 from http://www. umeshunkyo.or. jp/202/248/data.html

[12]   Shimazaki, T., Roles of ports in modern society (in Japanese), Centennial symposium report on port city Kagoshima, NPO Yume Minato Kagoshima, pp. 7-9, 2007.

[13]   Saito, U., Selected cases for civic design (category of ports) (in Japanese), Japan society of civil engineers, retrieved 08 November 2013 from http://www.nilim.go.jp /lab/bcg/siryou/tnn/tnn0434pdf/ks043407.pdf

[14]   Saeki, H., The unique facility of sea ice observation on the bottom of Okhotsk Sea (in Japanese), Journal of the Japan society of civil engineers, 81(1), pp. 2-5, 1995.

[15]   Hokkaido regional development bureau, Mombetsu port office web site (in Japanese),http://www.ab.hkd.mlit.go.jp/kouwan/monbetsuport/information /index.html, retrieved on 18 November 2013.

Section 3
Sustainable tourism assessment

Green meetings: ecocertification of sustainable events in conference and business tourism

L. Ranacher & U. Pröbstl-Haider
Department for Landscape, Recreation and Conservation Planning,
University of Applied Life Sciences Vienna, Austria

Abstract

Conference and business tourism is increasing in economic importance, and negative environmental impacts of associated events can be significant. One method of making such events more sustainable is the ecocertification of green meetings. Ecocertification is a common tool for the advancement of sustainability in the tourism industry, and some empirical research has already been dedicated to the perception of ecolabels, as well as to incentives for and inhibitors against joining ecocertification schemes. For the special segment of green meetings, however, such research is pending. This study, therefore, is dedicated to the perception of ecocertified green meetings and to the certification process involved. Qualitative and quantitative research methods are employed to investigate the perception of the congress facility manager, an event manager and the attendees of an ecocertified conference at the Congress Centre Alpbach in Tyrol, Austria. The congress facility manager and the event manager are interviewed via expert interviews. For the conference attendees, a standardised questionnaire is used. The results reveal the level of awareness concerning the existence of the Austrian Green Meetings Certificate and the perception of an ecocertified green meeting including its associated benefits. Furthermore, the perception of the certification process itself, the event manager's reasons for pursuing certification, the congress facility's role in the certification process, as well as limitations to encouraging environmentally friendly travel are reported. The paper is concluded with a discussion of preconditions and requirements necessary to increase the number of green meetings in Austria.
Keywords: Green meetings, ecocertification, sustainable event, sustainable tourism.

1 Introduction

Conference and business tourism is an emerging industry, encompassing events, conferences, meetings, conventions, fairs and exhibitions. Their negative environmental impacts are becoming increasingly known and attention is being paid to foster better environmental management strategies [1]. In the meetings industry, the term 'green meetings' is used for events in conference and business tourism that minimise environmental impacts using a triple bottom line approach [2].

Hosting a green meeting is accompanied by benefits such as image improvement, reduced costs and the raising of awareness for environmental issues [3]. Furthermore, sustainable event management can result in a competitive advantage, as it can be used as a differentiating tool to distinguish the event from those of conventional non-green meetings [4]. On the other hand, green meetings are said to be time consuming, difficult to organise and can even lead to an increase in costs. Additionally, lack of information and a certain sustainability-weariness are often considered inhibitors [5], and even scientists remain sceptical of attempts to make conferences sustainable [6].

It can be agreed upon that actions to make events more sustainable are laudable. However, the question arises of how to support the proliferation of green meetings in conference and business tourism? Scholars argue that more research in the area of green events is required to identify success factors as well as barriers for their implementation [7].

Ecocertification for green meetings is one way to go: It is a popular tool to promote sustainability in tourism, and describes a procedure that audits tourism facilities or services and gives written assurance that they meet specific standards and are thus awarded a marketable logo [8]. Such certification schemes are increasingly available for events too: International standards such as BS 8901, ISO 20121, and other green meeting guidelines are currently considered to be leading [9].

Ecocertification aims to influence tourists to purchase greener holidays and hotel managers to implement environmental measures [10]. Thereby they create a balance between maintaining profitability and reducing environmental impact [11]. Ecocertification helps establish trust, as greenwashing – the unjustified advertising and marketing of products or policies as environmentally friendly to gain an economic advantage – is a common problem [12]. The availability of ecocertification for green meetings is therefore considered to promote sustainability in the meetings industry by generating benefits for the event manager whilst minimising environmental impacts and avoiding reproaches of greenwashing.

For every ecocertification to function properly, consumers need to have confidence in the credibility of ecolabels, and producers need to believe that obtaining an ecolabel will benefit their sales [13, 14]. Empirical research reveals controversial results about the effectiveness of ecocertification for promoting sustainable tourism: There are more than 60 ecolabels in Europe [15] and, owing to the number and variety of available certification schemes, tourists have difficulties identifying which certifications are trustworthy. They differ in intention, criteria, geographical scope, send confusing messages and are often of low quality [16]. As a result, confusion, negative attitudes, and ignorance among tourists have been reported [17, 18].

Environmental responsibility is a strong motivator for implementing environmental measures and for pursuing ecocertification [19]. Nevertheless, ecocertification also serves as a key to the green market. Thus, the proliferation of ecolabels is not only the result of hoteliers' increasing environmental awareness, but also of them addressing different market segments [20]. Barriers against ecocertification of tourism facilities are high certification costs, the fear of jeopardising consumer satisfaction, lack of time, knowledge and environmental awareness, as well as difficulties to involve staff [18].

In Austria, the 'Austrian Ecolabel for Tourism' was launched in 1996 as the first official nation-wide certification system for tourism in Europe, and it soon became one of the most sophisticated ecolabels in Europe [21]. Since 2010, an adapted version – the 'Austrian Green Meetings Certificate' – is available for congresses, company meetings, trade fairs and seminars [22]. For Austria, being a popular destination for congresses and similar events, this step towards green meetings is promising.

In order to investigate how ecocertification contributes to the proliferation of green meetings in Austria, it is crucial to understand how an ecocertified green meeting and the certification process is perceived by its attendees, event manager and the hosting facility.

2   Methodological approach

2.1 Selection of case study

The Congress Centre Alpbach in Tyrol, Austria is located in a popular tourist destination. The congress facility is Green Globe certified and a licensee of the Austrian Green Meetings Certificate. One of the many events hosted at the Congress Centre Alpbach in 2012 was the '1st International Conference on Forests for People', which received the Austrian Green Meetings Certificate.

The proliferation of ecocertified green meetings is considered to be dependent on event managers' perception of the certification process, as they are the ones deciding on whether to pursue ecocertification for a meeting or not. Furthermore, the congress facility is considered to play a decisive role in the certification process, as they are the licensees who host the conference and handle the certification process. Last but not least, the perception of the conference attendees is important to identify whether environmental measures are noticed and how they are evaluated. Acknowledging the importance of these three stakeholders, the following aspects will be covered:

- What is the level of awareness concerning the Austrian Green Meetings Certificate?
- In which ways is a green meeting beneficial for event managers?
- How is a certified green meeting perceived by the attendees?

- How is the certification process perceived?
- Who sets the impulse for ecocertification?

2.2 Interviews with the event manager and the facility manager

Expert interviews were conducted with the hotel manager and event organiser to gain insight into their perception of the ecocertification process. The interviews were conducted face-to-face and via telephone, using a guideline specified to the expert's role in the ecocertification process. The interviews were transcribed and analysed using extraction to structure them around the key research themes.

2.3 Questionnaire for the conference attendees

The conference attendees were handed out a standardised questionnaire, asking whether they were aware that the conference was certified, whether they had noticed the environmental efforts and how they had travelled to the conference. The data was coded and analysed with SPSS using relative frequencies and chi-square tests.

3 Main findings

3.1 Interview with the event manager

3.1.1 Perception of the Austrian Green Meetings Certificate

The event manager knew the Austrian Ecolabel for Tourism and about green meetings, but the availability of a national label was considered a novelty. Despite the fact that a trend for sustainable conferences and international green meeting initiatives was identified, green meetings were considered to present a niche market:

> "I think there is a specific clientele or target group who knows about green meetings. Especially people coming from natural sciences or social sciences, who do research on sustainability."

The availability of the Austrian Green Meetings Certificate was considered a positive development in the Austrian meetings industry, but the demand for ecocertification was estimated to be only limited, as sustainability in event management only plays a minor role for the majority of event managers.

3.1.2 Perception of the environmental efforts

Environmental efforts were considered to contribute to the overall quality and sustainability of the conference. Especially the efforts concerning catering (i.e. local and organic foods) were very positively perceived, as they contributed to the whole atmosphere of the conference.

The reduction of plastic waste, promotional gifts and paper, as well as the efficient use of renewable energy in the conference facility were acknowledged. Field trips were conducted via shuttle bus and accommodation was in walking distance from the congress facility, to reduce emissions. However, concerning travel to the congress facility, the environmental benefits were considered to be limited:

> "Alpbach is located remotely in the Alps and therefore difficult to reach with public transportation. Through offering a shuttle service from Munich airport to Alpbach we were able to reduce emissions. But I think, in terms of environmentally friendly travel, there is still room for improvement."

The event manager was aware that international conferences are important for the scientific community to engage in networking and therefore will always depend on people travelling by plane.

3.1.3 The role of event manager in the certification process

It was important for the event manager to support the green image of her research facility, and the conference was planned from the beginning to be as green as possible. The conference had to be consistent with the university's profile. Apart from image reasons, the support and personal commitment of employees also provided a significant incentive for hosting a green meeting:

> "This is what we want and that is also the attitude of our employees. Because in everyday life we are always dealing with topics such as Fair Trade, local products and waste separation – of course we organise a green meeting."

The green meeting was also intended to create awareness for the issue of sustainability, so that every single conference attendee would become aware of her or his environmental impacts. In total, image reasons and personal moral responsibility were the main reasons for hosting a green meeting.

3.1.4 The event manager's perception of the certification process

Despite the event manager's intention to host a green meeting, the actual impulse to ecocertify the conference came from the congress facility. The event manager was informed about ecocertification and was offered expertise in the form of a green meetings manager. It was considered a great advantage that the congress facility already fulfilled many criteria required for certification, and the facility was considered to significantly contribute to the general feasibility of the certification process. Concerning ecocertification itself, the flexibility of criteria – some are obligatory others can be chosen from a given set of criteria – was considered to ease the ecocertification process. No major obstacles or difficulties were identified, but the event manager was aware that cost limitations or some criteria could present an obstacle:

> "Scientific conferences, especially, are very budget oriented, and the question automatically arises wether additional expenses for certification can be allowed. If the cost would have increased significantly, we could not have done it. Also, if we had had to fulfil all criteria, it would not have been possible."

Overall, the ecocertification process was perceived as requiring some extra effort, but as being definitely feasible due to the flexibility of criteria, the facility's assistance during the whole ecocertification process and because the facility already fulfilled some of the required criteria.

3.2 Interview with the facility manager

3.2.1 Benefits associated with the Austrian Green Meetings Certificate

When the congress facility started to offer green meetings, they soon realised that an external verification of environmental claims would be necessary, because customers increasingly asked for it. The Austrian Green Meetings Certificate was chosen for this purpose, because it is a well-known certificate and certifies both the facility and the hosted events. This is of central importance because, within Austria, the certificate is considered to have the status of a brand:

> "Ecocertified green meetings can be used for marketing purposes, public relations or corporate social responsibility reporting. The certificate allows events to differentiate themselves from others, and to position themselves on the green market to gain competitive advantages."

Although it is considered to be of limited international relevance, it is still seen as a useful tool to raise awareness for environmental issues, as nearly half of all visitors attended a green meeting at Alpbach and take this idea home.

3.2.2 Perception of the environmental efforts

Feedback on ecocertified green meetings was reported to be overwhelmingly positive. Environmental efforts are differently perceived and therefore have to be communicated in various ways. For example, concerning renewable energy supply and energy saving devices, active information through a tour upon attendees' arrival is necessary. On the other hand, green meeting attendees were found to be very sensitive towards environmental efforts surrounding food. Food is labelled (e.g. as organic) and noticed immediately. Concerning environmentally friendly travel, the facility manager is aware that international attendees will always remain part of this business:

> "We cannot exclude attendees who have to travel by plane to get to Alpbach, or ask them to travel by ship instead. But we try to optimise environmental measures where it is feasible to do so."

Attendees are actively informed about environmentally friendly travel and the possibility to travel with public transportation, and carbon offsetting is encouraged.

3.2.3 The role of the congress facility in the certification process

The Congress Centre Alpbach is usually chosen because of its complete offer as an international congress facility. The integration of green meetings in their offers and the possibility to ecocertify meetings are considered cherries on the icing:

> "Ecocertified green meetings are largely the result of our initiative. Event managers choose Alpbach because of its complete offer. To win them over for ecocertification, we need to actively inform them and ease their fears of escalating bureaucracy and costs."

Through the facility's active role, by providing information and offering expertise, they make ecocertification palatable for event managers. Event managers are informed about the possibility of ecocertification and are encouraged by the provision of expertise and precise information on the expected workload and the obtained benefits.

3.2.4 The facility manager's perception of the certification process

Event managers are often afraid of increased costs and workload linked to ecocertification. According to the facility manager, these fears are unfounded:

> "Because we have already implemented many criteria in our congress facility, ecocertification for green meetings is proffered on a silver platter. Of course the event manger has to ensure compliance with the criteria, which is associated with some extra effort. But this is just a question of willingness, as the certification was designed to be attractive for event managers, and not to scare them off."

A cost increase is often considered a barrier for certification, but in comparison to the overall costs of a conference, these additional expenses are minimal and contribute directly to the quality of the event. For example, catering according to certification criteria is more expensive, but is composed of high quality products.

The flexibility of certification criteria and the handling of the ecocertification process by the congress facility were considered advantages. The facility manager identified no significant obstacles needing to be faced in the ecocertification process. The decision for or against ecocertification was not considered to be a question of available resources, but rather a question of willingness.

3.3 Questionnaires for the conference attendees

3.3.1 Attendees' awareness of the Austrian Green Meetings Certificate

In total, 79 questionnaires were received, constituting a 50% return rate. 51% of the conference attendees came from Europe, and 18% from Austria. International attendees from other continents made up nearly one third. Figure 1 illustrates that

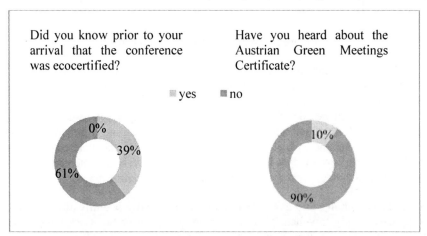

Figure 1: How many attendees knew about the ecocertification?

39% of the attendees knew prior to their arrival that the conference was ecocertified, and that 10% had heard of the certificate before. According to comments made on the questionnaire, attendees knew about the ecocertification via e-mail, the conference homepage and the conference outline.

3.3.2 Attendees' perception of the environmental efforts

The environmental efforts of the conference were noticed by the majority of attendees and evaluated as positive (99%) and contributing to the quality of the conference (87%). However, they were noticed to a different degree, as illustrated in figure 2.

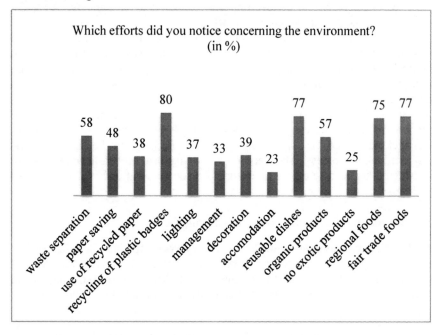

Figure 2: Which efforts were noticed?

Efforts concerning the plastic badges (80%), dishes (77%), fair trade (77%) and local products (75%) were noticed most, whereas no exotic produce (25%) and accommodation (23%) scored lowest.

Comments made on the questionnaire revealed scepticism about the 'greenness' of the conference due to its remote location. Furthermore, the availability of bananas, which obviously did not fit in with the claimed effort 'no exotic produce,' explains its low score and was negatively commented on. This reveals that attendees are very sensitive towards green claims made.

3.3.3 Travel choice and evaluation of environmentally friendly alternatives

Attendees mainly travelled to the conference via train or bus (48%) and plane (47%). In total, one third came to the conference by car, travelling either with their own car (13%) or as a passenger in a car (20%), as illustrated in figure 3.

The high use of public transport is explained by attendees who used both plane and public transport and therefore made double entries.

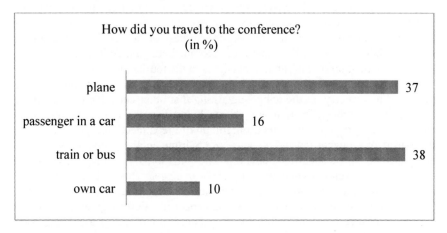

Figure 3:   How did the conference attendees travel to Alpbach?

The majority of attendees who travelled with public transport were either very satisfied (41%) or satisfied (41%) with the service. However, comments on the questionnaires revealed that there had been some difficulties understanding the schedule and travel options to the conference.

4   Conclusion

Ecocertification for green meetings is considered a promising tool to reduce environmental impacts of events associated with conference and business tourism. In order to investigate how ecocertification can contribute to the proliferation of green meetings in Austria, it is essential to understand the feasibility of the ecocertification process and the perception of green meetings.

Awareness: The Austrian Ecolabel for Tourism is a well-established brand. Its adapted version – the Austrian Green Meetings Certificate – is considered to profit from that popularity. Nevertheless, awareness of the availability of this certification among event stakeholders is low. This can be explained by the international background of the conference attendees, the ecolabel's recent establishment, and its application in a specific niche market tourism segment, supporting research on the general low awareness of ecolabels in tourism [23].

Perception: The majority of attendees perceive an ecocertified green meeting overwhelmingly as positive and as a contribution to the quality of the conference. Green elements concerning catering raised more attention than those concerning waste management and energy efficiency, and are useful vectors for transporting environmental awareness. However, some attendees were sceptical about the green claims made. This is considered to be linked to the attendees' expanded knowledge of sustainability issues, just as environmentally aware consumers have been found to be the most sceptic [24].

Benefits: An ecocertified green meeting is considered to be beneficial for the event manager's organisation or company, as it can be used for image and marketing purposes. Moreover, the certificate's function as an external verification for environmental claims is appreciated. This supports the argument that, even though there are numerous studies of tourists' scepticism of ecocertification, it is still the most preferred attribute, and reflects the need for external verification of environmental claims in the tourism industry [25].

Reasons to ecocertification The ecocertification of green meetings is perceived as a cherry on the icing, suggesting that other considerations than the availability of ecocertification and its attributed benefits are important when choosing a congress facility. The proliferation of green meetings is considered to be dependent on event managers' sense of environmental responsibility. As this is influenced by personal, sociocultural and situational factors [26], there are many different factors explaining why event managers choose to ecolabel their meetings, and future research should be dedicated to these factors.

Barriers: The main barrier against the ecocertification of green meetings is their *perceived* resource intensity. Event managers are afraid of escalating costs and workload associated with the certification process. An ecocertified green meeting at the researched facility was found to involve only a small increase of costs and workload, in comparison to the overall effort required to organise a conference. No significant barrier for the ecocertification of green meetings was identified, but rather a lack of event managers' willingness was made out. Nevertheless, budget restrictions and some criteria can present an obstacle.

Impulse: A push from the congress facility to encourage the ecocertification of green meetings was needed. The facility informs event managers about the environmental impacts associated with their planned event, the required resources, as well as the benefits they will derive from certification, and provides assistance throughout the certification process. Thus, the facility is considered to play a vital role in the decision process for or against pursuing certification. This suggests that, if congress facilities provide in-depth information about environmental impacts and assist event managers in the organisation, they have the ability to encourage ecocertification for green meetings.

Travel: Incentivising environmentally friendly travel to the congress facility remains a challenge. Potential lies in encouraging the use of public transport or car sharing possibilities. Both facility manager and event manager accept that there is a divergence between their sense of environmental responsibility and business reality, and both focus on the areas that are economically viable and possible to implement.

The discussion shows that the Austrian Green Meetings Certificate is an attractive ecolabel for event managers. Gaining ecocertification is considered to come down to a question of willingness, provided the congress facility supports event managers throughout the whole process. This successful example from Austria shows that ecocertification for green meetings can be a feasible and attractive tool for the advancement of sustainability in the meetings industry.

Future research should investigate ecocertification for green meetings on a broader scope. For example, several ecocertified green meetings should be examined to gain insight into the experiences of various event managers, attendees, and managers of licensed congress facilities.

References

[1]   Getz, D., Event tourism: Definition, evolution and research. *Tourism Management*, **29(3)**, pp. 403-428, 2008.

[2]   CIC, www.conventionindustry.org/standardspractices/GreenMeetings.aspx

[3]   Green Meeting Guide 2009 Roll out the Green Carpet for your Participants; United Nations Environment Programme, Online. www.unep.fr/scp/publications/details.asp?id=DTI/1141/PA

[4]   Henderson, S., The development of competitive advantage through sustainable event management. *World Wide Hospitality and Tourism*, **3(3)**, pp. 245-257, 2011.

[5]   Aase, S., A Guide to Greener Meetings. *Journal of the American Dietetic Association*, **109(5)**, pp. 800-803, 2009.

[6]   Guterman, L., Seeing Green in Conference Season. *Cell*, **137(7)**, pp. 1169-1171, 2009.

[7]   Laing, J., & Frost, W., How green was my festival: Exploring challenges and opportunities associated with staging green events. *International Journal of Hospitality Management*, **29(2)**, pp. 261-267, 2010.

[8]   Honey, M., & Stewart, E., Introduction. *Ecotourism & Certification Setting Standards in Practice*, ed. M., Honey, Island Press: Washington, pp. 33-71, 2002.

[9]   Sustainable Event Standards – Summary; Green Meetings Industry Council, Online. www.gmicglobal.org/resourace/collection/2A2E3AF1-0514-4AC9-B540-77016F1DB197/GMIC_Sustainable_Event_Standards_Summary.pdf

[10] Buckley, R., Tourism Ecolabels, *Annals of Tourism Research*, **29(1)**, pp. 183-208, 2002.

[11] Musgrave, J. & Raj, R., Introduction to a Conceptual Framework for Sustainable Events (Chapter 1). *Event Management and Sustainability*, eds. J., Musgrave & R., Raj, CABI Publishing: Oxfordshire, pp. 1-12, 2009.

[12] Marcus, A., Green Advertising and Marketing, *Environmental Encyclopaedia*, **4(1)**, pp. 789-790, 2005.

[13] Hale, M., Ecolabelling and cleaner production: principles, problems, education and training in relation to the adoption of environmentally sound production processes, *Journal of Cleaner Production*, **4(2)**, pp. 85-95.

[14] Toth, R., Exploring the Concepts underlying Certification, *Ecotourism & Certification Setting Standards in Practice*, ed. Honey, M., Island Press: Washington, pp. 73-101, 2002.

[15] Sloan, P., Legrand, W., & Chen, J.S., *Sustainability in the hospitality industry. Principles of Sustainable Operations*. Routledge: London, New York, 2011.

[16] Font, X., Regulating the Green Message: the Players in Ecolabelling, *Tourism Ecolabelling: Certification and Promotion of Sustainable Management,* eds. Font, X., & Buckley, R., CABI Publishing: Cambridge, pp. 1-17, 2001.

[17] Buckley, R., Tourism and the Environment, *Annual Review of Environment and Resources,* **36(1),** pp. 183-208, 2011.

[18] Ayuso, S., Comparing Voluntary Policy Instruments for Sustainable Tourism: The Experience of the Spanish Hotel Sector, *Journal of Sustainable Tourism,* **15(2),** pp. 144-159, 2007.

[19] Vernon, J., Eddex, S., Pinder, D., & Curry, K., The 'greening' of tourism micro businesses: outcomes of focus group investigations in south east Cornwall, *Business Strategy and the Environment,* **12(1),** pp. 49-69, 2003.

[20] Pröbstl, U., Müller, F., Hotel certification and its relevance for sustainable development: examples from the European Alps; *Sustainable Tourism V,* ed. Pineda, F.D. & Brebbia, C.A., WIT Press: Southampton, pp. 3-15, 2012.

[21] Hamele, H., Ecolabels for Tourism in Europe: The European Ecolabel for Tourism?; *Tourism Ecolabelling: Certification and Promotion of Sustainable Management,* eds. Font, X., & Buckley, R., CABI Publishing: Cambridge, pp. 175-189, 2001.

[22] Bundesministerium für Land- und Forstwirtschaft, Umwelt und Wasserwirtschaft; Green Meetings und Green Events Richtlinie UZ 62, Online. http://www.acb.at/greenmeeting/files/UZ62_R1.2a_Green Meetings_2010.pdf

[23] Millar, M., & Baloglu, S., Hotel Guests' Preferences for Green Guest Room Attributes, *Cornell Hospitality Quatery,* **52(3),** pp. 302-311, 2011.

[24] Virgil E., & Burton, L., Green Marketing, *Encyclopaedia of Small Business,* **1(4),** pp. 630-633, 2011.

[25] Tomescu A.M., Aspects of service quality and ecolabelling of Romanian lodging services, *Annals of the University of Oradea: Economic Science,* **1(1),** pp. 693-699, 2011.

[26] Tzeschentke, N.A., Kirk, D., & Lynch, P.A., Going green: Decisional factors in small hospitality operations, *International Journal of Hospitality Management,* **27(1),** pp. 126-133, 2008.

A sustainable urban tourism indicator in Malaysia

M. K. Razali & H. N. Ismail
Faculty of Built Environment, Universiti Teknologi Malaysia, Malaysia

Abstract

This paper presents a critical review on indicators for measuring sustainable urban tourism development in Malaysia. It has been debated that the contribution of urban tourism in the economy and local community's development are difficult to be determined due to the multiple discipline that clouds the existence of urban tourism as an independent sector. Arguably, these indicators failed to measure the level of achievement for urban tourism activities, and the economic terms are less justified. Since the concept of sustainable tourism is introduced, the role of indicator is increasingly important in measuring economic and social advantages, thus the development of the city also needs to be monitored with suitable indicator. The idea is to assess and monitor changes in urban economies for tracking the progress towards sustainable development. Therefore, the center of debate in developing urban tourism indicators are (1) to identify and measure the entire range of interrelated environmental, social and economic impacts in tourism development, and (2) to obtain accurate information for responsible decision. Several approaches have been made in the context of Malaysia although the indicators are not directly related to the perspective of urban tourism, such as Malaysian Quality of Life Index (MQLI) and Malaysian Urban Indicators Network (MURNINet). For example, MURNINet identified heritage and tourism as a sub-component of the indicator. As there is need to improve these indicators, situational analysis based on literature review in this paper will highlight the use of existing sustainable indicators and their relevancy to urban tourism development and economy.
Keywords: sustainable tourism, urban tourism, urban development, indicator.

WIT Transactions on Ecology and The Environment, Vol 187, © 2014 WIT Press
www.witpress.com, ISSN 1743-3541 (on-line)
doi:10.2495/ST140111

1 Introduction

Sustainable development has become a common buzzword in the developmental studies since the industrial revolution in the 19th century, while sustainable tourism term has been widely used since two decades ago [1]. There have been many studies and researchers on sustainable development in general, as well as in specific industries around the world. In tourism industry, sustainable development started to grow after the 1980s (Page and Hall [2]). Numerous authors have contributed in providing studies on different perspectives and in different regions. The common purpose for countries to sustain the tourism is to host tourists [3] and protect the environment [4].

Tourism brings economic benefits, while preservation of natural environment has been the global main concern. The urban development in Malaysia started soon after the government proposed its Vision 2020 and they consistently executed the Master Plan [5]. The vision is to develop country's economic and social condition, and bring forward the vision to become a developed nation by year 2020. For this purpose, the government has been implementing many strategies alongside the Master Plan, and tourism is one of the main concerns for the country. In this perspective, Malaysian government has developed indicators that monitor and evaluate the progress of sustainable tourism in Malaysia. This study brings forward a critical review to highlight indicators for measuring sustainable urban tourism development in Malaysia.

2 Literature review

This section presents the review of previous research journal articles that discussed sustainable development, urban development, sustainable urban tourism and related concepts regarding sustainable development, with the focus on urban tourism.

2.1 Sustainable development

The concept of sustainable development was introduced in 1987 by the Brundtland Commission. It is defined as the development that meets the need of the present without compromising the ability of future generations to meet their own needs (Haghshenas and Vaziri [6]). Sustainable development consists of three elements, namely environmental, economic and social development [6]. The concept of sustainable development was introduced to minimize the impact of development especially in environmental issues and helped to reduce poverty among poor countries (WCED [7]). Thus, there will be positive impact towards development when the suggestion from WCED is applied.

2.2 Sustainable development indicator

The need of sustainable development indicator (SDI) was raised during World Summit in Rio 1992, where the action plan Agenda 21 was used to formulate indicators necessary for monitoring sustainable development [8]. SDI has been used to measure the growth and impact of development in a country. An indicator can be described as something that helps us to understand the previous and current position and future state or position [9]. There are many functions of indicators, such as helping policy makers to make better decision and to execute effective actions [10]. Regardless of being a developing country, Malaysia has been very attentive in applying the concept of sustainable development whenever needed. Othman and Pereira [11] believed that the government first introduced the principles of sustainable development in the Third Malaysia Plan (1976–1980), and later in the Eighth Malaysia Plan (2001–2005), where the government focused on environmental issues.

2.3 Urban development

The Concise Oxford Dictionary [12] stated that the word "development" represents growth, evaluation, and stage of advancement. Urban development denotes the growth or transformation of the city or town area. In addition, Allan [13] has provided three criteria while defining the word "development", which are vision, historical process and action. Since Malaysia became independent in 1957, there is a lot of development made until today, notably in terms of the transformation of economic growth, increasing in employment, and vibrancy in foreign exchange, where these factors give impact on the nation's development process [14]. However, the growth in urban development also contributes to negative impacts, such as environmental pollution and traffic problem [15]. As a result, a sustainable development report, "Our Common Future" was presented in Bruntland by the World Commission on Environment and Development [7], where the concept of sustainable development was introduced in urban development. Furthermore, Agenda 21 has been introduced during Earth Summit in Rio de Janeiro in 1992, which provided suggestions for action or changing the traditional patterns of development to achieve sustainability, especially in the urban area [16].

2.4 Urban sustainability

Urban sustainability is a combination of the words "urban" and "sustainable". Previously, the concept of sustainability focused mainly on rural area or area with environmental sensitivity (Barke and Newton [17]). Urban or city is the place with an increasing statistical proportion of population within the area [11]. Sustainability can be defined as meeting the needs of a community, i.e. physical, social, economic and environmental, without limiting the capacity of future generation to meet their own needs (Pierce et al. [18]). Furthermore, the concept of urban sustainability strategies are helpful in increasing the urban efficiency in consumption and in reducing negative externalities (Finco and Nijkamp [19]). In Malaysia, the federal government, state government and local authorities cooperate together during the planning and development of an urban area.

2.5 Urban tourism

Urban tourism can be defined as tourism within cities and towns [20]. Researchers [21] have mentioned that cities are places where various major facilities such as transport, hotel and event infrastructure are located. This means that urbanization is a contributor for the development of towns and cities where people live, work and shop [2]. In fact, during the development period, town or city tends to improve the living standards and the area becomes location for tourism activity that has the accommodation and entertainment function [2]. The development of urban tourism has increased in the late 1970s [2].

In the early 1980s, the research on urban tourism started to gain attention [2] Researchers [21] came up with five major factors that characterize cities as tourism destinations: (1) Major travel nodes that serve as gateways or transfer points to other destinations; (2) High populations which attract large numbers of tourists who are visiting friends and relatives; (3) Focal points for commerce, industry and finance; (4) Concentrations of services such as education, health and government administration center; and (5) Places that offer a wide variety of cultural, artistic and recreational experiences.

In Malaysia, most of the tourist attractions are located in the towns and cities, especially the capital cities in federal territories and states. In the early 1980s, the government introduced urban conservation in the development of urban area in several heritage cities such as Kuala Lumpur, Georgetown, Malacca and Kota Bahru (Ahmad [22]). It shows that cities became a tourism product, especially those with rich heritage and multicultural society, and the cities also became famous tourist destinations in Malaysia [22].

2.6 Sustainable tourism development

World Tourism Organization (WTO-OMT) has practiced the concept of sustainable development in tourism. Sustainable tourism development (STD) is a process of meeting the needs of present tourist and host region, whilst protecting and enhancing opportunities for the future (Cernat and Gourdon [3]). However, tourism activities have caused environmental and socioeconomic problems [4]. For this purpose, sustainable tourism principles can help planners to make strategic planning to overcome the problems.

Furthermore, WTO is actively promoting the concept of sustainable tourism among its members. WTO has introduced and developed sustainable tourism indicators to measure and monitors the progress of sustainable tourism. WTO defines sustainable tourism indicators (STI) as *"the set of measures that provides the information for better understanding of the link between the impact of tourism on the cultural and natural setting that takes place, and on the cultural and natural setting in which this take place, and on which it is strongly dependent"* [23]. Sustainable tourism indicators have three basic functions: (1) the formulation of general action plans at a regional level; (2) the definition of short-term strategies for destinations; and (3) the establishment of destination benchmarking practices [23]. In addition, WTO has compiled a database of indicators in its guidebook as a reference to help policy makers in the planning of sustainable tourism [4].

2.7 Sustainable tourism indicator

The purpose of the development of indicator is to assess and monitor changes or progress of sustainable development (Roberts [24]). Indicators quantify change, identify processes and provide a framework for setting targets and monitoring performance [25]. Thus, indicator is a tool to measure the performance or tracks the progress of development. In addition, indicator has also becomes a tool for communication to promote information exchange regarding the issues (White *et al.* [25]). Nevertheless, it is very important to develop indicator as the tool to track the progress or monitor the performance, as well as the impact towards the development of sustainable tourism. Previous research have listed several criteria of good indicators, such as measurable, sensitive, economically viable, acceptable and accessible, useable and easily interpreted, reliable, verifiable and replicable, participative process, specific, timely, transparency, relevant and scientifically well-founded [25].

2.8 Sustainable urban tourism

The concept of sustainable urban tourism is relatively new in the area of sustainable tourism. Previously, urban tourism did not consider sustainable issues until the World Tourism Organization introduced the indicator of sustainable development for tourism destinations (WTO [26]). Since then, most of the researches on sustainable tourism have focused on rural tourism and community-based tourism [17]. Nevertheless, it is very important to bring the concept of sustainable tourism to the urban area for long-term sustainability.

2.9 Sustainable urban tourism indicator

Indicator is very important to measure the progress of the development in sustainable urban tourism. Indicator can be define as *"something that helps you to understand where you are, which way you are going and how far you are from where you want to be"* [9]. A previous historical indicator developed in the mid-1960s denotes that William Ogburn developed statistical measurement to monitor changes in social trends [27]. This means that indicator can be used as a tool to measure the existing issues, signals of problems, measures of risk and potential need for action, and as a means to identify and measure the results of our actions [26].

In the concept of urban tourism, it is very important to measure the current situation of the development of urban tourism area, which are the major attractions in the country. The results from the indicator can help developers in planning sustainable tourism, particularly for tourism destinations. There are three important dimensions in sustainable development, which are economic, social, and environment [28].

2.10 Urban development in Malaysia

Malaysia is located in Southeast Asia and consists of eleven states and three federal territories [29]. The country became independent in 1957, and since then the country has started its development. The government invested a lot of money in developing infrastructures and executed different projects to provide better facilities to the citizens by implementing the properly planned National Master Plan [5].

Previously, the Malaysian government focused on the development of infrastructure, such as airport, and accommodation in and around the capital city of Malaysia, Kuala Lumpur Ismail, Baum, and Kokranikkal [30]. Later, the government realized that Malaysia could become a major tourism destination in the world as the country received 25.03 million tourists and received RM 60.6 billion from tourism activity. The tourism sector in Malaysia has contributed in providing the second largest foreign exchange earnings and helped the country to strengthen the economy [31]. In addition, there are a lot of benefits from the development of tourism industry towards the community, such generating income, taxes, currency and jobs (Choi and Sirakaya [27]).

3 Initiatives of the sustainable development indicator in Malaysia

The concept of sustainable development in Malaysia started with the Malaysia Plan since 1970, which includes both long and short term plans [11]. At the beginning of sustainable concept, the government focused on environmental issues. Moreover, the researcher [32] stated the need for the environmental database and information systems in the Seventh Malaysia Plan towards sustainable development. Thus, indicators have been developed for monitoring and evaluating the progress of sustainable development in Malaysia.

In Malaysia, the development of an indicator was started in 1995 by the Institute for Environmental and Development (LESTARI), Universiti Kebangsaan Malaysia [33]. The indicators for sustainable development have been formed by federal government agencies, state governments and non-governmental organization (NGO), and Malaysia has several sustainable development indicators. Table 1 shows the summary of sustainable development indicators in Malaysia.

From the literature review, there are eleven (11) indicators established in Malaysia. The first indicator was developed in 1997 by Department of Health, Municipal Council of Kuching, Johor Bahru and Malacca. The latest indicator was developed in 2013, namely MURNInets, which is a rebrand of Malaysian Urban Rural National Indicator Network. The selected indicators are used as the benchmark for the present indicators implemented at all levels of planning in the country, for example National Physical Plan (NPP), National Urbanisation Policies (NUP), and Sustainability Assessment (SA) [34]. It shows that the Malaysian government has taken the initiatives to develop the indicator as the benchmark or as the tool in developing the country.

Table 1:   Summary of the sustainable development indicator in Malaysia.

Year	Authority/developer	Indicator	Summary
2013	Federal Department of Town and Country Planning, Peninsular Malaysia	Malaysian Urban Rural National Indicators Network on Sustainable Development (MURNInets)	The new MURNInets consists of 36 sets under 21 themes and 6 dimensions. The goal of MURNInets is to establish sustainable urban environment by improving the quality of housing and services.
2009	Malaysian Institute of Architects (PAM)	Green Builiding Index (GBI), Malaysia	GBI contains six different rubric aspects such as energy efficiency, indoor environmental quality, sustainable site planning and management, material and resources, water efficiency and innovation.
2004	Federal Department of Town and Country Planning, Peninsular Malaysia	Malaysian Urban Indicators Network (MURNInet)	MURNInet consists of fifty five (55) indicators to evaluate the sustainability of a city and region through eleven (11) planning sectors.
2003	Federal Territory Development and Klang Valley Planning Division, Prime Minister's Department	Klang Valley Regional Sustainable Quality of Life Index (KVRSQLI)	The goal of KVRSQLI is to develop stress ratio for the allocation of resources within Klang Valley. The formulation for the indicator is completed and it focused on regional planning.
2001	Sarawak Natural Resources Board	Sustainable Urban Development Indicators (SUDI)	The goal of SUDI is to assess the improvement in urban issues such as water quality and waste management by using Environmental Management Systems (EMS) as the guiding framework.

Table 1: Continued.

Year	Authority/developer	Indicator	Summary
1999	Economic Planning Unit, Prime Minister's Department	Malaysian Quality of Life Indicator (MQLI)	The goal of MQLI is to measure Malaysian success beyond economic achievement. MQLI consists of fourteen (14) theme indicators.
1998	Selangor State Government	Sustainable Development Indicators for the State of Selangor (SDIS)	The main objective of SDIS is to formulate strategies and action plan for implementing development, and the indicators used a 'fitness-for-purpose' strategy as the frameworks. There are 30 sets of indicators to measure sustainable development, which are divided into four sustainability classes such as economy, environment, natural resource and social.
1998	Environmental Statistics Section, Department of Statistics Malaysia	Compendium of Environment Statistics (CES)	The focus of CES is on the integration of socio-economic information with environmental parameters and it is based on the approach of Pressure-State-Response (PSR) model.
1997	Department of Health, Municipal Council of Kuching, Johor Bharu, and Malacca	Healthy Cities Indicators (HCI)	The goal of HCI is to create social and physical environment for healthy urban population and it is developed based on World Health Organisation framework, however the development is still at an early stage.

Table 1:   Continued.

Year	Authority/developer	Indicator	Summary
1997	Penang State Government	Sustainable Penang Initiative(SPI), Penang Report Card (PRC)	SPI has identified 40 indicators which represent the environment, community, culture and public participation, and then People Report Card (PRC) is produced.
1997	Environment and Natural Resource Section of the Economic Planning Unit, Prime Minister's Department	Malaysian Sustainable Development Indicators (MSDI)	The goal of MSDI is to develop a national system for tracking progress towards sustainability and aims to integrate sustainability elements into national level development planning. However, it is still under the identification stage.

In the tourism industry, ecotourism has gained more attention in Malaysia compared to other types of tourism such urban tourism, rural tourism and others. Following the development of ecotourism in Malaysia, the Ministry of Tourism and Culture (previously the Ministry of Culture, Arts and Tourism) developed the National Ecotourism Plan in 1996 to assist the government in developing the potential ecotourism [35]. The plan also indicates the benchmark or indicator for successful ecotourism sites, which should be followed by the tourism stakeholder. Moreover, tourism sector only becomes a sub-theme in the previous developing indicators such as MURNInet and Malaysian Quality of Life Index (MQLI) [33]. It shows that tourism plays an important role in urban development. Apart from that, the development of indicator is very important in dealing with environmental issue such as Compendium of Environment Statistics (CES) that is used as a tool to monitor pollution, depletion and degradation of environmental quality. It is very important because Malaysia has a lot of natural resources as tourist attractions. In addition, Malaysia is one of the 12 mega-diversity countries in the world that accepts the importance of preserving its social, environmental and cultural wealth heritage [36].

4   Discussion and conclusion

The Malaysian government has been taking action in developing sustainable development indicator (SDI). Table 1 shows the list of sustainable development indicators in Malaysia since 1997 until 2013. Malaysia has started the efforts in sustainability development since 1970 as stated in the Malaysia Plan [11].

However, the development of sustainable indicator started later in 1995 by Institute for Environmental and Development (LESTARI), Universiti Kebangsaan Malaysia [35].

The development of indicators in Malaysia was carried out by federal government, state government and non-governmental organization, where the indicators have different objectives or goals. By referring to Table 1, some indicators are just at the early stages, such as Healthy Cities Indicator (HCI) and Malaysian Sustainable Development Indicators (MSDI) (Hezri [37]).

Most of the indicators measured the development in urban or city areas, for example Malaysian Urban Indicator Network (MURNInet) and Malaysian Quality of Life Index (MQLI). The early development indicator only focused on environment and social issues. For that reason, Malaysian Statistic Department has developed the Compendium of Environment Statistics (CES) indicator that focuses on environmental issues, such as depletion of natural resources and neglect of new scarcities, and degradation of environment quality [36]. Also, a professional institute such as the Malaysian Institute of Architects (PAM) has developed the Green Building Index Malaysia with the objective to implement sustainability in the development plan [38].

In 2013, the Federal Department of Town and Country Planning, Peninsular Malaysia had previously reviewed MURNInet and rebranded the indicator as Malaysian Urban Rural National Indicators Network on Sustainable Development. The objective of MURNInets is to establish sustainable urban environment by improving the quality of housing and services. There are some issues emerging from previous indicators such as the lack of local authority's participation and the choice of indicators' characteristics needs to be reviewed by the department. In addition, MURNInets have six dimensions which include competitive economy, sustainable environmental quality, sustainable community, optimum use of land and natural resources, efficient infrastructure and transport, and effective governance [33]. In context of sustainable tourism, there is no specific indicator to measure sustainable development of tourism in Malaysia. The tourism sector is only a sub-theme indicator in current sustainable development indicator, such as Malaysian Urban Indicator Network (MURNInet), Malaysian Quality of Life Index (MQLI) and Compendium of Environment Statistics (CES).

This has created difficulty in measuring the level of sustainable development and contribution of tourism in Malaysia. In addition, current indicator has failed to measure the contribution of urban tourism towards the economy and local communities. As a conclusion, the issues arise from current indicators are very important to develop indicators for sustainable urban to assess and monitor changes in urban economies, as well as to track the progress of sustainable development. The development of suitable indicator, especially in urban tourism, will give a lot of information regarding current status of sustainable concept in urban development.

References

[1]   Buckley, R., Sustainable Tourism: Research And Reality. *Annals Of Tourism Research*, *39*(2), 528–546, 2012

[2]   Page Stephen J and Hall C Michael, Managing Urban Tourism, Prentice Hall, 15–17, 2003

[3]   Cernat, L. & Gourdon, J., Paths To Success: Benchmarking Cross-Country Sustainable Tourism. *Tourism Management*, *33*(5), 1044–1056, 2012

[4]   Tanguay, G. A., Rajaonson, J., & Therrien, M.C,Sustainable Tourism Indicators: Selection Criteria For Policy Implementation And Scientific Recognition. *Journal Of Sustainable Tourism*, 1–18, 2012

[5]   The Malaysia Plan Retrieve online www.pmo.gov.my

[6]   Haghshenas, H. & Vaziri, M., Urban Sustainable Transportation Indicators For Global Comparison. *Ecological Indicators*, *15*(1), 115–121, 2012

[7]   WCED, *Our Common Future*. Oslo. 1987

[8]   Hak, T., Kovanda, J., & Weinzettel, J., A Method To Assess The Relevance Of Sustainability Indicators: Application To The Indicator Set Of The Czech Republic's Sustainable Development Strategy. *Ecological Indicators*, *17*, 46–57, 2012

[9]   Miller, G., The Development Of Indicators For Sustainable Tourism: Results Of A Delphi Survey Of Tourism Researchers. *Tourism Management*, *22*(4), 351–362, 2001

[10]   Nations U. *Indicators Of Sustainable Development: Guidelines And Methodologies Indicators Of Sustainable Development*, 2007

[11]   Othman, A., & Pereira, J. J., Sustainable Development Indicators – Providing Environmental Statistics For National Reporting. Proc. of the *14th Conference Of Commonwealth Statisticians*, Cape Town, 1–13, 2005

[12]   Haget, S.,*Barriers For Tourism Sustainability In Destination By Sylvain Haget*. Bournemouth University, 2009

[13]   Allan, Meanings and Views of Development. Oxford: Oxford University Press, 2000

[14]   Nunkoo, R., & Smith, S. L. J. Political economy of tourism: Trust in government actors, political support, and their determinants. Tourism Management, 36, 120–132, 2013

[15]   Hugentobler, M., & Brändle-Ströh, M., Sustainable Urban Development: A Conceptual Framework And Its Application. *Journal of Urban Technology*, *4*(2), 85–99, 1997

[16]   Kamarudin Ngah, Jamaludin Mustafa, Zaherawati Zakaria, N. N. and M. Z. H. M. S, Formulation Of Agenda 21 Process Indicators For Malaysia. *Journal Of Management And Sustainability*, *1*(1), 82–89. 2011

[17]   Barke M. & Newton M, Promoting Sustainable Tourism is an Urban Context, Research Development in Malaga City, Andalusia, *Journal of Sustainable Tourism*, Vol 3 (3) 115–134, 1995

[18]   Pierce, J. C., Budd, W. W., & Lovrich, N. P., Resilience And Sustainability In Us Urban Areas. *Environmental Politics*, *20*(4), 566–584, 2011

[19] Finco, A. & Nijkamp, P., Pathways To Urban Sustainability. *Journal Of Environmental Policy & Planning*, 37–41, 2001

[20] Selby Martin, Understanding Urban Tourism, Image, Culture & Experience, I.B. Tauris, 11–12, 2004

[21] Ismail, H., & Baum, T. O. M, Anatolia : An International Journal Of Tourism And Urban Tourism In Developing Countries : In The Case Of Melaka (Malacca) City, Malaysia, 211–233, 2006

[22] Ahmad, G. Urban Tourism In Malaysia : Heritage Cities Of Georgetown, Malacca And Kota Bharu. Proc. of the *2nd. International Seminar On European Architecture And Town Planning Outside Europe (Dutch Period)*. Malacca 1–16, 1998

[23] Lozano-Oyola, M., Blancas, F. J., González, M., & Caballero, R., Sustainable Tourism Indicators As Planning Tools In Cultural Destinations. *Ecological Indicators*, *18*, 659–675, 2012

[24] Roberts, S., Sustainability Indicators For Small Tourism Enterprises – An Exploratory Perspective, *16*(5), 2008

[25] White, V., Mccrum, G., Blackstock, K. L., & Scott, A., Indicators and Sustainable Tourism : Literature Review, 2006

[26] WTO, *Indicators Of Sustainable Development For Tourism Destinations A Guidebook*. Madrid: World Tourism Organization, Madrid, 2004

[27] Choi, H. C., & Sirakaya, E., Sustainability Indicators For Managing Community Tourism. *Tourism Management*, *27*(6), 1274–1289, 2006

[28] Saadatian, O., Haw, L. C., Mat, S. Bin, & Sopian, K.. Perspective Of Sustainable Development In Malaysia. *International Journal Of Energy And Environment*, *6*(2), 260–267, 2012

[29] About Malaysia In Brief Online www.tourismmalaysia.gov.my

[30] Ismail, H., Baum, T., & Kokranikkal, J, Urban Tourism In Developing Countries : A Case Of Malaysia. Proc of the *"Urban Tourism – Mapping The Future" Ttra Europe Conference*, Glasgow, 1–12, 2003

[31] Hafiz, M., Hanafiah, M., Fauzi, M., & Harun, M.,Tourism Demand In Malaysia : A Cross-Sectional Pool Time-Series Analysis, *1*(1), 2010

[32] Hasan, M. N. H., Indicators Of Sustainable Development: The Malaysian Perspective. In *Proceedings of Regional Dialogue on Geo-Indicators for Sustainable Development. Institute for Environment and Development (Lestari), Geological Survey Department of Malaysia, and The Commission on Geological Sciences for Environmental Planning*, 1–16, 1998

[33] Hasan, M. N., & Adnan, A. H., Sustainable Development Indicator Initiatives In Malaysia – Novel Approaches And Viable Frameworks. *Lestari UKM*, 2004

[34] Shamsaini Shamsuddin & Azmizam Abdul Rashid, Malaysian Urban Rural National Indicators Network On Sustainable Development (Murninets). Proc of the *43rd Annual Conference Of The Urban Affairs Association*, San Francisco California, 1–13, 2013

[35] Hassanal, A., Success Indicators Development for Ecotourism Ventures. In *Akepts 1st Annual Young Researchers Conference And Exhibition.* Kuala Lumpur, 2011

[36] Wahid, N. A., Amran, A., Haat, H. C., & Abustan, I., Towards A Sustainable Tourism Management In, 301–312, 1998

[37] Hezri, A. A., Sustainability Indicator System And Policy Processes In Malaysia: A Framework For Utilisation And Learning. *Journal of Environmental Management, 73,* 357–371, 2004

[38] Mun, T. L. The Development of GBI Malaysia (GBI). *PAM/ACEM,* 1–8, 2009

Strengths and weaknesses in the assessment of sustainable tourism: a case study of the Nabq protected area in Egypt

M. M. Tolba
Department of Architecture, El Shorouk Academy, Egypt

Abstract

Talks over the past decade have been concerned with achieving a more sustainable form of tourism; however, the problem is that the largest sector of tourism is that of mass tourism, which continues to be the worst form of tourism in terms of sustainability. Previous studies have focused on defining the term 'sustainable tourism'. However, these studies have not been able to agree on a single definition for the term, which has dozens of definitions. This research aims to discuss and analyze the concept of 'sustainable mass tourism' and its effects on the Nabq protected area. In addition, this research aims to focus on mass tourism in terms of three separate aspects for its development, which are: economic sustainability, social sustainability and environmental sustainability. Each of these aspects will be discussed separately. By dividing the concept into three different parts, each part will be studied so as to relate to or isolate from each other to determine the safest and most successful path to be used by developers of mass tourism with the aim of applying the results of this research to the Nabq protected area.

Keywords: sustainable tourism, mass tourism, sustainability of mass tourism, economic sustainability, social sustainability, environmental sustainability, Nabq protected area.

1 Introduction

A number of research concepts concerning sustainable development, sustainable tourism and the development of sustainable tourism are examined in this paper. It is important to begin by pointing out the definition of 'sustainable

WIT Transactions on Ecology and The Environment, Vol 187, © 2014 WIT Press
www.witpress.com, ISSN 1743-3541 (on-line)
doi:10.2495/ST140121

development', which is 'a development that meets the needs of the present without compromising the ability of future generations to meet their own needs [1]. After the publication of this definition in 1987, discussion about the concept of sustainability began and the general debate on sustainability covered three main areas, namely: economic, social and environmental sustainability. In 1992, the Rio Declaration [2] concluded the discussion that began in 1987 by the Brundtland Commission. Tourism was initially included in the general debate on sustainability; however, it evolved over the past two decades and assumed a space of its own. Researchers had initially focused on sustainable development, but later turned their focus towards sustainable tourism and the development of sustainable tourism, both of whose definitions can be found here.

The term 'sustainable tourism' focuses on a product and/or service that aims to attract tourists, while the term 'development of sustainable tourism' is concerned with incorporating the development of tourism in the region to make it sustainable; thus bringing about a broader definition of development. 'Sustainable development' is therefore discussed on a broader scale in the tourism industry [3].

Over the past two decades, debates focused on how to achieve a more balanced approach in the overall development of tourism. The main conflict continues between tourism and the natural environment [4]. Since the 1980s, the debate has focused on the positive and negative effects of tourism on touristic areas, and how the economic, social and environmental impacts of tourism depend on the size of the touristic area.

Tourism often has a significant impact on the gross domestic product (GDP) – of any country – and the flow of foreign exchange, which gives precedence to the economic factor over the other factors. Tourism also has significant effects on both culture and the environment. The endurance of touristic sites and their ability to accommodate increasing numbers of tourists has become an important matter in recent years. It is, therefore, important that tourism developers, government and non-government agencies and organizations, as well as individuals that benefit from tourism and the tourists themselves be more responsible, because in the future mass tourism will become a major influential factor. It will also lead to an increase in demand to visit and enjoy nature as well as other cultural and social experiences, which will result in creating additional touristic destinations, and which also result in increasing both the positive and the negative effects on the environment.

The purpose of this introduction is to discuss and analyze the evolution of the concept of 'sustainable mass tourism' from the perspective of the different concepts that both affect and get affected by it.

2 The concepts of sustainability and sustainable development

As a concept, sustainability can be associated with all types of tourism. The problem, however, lies in the method for using or applying this 'sustainability'. While researches argue that 'sustainable development' is now an established term, adapting and implementing it are not often successful. The concept of 'sustainable development' consists of two contradictory parts. The first part is concerned with growth (movement), while the second part that is concerned with maintaining the status quo (steadiness) is not clear due to the various definitions used in different contexts. For this reason, it is unlikely that in the future there will be single explanation for the concept of sustainable development, which should be divided into two separate terms to provide an equation:

Sustainable Development = Development + Sustainability [5].

Researchers have tried to define the concepts of 'sustainable tourism' and 'mass tourism development' over the past decade with reference to their origins in the Brundtland report of 1987 in achieving sustainable development [6].

Accordingly, sustainable development studies have evolved and focused on three separate aspects within the definition, namely: economic, social and environmental sustainable development. In the application of sustainable tourism development, studies have found a contradiction between the three aspects of sustainability, which continue to be a challenge for researchers. How can there be an economic development without both an environmental and a social development in touristic sites? [6]. C. Hunter suggests that sustainable tourism means maximizing economic, social and environmental benefits in tourism while reducing costs at the same time, and with the need to find a balance between the three aspects without giving priority to the economic aspect over the others. In addition to maximizing profits, tourism developers need to address their environmental responsibilities. Where developers prefer mass tourism in order to achieve high returns and low costs, tourists prefer their own perspective of productivity which is to enjoy the social and cultural aspects of their destinations. So, the question remains: how can tourists and tourism developers find a balance between their different goals?

3   Sustainable tourism

Sustainable tourism is a positive approach to bring together the different parts of the tourism industry to include tourists, the environment and development. This is considered a long-term approach to plan for the quality of both natural and human resources. Therefore, sustainable tourism must include, through long-term development-planning, the various groups of stakeholders concerned when we discuss tourism, the environment, urbanization and the local community in tourist destinations. And because 'sustainability' entails environment protection, it is, therefore, important to maintain a balanced view of this concept by not limiting the growth of tourism, but by dealing with it along with tourists, the environment and the local host community [7]. Since the first issue of sustainability is the quality of the product or service provided, tourism can be better sustained and maintained through partnerships with local communities in tourist destinations.

3.1 Concept of sustainable tourism

The concept of sustainable tourism is seen as a new subject and is formulated in four approaches [8]. It is believed that mass tourism and sustainable tourism are polar opposites, and that the first is negative while the second is positive.

- Sustainable tourism, ranging from weakness and strength, results in very weak economic growth and technical innovation, but is also strong in protecting the resources of the site.
- The direction of sustainable tourism should include all types of tourism as well as working to improve them. Recognizing this shows the enormity of the problem and extent of mass tourism.
- An arguable point asks if all kinds of tourism should be sustainable.

The principle of sustainable tourism is subject to the process of rapid development, but developers are not keeping pace with the mandates of this concept. The reason is that developers are ready to apply this concept only when it serves their benefit by increasing their revenues and improving their public relations and public image; sometimes it is part of their marketing strategy. For example, in areas where water is scarce and where energy is deficient, developers invest in energy-saving and water-reduction systems. Developers view sustainability as a means of:

- Saving money.
- Having good public relations and maintaining a suitable public image to show that their companies come bearing good intentions. This image helps developers to construct buildings that are environmentally unfriendly and harmful to touristic sites without expecting the public or local community to object.
- Marketing because it can be a tool to attract tourists.

3.2 Sustainable tourism as an ideology

Applying sustainable development on tourism is discussed through three techniques:

1. Technique based on resources and focuses on the need to protect nature (environmental approach).
2. Technique based on activity and focuses on the need for the tourism industry as a means to acquire resources (economic approach).
3. Technique based on community traditions and focuses on the empowerment of different groups of people in tourism (social approach).

These techniques represent the advantages and disadvantages of the process of sustainable tourism. Since the late 1980s, rapid growth in the tourism industry has led to increased demand for more sustainable tourism, especially when it comes to mass tourism.

The development of sustainable tourism can be summarized in two key approaches:

- The first believes that environmentally sustainable tourism is a harmless economic activity. It focuses on tourism as a part of a broader policy for sustainable development.
- The second sees sustainable tourism as a tool for the development of tourism, and that the economic factor for the tourist destination is the most important factor in order to preserve the natural resources. This is the developers' point of view [8].

4   Sustainable mass tourism

The tourism industry differs from other industries in three aspects:
1. It must bring touristic activity for the tourist destination.
2. The tourist is the participant who plays an active role in production and consumption.
3. Tourist destinations include various groups who compete to attract tourists looking for entertainment. Generally, touristic programs are fixed when it comes to mass tourism. Developers look for short term gains and profits without long term planning when it comes to tourist destinations.

4.1 Sustainable development and mass tourism

Sustainable development for sustainable tourism is a four-stage process [8] Identifying and establishing the concept of sustainable tourism.
1. Determining the conditions required to achieve it.
2. Developing criteria for measuring its progress.
3. Developing a set of techniques for maintaining sustainable tourism in many destinations that are subject to growth and to the environmental effects of mass tourism.

4.2 Effects of mass tourism

Tourist destinations all over the world go through different phases, beginning with exploration and early development and ending with recession; because each destination has a limit for growth thus resulting in recession after that growth limit is reached.

After reaching recession, tourist destinations can be changed through development by improving infrastructure, marketing, or production of domestic goods and other services. Developing tourist destinations results in generating more money and provides tourists with a sense of improvement at their respective destinations; it also provides more growth compared to the phase before development [5]. This should be implemented in Egyptian tourist destinations so that we can achieve the sustainable development of mass tourism and achieve the target of the Ministry of Tourism in having a sustainable and well-maintained tourism industry by increasing the number of hotel rooms thus increasing the generated income as well as providing more job opportunities.

The goals to be achieved by the year 2017 include attracting 14 million tourists and increasing the number of tourist nights to 140 million nights, in addition to having 240,000 hotel rooms. This would generate around 12 billion dollars as income from the tourism industry and would provide around 1.2 million jobs.

5 Applying the concept of sustainable and collective tourism in Egypt

There was, and still is, a conflict between the three elements that make up the concept of sustainability; a conflict that is difficult to overcome. There is, often, a need for economic development of the tourist destination as local communities want to work in tourism to increase their income and improve their standard of living. There should many projects that positively affect the environment; such projects are seen in Egypt in: South Sinai, Sharm El-Sheikh, and Nabq protected area.

5.1 Identifying and defining the study area of the Nabq protected area

The Nabq protected area is situated at the extreme southern part of the Sinai Peninsula on the Gulf of Aqaba. It covers an area of about 600 km² (with around 440 km² on land and around 130 km² in the water). It is 35 km north of Sharm El-Sheikh. It also covers an area of 3-5 km of deep coral reefs from the east passing through Om Adawy Valley. The Nabq protected area was declared a multi-purpose nature reserve in 1992 by the Egyptian Prime Minister's decree no. 1511 of 1992, amended by the Prime Minister's decree no. 33 of 1996. The Nabq protected area features various and magnificent ecosystems and habitats, the most important of which are the dunes located at the entrance to the Valley of Kid as well as the largest gathering of plant mangroves (Avesenaa Marina) on the Gulf of Aqaba. There are also other types of habitats in the mountainous areas of the reserve where conditions allow plants to grow. The area also contains 134 protected species of plants including 86 long-lived species. All desert areas are fragile and vehicles are banned from most areas except specific tracks. Figure 1 shows the Nabq protected area, Sinai, Gulf of Aqaba.

Figure 1:   Nabq protected area, Sinai, Gulf of Aqaba.

5.2 Resources for tourist attractions in protected areas

- Tourism depends on the natural resources in the region with around 2 million tourists visiting the South Sinai governorate annually. Around 13,600 tourists visited the Nabq protected area in 2010 (93% of that figure represented various foreign nationalities while only 7% were Egyptian).
- The Maria Schroeder shipwreck lies at a 24-meter-depth and is used as a dive site in an area called 'Al Gharkana' (the Sunken Ship) across from the fishermen's village. The Maria Schroeder was originally passing through Aqaba on its way to Germany when it sank in the forest of Nabq in the Red Sea in 1956.
- This site has attracted many foreign grants to preserve its natural resources.
- In late 2010, the protected area was used as a safe beach for tourists for swimming after shark attacks plagued the beaches of Sharm El-Sheikh.

5.3 Sustainable tourism and its application in Egypt in the Nabq protected area

As the number of tourists coming to Sharm El-Sheikh continues to grow, there is a persistent need to increase the number of hotel rooms to accommodate this rise in tourists. In 1985, there were 1500 hotel rooms. In 2010, the total number of hotel rooms surged to 49,500 rooms (according to the Tourism Development Authority, 2010). This shows the rapid growth in tourism which is looked at as mass tourism, and which cannot be tolerated by the environment.

The development of Sharm El-Sheikh began in a linear fashion from Umm El Sid Hill through Naama Bay towards Shark Bay, Ras Nasrani (which harbors the city's airport) to the protected area of Nabq instead of growing to the west of the city in the direction of the hills to minimize the cost of the infrastructure. This type of linear development has affected and continues to affect the southern boundary of the Nabq protected area.

Figure 2:   The buildings over the southern boundary of the protected area Nabq.

The social conditions of the local population have given rise to many problems due to the increase in population, which rose from 54,806 inhabitants in 1996 to 149,335 inhabitants in 2006, according to the Central Agency for Public Mobilization and Statistics (CAPMAS). This rise came due to high migration rates to the city and the demographics of the community. In addition, the indigenous population working in environment-related professions such as fishing and grazing began searching for work in the field of tourism as touristic activities have various economic benefits. An example is shown in Fig. 3 after the fishermen abandoned the Fishermen's Village Park.

Figure 3:   The Fishermen's Village Park after it was abandoned by the fishermen.

The city of Sharm El-Sheikh has a high income per capita, making it have the highest standard of living in all cities in the area and amongst the top paid areas in the Arab Republic of Egypt. This feature has economically benefited the city alone [9].

An analysis of tourism developers in different areas in Egypt and a study of the opinion of J. Saarinen have indicated that tourism developers are always interested in the sustainability aspect which often affects other aspects, for example:

- **Egypt: Red Sea Governorate – City of Hurghada**

Tourism developers are interested in environmental factors that attract tourists and cause them to revisit these destinations. Coral reefs have been eroded due to either building over them or neglecting them, in addition to the increased number of visitors from 1985 to 2010. This rise in tourists has also resulted in a demand for more hotel rooms. However, as a result of coral reef erosion, many tourists have changed their destination and began going to places such as Marsa Alam, which lies in the south of the city of Hurghada. This shift in tourist destination has resulted in a decline in tourists and accordingly in a drop in revenues. Tourism developers need to work on improving the environment in the hope of bringing back economic growth to the city. Fig. 4 shows a satellite image of building on coral reefs in Hurghada.

- **Egypt: Luxor Governorate – City of Luxor**

Tourism developers are interested in cultural aspects, which are the main attraction in Upper Egypt and which have positive effects on both the economy and the society. This concept has led to the redevelopment of the city such as through the re-opening of the Rams Road (Tareeq El-Kebash) linking the largest temples in Luxor, namely the Karnak and Luxor temples, the development of the Nile marinas as well as the development of Nile transportation from Cairo to Luxor.

Tourism developers should work on improving the environment in the hope of redirecting economic growth to the city once more. Fig. 5 shows the proposed Rams Road (Tareeq El-Kebash) with its final layout, while Fig. 6 shows the current image of Rams Road.

Figure 4:   Building on coral reefs in Hurghada (satellite image).

Figure 5:   Proposed   Rams   Figure 6: Current   image   of
              Road   (El-Kebash)   Rams Road (El-Kebash).
              with final layout.

- **Egypt: Marsa Matruh Governorate – Siwa Oasis**

In the western part of Egypt, the main attraction is social tourism as seen in the Bedouin lifestyle, which even includes the treatment of diseases by burial in the sand or the use of sulfur hot water or simply by staying in Bedouin homes. There are some environmental hotels in the area such as Adrere Amellal Ecolodge.

- **Mass tourism and its various effects in Egypt**

As shown in the above examples, constructing new buildings is often carried out in tourist destinations without considering the social and environmental aspects in those areas, which results in harming the natural resources of those areas (the plants in Nabq and the coral reefs in Hurghada). Tourism developers should consider constructing buildings that are more environment friendly and which use solar energy instead of geothermal energy. Figures 7 show the negative impact of tourism in the future. It will be hard to predict what tourists will want for their future entertainment destination. Accordingly, there should be means to create a more sustainable tourism in all three aspects for the various tourist groups. Tourism is an essential part of development and growth in the world, and many countries, including Egypt, depend heavily on tourism to maintain and increase the level of income and employment opportunities.

Figure 7:   Environmentally unfriendly construction with expected negative impact on tourism.

Statistics in 2011 showed that overall tourism in Egypt represented 49.2% of service exports, a 20% of foreign cash flow, and a 11.30% in the country's gross domestic product (GDP). Tourism represents 2% of the total implemented investments, 7.8% of the total investment in the services sector and 25% of the total taxes on services.

The seasonality of the demand on tourism in terms of tourists and tourist agencies or bodies results in high demand for only a few months each year, making tourism unsustainable in terms of economic, social and/or environmental respects. Tourists are considered consumers of the environment as their presence in a destination is considered a type of consumption. This currently coexists alongside the rapid and unplanned development. Thus, the development of mass tourism should be sustained from a global perspective but only environmentally sustainable on the local and regional levels. Mass tourism has grown along with the developments in the transport sector. There can be no tourism without travel. Accordingly, travel problems negatively affect tourism. Travelling requires various means of transportation. For example, we find that the phenomenon of mass tourism began with the rise in privately-owned cars in the United States in the 1920s and 1930s, and in Europe in the 1950s. Using private cars, tourists can visit local areas like beaches and rural areas. International travel started with the development of commercial aircraft and with the development of low cost airlines, group tourism developed to remote destinations. The use of aircrafts in tourism represents about 30% of all transport-related tourism [5]. We find that one of the major problems with the comprehensive development of tourism is transferring tourists to their destinations. Studies show that 40–60% of problems affecting the environment result from means of transport in tourism. In addition, climate change affects air traffic, which is an important factor when discussing sustainable tourism. The issue is not the consumption of energy, but it is the noise and the pollution, as well as the waste and abuse of the landscape and residential areas. Only 20–30% of environmental damage caused by tourism is a result of tourism activities in places such as housing, restaurants and other services provided. So far we have discussed the concept of sustainable tourism without focusing on the means of transport [5]. Sharm El-Sheikh International Airport is located 10 km away from the borders of the Nabq protected area, which causes much environmental damage due to noise and general pollution on the reservation.

6 Conclusion

Creating a new model of sustainable tourism can develop tourism but cannot be completely sustainable; it can improve mass tourism but it is difficult at the same time to achieve economic, social and environmental sustainability. Previous studies have reached the same results, as tourism developers do not work with all three aspects of sustainability at the same time. They focus on one aspect, which in the end affects the others [8]. In order to develop the concept of sustainable tourism we have to separate the three components (economic, social and environmental) because grouping them as one concept creates contradiction. To be constructive and conclusive, we have to treat and analyze each concept individually. By focusing solely on environmental sustainability, sustainable mass tourism becomes a reality and not a fantasy. This study should be considered as a first step in acquiring a new perspective to change the focus in research on sustainability, because the world wants to continue the process of achieving a more sustainable tourism development in the future but with different approaches of study. More studies should be conducted to explore more views to achieve sustainable tourism. Instead of trying to use the concept of the report by the Brundtland Commission in 1987, which has not worked so far and is difficult for tourism developers to implement, we need a new perspective and a new starting point for sustainable tourism.

References

[1] World Commission on Environment and Development, Our common future, Report of the Brundtland Commission, 1987.
[2] United Nations Conference on Environment and Development, Agenda 21Rio, (1992).

[3] R. Sharpley. Tourism and Sustainable Development: Exploring the gap theory. Journal of Sustainable Tourism. Volume 8, Issue 1, pp. 1–19, 2000.

[4] H. Erkus & A. Eraydin, Environmental Management for Sustainable Tourism Development Cooperative and networking organization in the region of Antalya tourism. Journal of sustainable tourism, 31, pp. 113–124, 2000.

[5] D. Scott, Why Sustainable Tourism Must Address Climate Change. Journal of Sustainable Tourism, 19 (1), pp. 17–34, 2011.

[6] C. Hunter, Sustainable Tourism as a Model to Adapt. Annals of Tourism Research, Volume 24, No. 4, pp. 850–867, 1997.

[7] Z. Liu, Sustainable Tourism Development: A Critique. Journal of Sustainable Tourism, Volume 11, No. 6, pp. 459–475, 2003.

[8] J. Saarinen, Tradition of Sustainability in Tourism Studies. Annals of Tourism Research, Volume 33, Issue 4, pp. 1121–1140, 2006.

Section 4
Tourism and
protected areas

Environmental valuation by the local population and visitors for zoning a protected area

D. G. G. Matos[1], P. Díaz[2], D. Ruiz-Labourdette[1], A. J. Rodríguez[2], A. Santana[2], M. F. Schmitz[1] & F. D. Pineda[1]
[1]Complutense University, Spain
[2]La Laguna University, Spain

Abstract

Protected natural areas have traditionally played an important role in tourist destinations. There are over one hundred thousand of these areas throughout the world and to date, their landscapes and biodiversity have constituted the main factor attracting visitors. Although these components have not lost their power to attract, many tourist destinations now highlight the relationship between nature and traditional culture. On one hand, the planning and management of natural areas have fundamentally been based on biophysical aspects; hence, their name. But, on the other, the socioeconomic perspective is of great importance and should be incorporated further into this management. The professional field of the sciences of 'nature', which so far has played a major role in these areas, along with the disciplines of social sciences and humanities, faces the challenge of integrating their analysis methods, which can be directly applied to an understanding of the dynamics of present-day tourism. This integration could consider protected areas and territories beyond their physical boundaries. Our team, with experience in the development of environmental analysis models applied to the zoning and subsequent declaration of these areas, has proposed a new procedure for evaluating carrying capacities and tourism potentialities, integrating environmental (landscape), anthropological (local society and visitors) and socioeconomic (living standard and quality of life of local population) perspectives. The research relates this kind of components through multivariate analyses, geo-referenced databases and questionnaires. The pathway

WIT Transactions on Ecology and The Environment, Vol 187, © 2014 WIT Press
www.witpress.com, ISSN 1743-3541 (on-line)
doi:10.2495/ST140131

of the model is landscape functioning (ecosystem) and its function for society (ecosystem services).

Keywords: carrying capacity, cultural landscape, environmental planning, landscape assessment, local population preferences, natural landscape, protected area, tourism, visitors' preferences.

1 Introduction

Environmental land planning constitutes a previous framework that should be available for administrative policies and, within these, for decision-making and specific protocols for managing natural resources. These resources are material ones, such as those relating to mining or agriculture, energy, like coal or wind, and spatial ones, such as the different manifestations of the landscape. Both the historical and current forms of use of these resources, as well as the socioeconomic relationships at play, provide the cultural resources of the territory. These forms and relationships constitute an 'added value' which can be of great importance in counties that are economically quite undeveloped, and they are unequivocal actors in the function of the landscape in territories developed under the auspices of different policies.

The present paper addresses the interaction of three scopes: environmental planning of a territory, zoning of a new protected area into the activities provided for this territory, and perception of this new activity by society. The territory (i) involves the island of Fuerteventura (Canary Isles), which is of great interest to tourists, mainly from Europe. The protected area (ii) will be a national park to be added to other protected spaces on the island. As for the society, (iii) considering that economic activities, in particular tourism, call for natural resources to be well safeguarded, we incorporated:

- perception of the resources of the island's landscape by its users, both native and resident, on one hand, and visitors on the other.
- the quality of life and standard of living of these local populations.

We considered the pre-existing socioeconomic activities, as well as the new ones, weighing up the pros and cons of their spatial localisation.

A territory is rarely homogeneous (Forman and Godron [1]) and each place presents different carrying capacities; thus, on the one hand, there is a need for a Cartesian, a cartographic, framework showing the natural and cultural features of the landscape and, on the other, decisions ought to contemplate the localisation of the new land uses. That is to say, the situation of each new activity should consider this capacity of the territory, foreseeing the environmental costs and benefits involved – see, for instance, the classical studies by McHarg [2] and Leopold et al. [3] or, among more recent ones, Montalvo et al. [4]. Among the socioeconomic activities, the tourism industry not only calls for increasing involvement by the economy of practically any given country; rather, the success of tourist destinations requires careful planning and management of the land uses. Conservationists are becoming increasingly vehement in calling for natural areas to be protected, given the different capacities of territories to harbour different activities, and there is increasing demand for cost and benefit analyses

(SCBD [5], Le Saout *et al.* [6]). Moreover, these areas are in themselves a tourist attraction (Schmitz [7]), are therefore constitute very important elements in planning and analysis of sustainability. Our research is related to the interest of the Canary Isles Regional Govt. in declaring a national park in Fuerteventura. For ecological and economic reasons, as well as the attractiveness of the island for tourism, there is a pressing need to protect the natural and, in general terms, landscape values of this territory.

2 Planning with people

Fuerteventura is the second biggest island in the Canary Isles (1,731 km^2). Together with Lanzarote, its morphology is relatively flatter than that of the other islands, due to its geological age and the role played by the accentuated erosion in shaping the landscape (Hernández [8], Paredes and Rodríguez [9], Pineda *et al.* [10]). The climate, quite unaffected by the action of the Trade Winds, is more uniform than on the other islands (it is a desert climate and the key to a homogeneous landscape; Matos *et al.* [11]). In the last three decades, tourism has become an activity of growing importance in politics, orienting the island's current socioeconomic development, and notably influencing the character and personality of the rural cultural landscape, typical of an island with a desert landscape that to date has been quite unpopulated (Burriel [12]).

2.1 Planning and ecology

The different schools of geography have historically developed systems for sectoring a given territory by means of different methods. When ecologists have studied the carrying capacity of a region providing for new land uses, they have classically estimated this capacity by orienting the sectoring towards an analysis of the correspondence between the 'intensity' of foreseen disturbances (those of the new uses) and the 'severity' of these, that is to say, their incidence taking into account the ecological characteristics of the territory. This involves features resulting from mesoclimate, lithology, vegetation, hydric flows, etc., including cultural parameters such as existing agricultural uses, industrial facilities, etc. (McHarg [2], Leopold *et al.* [3], Pineda *et al.* [13], Roberts and Roberts [14]).

All these features can be considered as environmental 'themes' that can be mapped, and upon whose spatial units can be estimated the ecological reaction to new land use perspectives. The reaction provides information on the 'impact', ecological cost or benefit of each use in each theme (partial or thematic impacts of new uses; Leopold *et al.* [3], Pineda *et al.* [13], Hernández and Pineda [15]). Calculation of coefficients to characterise each thematic reaction to each hypothetical use enables us to weight the responses of the territory and to establish the magnitude as a weighted sum (the renamed 'environmental impact assessment'). This weighting enables us to estimate and map the carrying capacity of each of the sectors of the territory as objectively as possible (Montalvo *et al.* [4], Ruiz-Labourdette *et al.* [16], among other studies on ecological planning).

2.2 Planning and users of landscapes

In the planning process, inclusion of the local population, both native and resident, as well as visitors as users of the natural resources, constitutes an important goal of the present study and is therefore the focus of this paper. To date, there has been some interest in the theme, but rather methodological difficulties with regard to integrating locals or visitors in ecological assessments of the territory. However, there have been some studies in this sense (Díaz *et al* [17], Ruiz-Labourdette *et al.* [18], Rodríguez *et al.* [19], Aguilera *et al.* [20], Schmitz *et al.* [21, 22]). Even less common is the incorporation of the quality of life and standard of living into the above mentioned assessment of thematic and environmental impact. This is despite the fact that the planning attempts to manage the territories in which these people reside. In the case at hand, we address the incorporation of this society into the localisation and demarcation process of a national park as a new occupation and land use.

Considering social perception in the environmental assessment of the territory, the present paper incorporates appraisals and preferences of the landscapes by the local population, both native and resident, and by visitors, the latter being related to Fuerteventura's attraction as a resort, as well as the quality of life and standard of living of the local societies. The landscape served as a reference for the contrast between environmental values and carrying capacity; it was evaluated by means of questionnaires implemented through simple random sampling in relation to activities that are to form a part of the uses and maintenance of a territory harbouring a national park.

2.2.1 Landscape preferences of the local population and visitors: spatial interaction

The numerical relationship between the landscape preferences of the local population and visitors, on one hand, and the landscape features, on the other, enabled us to obtain spatial patterns of landscape assessment by the human society in the study area. We began with a spatial method involving quantitative and qualitative natural and cultural features, in a similar way as in previous studies (Schmitz *et al.* [22], De Aranzabal *et al.* [23, 24]).

The units for description of the territory were the population nuclei of the island (population sectors within the municipalities, Table 1), at which scale the socio-economic information is recorded (INE [25]). At this scale, we considered the landscape characteristics that can easily and rapidly be perceived by people and that facilitate the landscape evaluation process in relation to nature conservation, supply of natural resources, leisure, taking into account that the task involves zoning a national park (Schmitz *et al.* [22], Zee [26]). Landscape features are shown in Table 2.

The spatial influence area of the population nuclei was calculated by means of Thiessen polygons, based on Euclidean geometry. Each polygon defines an area of influence around each population nucleus (any location inside the polygon is closer to that point than any of the other sample points). For each polygon, we

Table 1:   Population nuclei differentiated in Fuerteventura.

1. Agua de Bueyes	17. Parque Holandés	33. Puerto del Rosario
2. Antigua	18. Cardón	34. Puerto Lajas
3. Casillas de Morales	19. Latija (La)	35. Tefía
4. Triquivijate	20. Morro Jable	36. Tesjuates
5. Valles de Ortega	21. Pájara	37. Tetir
6. Caleta de Fuste	22. Toto	38. El Time
7. Betancuria	23. Ajuy	39. Estancos (Los)
8. Valle de Santa Inés	24. Esquinzo	40. Giniginamar
9. Vega del Río Palma	25. Pared (La)	41. Gran Tarajal
10. Caldereta	26. Solana Matorral	42. Playitas (Las)
11. Corralejo	27. Ampuyenta (La)	43. Tarajalejo
12. Cotillo (El)	28. Asomada (La)	44. Tesejerague
13. Lajares	29. Casillas del Ángel	45. Tiscamanita
14. Oliva (La)	30. Guisguisey	46. Tuineje
15. Tindaya	31. Llanos	47. Juan Gopar
16. Villaverde	32. El Matorral	48. Tequitar

calculated *(i)* the spatial cover of the variables of each thematic landscape feature. Thus, each point of the territory is a vector containing quantitative data on the landscape variables. A matrix (A), 48 observations (polygons) × 22 landscape variables (features) enabled us to order data representing the spatial cover of each landscape feature in each polygon. We conducted *(ii)* a survey based on questionnaires given to the local population and visitors (B, C). These questionnaires, based upon a limited number of questions regarding people's attitudes and preferences, also include aspects of their sociological profile.

We designed two matrices of 1,556 observations (local people interviewed) × 22 variables (local population answering the questions; matrix B), and 1,554 observations (visitors interviewed) × 22 variables (their answers to the questions; matrix C). We calculated *(iii)* the relationship between landscape features and landscape preferences, through the product of the matrices, A × D and A × E -being D the vector of weighted sums of local population preferences and E the corresponding vector of visitor preferences- which enables the spatial pattern of landscape preferences to be estimated by quantifying the valuation of the local

Table 2:   Types of territorial variables considered in the survey.

1. Climatic comfort	12. Beaches and dunes
2. Warmth in winter	13. Desert steppes
3. Cool in summer	14. Volcano landscape
4. Autumn and winter temperatures	15. Mountains with rocks
5. Strong winds	16. Vegetation, flora
6. Sun, intense sunshine	17. Shrublands, cactus fields
7. Rural landscape, agriculture, *gavias*	18. Coastal vegetation, brine basins
8. Natural landscape (wilderness)	19. Lava fields (*malpaís*)
9. Large open valleys	20. Patent animal wildlife
10. Closed agricultural valleys	21. Patent avifauna, birdwatching
11. Valleys with palm trees	22. Traditional architecture

people and visitors - vectors product of locals and visitors, respectively - in relation to the spatial variables (Schmitz *et al.* [22]; De Aranzabal *et al.* [24]). Spatial expression on maps of the product matrices enables us to establish the patterns of preferential valuation of the territory -different kinds of landscapes have been evaluated by different target groups with their specific preferences and attitudes-. From the perspective of a protected area, this method is useful for landscape zoning based upon the content of paragr. 2.1, as all these different kinds of landscapes constitute mappable 'themes'.

To estimate the quality of life and standard of living of the island's population, we considered the parameters accepted by the OECD [27] as descriptors of the degree of material comfort (living standard) and personal wellbeing or satisfaction (quality of life). We adapted the explanatory variables according to their availability from the secondary sources (INE [25]) and to the results of the survey conducted by means of simple random sampling involving 1,556 people identified according to socioeconomic aspects, daily activities and environmental perception.

2.2.2 Appraisal of the quality of life and standard of living of the local population

We conducted the appraisal of the quality of life and standard of living in the population nuclei (sectors within the municipalities) according to the importance given by each local individual, native or resident in each entity to each descriptor of each category according to a Likert scale, using values of each of these two parameters for each one of the 48 polygons. Thus, these polygons are considered according to these two 'themes'. The resulting values were contrasted with data from ethnographic fieldwork (2008 and 2013).

3 Diagnosis: assessment for designing the protected area

The diagnosis, a set of tools and approaches providing a landscape assessment, must derive from analysis of the ecological structure and processes, as well as the cultural situation (social and economic characteristics; Haase [28], Bastian [29], Schmitz *et al.* [30], De Aranzabal *et al.* [23], Bastian *et al.* [31]). Our research was based on *(i)* the valuation of four socio-ecological 'themes' -the landscape character, valuated both by the local population living within each polygon and by visitors, and two socioeconomic aspects, standard of living and quality of life of the local population, also applied inside each polygon-. We *(ii)* analysed the compatibility of each theme with the land uses and activities associated with the proposed national park, according to Ruiz-Labourdette *et al.* [16]. Five steps were considered:

1. Thematic valuation. This involves valuation of the landscape sectors (polygons) pertaining to the different attributes and preferences of the local people and visitors, and the standard of living and quality of life. We expressed the units of each kind of valuated landscape on two thematic maps. The thematic units were hierarchically valued from 10, the highest, to 1, the lowest.

2. Land use hypotheses. We selected a set of seven outdoor activities and associated infrastructures in national parks (visitor reception centres, scenic viewpoints, roads, hiking routes, trails for motor vehicles and picnicking and camping areas). In selecting land use hypotheses and subsequently estimating their degree of severity, we took into consideration the actual situations generated by these types of land uses in the eastern Canary Isles, in counties that had undergone a real transformation.

3. Partial impact estimation. This consisted of estimating the severity of each of these activities for the units of each landscape attribute (partial impacts, paragr. 2.1), ΔV_{ij}, assuming that each of the planned use hypotheses was theoretically implemented in each spatial unit, *j*, of each of the themes or attributes, *i*. The relative change in value of each unit of each attribute was considered as the cost or partial impact of the use hypothesis in question. The impact was estimated in reference to a previous ordinal scale established in the appraisal of the units in each attribute (Pineda *et al.* [13], Ruiz-Labourdette *et al.* [16]): $\Delta V_{ij} = V_f - V_a$, where V_f is the value on the polygon *j*, of the theme *i*, estimated after being subjected to that use (the new position it would occupy on the hierarchical scale) and V_a the actual value on the same scale. For the estimation we considered type and intensity of the expected landscape disturbance and the foreseeable severity thereof, considering the ecological fragility and reversibility of each spatial unit and attribute, or loss of value in the case of standard of living and quality of life.

4. Calculation of socioecological impacts. This consisted of estimating the change in value caused by each of the activities in the themes considered. The impacts were calculated by means of multivariate ordination analysis. The loadings of the themes (weighting coefficients) serve as key references for zoning the territory according to conservation categories coherent with the landscape compatibility in relation to the above mentioned different activities. We analysed a data matrix containing 48 polygons × 4 partial impacts × 7 activities.

I_k, being the global value of each polygon (hypothetical 'sacrifice scale' if each polygon has to be drastically transformed by consensus of the team), the coordinates of the polygons according to the ordination analysis indicate the importance of each theme in the value of the set of polygons in relation to each hypothesis, $I_k = b_{kl} \Delta V_l + b_{kv} \Delta V_v + b_{kst} \Delta V_{st} + b_{kq} \Delta V_{kq}$, where *b* represents the calculated weighting coefficients of the partial impacts of activity *k* (the relative contribution of the impact of activity k in each of the study area's polygons (*l*: landscape valuation by the local people, *v*: landscape valuation by visitors, *st*: standard of living, *q*: quality of life). The values for ΔVi were mapped for each 0 polygon and activity, standardized and ordered, and ranged from −1 (maximum impact; most severe activity for a theme) to +1 (maximum positive impact; best activity increasing the value). The co-ordinates of the polygons along the first axis of the analyses were considered as the values of *I*: the polygons with co-ordinates at the positive or negative ends of this axis represent the places most vulnerable or most resilient to each proposed land use, respectively.

5. Zoning process. The coordinates of the polygons on the first axis serve to differentiate the groups of polygons which, due to their sensitivity to the use hypotheses considered, should correspond to different protection categories.

4 Results and discussion

The zoning conducted considers incorporating the social component into procedures previously employed – above quoted – for planning the territory. Herein, the reason for declaring a national park in Fuerteventura is the high naturalistic values encountered therein (Hernández [8], Pineda [10], Lorenzo [32], Del Arco [33], Rodríguez-Delgado [34]), as well as the fact that the study area is a tourist resort that is attractive, but also classical (*four s* tourism), still presenting a low cultural value (Hernández and Pineda [15], Díaz *et al.* [17], Ruiz-Labourdette *et al.* [18], Rodríguez *et al.* [19]). This fact is recognised by the tourism industry.

These are all good reasons to include ecological and socioeconomic aspects in one single framework planning procedure. The present document addresses and describes an ecology-based procedure (consideration of partial territorial themes or aspects, paragr. 2.1), which is not elaborated upon in this book, due to issues relating to space. It therefore only deals with socioeconomic components, and the integration of both the ecological and socioeconomic aspects therefore remains to be addressed. This could involve global integration, incorporating as information into the aforementioned numerical analysis the different types of themes, or a procedure could be followed that involves comparison of the results obtained by the same method, but separating the ecological and social perspectives. This task remains to be tackled here. The method allows a certain degree of subjectivity in the evaluation of the standard of living and quality of life, depending upon the global parameters habitually accepted and used, and the conditioning caused by the existence of data provided by small-sized sampling units. This individualised information can be created by deducing it from certain valid descriptors at the local scale in order to avoid homogenisation of the datum for the territory and making use of a previous qualitative approach.

Correspondence between the results of a quantitative analysis and the final decision should always involve collective cabinet debate entailing participation by the Administration (who have ultimately to implement management of the natural resources) and the Academic Stakeholders (at least the team of investigators, who must provide conclusions, avoiding their own personal opinions). As results can clearly differ, the aim of this debate is to reach a consensus and to put forward a proposal, which is to be objective (scientific), and to facilitate a political decision which will also involve other dimensions (Ruiz Labourdette *et al.* [16]) that can all too often produce results that are not easily explained.

Studies such as most of those cited herein attempt to optimally localise a protected area considering almost exclusively biophysical features. Protecting an area can involve transformations in the perception of the landscape's resources, changes in the day-to-day peculiarities of the people living in the area and its surroundings, and in their habitual practices. There are not many examples of local people's circumstances being taken into account (Schmitz *el al.* [35, 36]). The task described herein is based upon four socioeconomic thematic aspects, but it remains subordinate to the results of a considerable number of biophysical aspects not included in the analyses. Thus, Figure 1 shows the partial results of the procedure described. There are noteworthy

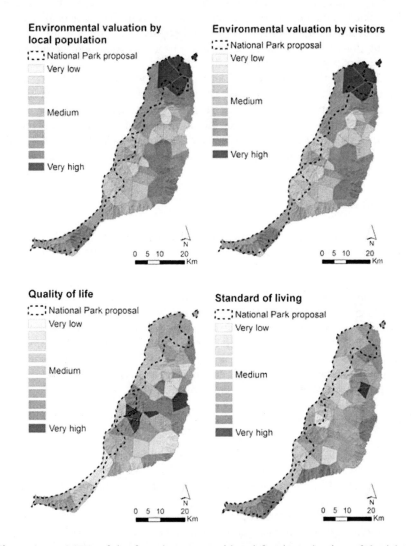

Figure 1: Maps of the four themes considered for the valuation of the island according to socioeconomic variables recorded in population nuclei (polygons). The Administration proposed the area in the West (dashed line) as a national park.

differences in the standard of living and quality of life of the populations. The high values of the former correspond to more urbanised places with more tourism, with better public services and tertiary production activities. The higher quality of life generally corresponds to the more ruralised character and, although these populations can constitute tourist attractions, there are much fewer and more temporary residents and visitors. This avoids costs to the traditional values caused by tourism (loss of privacy, identity, overcrowding,..) and urban development (pollution, stress, prices,...), but key infrastructures tend to be lacking, including those associated with tourism. The poor quality of life reported in the questionnaires by some rural populations reveals indifference by the institutions in relation to infrastructures, health or education, because these aspects do not respond to the profitability of tourism.

Furthermore, the preferences of local people and visitors for the landscape present significant similarities. There are interesting areas in the surroundings of the better developed tourism nuclei, which accounts for the fact that tourists know these areas better and for the incidence of classical sun-and-sand stereotypes projected beyond the island by the tourism industry, which includes studied images of the local population. Local people, however, value the island much more positively than visitors.

5   Conclusion

We have employed the aforementioned previous methods of ecological planning, now incorporating socioeconomic perspectives (social perception of the landscape and the natural resources, standard of living and quality of life of local population). With this in mind we have valued the territory and, in particular, we try to zoning a national park.

We found very marked differences between zoning the national park initially proposed by the Administration and the result of incorporating these perspectives. Zoning a protected area according to purely ecological considerations would be fine, but Canary Islands are a prime tourist destination and the perception of the local community and visitors is essential and inescapably must be taken into account in planning.

References

[1]   Forman, R.T.T. & M. Godron, Patches and Structural Components for a Landscape Ecology. *BioScience* 31(10): 733–740. 1981.

[2]   McHarg, I.L. *Design with nature.* Doubleday & Company INC: Garden City. NY. 1969.

[3]   Leopold, L.R., Clark, F.A., Henshaw, B.R. & Balsey, J.R. *A Procedure for Evaluation of Environmental Impacts.* US Depart. Interior. Geological Surveys Circular 645. USGS, IANA S 946 L45, Washington. 1971.

[4]   Montalvo, J., Sanz, L.R., De Pablo, C.L. & Pineda, F.D. Impact Minimization   through   Environmentally-based   Site   Selection: a

Multivariate Approach. *Journal of Environmental Management* 38(1): 13–25. 1993.

[5]   SCBD. COP 10 Decision X/2. *Strategic Plan for Biodiversity 2011–2020* (Secretariat of the Convention on Biological Diversity, Nagoya, Japan). 2010.

[6]   Le Saout S., Hoffmann M., Shi, Y., Hughes, A., Bernard, C., Brooks, T.M., Bertzky, B., Butchart, S.H.M., Stuart, S.N., Badman, T. & Rodrigues, A.S.L. Protected areas and effective biodiversity conservation. *Science* 342: 803–805. 2013.

[7]   Schmitz, M.F. (ed.). *Tourism and Natural protected Areas.* WIT Press, Southampton. 139 pp. 2013.

[8]   Hernández, C.C. *La evolución del relieve de Fuerteventura.* Cabildo Insular, Puerto del Rosario. 1992.

[9]   Paredes, R. & Rodriguez, R. (eds.) *Fuerteventura.* RAI Ediciones, Antigua. 2002.

[10] Pineda, F.D. (dir.). *Estudio para el Plan de Ordenación de los Recursos Naturales (PORN) de la propuesta de Parque Nacional de Fuerteventura. Primera Fase.* (Proy. 314/2006; 228/2008, UCM). Puerto del Rosario-Madrid-La Laguna, Cabildo de Fuerteventura. 2010.

[11] Matos, D.G.G., Ruiz-Labourdette, Schmitz, M.F. & Pineda, F.D. Ecological zoning of a homogeneous territory. *Ecological indicators*, 2014 (reviewing).

[12] Burriel, E. *Canarias: población y agricultura en una sociedad dependiente.* Oikos-tau, Barcelona. 1981.

[13] Pineda, F. D., Escudero, J. C, Hiraldo, F., García-Novo, F., Bernáldez, F. G., Merino, J., Ramírez, L., Ramos, A., Ribero, J. C., Sancho, F. & Sainz, H. *Terrestrial ecosystems adjacent to large reservoirs. Ecological survey and impact diagnosis*, in *XI Congress of Internatational Commission on Large Dams: "ICOLD 73"* Dirección General de Obras Hidráulicas. Centro de Estudios Hidrográficos: Madrid. p. 38. 1974.

[14] Roberts, R.D. & Roberts, T.M. (eds.) *Planning and Ecology.* Chapman and Hall, London, 1984.

[15] Hernández, S. & Pineda, F.D. (dirs.). *Escultura de Eduardo Chillida "Montaña de Tindaya" (Isla de Fuerteventura).* Informe para la Consejería de Medio Ambiente y Ordenación Territorial, Gobierno de Canarias, Santa Cruz de Tenerife. 2007.

[16] Ruiz-Labourdette, D., Schmitz, M.F., Montes, C. & Pineda, F.D. Zoning a protected area: proposal based on a multi-thematic approach and final decision. *Environmental Modeling and Assessment* 15: 531–547. 2010a.

[17] Díaz, P., Ruiz-Labourdette, D., Darias, A.R., Santana, A., Schmitz, M.F. & Pineda, F.D. Landscape perception of local population: the relationship between ecological characteristics, local society and visitor preferences. In: C.A. Brebbia & F.D. Pineda (eds.). *Sustainable Tourism IV.* Wit Press, Boston: 309–317. 2010.

[18] Ruiz-Labourdette, D., Díaz, P., Rodríguez, A.J., Santana, A., Schmitz, M.F. & Pineda, F.D. Scales and scenarios of change in the anthropology-

landscape relationship: models of cultural tourism in Fuerteventura (Canary Isles). In: S. Favro & C.A. Brebbia (eds.). *Island Sustainability.* Wit Press, Southampton: 51–63. 2010b.

[19] Rodríguez, A. J., Díaz, P., Ruiz Labourdette, D., Pineda, F.D., Schmitz, M. F. & Santana, A. Selection, design and dissemination of Fuerteventura's projected tourism image (Canary isles). In: S. Favro & C.A. Brebbia (eds.). *Island Sustainability.* Wit Press, Southampton: 13–24. 2010.

[20] Aguilera, P., Schmitz, M.F., de Aranzabal, I., Castro, H. & Pineda, F.D. Characterization of visitors to natural areas in the Southeast of Spain. In: F.D. Pineda & C.A. Brebbia (eds). *Sustainable tourism.* Witt Press, Boston: 333–340. 2004.

[21] Schmitz, M.F., Ruiz Labourdette, D., Sañudo, P.F., Montes, C. & Pineda, F.D. Participation of visitors in the management design of protected natural areas. In: C.A. Brebbia & F.D. Pineda (eds.). *Sustainable tourism II.* WIT Press, Boston: 139–148. 2006.

[22] Schmitz, M.F., de Aranzabal, I. & Pineda, F.D. Spatial analysis of visitor preferences in the outdoor recreational niche of Mediterranean cultural landscapes. *Environmental Conservation* 34(4): 300–312. 2007.

[23] De Aranzabal, I., Schmitz, M.F., Aguilera, P., Pineda, F.D. Modelling of landscape changes derived from the dynamics of socio-ecological systems.A case of study in a semiarid Mediterranean landscape. *Ecological Indicators* 8: 672–685. 2008.

[24] De Aranzabal, I., Schmitz, M.F. & Pineda, F.D. Integrating landscape analysis and planning: a multi-scale approach for oriented management of tourist recreation. *Environmental Management* 44: 938–951. 2009.

[25] INE. Instituto Nacional de Estadística de España (INE). *Censo de Población y viviendas*, Madrid. 2010.

[26] Zee, D. The complex relationship between landscape and recreation. *Landscape Ecology* 4(4):225–236. 1990.

[27] OECD (Organisation for Economic Co-operation & Development). *How's Life? 2013. Measuring Well-being.* 2013.

[28] Haase, G. Approaches to, and methods of landscape diagnosis as a basis of landscape planning and landscape management. *Ekológia* 9: 11–29. 1990.

[29] Bastian, O. Landscape classification in Saxony (Germany) – a tool for holistic regional planning. *Landscape and Urban Planning* 50: 145–155. 2000.

[30] Schmitz , M.F., De Aranzabal, I., Aguilera, P., A. Rescia & Pineda, F.D. Relationship between landscape typology and socioeconomic structure. Scenarios of change in spanish cultural landscapes. *Ecological Modelling* 168: 343–356. 2003.

[31] Bastian, O., R. Krönert, & Z. Lipský. Landscape diagnosis on different space and time scales – a challenge for landscape planning. *Landscape Ecology* 21: 359–374. 2006.

[32] Lorenzo, J.A. (ed.). *Atlas de las aves nidificantes en el archipiélago canario.* M. Medio Ambiente- SEO/Birdlife, Madrid. 2007.

[33]   Del Arco, M. (ed.). *Mapa de Vegetación de Canarias*. GRAFCAN, S.C. de Tenerife. 2006.

[34]   Rodríguez-Delgado, O. (ed.). *Patrimonio Natural de la isla de Fuerteventura.* Cabildo de Fuerteventura, Puerto del Rosario. 2005.

[35]   Schmitz, M.F., Sánchez, I.A. & De Aranzabal, I. Influence of management regimes of adjacent land uses on the woody plant richness of hedgerows in Spanish cultural landscapes. *Biological Conservation* 135: 542–554. 2007.

[36]   Schmitz, M.F., Matos, D.G.G., De Aranzabal, I., Ruiz Labourdette, D. & Pineda, F.D.   Effects of a protected area on land-use dynamics and socioeconomic development of local populations. *Biological Conservation* 149: 122–135. 2013.

Analysis of the social, cultural, economic and environmental impacts of indigenous tourism: a multi-case study of indigenous communities in the Brazilian Amazon

C. N. Brandão[1], J. C. Barbieri[1] & E. Reyes Junior[2]
[1]Fundação Getulio Vargas – EAESP/FGV, Brazil
[2]Universidade Federal de Roraima – UFRR, Brazil

Abstract

Indigenous tourism does not yet figure on the agenda of public tourism policies in Brazil, neither is it regulated. There are, however, various tourism initiatives in indigenous areas throughout the country, mainly in the Amazon region, where most of Brazil's Indian population is concentrated. Considering tourism can lead to both positive and negative consequences the objective of this work is to analyze the social, cultural, economic and environmental impacts of tourism on Indian communities in the Brazilian Amazon region. A survey was carried out that comprised forty questions that were answered by Indians from the communities. The study revealed that tourist activities have proved to be sustainable in their social, cultural and environmental dimensions, according to the opinion of the local inhabitants. However, the result for economic sustainability was not representative, perhaps because the communities receive a reduced number of visitors because of their incipient infrastructure.

Keywords: sustainable tourism, indigenous tourism, tourism sustainability indicators, sustainable development.

1 Introduction

Indigenous tourism is not yet a segment prioritized by the Brazilian tourism industry, neither is it regulated. There are, however, various tourism initiatives in indigenous areas throughout the country, but it is not known for certain how the activity is organized and if it really produces benefits for the Indian people, because there are few empirical studies on this theme, particularly in the Amazon region where most of the Indian population in Brazil is concentrated.

This research was carried out in three Indian communities: Bananal, Nova Esperança and Boca da Mata, which belong to the São Marcos Indigenous Lands, which are located in the Brazilian Amazon region. Initially, Indian people lived mainly from growing manioc, hunting and fishing, but this reality has changed over the last ten years. There is an increasingly constant search for activities that make the social, economic, cultural and environmental sustainability of the communities feasible. The Indian communities mentioned above have seen tourism as an alternative for sustainable local development. These indigenous groups have shown themselves to be active entrepreneurs, who negotiate partnerships with private companies, prepare projects for obtaining financing and have started assuming a relevant role in the structure of the sector. Starting from the premise that tourism, depending on the way in which it is carried out, can promote sustainable local development for indigenous people, the objective of the research is to analyze the social, cultural, economic and environmental impacts on indigenous communities living in the Brazilian Amazon region.

The study is justified because of the concern with the impact that tourism might have on indigenous areas if measures are not taken that include the sustainability dimensions in their development. Various academics have debated the positive and negative effects of tourism on indigenous cultures [1, 2]. In the Brazilian Amazon region it is seen that the Indians have chosen tourism as an activity that is capable of providing those living in the community with autonomy while preserving their culture and traditional values.

2   Sustainable local development

Numerous reports have been published since the 1970s that mention the concern there is with maintaining economic growth without destroying the natural and social environment. The World Commission on Environment and Development (WCED) was created by the General Assembly of the United Nations Organization (UNO) in 1983, and its report entitled "Our Common Future", which was published in 1987, emphasizes the need for a new development model that is capable of making economic growth, wealth distribution and environmental preservation compatible. Sustainable development is defined as that which satisfies the needs and aspirations of the present, without compromising the ability of future generations to satisfy their own needs [3]. The central points on sustainable development that were presented in the "Our Common Future" report became the basis for preparing Agenda 21, which can be defined as a "planning instrument for the construction of sustainable societies in different geographic bases, which reconciles methods of environmental protection, social justice and economic efficiency" (UN Conference on Environment and Development, 1992) [4].

Segmentation by activity or by sector, as [5] highlight, is a way of operationalizing sustainable development proposals. Sustainability can be found in civil construction, sustainable architecture, sustainable tourism and in other economic sectors. Even though each of the dimensions are broken down to facilitate an understanding of sustained development, they cannot be developed in isolation because they are inter-related. From this perspective, the reach of sustainable local development in indigenous communities may result from the integration of tourism, provided that the planning and management of the activity are carried out in a participative way and include the strengthening of an endogenous power on the part of the communities.

2.1 Indigenous tourism and sustainability

It is a well-known fact that the tourism industry depends on natural and cultural resources for attracting tourists. As [6] define it, indigenous tourism is tourism in which the Indians are directly involved and the main attraction are their culture and tradition.

The concept of sustainability in tourism was initially established as a notion that there is a need to balance the inter-relationship between tourism and environment; that there must be a commitment to minimizing conflict; and that planning must be exercised in such a way that the long-term feasibility of the industry is safe-guarded [7]. Whatever the position, a common theme running through these perspectives is that the development of sustainable tourism includes a focus on achieving some level of harmony among the groups of stakeholders in order to develop long-lasting quality of life [8, 9].

The [10] conceives of sustainable tourism as a process that meets the current needs of tourists and the receiving communities, without compromising the ability to meet the needs of future generations. [8] defines it as "tourism that is economically viable, but that does not destroy those resources on which tourism of the future will depend, particularly the physical environment and the social fabric of the local community". In this context, the development of sustainable tourism requires the participation of all those interested – citizens, businesspeople and community leaders – in order to guarantee there is consensus with regard to the decisions taken [11]. The focus on stakeholder participation underlines even more the capacity to deal with the various problems that crop up [9, 11, 12].

Achieving sustainable tourism requires constant monitoring of the impacts and the introduction of preventive and/or corrective measures whenever necessary. Tourists must also be guaranteed a significant experience in order to raise their awareness of the issues of sustainability [11, 13, 14]. For this to happen, it is necessary to use accurate and reliable indicators that are capable of testifying to the sustainability of the tourism as well as its monitoring.

2.2 Sustainable tourism indicators

According to the [11] indicators are sets of formally selected information to be used on a regular basis in such a way as to measure important changes in the development and management of tourism. They are measures that help discover the existence and seriousness of current problems, signs of future problems, and means of identifying and measuring the results of anthropic actions in order to facilitate the decision-making process [15]. It is within this context that [16] adds that indicators are developed as a simplified tool that facilitates communication, serving as the basis for political decisions in the pursuit of sustainability.

Indicators normally correspond to questions relating to the natural resources of a destination, concerns with its economic sustainability, questions relating to its cultural heritage and social values and broader questions to do with the organization and management of the destination [11].

3 Methodology

This study is characterized as being exploratory-descriptive, since it describes and analyzes in what way the phenomenon occurs, as well as its characteristics and nature. The research strategy adopted was that of the case study, whose contribution, according to [17], is knowledge of individual, organizational, political, social, group and related phenomena, evoked by the desire to understand complex social phenomena.

The research was carried out by applying a survey, which comprised four questions adapted from the Workshop on Indicators for the Sustainable Development of Tourism, [18]. The instrument comprised two sections: one referred to the socio-demographic characteristics of those interviewed, like their age, gender, employment situation and earnings from tourism. The second checked the environmental, cultural, social and economic impacts arising from tourism in indigenous communities. A pre-test was carried out to check for clarity and understanding of the questions in the questionnaire.

The research sample was constituted by 210 valid responses. As the questionnaire consisted in 40 statements this provided a ratio of 5 cases per variable, using a 5-point interval scale (5 – I fully agree, to 1 – I totally disagree). [19] alleges that a minimum of five cases per variable is acceptable, but for greater analysis reliability it is preferable to have a proportion of more than ten cases per variable. Because of this, intrablock factor analysis was chosen, in order to evaluate the unidimensionality of the construct, as Mondadori and Ladeira (2007) mention [20]. Categorical Principal Components Analysis (CAPCA), as indicated by [21], was used. This is a method that aims to summarize a set of data in a manner that is similar to the conventional analysis model. This is an alternative option when the suppositions of linearity between variables, interval scales and normal distribution are not met.

Subsequently it was decided to compare two groups. As the normality assumption was not confirmed, a Mann-Whitney statistical test was carried out. The statistical test shows the mean-rank values that are used for identifying which of the groups had a positive opinion about sustainability in tourism in the social, cultural, environmental and economic aspects. In this case the p-value (Asymp. Sig.) is a criterion for defining if there are significant differences between the groups or not. The analyses were made feasible by way of the SPSS software, Version 18.0.

4   Results

The first part of the questionnaire refers to the socio-demographic data and the second stage refers to the analysis of the impact of tourism on social, cultural, environmental and economic dimensions in the view of the residents. It was found that there is not a large difference between the genders in terms of the numbers of those responding. Female respondents represented 48% of the sample, while male respondents represented a little more than 51%. As for the age band, it was observed that in those indigenous communities where the survey was carried out young people in the 150–25 year band represent 32.38% of the population, as shown in Figure 1. People in the 25–34 and 35–44 age bands totaled a little over 20% each. People in the 45–54; 55–64, 65–74 and over 75 bands totaled less than 10% each.

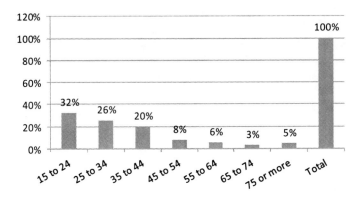

Figure 1:   Age.

Community income derives predominantly from agriculture, according to 40% of the respondents. The second activity is tourism, with 33% of the replies. However, the respondents did not choose the 'tourism' option as their only activity; it is always accompanied by some other activity. In the majority of cases tourism is the second most important source of income for the respondents. This was followed by the 'Other areas' category, which totaled 14%. And 'Education', which totaled 9%. The categories 'Trade' and 'Fishing' totaled 2% each.

As far as concerns the percentage of income coming from tourism, most of the interviewees (139 people) were unable to say how much of their income comes from tourism or they have no income from tourism, as can be seen in Figure 3. This result may seem contradictory when compared with what was presented in Figure 3, in which tourism appears as the second most practiced activity. However, less than half of the residents from the three communities are able to calculate how much of their income comes from tourism. Most, perhaps because of the sporadic nature of the activity, cannot say what percentage they earn from tourism. As can be seen, 39 respondents state that 5% of their income comes from tourism activities. A further 25 people said that 10% of their total income comes from tourism. Four respondents said that their income coming from tourism is 20%. Finally, three respondents said that tourism corresponds to 30%, 50% and 80% of each of their incomes.

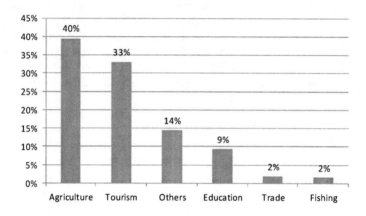

Figure 2: Area of work.

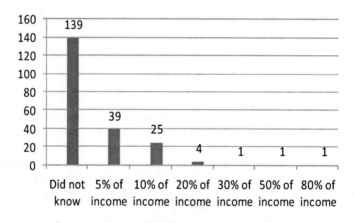

Figure 3: Percentage of income coming from tourism.

The second stage of the questionnaire refers to the intrablock Exploratory Factor Analysis (intrablock EFA), which was used to analyze the undidimensionality of the 40 statements about tourism sustainability that were placed in each of the 4 dimensions studied in the research: social, cultural, environmental and economic. Below are the analysis summary measures, which are: the dimension studied, Cronbach's alpha and the percentage of explained variance. It was expected that each of the dimensions would have a Cronbach's alpha over 0.6, an eigenvalue over 1 and a variance percentage over 0.5, according to [19]. Table 1 shows the summaries of the EFAs. All dimensions have a Cronbach's alpha over 0.6; an eigenvalue over 1 and a variance percentage over 0.5.

Table 1: Intrablock Factor Analysis summary.

Dimension	Cronbach's alpha	Explained variance	
		Eigenvalue	% of explained variance
Social	.695	2.089	52.22
Cultural	.662	1.709	56.96
Environmental	.869	2.874	71.85
Economic	.725	2.193	54.84

Table 2 gives the weightings of the dimensions studied. The results were significant for forming the social dimension, using four of the ten statements in the questionnaire. Three of the ten statements were used to form the cultural dimensions.

Table 2: Weightings of the dimensions.

Dimension	Factor loads	
Social	DIM_SOC2	.718
	SOC_DIM5	.728
	SOC_DIM8	.735
	SOC_DIM9	.709
Cultural	INV_CUL_DIM7	.780
	INV_CUL_DIM9	.749
	INV_CUL_DIM10	.734
Environmental	INV_AMB_DIM2	.770
	INV_AMB_DIM3	.893
	INV_DIM_AMB4	.871
	INV_AMB_DIM8	.851
Economic	ECO_DIM3	.737
	ECO_DIM4	.899
	ECO_DIM5	.785

Four of the ten statements were necessary to compose the environmental dimension. Finally, to form the economic dimensions three of the ten statements were necessary.

4.1 Comparison of groups

A non-parametric Mann-Whitney test was used to test the differences between the two groups. The differences between the opinions of the respondents were analyzed, by dividing them into two groups by economic activity. The differences between agricultural activities were first analyzed and then the differences between tourism activities. With this it was possible to show the respondents' opinions with regard to which dimensions are significantly important to sustainability in tourism.

After the analyses it was seen that the respondents who are active in the agriculture area were more positive as to sustainability in tourism within the cultural dimension, as shown in Table 3, with a mean-rank value of 107.46.

Table 3: Analysis of dimensions by activity (agriculture).

Agriculture	No	Yes	Asymp. Sig. (p)
Social dim (mean-rank)	116.310	97.850	0.026
Cultural dim (mean-rank)	102.720	107.460	0.547
Environmental dim (mean-rank)	113.630	99.750	0.050
Economic dim (mean-rank)	110.490	101.970	0.250

However, when observing the p-value, it can be seen that this difference is not significant between respondents. There were, however, significant differences in the social and environmental dimensions, with values of 0.026 and 0.05 respectively.

Those respondents who are active in the tourism area proved to be more positive with regard to sustainability in tourism in the cultural dimension, as can be seen in Table 4, with a mean-rank value of 120.96.

Table 4: Analysis of dimensions by activity (tourism).

Tourism	No	Yes	Asymp. Sig. (p)
Social dim (mean-rank)	122.670	87.660	0.000
Cultural dim (mean-rank)	90.620	120.960	0.000
Environmental dim (mean-rank)	108.250	102.640	0.421
Economic dim (mean-rank)	105.300	105.700	0.956

When observing the Asymp. Sig. value it can be seen that there is a significant difference between the respondents; in other words, for those who work in the tourism area, tourism is sustainable in the cultural dimension. There were significant differences in the social dimension, with a value of 0.000. But the lowest mean rank value (87.66) related to the tourism area, which shows that the other areas are more positive with regard to sustainability in the social dimension.

The social, cultural, environmental and economic dimensions were used for carrying out the group comparison tests. The scores were estimated in accordance with the categories found in the factor analyses, which generated the variables in the dimensions mentioned.

5 Conclusions

The intention behind carrying out this research was to verify the opinion of Indians as to the sustainability of tourism, by checking this activity's positive impacts on the social, cultural, environmental and economic dimensions. Given the results of the group comparison it was seen that tourism has had a positive impact on the indigenous communities as far as the social, environmental and cultural dimensions are concerned, according to the opinion of the residents. Results indicated that the impacts coming from tourism, according to the opinion of the residents, have been positive so far – at least in the social, cultural and environmental dimensions. However, the result for economic sustainability was not representative. One of the reasons for this result may be due to the fact that the communities have a reduced number of visitors. Generally speaking, however, it was found that there was an increase in income in indigenous communities. As several residents mentioned, this increase in income is perceived more at the individual level than collectively.

This result might be different if there was a more constant and greater flow of tourists to these locations. The [22] emphasizes that the principles of sustainability refer to an adequate balance between the environmental, economic and socio-cultural aspects of tourism, in such a way as to guarantee its long-term sustainability. According to the result as analyzed, this is not yet happening in all the dimensions in the communities surveyed.

With regard to the socio-cultural aspect the indigenous people have noticed improvements in self-esteem and in valuing the culture and an increase in the interest among the young to learn their mother tongue. Typical festivals and handicraft work have also become more popular and widely sought after. With regard to the environmental aspect there was an interest in conserving the environment, in reducing burning, in maintaining trails and in cleaning the area surrounding the community.

The Bananal, Nova Esperança and Boca da Mata communities can be considered to be emerging indigenous tourist destinations in the Brazilian Amazon region. But local government needs to intervene to regulate the activity and provide support for planning and monitoring the activity.

It is suggested that actions be prioritized that transform existing initiatives into excellent indigenous tourism destinations, thus creating the conditions needed for other communities to draw their inspiration from these models.

Finally, it is hoped that the findings of this research can contribute to a better understanding of this as yet little studied activity in Brazil, but one that represents an emerging segment of tourism and that is fast becoming a new opportunity for achieving the objectives of sustainable local development.

References

[1] Smith, T. Welfare, enterprise, and aboriginal community: the case of the Western Australian Kimberley region. *Australian Economic History Review*. 46(3), 2006.

[2] Weaver, D. Indigenous tourism stages and their implications for sustainability. *Journal of Sustainable Tourism*. 18(1), 43-60, Jan., 2010.

[3] CMMAD – Comissão Mundial sobre Meio Ambiente e Desenvolvimento. *Nosso futuro comum*. 2 ed. Tradução de *Our common future*. 1a ed. 1988. Rio de Janeiro: Fundação Getulio Vargas, 1991.

[4] CNUMAD. *Conferência das Nações Unidas para o Meio Ambiente e Desenvolvimento*. Rio de Janeiro, 3–14 jun, 1992. http://www.un.org/geninfo/bp/enviro.html, acessado em 23 de janeiro de 2012.

[5] Brandao, C. N., Barbieri, J. C., Reyes Junior, E.. *O Campo de Estudo do Turismo Sustentável em Comunidades Indígenas*. In: XIII Anais ENGEMA – Encontro Nacional sobre de Gestão Empresarial e Meio Ambiente. São Paulo, 2011.

[6] Hinch, T.; Butler, R. *Indigenous tourism: A common ground for discussion*. London: International Thomson, Business Press, 1996.

[7] Hunter, C; Green, H. *Tourism and the environment: a sustainable relationship?* London; New York: Routledge, 1995.

[8] Swarbrooke, J.. *Turismo sustentável: conceitos e impacto ambiental*. Vol.1. Tradução de *Sustainable tourism management*. Oxon: CABI. São Paulo: Aleph, 2000.

[9] Byrd, E. T. Stakeholders in sustainable tourism development and their roles. *Tourism Review*. 62(2), 2007.

[10] WTO. *Making tourism more sustainable: a guide for policy makers*. United Nations Environment Programme and World Tourism Organization. France; Spain, 2005.

[11] WTO. *Indicators of Sustainable Development for Tourism Destinations: a Guidebook*. World Tourism Organization, Madrid, Spain, 2004.

[12] Butts, T.; Singh, S. Sustainable tourism as a tool for conservation and protection of the Amazon rainforest in Guyana? *Sustainable tourism*. 2(2), pp.173-185, 2010.

[13] Johnston, J.; Tyrrel, J. Management exercises and trainer's note in sustainable tourism and dynamics. *International Journal of Culture, Tourism and Hospitality Research*. 1(4), 2007.

[14] Jayawardena, C. *et al*. Sustainable tourism development in Niagara Discussions, theories, projects and insights. *International Journal of Contemporary Hospitality Management*. 20(3), pp. 258-277, 2008.

[15] United Nations – UN. *Indicators of Sustainable Development: Guidelines and Methodologies - 2001*. UN: New York, 2001.

[16] Ciegis, R. *et al*. Theoretical Reasoning of the Use of Indicators and Indices for Sustainable Development Assessment. *The Economic Conditions of Enterprise Functioning*, 3(1), 2009.

[17]   Yin. R. K. *Estudo de caso: planejamento e métodos.* 3 ed. Porto Alegre: Bookman. 2010.

[18]   WTO. Final report -Workshop on Sustainable Tourism Indicators for the Islands of the Mediterranean Kukljica, Island of Ugljan, Croatia 21–23 March, 2001.

[19]   Hair JR, J.F. *Fundamentos de métodos de pesquisam em administração.* Tradução: Lane Belon Ribeiro. Porto Alegre: Bookman, 2005.

[20]   Mondadori, M. G.; Ladeira, W. J.. Validação de um instrumento quantitativo em pesquisa de empreendedorismo e inovação: um estudo no contexto dos recursos tangíveis e intangíveis. Proc. of *Anais do Encontro da Anpad, XXXI, 2007,* Rio de Janeiro: Enanpad, Sep, 2007.

[21]   Meulman, J. J.; Heiser, W. J. *SPSS Categories 14.0.* SPSS Inc. Chicago, 2005.

Planning for sustainability at the destination level through limiting accessibility on the island of Spetses, Greece

A. Vassi & G. Christodoulopoulou
National Technical University of Athens, Greece

Abstract

Spetses is the only Greek settlement which has a complete ban of traffic. Excessive use of motorcycles puts in danger not only the development of tourism on the island but also the island itself. This study aims at preserving the shape of the settlement, its natural and urban environment, improving the quality of life and promoting the development of tourism.
Keywords: sustainable tourism, areas of controlled accessibility, limiting accessibility.

1   Introduction

During the 1990s, the issue of sustainability was the subject of a discourse which resulted in the term "sustainable tourism". The Fifth Environmental Action Programme: Towards Sustainability, adopted by the European Commission in March 1992, was employed by the European Union to implement Agenda 21. Wilkinson [1] points out that the backbone of the Action programme was the need to integrate the needs of the environment into the development and implementation of other policies: agriculture; energy; industry; transport; tourism. Lane [2] describes the term of sustainable development as all the components chart a path for tourism development such that a destination area's environmental resource base (including natural, built, and cultural features) is protected for future development. Hunter [3] proposes 4 ways of interpreting sustainable tourism: 1. sustainable development through a "Tourism Imperative"; 2. sustainable development through "product-led tourism"; 3. sustainable development through "environment-led tourism"; 4. sustainable development through "'Neotenous Tourism". Some researchers, such as Butler [4], prefer the

WIT Transactions on Ecology and The Environment, Vol 187, © 2014 WIT Press
www.witpress.com, ISSN 1743-3541 (on-line)
doi:10.2495/ST140151

term 'sustainable development in tourism', involving the ideology of sustainability and which does not necessarily refer to a tourism-centric approach in development discussions and practices in which the evaluation is focused on the needs of the tourist industry [5]. Inskeep [6] points out that: "the sustainable development approach can be applied to any scale of tourism development from larger resorts to limited size special interest tourism". Leiper [7] highlights the fact that the inextricable relationship between transport and tourism is of fundamental importance in explaining the tourism system. Lumsdon and Page [8] and Page [9] realize that, within the academic discipline of transport, studies that focus on leisure or tourism settings are limited and yet leisure traffic can be significant. In the UK it accounts for 30% of all trips and 40% of all trip miles if visits to friends and relatives are included and it is dominant in the long-distance market, accounting for 58% of all UK trips over 50 miles (Department for Transport, 2005 [19]). This situation is not unique to the UK. German figures estimate that leisure trips account for 48% of all passenger kilometres [10]. Dickinson and Robbins [11] explore the contradiction in policy objectives as national governments are keen to promote tourism and leisure for their economic benefits (whilst at the same time there is an agenda to reduce congestion, greenhouse gas emissions and tackle other environmental problems associated with travel by car by reducing road traffic growth).

2 Background

Spetses is the only Greek settlement which has a complete ban of traffic. Prohibiting cars is not an arbitrary policy, nor an exception in a world that considers driving to be the foundation for the operation of the city. It is absolutely in line with the shift toward solutions closer to the community, to the environment, to the conservation of resources and the preservation of the natural landscape. On the island of Spetses, in the absence of cars, the inhabitants and tourists, without exception, have resorted to motorcycles. While the users of motorcycles are safe on roads without cars, that does not apply to pedestrians, particularly under conditions of the almost total absence of sidewalks. The extended use of motorcycles causes pollution, noise pollution and degradation of the landscape in the settlement. The movement of motor vehicles on the roads of the settlement is very difficult and highly dangerous due to their topography and due to the number of motorcycles during the summer months. The unlimited use of motorcycles is due to easy accessibility.

3 Sustainability at destination level

Much of the current tourism research has focused on investigating ways of making energy intensive transport systems more environmentally sensitive, or how to lessen impacts stemming from increased tourist traffic. Cullinane and Stokes [12] examine ways to minimise the impact of the car in environmentally sensitive areas, which have recreational or tourism appeal. The European project "CUSTODES" specifically relates the sustainable touristic development with sustainable mobility and accessibility: "sustainable mobility stands at the basis of more sustainable tourism, the tourist movement should transfer towards more sustainable modes of transport, and accessibility planning has become a statutory requirement of local authorities". Although widely used, the concept of accessibility is hard to fully define. Gould [13] referred to accessibility as a slippery notion, a common concept that everyone uses until faced with the problem of defining it and above all measuring it. Two widely accepted definitions demonstrate its richness. According to Bhat *et al.* [14]: 'accessibility is a measure of the ease of an individual to pursue an activity of a desired type, at a desired location, by a desired mode, and at a desired time'. Geurs and Van Eck [15] define 'accessibility as the extent to which the land use-transport system enables (groups of) individuals or goods to reach activities or destinations by means of a (combination of) transport mode(s). Accessibility does not simply relate to the qualities of the transport system (e.g. travel speed or costs), but also to the qualities of the land use system (e.g. densities and mix of opportunities). Accessibility becomes both a feature of the spatial system and the traffic and transport. Medlik [16] connects the term of accessibility with tourism: "in tourism, accessibility is a function of distance from centers of population, which constitute tourist markets and of external transport, which enables a destination to be reached. It is measured in terms of the distance traveled, the time taken or the cost involved".

Accessibility is the tool to facilitate people who live and move in areas where it is desirable to give priority to public transport, walking and cycling. After research, three types of areas of controlled accessibility can be defined: 1. cities, towns, villages, islands and territories which belong in this category, do not allow the free passage of motor vehicles, except in an emergency. Usually, these towns have been developed before the advent of cars, such as Venice and they retain their character today. The islands have an additional advantage as they are surrounded by sea, which is itself a factor of isolation, but it is also due to their limited size and thus the lack of available space to create an extensive road network; 2. A second category includes cities or large areas in them, which are areas in which the traffic is regulated in order to reduce the problems which occur from extensive car use. Walking, cycling and more environmentally friendly forms of travel, are prioritized here, but there are a few cases where they have to co-exist and share the space with cars; 3. The areas that fall into this category are the areas of controlled accessibility. These are in fact pedestrianized areas corresponding to the older parts of cities around which the newer parts of the town have been developed later or even to individual shopping streets. Priority is given to cyclists and pedestrians, to the creation of shared public space and to the aesthetic enhancement of the landscape.

A large number of islands and resorts are located in the lists of cities of controlled traffic. The islands are cut off from the mainland and can easily keep cars away. Measures are required in order to regulate freight transport, emergency vehicles, etc., especially in the case of large islands with scattered villages and settlements. The tourist resorts, mainly for economic reasons, are developed as areas of controlled motorized traffic because it is understood that the use of motorized vehicles reduces the profits of traders and shopkeepers, as they are seen as less attractive destinations for visitors. Alayo [17] points out that the growing increase in motor vehicle use is burdening cities with increasing problems and costs related to congestion, accidents, loss of amenity and space, noise, poor quality of life, poor accessibility, pollution, poor urban air quality and energy consumption, which have adverse effects on both the natural and built environment. Public transportation, bicycles, walking or electric vehicles are the main solutions in such cases, and even boats, fishing boats and ships can serve the coastal settlements. 'Green' transport is often an important consideration in the amelioration of urban transport problems. However, as Whitelegg [18] highlights: "vehicles with zero emissions, zero fuel consumption and virtually zero impact on pedestrians, cyclists and urban population densities might be 'green' but then we might as well have rediscovered the bicycle or feet".

Tourists wish to rest and get to know the place and its history. The presence of the car is a barrier that prevents the realization of their desires. It is a synonym to noise, pollution, and accidents and to the distortion of urban and architectural aesthetics and physiognomy. The argument that comes with the car is that it serves the transportation needs of tourists. However, in small places where distances are limited, there are many alternative mobility solutions, such as cycling, walking or electric bikes. Walking allows tourists and residents to discover the streets of the village through an enjoyable physical activity. It is accessible to all and the aesthetic parameter of space, the quality of life, the quality of air, peace, health, safety and the social environment can be enjoyed. By bicycle, transport is converted into an opportunity for enjoyment and getting better acquainted with the place in which you live or visit. The first priority for visitors is not a fast means of transport but to stop in public places that are really attractive due to their character. The main desire of the visitor is not speed but the joy of moving around.

4 Methodology application and results

The starting point of the research was the investigation of the European experience on issues regarding the areas of controlled accessibility. Three main categories of areas of controlled accessibility were identified as mentioned above. Their relation to tourism was analyzed through the urban and transport framework of each city, focusing on the planning principles, the technical characteristics in relation to accessibility and the promotion of tourism. The results formed a useful reference point for the future steps of research, especially for important decisions such as the shape of the network, and the basic design principles. In the next phase, a methodology leading to a proposal for a clear, functional and safe network and a pleasant environment was developed. The aim was to involve the citizens in the decision making process concerning the future of their city, in order to avoid a top-down approach. Specifically, the methodology comprises four successive steps:

1. Identification of urban and social characteristics.
2. Identification of problems.
3. Development of scenarios.
4. Participatory evaluation/choice of scenarios.

4.1 Identification of urban and social characteristics

Land use: Land use has a significant impact on transport. The hotels and the "rooms-to-let" are of particular interest for tourists. Other places of interest which are usually visited on a daily basis are the shopping and entertainment areas. Archaeological places and museums are not visited on a daily basis, but are of great importance. The most crowded area is close to the port due to the high concentration of land use that attracts a lot of people. The spatial distribution of land use is shown in Figure 1.

Source: Own elaboration

Figure 1:   The spatial coverage of land use.

Built environment: The town of Spetses has been identified by the Ministry as a traditional settlement, which has maintained intact the image it had in the past, and the local characteristics. The buildings have a common architectural style, the maximum number of floors is two, and the maximum height of the building is up to 7 meters. Inside the village, artisanal and industrial units are not allowed, apart from small family businesses, laboratories and shops. According to the census of 2001, 3,880 permanent and holiday houses were registered.

Geometry of the network: The roads are made for walking and perhaps for transporting animals. They are complex and unsuitable for cars. The geometry of the network is irregular, the width of the road is constantly changing (Figure 2), straights roads are rare and there are many deadlocks. Few roads continue through a large part of the city. Travelling in the city is characterized by continuous curves and low speeds.

LEGEND

WIDTH <3m
WIDTH 3-4m
WIDTH 4-5m

Source: Own elaboration

Figure 2: Roads according to their width.

Visibility in nodes/intersection: A node is defined as the intersection of a route with a road of equal or higher hierarchical level. Most of the nodes/intersections of the settlement are considered dangerous even when moving at 30 km/h (red intersections in Figure 3). A visibility study was applied in all the intersections of the settlement.

LEGEND

PRIMARY ROAD
ROAD NETWORK
INTERSECTIONS WITHOUT VISIBILITY
INTERSECTIONS WITH SOME VISIBILITY
INTERSECTIONS WITH VISIBILITY

Source: Own elaboration

Figure 3: Classification of nodes according to their visibility.

Transportation and restrictions: Spetses is an island that belongs to the second category of areas with controlled accessibility, areas that do not allow the free movement of cars and trucks for the most part. For this reason they have adopted restrictive measures for traffic, which aim to ensure the convenience of the residents and visitors of the island, while protecting the natural environment and ensuring the enhancement of quality of life. Residents' cars may be parked but they are not authorized to travel around the island. The only vehicles that are allowed to move are emergency vehicles and ten cabs. The use of motorcycles is allowed almost everywhere across the island. There are some restrictions which vary depending on the season, in order to avoid the routes with a high concentration of people.

Commuting and traveling on the island: It was observed that a large part of the population uses motorcycles even for the shortest trips (< 500 m). Motorcycle users are all ages, but it should be noted that people over 65 years avoid motorcycle use. The phenomenon of the extensive use of motorcycles intensifies during the summer months because of the tourists. During the summer months when it is restricted to cross the coastal zone of the city for several hours, the roads in the settlement are filled with motorcycles. Something to be highlighted is the bad condition of most of the motorcycles as they are old and badly maintained.

4.2 Problems

Trying to overcome the difficulties faced by the movement of cars on the extremely difficult roads of the settlement, and by the ban of car traffic, residents have resorted to motorcycles. They are flexible in the narrow streets, easy to use, can be parked anywhere, are easy to get on and off, they stop and start without delay, have minimal fuel consumption and are affordable to buy. In the cases of other Greek cities the main deterring reason for using a motorcycle is the security problems due to the presence of cars. In Spetses, this problem does not exist. At the same time, due to the continuous curves of the roads, high speeds are not possible and this gives confidence to women and older people, who are more sensitive to matters of safety. While motorcycle users are safe, pedestrians are not, especially in roads with an almost total absence of sidewalks. There are also serious problems of visibility at intersections which increase due to the absence of sidewalks. Motorcycles travel very close to buildings, resulting in dangerous "meetings" with the pedestrians. This danger also applies to motorcycles traveling from different directions.

Does the motorcycle smoothly integrate on the streets of the village?

The answer is clearly negative because it is a vehicle that pollutes and makes a lot of noise. In conditions of large roads with more regular geometry, pollution and noise from motorcycles is suppressed for two reasons:

- the large width, the ventilation of roads and the turbulent flow of air facilitate the diffusion of pollution and noise;
- noise and pollution from cars create conditions where additional pollution from motorcycles becomes less noticeable.

In the case of the village of Spetses, where due to high temperatures house windows stay open almost all day long, pollution and noise is perceived by the tourists as an undesired degradation of a traditional settlement. The inclination of the roads in combination with the inadequate maintenance of the motorcycles aggravates emissions and noise. The road network which is unsuitable for car use in combination with the ban of car traffic creates a serious side effect. Cars were replaced by motorcycles and the environmental impact for those inside their homes is very serious, especially during the afternoon and night hours, and for pedestrians. The problem of safety for pedestrians and particularly for the elderly and children in the streets, which would normally be meeting places for conversation and entertainment, is also severe.

4.3 Development of scenarios

The issue therefore of the presence or exclusion of motorcycles does not arise as a technical issue. There is no transport model that could prove or reject the need for a road or an area to be pedestrianised. Such a decision depends on the priorities and values of the society in each place. It depends on general cultural issues that determine the decisions about what would be tomorrow's form of the city. The technique can make any decision functional. However, not all solutions are applicable, and their effects are not the same. They depend largely on geometric characteristics and the capacity of each road especially in historical settlements which were developed before the invention of the car. Assuming Spetses decided to allow cars to move freely in the settlement, their effects on the settlement and the economy would be dramatic. The mainstay in all scenarios was to enhance safety and to improve quality of life.

The criteria for the development of the scenarios were selected by the research team in collaboration with the representatives of the municipality.

Use of motorized and non-motorized means of transport: This describes the level of safety of a route. It was calculated as the quotient of the number of routes suitable for motorized and non-motorized means of transport.

Junction safety: This describes the level of safety of each intersection. It is calculated by the visibility study performed for the speed of 50 km and 30 km.

Natural environment: This describes the degree of presence of natural elements (e.g. stream, coastline, forest, urban park) along the route.

Built environment: This describes the quality of urban-architectural environment along a route.

Accessibility to the main uses: This criterion regards the number and type of urban activities that are accessible from a route. Accessibility is defined as the amount of services and jobs that people can access within a certain travel time, considering multimodal modes of transport such as walking, biking, driving and public transport. The examination concerned how many of them fall into a buffer zone of 250 m from the route.

Two scenarios were proposed, which have as their backbone the restriction on the movement of motorcycles. The objective of both scenarios was to optimize the movement of residents and tourists. New traffic arrangements are proposed which are oriented to the safety of pedestrians, to the promotion of cycling and walking and to the aesthetic and cultural promotion of the settlement.

4.4 Final selection

Through 2 community meetings the final scenario was selected. By bringing together a cross-section of viewpoints, a community meeting was the perfect setting to exchange ideas and information about the future of the island. In the meetings all the elected municipal counsellors, residents, representatives of the shop owners, hotel owners and taxi drivers were present. First, the research team presented the criteria and also presented the different scenarios which were the results of different weighting of the criteria. A discussion followed the presentation, where opinions were shared.

The scenario selected included the creation of two parking areas for cars, on the outskirts of the settlement in order to minimize the existence of cars in the settlement. A route towards the parking areas was specified based on the route with safer junctions and a minimum impact on the environment of the settlement.

There would be a gradually reduction of the number of cars entering the island.

There would be a re-organization of the road network in order to exploit the potentials of its geometry in favour of the residential areas and the areas of particular interest.

Ring routes are adopted in order for safer access to the central areas and to points of interest, as seen in Figure 4, where the reorganisation of the roads is pictured. Additionally, in order to protect the desired areas, small scale interventions for the road environment were proposed. Some impasses (similar to a "cul-de-sac") were created in order to reduce high speeds and the movement of motorcycles through residential areas. Traffic at the network level is optimized as the local roads are transformed into one way streets. This helps to ensure safer intersections for pedestrians, cyclists and users of motorcycles and in minimizing frontal collisions. It also contributes to organizing the space at road level by specifying a "traffic corridor" and utilizes the space on either side for planting. The rings routes remain two way roads as an alternative route cannot be provided due to the irregularity of the road network.

Source: Own elaboration

Figure 4: Reorganisation of the roads.

5 Conclusions

In Greece, that is hamstrung of the car, Spetses is the only Greek settlement which has imposed a total ban of cars. Nevertheless, the mobility options of its residents endanger the form of the settlement, its environment and its source of revenue. This study was an attempt to realize the desired form of the future settlement for residents and tourists.

 WIT Transactions on Ecology and The Environment, Vol 187, © 2014 WIT Press
www.witpress.com, ISSN 1743-3541 (on-line)

Source: Own elaboration

Figure 5: Design of obstacles for motorcycles.

The main contributions of this paper are three-fold. First, the process of planning aimed at offering public spaces to residents, which are safe, open and quiet. In their everyday life the quality of public spaces affects their lives and the measures proposed had as their objective the enhancement of the feeling of safety and comfort and to make them meeting points, reinforcing the social life of the settlement. There is also a strong tourist dimension in the selection of measures proposed. The purpose of planning is to make the place attractive and enjoyable for tourists. This happens when they come into contact with the place and its people, when they enjoy the details of the settlement and read its story through its roads and buildings. The objective was to rearrange space in order for the tourists to feel calm and welcome on the island, to enjoy the place and to invite them to stay and revisit it.

WIT Transactions on Ecology and The Environment, Vol 187, © 2014 WIT Press
www.witpress.com, ISSN 1743-3541 (on-line)

In addition, the preservation of the natural and built environment has succeeded through the scenario selected. Air and noise pollution will be limited and the image of the settlement will improve. The methodology is useful for all the tourist areas which are in danger due to the excessive use of motorized means of transport.

Finally, it is worth highlighting the importance of the effective participation of citizens in planning for sustainable mobility in cities. The involvement of the public in the final decision of the scenario aimed at familiarizing them with the possible solutions and gaining their acceptance as they are the ones who would be affected the most from the planning.

References

[1]   Wilkinson, D., 1997. Towards sustainability in the European Union? Steps within the European commission towards integrating the environment into other European Union policy sectors, Environmental Politics, 6(1), pp. 153-173.

[2]   Lane, B., 1994, Sustainable Rural Tourism strategies: A Tool for Development and Conservation, Journal of Sustainable Tourism 2, pp. 102-111.

[3]   Hunter, C., 1997, Sustainable tourism as an adaptive paradigm, Annals of Tourism Research, 24(4), pp. 850-867.

[4]   Butler, R., 1999. Sustainable Tourism: A State-of-the-Art Review, Tourism Geographies, 1, pp. 7-25.

[5]   Burns, P., 1999. Paradoxes in Planning: Tourism Elitism or Brutalism? Annals of Tourism Research, 26, pp. 329-348.

[6]   Inskeep, E., 1991, Tourism Planning: An Integrated and Sustainable Development Approach.

[7]   Leiper, N., 1990, Tourist attraction systems, Annals of Tourism Research, 17(3), pp. 367-384.

[8]   Lumsdon, L., Page, S. J. 2004, Progress in transport and tourism research: reformulating the transport-tourism interface and future research agendas, Tourism and transport: issues and agenda for the new millennium, pp. 1-27.

[9]   Page, S., 2005, Transport and tourism: global perspectives, Pearson Education.

[10]   Schlich, R. et al., 2004, Structures of Leisure Travel: Temporal and Spatial Variability, Transport Reviews: A Transnational Transdisciplinary Journal, 24(2), pp. 219-237.

[11]   Dickinson, J., Robbins, D., 2006. Using the car in a fragile rural tourist destination: a social representations perspective.

[12]   Cullinane, S, Stokes, G, 1998, Rural Transport Policy, Elsevier.

[13]   Gould, P. 1969. Spatial Diffusion, Resource Paper no. 4. Commission on College Geography, Association of American Geographers, Washington, DC.

[14]   Bhat, C., S. Handy, K. Kockelman, H. Mahmassani, Q. Chen, L. Weston. 2000. Development of an urban accessibility index: Literature review. Research project conducted for the Texas department of transportation. University of Texas, Austin, TX: Center for Transportation Research.

[15]   Geurs, K.T., J.R. Van Eck. 2001. Accessibility measures: Review and applications. Rijksinstituut voor Volksgezondheid en Milieu (National Institute of Public Health and the Environment, RIVM) and Urban Research Centre. Bilthoven/Utrecht, Netherlands: Utrecht University.

[16]   Medlik, S., 2003, Dictionary of travel: tourism and hospitality, Butterworth-Heinemann, pp. 273.

[17]   Alayo, J.A., 1998, The Walking City: An obsolete design or the city of tomorrow, PTRC Education and Research Services Limited, pp. 269-78.

[18]   Whitelegg, J., 1993, Transport for a sustainable future: The case for Europe, Belhaven Press (London and New York).

[19]   Department for Transport, 2005. Focus on Personal Travel, 2005 Edition. London: The Stationary Office.

The positive impacts of ecotourism in protected areas

P. Lanier
Friends of Sustainable Tourism International, USA

Abstract

Ecotourism is a topic that has been rapidly gaining interest globally in the last decade. Is ecotourism a viable means to increase economic development while protecting the environment, or is it an unrealistic ideal that leads to overdevelopment, pollution, and the introduction of non-native species to fragile ecosystems? This paper presents four documented case studies which serve as examples of successful protection of tourist areas, and that ecotourism, when sufficiently planned and properly managed, does generate positive impacts. A detailed review of Ecoventura in the Galapagos, Lapa Rios in Costa Rica, Camp Denali in Alaska, and Guludo Lodge in Mozambique illustrate the viability of ecotourism in generating economic development, advancing the interests of the environment, promoting cultural diversity, and encouraging community involvement and education.

Keywords: ecotourism, responsible tourism, environmental conservation, economic development.

1 Introduction

Tourism is accounting for an increasing portion of the world's economy. According to the World Travel and Tourism Council, in 2011 alone, travel and tourism made up 9% of GDP, employed 250 million around the world, and boasted a profit of 6 trillion USD [1]. As such a significant component of economic activity, travel and tourism have the potential to make a significant impact on the world.

Ecotourism, as defined by IUCN, is "environmentally responsible travel and visitation to relatively undisturbed natural areas, in order to enjoy and appreciate nature (and any accompanying cultural features – both past and present) that

WIT Transactions on Ecology and The Environment, Vol 187, © 2014 WIT Press
www.witpress.com, ISSN 1743-3541 (on-line)
doi:10.2495/ST140161

promotes conservation, has low visitor impact, and provides for beneficially active socio-economic involvement of local populations" [2]. As such, ecotourism has three pillars: sustainable business practices, community development and environmental stewardship.

Sustainable business practices are the practical means of minimizing an enterprise's environmental impacts and maximizing its self-sufficiency, which includes everything from building material selection to water usage. Community development entails the social, cultural and economic effects that the business and its visitors have on the local inhabitants. Not only should local culture, traditions and values always be respected while running a business, but there should also be a commitment to supporting and strengthening the local community. Environmental stewardship is comprised of the initiatives and programs to protect and conserve the surrounding natural environment.

The following paper will attempt to demonstrate that ecotourism is an effective way for businesses in tourism destinations to have a positive impact on their host communities and natural environment through four distinct case studies: Ecoventura in the Galapagos, Lapa Rios in Costa Rica, Camp Denali in Alaska, and Guludo Lodge in Mozambique.

2 Ecoventura

Giving back while providing intense, inspiring, hands-on wildlife experiences
The Galapagos Islands, home to an abundance of exotic vegetation and animal life, represent one of Earth's most precious and unique ecosystems. In 1959, 100 years after the publication of Darwin's *On the Origin of Species*, Ecuador declared 97 percent of the Galapagos' overall landmass to be a national park. In 2001, the nation also established the marine reserve of Galapagos. More importantly, in 2007, UNESCO declared the Galapagos Islands an at-risk World Heritage Site. Although the Islands were removed from the list in 2010, conservationists feel it happened too soon, as the Islands are still very much at risk due to illegal fishing, unsustainable tourism, illegal migration and population growth, and the unwelcome introduction of non-native species.

2.1 Offering authentic, intimate, green voyages since 1990

Ecoventura Cruises, a family owned expedition cruise line based in Guayaquil, Ecuador, seeks to make a difference. The company has been protecting and touring the Galapagos Islands since 1990, enabling thousands of travellers to experience the area's natural beauty [3]. The company's goal is to provide guests with authentic experiences in intimate groups and safe, memorable voyages. Ecoventura began focusing seriously on "greening" its Galapagos tours in 1999 by re-evaluating operational procedures and equipment – a move that enabled the company to become the leader in ecotourism in the Galapagos Islands.

2.2 Investing in green: from a hybrid yacht to knowledgeable, local crews

Since those first efforts, Ecoventura has invested more than half a million dollars to refurbish its company-owned fleet of private vessels to meet tough ecological standards. The company owns four expedition vessels; three identical first-class, 20-passenger yachts named *Eric*, *Flamingo*, and *Letty*; and a 16-passenger luxury dive liveaboard named *Galapagos Sky*. In keeping with the idea of local sustainability, each luxury vessel was custom-built in Ecuador. *Eric*, one the first-class yachts, boasts 40 solar panels and two wind generators, making it the first hybrid, carbon offset yacht in the Galapagos Islands.

Ecoventura also invests in its crew. Knowledgeable, friendly captains, often former members of the Ecuadorian Navy or Merchant Marine, lead expeditions, while local, onboard naturalists who speak fluent English educate guests about the Islands and its treasures. Most members of Ecoventura's crew have worked with the company since its founding; they are a united group, like a family, committed to doing everything possible to ensure guests enjoy a comfortable, memorable stay and return to their homes wiser about nature and the importance of conservation.

2.3 Inviting guests to fully experience the Galapagos' natural environment

Ecoventura aims not only to educate; it wants to please its passengers as well by offering intimate groups the most mind boggling, inspiring, hands-on wildlife experiences possible in the Galapagos Islands. Guests are treated to a host of memorable, eco-friendly activities, including hiking along volcanic formations, viewing nesting sea birds, visiting remote beaches peppered with sea lions, snorkelling with penguins and sharks, kayaking in secluded coves, and rafting in zodiacs to explore the surrounding wildlife. The company offers guided nature walks twice daily, led by naturalists trained to provide the ultimate intellectual and wilderness experience. While on their own, guests might choose to swim along the glorious beaches, or snorkel in deep water coves. Experienced scuba divers can explore the waters along Wolf Island and Darwin Island, two of the northernmost islands in the Galapagos archipelago, from the 16-passenger dive boat, the *Galapagos Sky*, which promises divers an amazing liveaboard experience.

Ecoventura keeps its guide to passenger ratio low to ensure guests return home with unforgettable memories. At one guide per ten passengers, the company offers the smallest ratio among Galapagos tour operators. Groups depart each Sunday, following one of two different routes through the Islands crossing the equator up to five times! The company also offers families with children under seventeen special Galapagos expeditions over school breaks which feature age-appropriate experiences and adventures that are just as memorable as are those for adults.

2.4 Giving back: partnering and investing in education and local communities

Guests, although critical to the company's success, are not Ecoventura's sole focus; the company also strives to partner with and invest in its local communities. For instance, in 2000, Ecoventura volunteered to be the first cruise-line company certified by Smart Voyager, an ecological program developed by The Rainforest Alliance, an international non-profit that works primarily in the Americas [4]. In another example, Ecoventura partnered with the World Wildlife Fund to create the Galapagos Marine Biodiversity Fund. Through the fund, the company has raised more than $300,000 for marine conservation efforts and to educate local children about the environment [5].

In 2012, Ecoventura also partnered with the Ecology Project International to allow local teens to participate in a field conservation course, which equips them with knowledge and hands-on environmental experiences in the Galapagos Islands [6]. The company has also supported the Alejandro Alvear School for at least a decade by providing salaries for teachers, as well as physical therapists for hearing-impaired adults and children with physical disabilities [7]. To involve guests in its sustainability efforts, Ecoventura partners with "Pack for a Purpose", a program that allows passengers to bring supplies needed by local schools.

From vessels to crews to guests to communities, Ecoventura is a company worth supporting and emulating, as it takes its commitment to conservation, preservation, and sustainability seriously.

3   Lapa Rios

A "five-leaf," tropical beach resort protecting the culture, the rainforest and rare, native species
The Lapa Rios Ecolodge and Nature Reserve, next to the Pacific Ocean in southwestern Costa Rica, sits on the lavishly green Osa Peninsula. The Osa Peninsula, filled with magnificent waterfalls and beautiful white beaches, is home to 2.5 percent of the world's biodiversity and serves as a wildlife passage or connection for rare Costa Rican species struggling to survive harsh developmental conditions in their natural habitat. The Osa Peninsula is also home to the Corcovado National Park, a special sanctuary to various rare and endangered species, such as pumas, scarlet macaws, and the harpy eagle. While the ecolodge offers respite to guests in search of a Costa Rican beach and rainforest experience, the nature reserve offers a natural buffer for the national park and a home to many rare species native to the region.

3.1 Meeting the natural treasures of the Osa Peninsula, including rare wildlife and trees

For instance, the Osa Peninsula is the jaguar's last refuge in Central America, while the reserve itself is home to 80 percent of the total population of the sangrillo colorado tree, one of 37 species of tree heading toward extinction [8]. Guests visiting the ecolodge and reserve may hear the chatter, whoops, and screeches of four native species of Costa Rican monkey – the squirrel monkey, white-faced capuchin, mantled howler, and the spider monkey – and spot other intriguing native creatures as well, such as the poison dart frog, the silky anteater, and the three-toothed sloth. Bird lovers visiting the reserve enjoy the challenge of identifying more than 300 bird species who call the reserve home, including the toucan and the reserve's beautiful namesake, the scarlet macaw.

3.2 Ensuring permanent conservation for a "River of Scarlet Macaws"

The Lapa Rios Ecolodge and the Lapa Rios Nature Reserve take their names from the scarlet macaw, or known simply as "lapa" in Costa Rica. It's reported that when the owners of the 1000-acre nature reserve rainforest toured the landscape for the first time, a 'river of scarlet macaws' flew overhead. Perhaps considering the flight serendipitous, the owners named this unique part of the rainforest "Lapa Rios," or "River of Scarlet Macaws".

The owners of Lapa Rios also believed that, in a time of overly zealous development, the treasures of their land needed preservation. With that in mind, they generously signed a conservation easement, which resulted in the permanent protection of the 1000 acres of tropical rainforest. The agreement also created a binding partnership between The Nature Conservancy and a leading Costa Rican land conservation organization, ensuring that Lapa Rios would be preserved indefinitely. The restrictions set forth in the agreement are intense, stating that, on Lapa Rios, there shall be no mining, forestry, hunting, and building of tourism facilities. The agreement does, however, allow for educational and scientific activities throughout the reserve.

For instance, the Lapa Rios Nature Reserve supports The Wildlife Conservation Program, which works to further develop the feline populations on the Osa Peninsula [9]. In this endeavor, researchers are using videos and cameras to capture wild felines in action, studying their moods, actions, and behaviors to help save and protect them and other highly endangered species. Lapa Rios, in addition to providing access to the land, also donates funds to the Program, enabling researchers to purchase equipment and continue their studies.

3.3 Winning the five-leaf sustainability award: inviting guests to join the efforts

Amidst the land and its wildlife is the Lapa Rios Ecolodge itself, where sustainability is a key value. In 2003, Lapa Rios became one of the first hotels in Costa Rica to receive a Certificate for Sustainable Tourism and to be awarded five-leaf status from the Costa Rica Tourism Board. This organization evaluates and rates a property's sustainability on a scale of one to five leaves, with five leaves being the highest achievement.

Although the public recognition is satisfying, even more so is being able to share the protected rainforest and its inhabitants with visiting guests. The ecolodge offers guided hiking and waterfall tours, during which visitors can experience Costa Rican wildlife in its natural habitat. Guests can kayak and surf, viewing a magnificent variety of colorful birds and fish, and contribute to preservation efforts by transplanting the primary seedling of a rare plant to an area of secondary growth. The ecolodge's well-informed local guides also steer guests in the direction of native craftspeople, spurring on and supporting the local economy. Costa Rica is renowned for its wildly colorful arts and crafts, including handmade musical instruments, oxen carts, pottery, and greeting cards and notepaper made from either bananas or coffee, both of which grow bountifully throughout the land.

3.4 Giving back to the community and strengthening the conservation message

Because ecotourism is about preserving and supporting native peoples as much as it is about environmental conservation, the owners of Lapa Rios are also involved in local educational efforts. For instance, they helped to create the Carbonera School, which has neighbored the Nature Reserve since the early 1990s, supporting elementary-school-aged children through donations, summer school programs, and educational outreaches related to the environment. Thanks to the success of the Carbonera School, the Osa Peninsula is now home to ten additional schools, all of which have been outfitted with dining rooms and school supplies. Overall, the educational programs supported and created by Lapa Rios's donors and researchers have positively affected more than 120 schools in the area.

Guests at Lapa Rios are invited to get involved in the ecolodge's education efforts as well by touring with the children of the Carbonera School community, a gesture that lingers long, strengthening Lapa Rios's conservation and preservation message that guests take back home.

4 Camp Denali

Bringing guests closer to the land without changing or disturbing the environment and wildlife
Camp Denali sits squarely in the heart of Denali National Park and Preserve, which spans six million acres. This eco-friendly and family-owned retreat delights visitors with clear views of Denali and the Alaska Range, Wonder Lake, and the 95 mile Denali Park Road.

Celia Hunter was one such visitor. After hiking and touring the surrounding landscape, she staked claim in 67 acres of an isolated, rocky ridge with a pond, acreage that would soon become Camp Denali. Celia, along with two like-minded explorers, Ginny and Morton Wood, founded Camp Denali to fulfil their life-long dream of owning a simple, rustic lodge where park visitors could stay and, according to the camp's website, "savor the vigor and freshness of this young country and absorb its spacious tranquility" [10].

4.1 Conservation: a family tradition

The three founders built the lodge using reclaimed supplies from the National Park Service, and ran it for 25 years before selling to Wallace and Jerryne Cole in 1975. Wallace and Jerryne Cole, always directly involved with lodge guests, ran Camp Denali for another 30 years before handing over the reins to their daughter and her husband in 2005. The new Cole owners, like their predecessors, consider caring for the lodge, its guests, and the surrounding landscape as part of the Cole family tradition.

So far, they've been successful: the camp remains remote, with a small amount of foot and vehicular traffic, allowing visitors to experience the natural Denali habitat as much as possible. Minimizing fuel and emissions on the grounds of Camp Denali also preserves a sense of peace and quiet for guests and employees.

4.2 Renovating to improve conservation efforts

The lodge itself is a true conservation effort, as its structure has changed very little due to various preservation efforts and the remote setting. The owners across generations have made few renovations to the foundation and lodging to maintain a remote and sustainable environment for guests. For instance, when the latest Coles added a new dining hall to the grounds of Camp Denali in 2008 to create more space, they also added more opportunities for energy conservation.

4.3 Relying on solar and water for renewable energy

Today, solar power and sustainable products power the dining hall, and water for the dining hall, bathrooms, and kitchen are preheated by the sun, which can raise the temperature to as much as 100 degrees Fahrenheit on a hot day. The solar power system, with photovoltaic panels collecting and storing the power of the sun all day long, also enables the lodge to use electrically powered generators as a backup, instead of as a prime power source. Camp Denali also gets energy from a hydroelectric system, added to the property in 1981 when the Coles gained control over access to free-flowing water on a mountainside adjacent to the lodge site.

4.4 Conserving through everyday initiatives

The Cole family is proud of their ability to reduce energy consumption through simple tasks, such as line-drying all laundry on the grounds, composting food and yard scraps, and using reusable products, such as cloth napkins, lunch bags, and water bottles. The camp also uses non-toxic, concentrated cleaning products to minimize its footprint more [11]. One of the major accomplishments of Camp Denali is that the few items that they do not completely consume or reuse are made of recyclable materials such as paper, aluminum, tin, cardboard, and recyclable plastic.

4.5 Sourcing food locally to reduce the footprint even more

In the last decade, small-scale farms in Alaska have become increasingly successful in raising pork, elk, reindeer meat, and fish and shellfish – all common in Alaska. Raising animals in Alaska is a serious business, and Camp Denali is fortunate enough to receive some of its meat and sausages from Delta Meat and Sausage Company, a family business that raises its own cattle and pigs in addition to running a USDA-certified meat-processing operation.

Several small, local farms provide Camp Denali with basic food supplies, such as lettuce, greens, onions, potatoes, squash, carrots, and more. Camp Denali orders food and other needed culinary goods locally to further reduce its environmental footprint. Organic farmers in the area provide flowers, herbs, fruits, and vegetables to Camp Denali as well. Camp Denali is also known for its on-site greenhouse and outdoor, raised-bed, kitchen gardens.

4.6 Working together to instil in guests a desire to respect and care for the environment

In many ways on a daily basis, the owners and employees of Camp Denali act on a core belief that it's important for guests to experience both conserving and preserving the environment, as well as to experience nature and wildlife in as close to its natural state as possible. The overarching goal is that guests are changed when they return home; that they are equipped with a mindset that nature not be disregarded as background, and that each one of us are partners in creating a sustainable environment. To help further instil these values in guests, Camp Denali also offers engaging activities, such as learning adventures and hiking vacations, led by local naturalists, who guide guests into experiencing the park and its environment intellectually as well as leisurely with the hopes of changing attitudes.

5 Guludo Beach Lodge

A sustainable business and sister organization restoring hope and rebuilding communities

The Guludo Beach Lodge, a balmy tourist destination in Mozambique's Quirimbas National Park, began as a dream in the minds of Neal and Amy Carter-James. The pair visited the poverty-stricken area in 2002, envisioning a blend of tourism and philanthropy that could lift the veil of poverty that had long since settled over the people of Mozambique.

Today, Guludo Beach Lodge acts as an area resource by donating five percent of its profits to the Nema Foundation, a sister organization the Carter-Jameses created with the intention of supporting the local community and economy. The Nema Foundation cooperates with sixteen local communities near the Guludo Beach Lodge, creating projects that benefit the area economically and culturally.

5.1 Bringing help and hope where it is most needed

The assistance is needed, as Guludo, although rich in beauty with its 7.5 mile palm-fringed beach, is situated in one of Mozambique's poorest areas. The life expectancy of local adults is only 38 years, and one in three children do not reach their fifth birthday [12]. Before the Carter-James came along, the community lacked guaranteed access to clean water, and the education system was almost non-existent since very few children attend school. People also lacked a sense of cultural identity, and had to rely on threatened and endangered resources. Without the help of outside hands, the people living in the Guludo area of Mozambique would not have had the ability to thrive or to cause change in their environment, both financial and natural.

5.2 Restoring access to a land rich in beauty, wildlife, and culture

The natural environment itself is worth respecting and saving. Quirimbas National Park, the largest marine-protected area in Africa and home to five species of turtles, calving humpback whales, grazing dugongs, and beautiful coral reefs, is an ideal setting for conservation and tourism. The park encompasses eleven islands of the Quirimbas Archipelago, which stretches north to bordering Tanzania. These tropical islands act as a vast reservoir of Africa's historical and cultural past, and illustrate the influences of the Arab and Portuguese cultures on the land as well.

Quirimbas National Park also encompasses land on the continent, protecting plentiful coastal forest inhabitants that once populated the East African coastline but have since moved inland: elephants, lions, leopards, crocodiles, and even wild dogs [13]. Historically, the country's decades-long civil war cut off the remote region now reserved for the park, leaving it a grey area in both Southern and East African field guides. Thanks to Guludo and other tourism and ecologic efforts, the park is blossoming and is rejoining society, opening its land where new species and treasures wait to be discovered.

5.3 Achieving recognition and offering guests the best of Africa

Northern Mozambique and Guludo are being noticed, having been called next travel hotspots with world class beaches and hotels. It's no wonder, as Northern Mozambique lays claim to the best beaches in Africa, pristine coral reefs, and a rich cultural heritage.

Guludo Beach Lodge invites guests to experience all that the locals have to offer, from land and nature to local gifts, foods, and customs. Guests can scuba dive, snorkel, visit Quirimbas National Park, visit Guludo village, partake in bush lookouts, and more. The lodge positions itself in the luxury class, offering guests anything and everything they need to enjoy a barefoot retreat complete with endless beach views and gentle sea breezes.

5.4 Shifting tourism gains to lift local peoples and communities

Winner of several international awards, Guludo Beach Lodge is responsible for a significant influx of tourism to Mozambique year round. Tourism has deeply affected the area's surrounding local communities, which is exactly what the Carter-Jameses intended. The lodge inspires and fuels the local economy, while the Nema Foundation tackles the leading causes of poverty and the environmental problems that have for years stunted Mozambique's prosperity. [14] In that regard, Guludo Beach Lodge is an example of a successful, sustainable business with a sister organization that supports community development projects and highly impactful conservation efforts.

5.5 Measuring results with clean water, meals, mosquito nets, and education

The Carter-James's success is supported by numbers. Since Guludo Beach Lodge opened, more than 20,000 people have gained access to clean water, and more than 900 malnourished children receive education and a school meal each day. Nearly one hundred thirty young scholars have received a secondary education. The Nema Foundation has also been responsible for providing 9,500 mosquito nets, building two primary schools, and educating local families about nutrition, malaria, HIV, hygiene, and sanitation. The effects of Guludo extend into the local business community as well, with the lodge supporting more than one hundred fifty local suppliers, employing seventy staff members, and enabling eight local businesses to sell products directly to lodge guests.

5.6 Combining green efforts with tourism and philanthropy for eco-success

Today, a new and growing sense of optimism is alive in the communities surrounding Guludo, which prospers by drawing tourists from near and far. With more tourism and profits, the more that Guludo could contribute to the Nema Foundation and to the local economy. From 2009 to 2012, a time of great struggle for many businesses in the tourism industry, Guludo Beach Lodge experienced exceptional growth. The Carter-Jameses plan to continue to expand the lodge's and the foundation's efforts to bring more prosperity and hope and environmental conservation to the region in the years to come.

6 Conclusion

Through these case studies of eco-resorts and their best practices, we have endeavored to show how conscious, careful development, while certainly not a panacea, especially when transit to these far-flung destinations burns fossil fuels, is nonetheless the best hope that the ever-expanding reach of world tourism will have positive effects on the environment and the local people. With the environment uppermost in their minds, ecotourism enables travelers to learn about sustainable practices and serve as examples to their peers.

While empirical data is just now emerging that "deep green" carefully conceived and executed ecotourism provides conservation benefits, it is imminently apparent that hosting adventurous travellers in fragile areas provides a positive alternative to the destruction of habitat and decimation of animal and forest resources through other sources of income- logging, mining, overfishing and endangered animal sales- available to communities struggling to survive and maintain their cultural heritage. Employing and supporting education for community stakeholders is one of the most obvious as well as long-lasting results.

As environmental visionary Paul Hawken said in his speech to the San Francisco Commonwealth Club in 1992, "Business is the only mechanism on the planet today powerful enough to produce the changes necessary to reverse global environmental and social degradation" [15]. Eco-travel is a leading example of this principal at work today.

References

[1] World Travel & Tourism Council, *Benchmarking Travel & Tourism, Americas Summary: How does Travel & Tourism compare to other sectors?* April, 2012.

[2] IUCN, Resolution CGR 1.67 'Ecotourism and Protected Area Conservation'. *1st World Conservation Congress*: Montreal, 1996.

[3] Ecoventura, "Social and Environmental Responsibility". www.ecoventura.com/galapagos-sustainability/social-environmental-responsibility

[4] Ecoventura, "Smart Voyager Certification". www.ecoventura.com/galapagos-sustainability/smart-voyager-certification

[5] Ecoventura, "Galapagos Marine Diversity Fun". www.ecoventura.com/galapagos-sustainability/wwf-galapagos-marine-biodiversity-fund

[6] Ecoventura, "Ecology Project International". www.ecoventura.com/galapagos-sustainability/ecology-project-international

[7] Ecoventura, "Pack with a Purpose". www.ecoventura.com/galapagos-sustainability/pack-purpose

[8] Lapa Rios, "Conservation at Lapa Rios". www.laparios.com/conservation.html

[9] Lapa Rios, "Join a Wildcat Expedition". www.laparios.com/wildcat.html

[10] Camp Denali, "Our History" www.campdenali.com/live/page/our-history

[11] Camp Denali, "Sustainability" www.campdenali.com/live/page/sustainable-practices

[12] Guludo Beach Lodge, "About Us" www.guludo.com/content/about-us

[13] Guludo Beach Lodge, "Quirimbas National Park" www.guludo.com/content/quirimbas-national-park

[14] Guludo Beach Lodge, "Guludo Beach Lodge" www.ecogo.org/th_gallery/guludo-beach-lodge

[15] Hawken, P., Speech to the Commonwealth Club, 1992, San Francisco, California.

Section 5
Rural tourism

Accessing the attitudes of successors in dairy farms toward educational tourism

Y. Ohe
Department of Food and Resource Economics, Chiba University, Japan

Abstract

Educational activities provided by farmers have recently been gaining attention and enabling consumers to learn about food, life and rural heritage. This paper reports the attitudes of the next-generation successors of Educational Dairy Farms (EDF) who are now working on-farm, in comparison with their counterparts working on ordinary dairy farms in Japan, as determined by questionnaire surveys. First, the main findings were that the EDF successors tended to have wider job experience, and longer and more varied training experience across the country and/or abroad than their counterparts in ordinary dairy farms. This means that EDF successors have both a wider perspective and more extensive human networks from social learning opportunities. Second, EDF successors gained high psychological rewards and strengthened their identity as a dairy farmer from the educational activity of the farm, including more self-confidence and pride as a dairy farmer. Third, most successors, however, did not consider the educational service to be economically viable. Thus, in the long term, it will be necessary to levy a service charge to make the educational activity viable. Quality improvement was considered to be a necessary measure for this purpose.
Keywords: educational tourism, rural tourism, dairy farm, farm tourism, agritourism.

1 Introduction

Educational activities provided by farmers are gaining popularity and are included in the category of experience-oriented tourism. Examples of such activities that have been already implemented include the Farming And Countryside Education (FACE) program in the UK [1], (for more recent

WIT Transactions on Ecology and The Environment, Vol 187,© 2014 WIT Press
www.witpress.com, ISSN 1743-3541 (on-line)
doi:10.2495/ST140171

developments [2], Ferme Pédagogique in France, Fattorie Didattiche in Emilia-Romagna in Italy [3], children's gardening in the USA [4] and educational dairy farms (EDFs) in Japan [5]). Through farm visits, children and adult consumers can learn how food is produced from land and livestock, and what jobs are performed for this production. Especially in dairy farming, the presence of livestock enables visitors to realize the connection between life and food – a fundamental link that is related to the meaning of life but is often forgotten daily.

In this context, it is expected that the educational activity provided by farmers can create a new social role for dairy farming and might eventually generate a new income source to counter stagnant demand for dairy products. So far, however, such educational activities have not become economically viable [6]. Thus, how to attain viability is a crucial issue for the development of educational tourism in agriculture. Because educational tourism in agriculture is a relatively newly emerging topic, this issue has been seldom addressed except for a bunch of studies by [6–8], which examined the attitudes of the EDF operators toward the educational activity and disclosed their reasons for becoming an EDF, in addition their satisfaction with the educational service and issues for future development.

Because EDFs mostly comprise family farms, it is essential to clarify how the next generation of successors views the educational activity in terms of its sustainable development. As yet, however, this issue has not been explored. From this perspective, this paper examines the attitudes of farm successors who have already taken a full time job on-farm toward the educational activity by focusing on EDFs in Japan, which provide one of the most well-organized educational services in agriculture.

To achieve this aim and following on from previous studies, this paper has investigated the experience and views of EDF operators of the younger generation toward the educational activity on the basis of data collected by questionnaire surveys directed toward the successors of both EDFs and ordinary dairy farms. To clarify the point, I have compared the attributes of respondents between EDFs and ordinary dairy farms. Finally, I discuss policy implications regarding the viability of educational tourism in agriculture.

2   Trend of Educational Dairy Farms

2.1 Outline of the program of Educational Dairy Farms

The EDF program was established in 2000 by the Japan Dairy Council, which is a national organization that conducts promotional activities for dairy farms. The purpose of this program is to provide accurate information on what dairy farms do in order to improve the public's understanding of the role of dairy farming in society. The aim of the EDF is not only to promote an open-door policy for the farmyard toward the general public, but also to enhance the educational value of dairy farming through teaching where milk comes from and the life of the milk cows on the farm. In this respect, the farmers' role is crucial and thus they are called facilitators in this program. For instance, when visitors experience milking, they learn that warm white milk comes from the udder of a cow, which is a simple fact, but is quite different from the cool milk in a carton in the refrigerator that they are used to drinking every day. A facilitator explains to visitors that 'white' milk is generated in the udder from 'red' blood, which symbolizes life, and that the same process also happens in humans. When visitors are lucky enough to come across the birth of a calf, they gain a lifelong impression of the meaning of life. The Council administers the certification for recognition as an EDF and, together with teachers, develops educational materials both to enhance the effects of this activity and to provide seminars to improve skills of facilitators. When the last survey was conducted in 2012, 309 farms were designated EDFs.

Interestingly, the number of visitors increased year on year to reach more than 880 thousand in 2009. Particularly, the number of visitors from April to September, i.e. summer time, increased more rapidly than that from October to March, i.e. winter time. Nevertheless, the number of visitors dropped suddenly in 2010 due to an outbreak of foot and mouth disease, which is highly contagious to cloven-hoofed animals such as cows and pigs. If it spreads, it has a devastating effect on the local livestock industry. Because of this outbreak, many operators closed their farms to visitors to reduce the risk of this disease. Fortunately, the drop in numbers did not last, and the number of visitors picked up again despite another disaster in March, 2011, when a gigantic earthquake hit northern Japan. As of the end of 2012 when the current questionnaire survey was conducted, the number of visitors had returned to 95% of the level in 2009. It is expected that the demand for farm visits will increase in the future, along with a growing demand for experience-oriented tours in general.

3 Data

Data were collected by a questionnaire survey directed only toward EDFs that were mainly run by families to narrow data variation. Although the majority of EDFs are family farms, the EDF program also includes public ranches, ranches run by cooperatives and the dairy industry, college ranches and agricultural high schools. These types of non-family farm were not included in the present survey. The survey was implemented jointly with the Japan Dairy Council, which selected farms and is the founding body of this survey. The survey was sent by surface mail from the author's office to 248 farms and returned between September and December 2012. The response rate was 141 farms (56.8%).

Over the same period, another questionnaire was distributed by surface mail to ordinary dairy farms through regional dairy cooperatives, which selected 470 mainly family-run farms across the country for comparison with the EFDs. The response rate was 48.5% (228 farms).

4 Results

4.1 Attributes of respondents

First, the attributes of all respondents were tabulated in order to compare them between respondents from ordinary dairy farms, termed "ordinary respondents"

hereafter, and those from EDFs (Table 1). The average age of the ordinary respondents was younger than that of the EDF respondents. In this sense, the EDF respondents were more experienced than the ordinary respondents. Interestingly, the proportion of females was much higher, nearly 20%, among EDF respondents than among ordinary respondents (18.4% and 3.5%, respectively). This fact indicates that female successors will play an important role in EDF activity.

Table 1:   Respondents' attributes and dairy production.

Item	Ordinary dairy farm		EDF	
Age on average	34.5		43.1	
Age of starting farming	23.9		25.0	
Sex	%	No. respondents	%	No. respondents
Male	94.7	216	78.0	110
Female	3.5	8	18.4	26
No answer	1.8	4	3.5	5
Total	100.0	228	100.0	141
Item	Mean	No. respondents	Mean	No. respondents
Amount of milk production (t)	400.6	202	561.2	131
No. milk cows (Holstein cow)	55.1	221	72.4	133
Type of farm	%	No. respondents	%	No. respondents
Family farm	91.2	208	70.9	100
Corporate family farm	5.7	13	17.0	24
Jointly run non-corporate farm	0.0	0	0.7	1
Jointly run corporate farm	0.4	1	3.5	5
Others	1.3	3	5.7	8
No answer	1.3	3	2.1	3
Total	100.0	228	100.0	141

Source: Questionnaire surveys completed by successors who had taken jobs on-farm at EDFs and ordinary dairy farms sent out between September and December 2012 by surface mail. The number of respondents was 141 of 248 EDFs (56.8%) and 228 of 470 ordinary farms (48.5%).

In terms of milk production, EDFs were larger. With respect to the type of management, the proportion of corporate family farms was higher among EDFs (17%) than among ordinary farms, of which more than nine out of ten were non-corporate family farms.

Second, academic background, job history and job-training experience were compared between the two categories of respondents (Table 2). The proportion of those who finished university and graduate school was slightly higher among EDFs than among ordinary farms, and the EDF respondents had gained wider job experience before taking a job on their own farms. Put differently, the EDF respondents were less likely to take their jobs on their home farm directly after finishing school. Furthermore, the EDF respondents had more experience abroad and/or across the country in terms of their job-training experience in dairy; that is, over 70% of the EDF respondents had job-training experience, whereas 36% of the ordinary respondents had no job-training experience (Table 3). In terms of job-training abroad, more EDF respondents went to Europe, where farm activity tends to be more diversified than other areas, as compared with ordinary respondents (40% and 25%, respectively). Furthermore, the EDF respondents tended to stay abroad for a longer period than the ordinary respondents. Another interesting difference between the two groups was observed in the content of the job-training; the EDF respondents were more eager to learn processing skills and skills related to the exchange with consumers, whereas the ordinary respondents were more inclined to learn dairy production skills.

Table 2:   Academic background and jobs before farming.

Item	Ordinary dairy farm		EDF	
Academic background	%	No. respondents	%	No. respondents
Jr High school	1.8	4	0.0	0
High School	30.7	70	27.0	38
Jr college/ Vocational school	36.4	83	36.2	51
University	28.5	65	32.6	46
Graduate school	1.8	4	1.4	2
No answer	0.9	2	2.8	4
Total	100.0	228	100.0	141
Occupation before farm-job taking (multiple answers)	%	No. respondents	%	No. respondents
Student	47.8	109	39.0	55
Company employee	25.4	58	24.1	34
Public-sector employee	3.1	7	2.1	3
Teacher	0.0	0	2.1	3
Agri. cooperative employee	8.3	19	2.8	4
Self-employed	0.9	2	5.7	8
No employment	1.3	3	2.1	3
Others	9.2	21	12.1	17
No answer	4.4	10	9.9	14
Total	100.4	229	100.0	141

Source: As Table 1.

In short, as compared with the ordinary respondents, the EDF respondents ran larger farms of a more corporate nature with more female involvement, and had more active job-training experience as well as longer and more varied job experience. These facts indicate that the EDFs respondents had a wider perspective on dairy activities. Table 4 supports this indication, which contrasted the method of public relations (PR) used by the farm between the two groups of respondents. The EDF respondents were very active in promoting their farms through various channels from having their own website to publicity in magazines, whereas nearly 80% of the ordinary respondents did not carry out

Table 3:   Experience of job training in dairy farms abroad.

Item	Ordinary dairy farm		EDF	
Place of training	%	No. respondents	%	No. respondents
Only in the country	49.1	112	39.0	55
Only abroad	1.3	3	6.4	9
Domestic & abroad	11.8	27	26.2	37
No experience either	36.0	82	24.1	34
No answer	1.8	4	4.3	6
Total	100.0	228	100.0	141
Region of training abroad (multiple answers)	%	No. respondents	%	No. respondents
North America	37.5	15	36.7	22
Europe	25.0	10	40.0	24
Oceania	17.5	7	18.3	11
Other	7.5	3	5.0	3
No answer	12.5	5	0.0	0
Total	100.0	40	100.0	60
Period of training	%	No. respondents	%	No. respondents
Les than three months	47.1	16	44.9	22
3 months-5 months	2.9	1	4.1	2
6 months-11 months	5.9	2	16.3	8
one-two years	26.5	9	30.6	15
more than three years	2.9	1	4.1	2
No answer	17.6	6	0.0	0
Total	102.9	35	100.0	49
Content of training (Multiple answers)	%	No. respondents	%	No. respondents
Dairy production skills	40.4	23	33.7	28
Dairy processing skills	3.5	2	12.0	10
Management skills	17.5	10	19.3	16
Exchange with consumers	1.8	1	12.0	10
Exchange with farmers	21.1	12	18.1	15
Other	5.3	3	4.8	4
No answer	10.5	6	0.0	0
Total	100.0	57	100.0	83

Source: As Table 1.

any PR activities. Although the majority of the ordinary respondents thought that they needed farm diversification, in reality they rarely had a chance to exchange directly with consumers (Table 5).

5   Activity of the Educational Dairy Farm

Here, I examined what the EDF respondents are doing, as well as the attitudes that they have, toward the educational activities of the farms. Table 6 shows the outcomes of EDF activity. There were large variances in the number of visitors and in the number of times that the educational activity was practiced. The

Table 4:   Public relations methods used by each farm (multiple answers).

Item	Ordinary dairy farm		EDF	
	%	No. respondents	%	No. respondents
Holding own website	2.1	5	19.5	43
Twitter/blog	3.0	7	10.9	24
Facebook	6.4	15	10.4	23
Distribution of fryer	0.4	1	9.5	21
Publicity	5.5	13	9.0	20
Nothing in particular	78.0	184	33.0	73
Other	3.4	8	7.2	16
No answer	1.3	3	0.5	1
Total	100.0	236	100.0	221

Source: As Table 1.

Table 5:   Attitude toward diversification (ordinary fairy farms).

Necessity of farm diversification	%	No. respondents
Think so	18.4	42
Think so a little	38.2	87
Do not think so much	24.1	55
Do not think so	14.0	32
Do not think so	3.1	7
No answer	2.2	5
Total	100.0	228

Experience of exchange with consumers	%	No. respondents
No experience	41.7	95
Once or twice a year	43.0	98
Once a few months	11.0	25
Once a month	1.8	4
More than a few times a month	0.9	2
No answer	1.8	4
Total	100.0	228

Source: As Table 1.

number of visitors and number of times were roughly distributed around 100 visitors and 10 times, respectively.

Table 7 lists the reasons for starting the EDF activities, which were evaluated via a Likert scale ranging from 5 to 1, indicating that the respondents agreed, slightly agreed, neither agreed nor disagreed, slightly disagreed, disagreed. The three reasons with the highest scores were 'to let consumers know what dairy farms do', 'as a community service', and 'to establish human networks', all three of which are not economic, but rather social reasons. Economic reasons, such as

Table 6:   Outcome of EDF activity.

No. visitors	%	No. respondents
-49	30.5	43.0
50-99	23.4	33.0
100-299	12.8	18.0
300-499	6.4	9.0
500-999	10.6	15.0
1000-1999	4.3	6.0
2000-	9.9	14
No answer	2.1	3
Total	100.0	141
No. of times of receiving visitors	%	No. respondents
zero	7.8	11
1-10	46.8	66
11-30	21.3	30
31-50	7.1	10
51-100	6.4	9
100-	8.5	12
No answer	2.1	3
Total	100.0	141

Source: As Table 1.

'a new income source', were not scored highly. After performing the EDF activity, the respondents experienced various positive changes in themselves. The top three changes were 'increasing self-confidence and pride', 'enjoyment of exchange with consumers', and 'increasing awareness of playing a social role'; by contrast, changes in economic aspects, such as 'as a viable activity', 'as a mean of sales promotion for dairy products', and 'as a new income source', were not scored highly. These observations indicate that the EDF respondents have a wider perspective that enables them to look at emerging social roles and to build their self-confidence through the educational activity, which in itself has an educational effect on farmers.

Table 8 shows how the EDF operators view the educational activity. Currently, the majority of them offer the educational activity on a voluntary or cost-covering basis. By contrast, those who have considered the activity from an economic viewpoint, such as means of marketing or as a viable enterprise, accounted for only 20%. In this respect, therefore, the EDF operators conduct the educational activity not as an economic, but as a social activity. Nevertheless, 40% of respondents expressed their intention to consider as the activity as an economic enterprise in the future.

Table 7:   Successors' attitudes toward EDF activity.

Reason for starting EDF (5-scale evaluation)	Point	No. respondents
Let consumers know what diary farms do	4.4	136
As community service	4.2	133
Making human network	3.8	132
Enlargement of activity	3.7	132
Wanted to do different from what has been done	3.2	126
As evolution of open farm policy	3.1	124
As a new income source	2.8	127
As parents started EDF	2.5	118
Wanted to do what was different from what parents did	2.2	117
Other	1.4	9
Change in consciousness after EDF started (5-scale evaluation)	Point	No. respondents
Enhancement of self-confidence & pride	4.3	132
Enjoyment of exchange with consumers	4.3	133
Increasing awareness of social role	4.3	132
Connection with local community	4.1	128
Revaluation of farm resource	4.1	129
Enjoyment of teaching experience	4.0	130
Enlargement of human network	3.9	131
Discovery of new material for EDF	3.9	130
As a viable activity	2.7	126
As a mean of sales promotion for dairy products	2.7	125
New income source	2.7	124
Nothing in particular	2.0	74
Other	1.0	6

Source: As Table 1.

There is no single answer regarding how the EDF operators should view the educational activity. Given the increasing demand for farm visits, it may be time to start gradually shifting the emphasis from a social activity to an economic activity. From this perspective, levying a fee will be essential to establish the economic viability of this service. Table 9 indicates the attitudes of the EDF respondents toward levying a service charge: one-third of respondents said no charge; about 30% would charge for the whole service, which was followed 24.1% who were already making a partial charge. Thus, operators' attitudes are split into dichotomous views on charging. The lower part of Table 9 lists the respondents' views concerning measures toward implementing a charge for the educational services. The top measure was quality improvement, which was followed by PR activity, and financial assistance.

Table 8:   Attitudes toward EDF activity (present and future).

Attitude toward EDF at present	%	No. respondents
Voluntary	28.4	40
Cost covering	32.6	46
Means of marketing	9.9	14
As a viable activity	9.2	13
Nothing in particular	11.3	16
Other	7.8	11
No answer	0.7	1
Total	100.0	141
Attitude toward EDF in the future	%	No. respondents
Voluntary	17.0	24
Cost covering	27.0	38
Mean of marketing	17.7	25
As a viable activity	22.7	32
Decrease/quit EDF activity	7.1	10
Don't know	2.8	4
Other	5.7	8
No answer	0.0	0
Total	100.0	141

Source: As Table 1.

Finally, issues regarding the EDF activity are given in Table 10. As mentioned earlier, the educational activity at the farm increases the risk of spreading highly contagious diseases among livestock due to the open door policy for visitors.

Table 10 clearly indicates that this is the biggest issue that EDF operators face, and it poses a deep dilemma for the sustainable development of the educational activity. Prevention measures are not only the responsibility of individual farms, but also that of the public sector, especially those in charge of the quarantine office. Thus, support measures for quarantine will become more essential in the future. The next greatest issues were related to on-farm facilities, i.e. toilets and lecture rooms. This is because inadequate toilet facilities can hamper the smooth implementation of the educational program, especially for a group of school children. A lecture room is also effective for enhancing the educational program given by operators.

Table 9:   Attitudes toward EDF service charge.

Levying service charge	%	No. respondents
Whole service	29.8	42
Partially	24.1	34
No charge	33.3	47
Variable	7.1	10
Other	3.5	5
No answer	2.1	3
Total	100.0	141
Measures toward implementing a service charge (5-scale evaluation)	Point	No. respondents
Quality improvement	4.0	121
PR activity	3.9	122
Financial assistance	3.5	119
Utilization of social media	3.3	118
As collateral service with selling product	3.3	118
Cooperation with mass media	3.3	118
Partnership with travel agency	3.0	117
NPO	2.9	116
No charge policy	2.5	122
Other	1.0	3

Source: As Table 1.

Table 10:   Issues of EDF activity.

Issues of EDFs (5-scale evaluation)	Point	No. respondents
Epidemic prevention	4.7	138
Toilet	3.9	104
Lecture room	3.9	107
Knowhow	3.7	125
Labour	3.5	132
Making compatible dairy and educational activities	3.3	133
Educational material	3.3	131
Development of educational program	3.1	129

Source: As Table 1.

6   Conclusion

Farms have been attracting a growing number of visitors from school and consumers in general. The present survey has shed light on the educational service that the EDFs offer to visitors and has investigated the experience and attitudes of EDF successors toward the educational activity, together with the issues that this younger generation has. To achieve this aim, differences between EDFs and ordinary dairy farms were compared by sending questionnaire surveys to both types of farm. The main findings were as follows.

EDF successors tended to have wider job experience, and longer and more varied job-training experience than their counterparts in ordinary dairy farms. In addition, female successors were more involved in EDFs than in ordinary dairy farms. These observations imply that EDF successors have a wider perspective and more extensive human networks from social learning opportunities, both of which are crucial aspects in the development of this emerging innovative educational service.

Through the educational activity, EDF successors gained satisfaction in terms of psychological reward and strengthened their identity as a dairy farmer. Nevertheless, the majority of EDF successors did not consider the educational service as an economically viable product, but rather a social behavior that offers benefit to the local community and society.

In the long term, levying a charge, rather than maintaining it as a voluntary service, will be necessary to make the educational activity viable. This is a step forward in enhancing the recognition of this service as a new social role that dairy farmers can play in a sustainable manner. Quality improvement was considered to be an important measure for this purpose. Consequently, there should be a training program not only for improving technical skills to enhance the educational program, but also for generating a positive attitude to raise viability. Finally, for the younger generations of farmers, it is effective and necessary to provide more opportunities for job-training involving wider aspects of dairy farming.

Acknowledgements

The questionnaire survey for this research was financed by the Japan Dairy Council and the subsequent analysis was funded by Grants-in Aid for Scientific Research No. 24658191, Japan Society for the Promotion of Science (JSPS).

References

[1]   Graham, B., The work of farming and countryside education (FACE). *J. Royal Agricultural Society of England*, 165, pp. 1-8, 2004.
[2]   Gatward, G., 'The society's charitable activities', Journal of the Royal Agriculture Society of England, 168, pp. 1-8, 2007.
[3]   Canavari, M., Huffaker,C., Mari, R., Regazzi, D., and Spadoni, R., 'Educational farms in the Emilia-Romagna region: their role in food habit

education', Symposium on 'Food, Agri-Culture and Tourism', University of Göttingen, December 15, pp. 1-24, 2009.

[4] Moore, R.C., Children gardening: first steps towards a sustainable future, Children's Environments, 12(2), pp. 222-232, 1995.

[5] Ohe, Y., Evaluating jointness of multifunctional agriculture: the educational function of dairy farming in Japan, *Environmental Economics and Investment Assessment*, ed. K. Aravossis, C.A. Brebbia, E. Kakaras & A.G. Kungolos, WIT Press: Southampton, pp. 337-346, 2006.

[6] Ohe, Y., Emerging environmental and educational service of dairy farming in Japan: dilemma or opportunity? *Ecosystems and Sustainable Development VI*, ed. E. Tiezzi, J.C. Marques, C.A. Brebbia & S.E. Jørgensen, WIT Press: Southampton, pp. 425-436, 2007.

[7] Ohe, Y., Evaluating Internalization of Multifunctionality by Farm Diversification: Evidence from Educational Dairy Farms in Japan. *J. Environ. Manage.* 92, pp. 886-891, 2011.

[8] Ohe, Y., Operators' attitudes on educational tourism in agriculture, Pineda, F.D. & Brebbia, C.A. eds. Sustainable Tourism V, Southampton: WIT Press, pp. 273-286, 2012.

Quality of experience in rural tourism: regional case studies in Austria and Germany

V. Melzer & K. Meyer-Cech
Department of Landscape, Spatial and Infrastructure Sciences,
University of Natural Resources and Life Sciences Vienna, Austria

Abstract

The conducted research deals with factors of quality of tourism in relation to rural touristic initiatives, which conjointly market their tourism products. Several touristic initiatives were selected based on five criteria (e.g. a regional embeddedness and existence of a trademark) and their touristic offers were analysed. The study aimed to work out how these initiatives highlight their regional characteristics and which quality components contribute to a high quality of tourism experience. Based on the literature, four main components were identified that contribute to the quality of tourism, namely: hardware, environment/culture, software, and quality of experience. These components were combined with the seven instruments of quality of experience (e.g. the focus on a specific topic) by Müller and Scheurer (*Tourismus-Destination als Erlebniswelt. Ein Leitfaden zur Angebots-Inszenierung*, 2004) and tabulated. In the case study analysis, the quality requirements the touristic initiatives impose on their members, as well as existing offers, were gathered and assigned to the above-mentioned components of quality of tourism. The case study analysis revealed that all regional initiatives provide offers in all four main components. The initiatives also apply several aspects of the quality of experience, to highlight their regional characteristics. Several offers exist, in particular in the subcategories accommodation, culinary and regional products, events, information and internet presence as well as social media. In the field of quality of experience, the conveying of authenticity, the creation of atmosphere, and approaches of storytelling are used to generate attractions and to constitute positive guest experiences. This article provides first points of reference for an implementation of a universal guideline for regional touristic initiatives.
Keywords: rural tourism, quality of tourism, quality of experience, Austria, Germany.

WIT Transactions on Ecology and The Environment, Vol 187, © 2014 WIT Press
www.witpress.com, ISSN 1743-3541 (on-line)
doi:10.2495/ST140181

1 Introduction

Rural tourism destinations distinguish themselves by the fact that the sector is extremely fragmented and dominated by small, generally family run, enterprises. On the one hand this may result in a competitive disadvantage or else in often challenging efforts in concerted marketing activities of small businesses. On the other hand it is this fragmentation and semi-professionalism that is viewed as the very attraction of rural tourism destinations (see e.g. [2, 3]). This paper argues that both the atmosphere of rural host enterprises as well as their regional embeddedness strongly contribute to the quality of the tourist experience.

"*Although there is much debate about the precise meaning of 'quality' in the context of sustainable rural tourism, there is general agreement among its key stakeholders that delivering quality is a key requirement for achieving success in rural tourism businesses.*" [3], p. 227. A review of literature on quality in tourism (e.g. [4–7]) gives insight into the main components of quality in tourism, such as material factors (e.g. natural and built environment), quality of service and even quality of experience – whereby the latter is not dealt with in the same level of detail and was therefore chosen as the main focus of this paper. Looking at rural touristic initiatives it is the goal of this article to identify quality components in terms of the staging of rural attractions and creating an intense and positive guest experience.

2 Methodology

A review of literature on topics such as tourist offer, quality in tourism, interpretation and creation of memorable tourist experiences as well as destination management was undertaken for two reasons: on the one hand in order to clarify the terms used in this paper and on the other hand to find those components of quality in tourism that are relevant for regionally embedded collective tourist initiatives. The extracted components of quality were illustrated in a chart (see Fig. 1) whose skeletal structure is based on Müller's [7] classification in hardware, environment/cultural aspects and software. These components were complemented by findings of Freyer [8], Opaschowski [5] and concerning heritage interpretation and the elements that enable a memorable tourist experience by the works of Beck and Cable [9] as well as Müller and Scheurer [1].

The empirical part of this paper draws on the examination of six case studies, namely collective tourist initiatives in Austria and Germany that can be considered as good practice examples in terms of staging special regional features (see 5). These case studies were chosen according to the following criteria: small scale, environmentally responsible collective initiative, strong relation to a regional entity or regional characteristics in terms of tourist marketing and branding, converting a special regional attraction into a memorable tourist experience, existence of a list of quality criteria that the members of the tourist initiative have to comply with, regional embeddedness (i.e. contribution to the regional economic value added), existence of a responsible organisation that is in charge of management and coordination and existence of a brand mark for the collective tourist offer in general and the destination in particular. The necessary data to describe the case studies and their lists of quality criteria was obtained in the year 2013 by reviewing the relevant websites, brochures and written communication with the persons in charge of managing the tourist initiatives.

The analysis of the case studies concentrated on finding good examples for staging regional characteristic features, such as an agricultural product, the cultural landscape, craftsmanship or life on a farm. These examples for successful staging were described according to the components of quality in Figure 1. By doing so, differences and commonalities between the case studies became evident (see 6.1). And it became clear in which areas many offers exist that enable a memorable tourist experience and in which areas there is a lack thereof. Finally recommendations were made for various stakeholders, e.g. tourist entrepreneurs or municipalities, on how to improve the quality of providing memorable tourist experiences with a strong regional relation in rural tourism.

3 Clarification of terms

Rural tourist initiatives
For the present paper, several tourist initiatives were selected as case studies. In most cases, the foundation of the tourist initiatives was initiated by the joint marketing of the respective tourist product. This product can be both a tangible good, one or more services or the marketing of an entire region. If several service providers (e.g. accommodation, farmers) incorporate and jointly offer a particular product (e.g. hiking or biking holiday, farm holiday), this can be seen as a tourist initiative, referred to as special interest group.

Characteristics of tourism quality
There is a lot of literature dealing with service quality (e.g. [4–8, 10]), where several determinants for service quality are defined. For this paper, three approaches are most relevant. The first approach comes from Opaschowski [5], who defines three main components of tourism quality, namely the natural quality, including i.a. landscape and climate, the tangible quality such as accommodation and restaurants, and the intangible quality, which comprises atmosphere, hospitality and friendliness. Freyer [8] describes similar categories. He divides the touristic product into original offer (e.g. landscape, culture, hospitality) and derived offer (e.g. accommodation, hiking paths, events). Furthermore, he mentions that the intangible offer such as experiences and atmosphere plays an important role for a high tourism quality. The third approach is Müller's [7] classification in hardware, environment/culture and software. Equipment, function and aesthetics are assigned to the hardware component. Landscape, pollution and culture/traditions belong to the component environment/culture and software involves service, information and hospitality.

Opaschowski ([5], p. 115) points out that *"the guest sets the standard for quality in tourism"*.

Regional branding

The term branding refers to the assignation of a brand to something, as in this case a tourist product. Trademarks serve to give a product, business, or an entire destination distinctiveness, they remain in the customer's mind [11]. A brand can give the guest an orientation aid, because it provides information on quality norms and standards, which makes it easier for the guest to assess the quality of the expected services. They provide information on quality norms and standards, as well as the benefits and guarantees [12]. All selected case studies of this paper have a recognizable brand name.

Quality of experience

Experiences are induced by specific environmental stimuli, especially by a change of the environment. The experience itself is a response to this stimulus. Experiences are often associated with the interaction with other people, but can also be created by other stimuli, such as odours, tastes or sounds, to which the person reacts with certain emotions [1]. The staging of experiences takes place at a certain location or in a particular environment, called "setting". The staging serves to design the experience setting, e.g. by highlighting a certain topic to create an appropriate atmosphere.

4 Components of quality in tourism based on literature

As a result of the literature review this chapter and figure 1 in particular give an overview over the components of quality in tourism. As mentioned above Müller's [7] classification in hardware, environment/cultural aspects and software was used as the skeletal structure. The "memorable tourist experience" (called "Erlebnisqualität" in German literature) is viewed as part of the software by Müller [7] and as part of the immaterial aspects by Opaschowski [5] and Freyer [8]. But in accordance with the focus of this paper the authors decided to depict the memorable tourist experience as a separate fourth component - even though some aspects of it can be viewed as part of the other three components. For example the accommodation (which belongs to the element of hardware) has to be designed in such a way that a certain atmosphere is created and the authenticity of the regional tourist offer is conveyed. Both atmosphere and authenticity are also integral parts of the memorable tourist experience.

The component hardware includes the sub items facilities, aesthetics/setting and function. A rural tourist destination may comprise of facilities for accommodation, catering, traffic and leisure activities. Facilities in rural tourism may be a winery, an alpine dairy or a handicraft business as well as local produce such as cheese or pumpkin seed oil.

The component environment/cultural aspects comprises of the landscape, socio-cultural aspects as well as litter and other forms of pollution. A landscape's scenery, its natural monuments as well as hiking and biking trails are predestined to be staged. By doing so attractive tourist experiences that involve all the senses are enabled. Local customs and events, which are ascribed to socio-cultural aspects, also offer manifold opportunities to stage the overall theme of the conjoint rural tourist initiative.

The quality element software is made up of the sub items service, information and hospitality. The latter not only includes the friendliness and skills of the staff, but also the external communication (e.g. a uniform appearance by establishing a corporate identity), which is another field in which the senses of the tourists are appealed to.

Finally the component of the memorable tourist experience involves all sorts of ways of staging the tourist offer: e.g. highlighting a specific theme, activating all the senses of the guests, getting the guests involved in activities and creating a certain atmosphere. Storytelling, i.e. all parts of the tourist offer represent pieces of an umbrella theme or story, is another instrument for successful staging [13]. In this context this paper also draws on the findings of heritage interpretation (see e.g. [9]), which focuses on the often interactive explanation of heritage sites using a wide range of modalities such as guided walks, staffed stations, signs, artwork, brochures, audio-guides and audio-visual media.

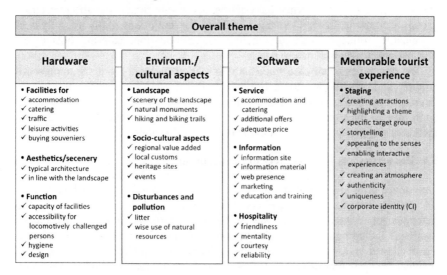

Figure 1:   Components of quality in rural tourism (based on [7], complemented by [5] and [8], revised by the authors).

5 Quality of tourism in the case studies

From the six selected case studies five are Austrian examples. Three case studies use an agricultural product for regional branding, namely a Wine Trail, a Cheese Trail and an umbrella organisation concerned with establishing so-called "Genuss Regionen" or taste regions. One case study is an umbrella organisation for marketing regionally typical craftsmanship and another for marketing farm tourism. The sixth case study was chosen from Germany, it is an organisation that conveys a quality label for socially and environmentally responsible tourism not only to single enterprises, but – and this is interesting for this paper - to towns and nature parks.

The Wine Trail in Lower Austria is one of the longest trails worldwide following the topic of wine. It has 830 km in length and guides through eight wine regions including more than 150 wine villages. The Cheese Trail, which is located in the Austrian state Vorarlberg, is an incorporation of businesses (e.g. farmers, cheese manufacturers), who conjointly market cheese products and want to display the cheese production, the cheese consumption and the landscape in such a way that memorable experiences for the guests are created. The "Meisterstrasse Austria" is not a specific trail, but an association of about 350 Austrian handicraft businesses in various industries (e.g. textiles, housing, jewellery). The organisation "Genuss Region Österreich" includes 110 regions in Austria, which promote a certain lead product that is typical for the respective region. The labelling as such a taste region is carried out by the Federal Ministry of Agriculture, Forestry, Environment and Water Management in Austria. The initiative promoting farm holidays consists of about 2600 farms providing specific offers (e.g. bio-farms, baby-farms, accessible farms) for different target groups. "Viabono" is a German certificate for environmentally friendly and sustainable holidays. Members include accommodation, catering businesses, destinations, towns and nature parks.

The objectives of all case studies are to market regional products, to preserve culture and traditions, to coordinate tourism activities and to promote interregional cooperation. Furthermore, the rural tourist initiatives want to contribute to the strengthening of regional identity and hospitable attitude of all members and partners as well as to the regional value added.

5.1 Requirements for members of the rural tourist initiative

Only those rural tourist initiatives were selected as case studies, which have a set of quality criteria their members have to respond to. For example the management organisation of the Wine Trail formulated a comprehensive catalogue including mandatory and optional quality criteria, whereas the Cheese Trail created a brochure containing guidelines for quality. Both documents include criteria for different actors (e.g. accommodation and gastronomy businesses, wineries, alpine dairies, hosts of events) concerning

- the overall appearance of the locality,
- the theme-specific touristic information for guests as well as signage,
- the regional and typical products,
- the qualified and friendly employees,
- the cleanliness and hygiene.

The quality requirements of the initiative "Genuss Region Österreich" concern the agricultural product, the region as well as the marketing, accommodation and gastronomy businesses within the taste regions. In order to become a taste region, an application must be submitted to the Ministry and a jury decides on the award. Subsequently, an agreement between the region and the Ministry is created.

The procedure to become a member of the initiative for farm holidays is similar. In a categorization process, the entire farm is reviewed in the areas of quality of equipment, quality of service, quality of memorable tourist experience as well as general farm condition and cleanliness. The farms are divided into three quality categories, which are illustrated by flowers. Two flowers represent a satisfying, three flowers a good and four flowers a very good quality.

To become a member of the "Meisterstrasse Austria", a craft business must complete the partner agreement and pay a membership fee. By signing the partner agreement, the owner of the craft business also obliges to comply with certain quality criteria. There are criteria concerning products, but also for the craft businesses.

"Viabono" has several certification concepts for their different members, e.g. hotels, gastronomy or nature parks, whereby the latter are most relevant for this paper. The application documents for nature parks include the categories of nature-based recreation, management, information and education, regional economic flows as well as mobility, waste, energy and climate, water, and architecture. An applicant is awarded points for fulfilling mandatory and optional criteria, whereby there is a minimum number of points that must be achieved.

5.2 Quality criteria and examples for staging

The touristic offer of the case studies was analysed and good examples for staging regional characteristics were collected based on the quality components in rural tourism shown in Figure 1.

Within the hardware component, all the examples generally have a good offer, but a few examples can be highlighted positively. The Wine Trail has several wineries, where guests can visit the wine cellar, find out interesting facts about wines and the production as well as tasting wines. The Cheese Trail also has dairies, which can be visited, including tasting and information about the typical traditional cheese production in the region. The accessibility for physically challenged people also belongs to the hardware component. Here the tourist initiative for farm holidays must be emphasized, as they provide specific offers for this challenged target group. Additionally, the font size of the homepage can be changed individually. The other examined case studies have at least some approaches relating to accessibility. The Wine Trail, the Cheese Trail and "Viabono" have barrier free hiking paths, but there is hardly any other information about this issue.

Regarding the component environment/cultural aspects, there is a huge offer of different events. On particularly beautiful sites in the middle of the wine yards a kind of banquet with a special menu, different wines and live music is organized by the Wine Trail Lower Austria. One member of the Wine Trail organizes a crime walking tour through the vineyards, where guests have to solve a murder case. Furthermore, the taste regions of the initiative "Genuss Region Österreich" take part in a series of events, so called "gusto weeks" at specified times each year, where seasonal menus are offered. Another event series of the taste regions is a tour with e-bikes to defined "gusto places". A good example for creating memorable tourist experiences is the Christmas market, organized by the "Meisterstrasse Austria", where handicraft businesses present their products.

Within the component software, most offers exist for the subcategory information. All case studies use the internet as an information platform, On the one hand, all examined rural tourist initiatives have one or more websites, but they additionally all use social media like Facebook on the other hand, where they present pictures or announce events. Furthermore, a wide range of printed information material is available for the Wine Trail (e.g. a detailed catalogue listing all members, their features and events) and for the taste regions (e.g. brochures about the lead product). The "Meisterstrasse Austria" and the initiative for farm holidays also publish catalogues listing their member businesses. Some initiatives provide an online shop, where the regional products can be bought.

6 Conclusions

In a first step in this following chapter, the differences and commonalities between the case studies are shown by comparing their respective quality components. This juxtaposition enables to determine those areas in which many offers exist and where there is a lack thereof. In a second step, recommendations for the future are stated.

6.1 Contrasting juxtaposition of the quality components of the case studies

The analysis of the case studies showed that there are offers in all four main quality components (hardware, environment/culture, software, quality of experience) and that all case studies use instruments of staging regional characteristic features.

Referring to the instruments for staging these regional characteristic features, it was found out that the initiatives put their emphasis on promoting authentic and regional embedded offers. All rural tourist initiatives highlight a specific topic (agricultural or handicraft product, life on a farm, nature park) and also include the landscape that is typical for the region. In this context it can be stated that all case studies display their tourist offer by means of telling a story: the story of where a certain agricultural or artisan product comes from and how the people live who produce it, the story of life on a farm or the story of the plant and animal inhabitants of a natural habitat. The element of storytelling used in this manner helps to fascinate the guests, lets them enter another world different from their everyday lives.

Examples, where staging is particularly well applied, are the crime walking tour example through the vineyards, as well as the banquets with wines and regional culinary specialties accompanied by live music. For these events, the staging instruments storytelling and creating atmosphere are implemented.

The possibility to visit wineries or alpine dairies creates memorable experiences for the guests by enabling the interactive participation in those activities. Furthermore, the traditional production methods are authentically conveyed to the guest by these visits. Some case studies offer tastings of their regional delicacies, thus appealing to the senses.

Figure 2 gives an overview of those instruments of staging regional characteristic features, which are used the most by the examined rural tourist initiatives.

Figure 2:   Most used instruments of staging of the examined case studies (compilation by the authors).

Differences between the case studies can be found concerning their inclusion of accommodation into the tourist offer in general and into their efforts of staging the tourist offer in particular. The spectrum ranges from the umbrella organization for farm holidays that deals with creating a certain atmosphere in the offered rooms in great detail over the Wine Trail, that has a few so-called wine hotels that set value on telling the story of wine, to the Meisterstrasse, that does not include accommodation in its tourist offer.

Another great difference between the case studies can be found in how they deal with regional embeddedness and geographical concentration. The first group consists of two case studies, namely the organization for farm holidays and the Meisterstrasse: they do place value on the local/regional setting, but their members are not all from the same geographical region. Rather they can be found throughout Austria. The next group places most emphasis on the geographical region, i.e. the label Viabono for the category of nature parks. And the last group contains the collective tourist initiatives that are made up of a whole group of regional stakeholders that all come from the same geographical region.

6.2 Recommendations

The research on this paper has shown that it is essential for rural tourist initiatives to strengthen the cooperation with regional stakeholders from different sectors (tourism, trade, agriculture, gastronomy, etc.) in order to persist in the tourism market. Additionally, successful tourist initiatives ensure the regional value added by national and international marketing of their products and services.

Rural tourist initiatives could also think about benefitting from new markets, such as social media and communication technologies (smartphones, tablets). There is already an extensive presence in social media, but applications for smartphones and tablets are hardly available.

Furthermore, the authors recommend to profile an umbrella organisation for rural tourist initiatives and to use strategies of destination management in order to coordinate the diverse actors and to guarantee certain quality standards. Some studies [12, 14] emphasize that a brand creates trust, conveys values and contributes to the identification of the guest with the brand/initiative.

Education and training of staff is also very important to meet the continually increasing demands of guests. Motivated and competent employees are substantial for a high quality of the tourist product, which is also confirmed by Opaschowski [5] and Müller [7]. In this context, the mandatory participation in training courses would prove as useful, as the Cheese Trail has already formulated in their quality criteria. Even regular information sessions and meetings to exchange experiences between the various stakeholders are recommended.

However, it is not sufficient only to formulate quality requirements for the members of the tourist initiative. To ensure that the quality of the tourist product can also be obtained, quality assurance is important. Opaschowski [5] claims a quality seal for quality tourism. Guest evaluation and feedback should also be part of the quality management in order to guarantee the maintenance of quality standards and to enable improvements. Müller and Scheurer [1] see guest evaluation as one of their seven instruments of quality of experience. Besides the guest evaluation, they outline that a concept for the staging of the specific topic should be created, including the objectives of the initiative, the subject, the lead products and a definition of the relevant target groups. It seems useful for rural tourist initiatives to include the aspect of quality of experience into the requirements for members.

When staging rural attractions, however, caution is advised, as an overstated staging may cause the loss of authenticity. In which way staging is carried out, is based on the natural conditions of the destination or region. It is important for the guest that the instruments used for staging regional characteristic features should be related to his or her stay and should be convincingly conveyed. Furthermore, the experience setting should also be based on the existing regional natural and cultural characteristics in order to enable a high quality of experience for the guest. The guest recognizes the difference between authentic, well-staged experience settings and inauthentic, overstated or poorly staged experience settings with certainty [13, 15].

References

[1] Müller, H., Scheurer, R., *Tourismus-Destination als Erlebniswelt. Ein Leitfaden zur Angebots-Inszenierung.* FIF Universität Bern, Bern, 2004.

[2] Meyer-Cech, K., *Themenstraßen als regionale Kooperationen und Mittel zur touristischen Entwicklung – fünf österreichische Beispiele,* thesis at the University of Natural Resources and Life Sciences Vienna: Vienna, 2003.

[3] Youell, R. & Wornell, R., Quality as a Key Driver in Sustainable Rural Tourism Businesses, Aspects of Tourism 26: *Rural Tourism and Sustainable Businesses,* Eds. Hall, D., Kirkpatrick, I., Mitchell, M., Channel View Publications, Clevedon, pp. 227-248, 2005.

[4] Parasuraman, A., Zeithaml V. A., Berry, L. L., A Conceptual Model of Service Quality and 1st Implications for Future Research, *Journal of Marketing* **(49)**, 41-50, 1985.

[5] Opaschowski, H.W., Das gekaufte Paradies – Tourismus im 21. Jahrhundert, B·A·T Freizeit-Forschungsinstitut GmbH (Ed.), Germa Press: Hamburg, 2001.

[6] Bruhn M., Stauss B. (Eds.), *Dienstleistungsqualität – Konzepte – Methoden – Erfahrungen,* 3. Auflage, Gabler Verlag: Wiesbaden, 2000.

[7] Müller, H., Qualitätsorientiertes Tourismus-Management. Wege zu einer kontinuierlichen Weiterentwicklung. Haupt Verlag: Bern Stuttgart Wien, 2004.

[8] Freyer, W. (Eds.), *Tourismus – Einführung in die Fremdenverkehrsökonomie.* 8th edition, Oldenbourg Verlag: München Wien, 2006.

[9] Beck, L., Cable, T.T., *Interpretation for the 21st Century – Fifteen Guiding Principles for Interpreting Nature and Culture,* Sagamore Publishing: Champaign, 2002.

[10] Voigt, H.D., Mockenhaupt, A., *Qualitätssicherung, Qualitätsmanagement. praxisnah – anwendungsorientiert.* 3rd, completely revised edition. Verlag Handwerk und Technik GmbH: Hamburg, 2010.

[11] Meffert, H., Burmann, C., Koers, M. (Eds.), *Markenmanagement – Grundlagen der identitätsorientierten Markenführung,* Gabler Verlag: Wiesbaden, 2002.

[12] Ferner, F-K., Pötsch, W., *MarkenLust und MarkenFrust im Tourismus – Techniken, Strategien, Design und Praxis beim Aufbau und Management von Tourismusmarken,* Österreichischer Wirtschaftsverlag: Wien, 1998.

[13] Egenter, S., *Natur in Szene gesetzt – das Erlebnis beginnt! Erlebnismanagement im naturnahen Tourismus,* VDM Verlag Dr. Müller: Saarbrücken, 2007.

[14] Deutscher Verband für Landschaftspflege (DVL) e.V., Landschaft vermarkten – *Leitfaden für eine naturverträgliche Regionalentwicklung,* DVL-Series "Landschaft als Lebensraum", Issue 10, 2006.

[15] Steinecke, A., Treinen, M. (Eds.), *Inszenierung im Tourismus – Trends – Modelle – Prognosen.* ETI-Studien Band 3, Europäisches Tourismus Institut GmbH: Trier, 1997.

Ecotourism: sustainable indigenous policies and its effects in Mayan communities, southern Mexico

S. E. Valle-García
Facultad de Ciencias Políticas y Sociales,
Universidad Nacional Autónoma de México, México

Abstract

In a sustainable development paradigm, the promotion of alternative tourism seeks simultaneously: preservation of nature, alleviation of poverty and consideration to ancestral culture. Nevertheless, in an analysis of multilateral and federal policies with methodological triangulation of surveys, in-depth interviews and participative observation, about the tourism market's dynamics in the ecotouristic Mayan community of Lacanjá Chansayab Chiapas, it was found that the aims of alternative tourism have not been achieved because the changes from a primary to a tertiary economic sector of indigenous' livelihoods has induced: 1) inter-ethnic struggles over economic natural resource management; 2) upward and downward spiral marginalization; 3) creation of urban environmental problems; 4) ancestral cultures have reconfigured their social function; 5) natural and cultural capitals have become global stock, less favoring indigenous people. The causes are, on the one hand, the intervention of multi-sectorial policies in Mexico is diffuse and without local participation in their design. On the other hand, the absence of impact assessment *ex-ante* to government interventions.
Keywords: sustainable tourism, poverty and environment, indigenous policies effects, rural and protected areas, socio-spatial transformations.

1 Introduction

The dominant discourse about sustainability is argued in equally among economic, social and environment systems. The most important activity that achieves the goal is tourism. First, this is because this service economic activity has no direct impact on natural resources, and second, it is an activity that can help to alleviate poverty with the Gross Domestic Product (GDP) increment at national level.

In recent years, "Sustainable Development" can be achieved not only through intense nature preservation but also with the high participation of local settlements. For this reason, Sustainable Tourism combines: Protected Natural Areas (PNAs) which are inhabited more by indigenous people in conditions of poverty. Therefore, the activity itself is implied to be the panacea that solves three big objectives: natural and cultural preservation with poverty alleviation [1].

Multilateral and supranational organizations like World Bank, International Monetary Fund, World Wildlife Fund, United Nations Development Programme and UNESCO promote sustainable tourism with international agreement. For this reason, in México the discourse is translated into promotion of services activities, and some farming activities in rural areas, with the implementation of the policies. Nevertheless, the well intentioned goal can be limited by scale factors: a local–regional context; the national political system; the global tourism market.

Consequently, in the present paper we will analyze the effects of indigenous policies that promote ecotourism as the solution of economic problems in southern Mexico. More specifically, the dynamic in the Mayan region mainly in the Lacandon rainforest is included as a case study: Lacanjá Chansayab. The document is divided into four sections: 1) sustainable tourism and ecotourism definitions; 2) implementation of Mexican ecotourism policies in rural areas; 3) empirical evidence of "Mayan World" Programme, Lacandon rainforest social dynamic and ecotourism effects in Lacanjá Chansayab; 4) socio-spatial transformation analysis.

2   Sustainable tourism and ecotourism

"Alternative tourism" as opposed to "conventional tourism", is a specialized practice developed in nature and promotes the active participation of tourists with a deep interaction with the exotic environment and preserved communities [2]. A ramification of alternative tourism is "low impact tourism" better known as "ecotourism" in the ecosystem and its preservation [3].

This sustainable tourism mode tries to seek the optimal use of natural resources, to preserve the essential ecological process; to respect communities' ancestral traditions and to guarantee the long-term economic benefits to the alleviation of poverty. In this sense, environment refers not only to the natural environment – flora, fauna, landforms, and atmospheric considerations – but also to social, economic, scientific, managerial, and political elements [2].

Moreover, it is possible to describe four fundamental elements of ecotourism [1–3]:
1) Travel should be restricted to Protected Natural Areas (PNAs).
2) It is not a business trip or conventional holiday to beach or cities.
3) The travel's interval is related to cultural and environmental awareness, environmental preservation and empowerment of the local people.
4) Includes a learning process about nature and, promotes pro-conservation sentiments and actions.

3 Mexican policies and ecotourism

The Mexican version of sustainable tourism is a mixture of economic activities developed with environmental and indigenous policies. Since the TLCAN Agreement, tourism is seen as a job generator and accelerator of growing economics [4].

This implementation includes multi-sectorial participation at local, regional and multilateral levels. In August 2007, the "General Agreement of Interinstitutional Collaboration for Sustainable Tourism Development in Mexico, 2007–2012" was signed and has as its goal:

"To use and preserve rationality the natural resource with the rural and indigenous development through direct participation and formal employments" [5].

In this sense, sustainable tourism is implemented with work joined to Mexican Secretaries in "Community-Based Sustainable and Heritage Tourism to Rural Development and Conservation Programme" at three levels:

1) Firstly, touristic promotion. The Tourism Secretary (SECTUR) only encourages rural tourism and supports the promotion of places to visit, the touristic infrastructure in communities, and training to indigenous people about touristic services [5].
2) Secondly, tourism with ecological management. The National Commission for Indigenous Communities Development (CDI); and Environment and Natural Resources Secretary (SEMARNAT) are trying to seek nature preservation and community-based alternative tourism through ecotourism certification, the touristic infrastructure with ecological equipment and training to indigenous people [6, 7].
3) Thirdly, complement with enhanced social and environmental conditions. The Social Development Secretary (SEDESOL) joined with SEMARNAT in order to seek simultaneously poverty alleviation and nature preservation with Conditional Cash Transfers – payments for Environmental Services (PES) by SEMARNAT and Oportunidades by SEDESOL – ensuring that people do not take natural resources, and complementing with natural resource management (SEMARNAT) and Food Safeguards (SEDESOL) [6, 8].

This is followed by international organizations:

1) Social and environmental attention: Agency for International Development (USAID), Organization International for Conservation (Pronatura), and Mexican Found for Nature Conservation A. C (FMCN).
2) The European Union with Sustainable and Social Development Project (Prodesis) and Programme Reducing Emission from Deforestation and Forest Degradation (REDD+plus).

In addition, it is more important that the state government issues subsidies on the one hand, and collaborates with federal actions on the other hand. Nevertheless, tourism in México is not free from contradictions, paradoxes, complexities and disappointments.

4   Mayan communities in southern Mexico

In this section, we will present the empirical evidence of ecotourism policy analysis and its effects in Mayan communities in Southern Mexico. The section is divided into two parts. The first shows hemerographic and bibliographic results of the one hand from the "Mayan World" and the other hand in the Lacandon rainforest.

The second part develops the study case: Lacanjá, Chiapas. Data arising were collected from May to July 2012. It includes an analysis comparative simulating three sceneries: before the people stared to join any governmental programme; during the flow of governmental subsides; and at present, to understand environmental policies' effects in rural communities (micro level) and the change attributable to government intervention (macro level). 18 surveys given to households were conducted for to discover conditions of well-being, and environmental problems.

Likewise, 23 in-depth interviews were implemented to recognize the socio-spatial transformation level of individual, family and community. At the same time, participatory observation in a settlement was conducted with three households to understand daily life and intersubjectivity, self-perception about the relationship between subjects, nature and the cosmos, through generational analysis.

4.1 Mayan world: dynamic macro-regional analysis

The "Mayan World" is shaped by México, Belize, El Salvador, Guatemala and Honduras. Mexico integrates 241, 784 km^2 within the states of Chiapas, Campeche Quintana Roo, Tabasco and Yucatán [5]. Its features are an amazing landscape, warm weather, extensive jungle and beaches in the Gulf of Mexico, the Mexican Caribbean or the Pacific Ocean. Ideal features to be designed as ultimate touristic destinations are building hotels, thematic parks, pubs, and resting places.

The activities along "The Mayan Route" are part of a recent creation, the Regional World Mayan Programme in 2011, the objective of which is:

"The strengthening of Mayan Region, on actions and strategies to improve touristic inputs in sustainable touristic development framework, with the participation of public and private sectors with local communities" [5].

Through: 1) building the infrastructure for service, railways and telecommunications that also connects all states on the Mayan route with the rest of the world; 2) promoting tourism investment in different levels and sectors; 3) promoting sustainability.

However, the intense promotion of first conventional tourism and then alternative tourism has caused high impact in this macro-region.

Firstly, cultural marginalization, because promoting Mayan culture leads to abandoning other important cultures like Olmec. Moreover, only one Mayan predominated, the Yucatec, other variations are excluded. Lastly Mayan culture also is less important in a traditional worldview in a globalization context [9]. The most important symbols are the pyramids, some drinks and traditional food and dress, and daily lifestyle is ignored.

Secondly, there has been no alleviation of poverty. In macroeconomic terms, 20 years ago the index marginalization showed no change in the states (see Table 1). Major poverty areas are concentrated in Chiapas, and there is less poverty in Quintana Roo.

Thirdly, environmental problems are great, for example, in Cancun and Yucatan that sees over-densification in rural areas; water and air pollution, forest and soil degradation, and endangered wildlife. For more details, see [10, 11].

Table 1: Poverty in the "Mayan World" (adapted by [12]).

State	Marginalization index			Marginalization grade		
	1990	2000	2010	1990	2000	2010
Campeche	0.47741	0.70170	0.43357	High	High	High
Chiapas	2.36046	2.25073	2.31767	Very high	Very high	Very high
Tabasco	0.51677	0.65540	0.47240	High	High	High
Quintana Roo	-0.19119	-0.35917	-0.41774	Medium	Medium	Medium
Yucatan	0.39959	0.38133	0.42295	High	High	High

4.2 Lacandon rainforest: nature space and struggle

The Lacandon rainforest is situated in the east of Chiapas (see Figure 1) and includes the municipalities Ocosingo, Las Margaritas, Marques de Comillas, Maravilla Tenejapa, Benemérito de las Américas and a little part of Palenque, Altamirano and Chilón [13]. It is a big mosaic of ecosystems with evergreen forest, coniferous forest and cloud forest, and a big collection of cultures and which constructs the natural space use [14].

Nevertheless, it is a regional space with a complex social, ecological and agrarian situation, caused by two very important institutional and official Declarations.

Firstly, the Agrarian Declaration by ex-president Luis Echeverria, who tried to attend to the pressure of land tenure of migrants or ancestral settlements [15], decided to reject land use planning and defined the Lacandon Community Zone (CZL) in 1972 with 66 lacandon households assigned 614,321 ha in three settlements: Naha, Metzabok and Lacanjá Chansayab [14]. Then in 1979 another settlement of choles and tzeltales households was recognized with property rights in this area [13]. However this assignation was unequal, because other settlements had petitioned agrarian regularization fifteen years ago without an answer from the state, therefore, they became irregular after the 1972 Declaration.

Secondly, the Ecological Preserved Declaration by ex-president José López Portillo, who joined international conservationist pressure to preserve the jungle, decided, in 1978, to reject the creation of PNA of Reserve Biosphere Montes Azules (REBiMA) whose polygon overlaps most settlements with CZL with 331,200 ha (see Figure 1).

Both are very important successes, because on the one hand it defined who can use natural resources, and on the other hand defined its use. Irregular settlements had to be removed from the Lacandon rainforest, and regular settlements can use the space but only with low farming, livestock, firewood, fishing but not hunting. The primordial use of the forest is for academic and scientific institutions and touristic, pharmaceutical, forest and energy markets [14]. Besides, communities have restricted access in their livelihood, paradoxically because they are blamed that their traditional activities jeopardize the Lacandon rainforest (see Figure 2).

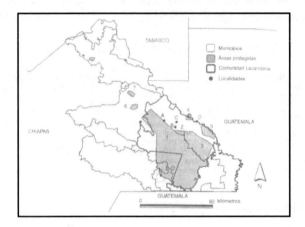

Figure 1:   Lacandon rainforest territorial planning (adapted by [13]).

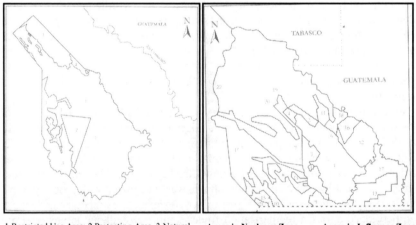

1 Restricted Use Area; 2 Protecting Area, 3 Natural Resources in Sustainable Use Area; 4 Traditional Use Area(Lacanjá).

Taken from SEMARNAT, REBiMA management Programme. National Ecology Institute Instituto 2000, p. 72

Areas in Nucleous Zone

1 Conservation and researching
2 Retrieval
3 Agricultural and Forestry
4-6 Cultural-Touristic

Areas in Influence Zone

7–10 Forest Preservation
11–13 Perennial Forest
14–17 Agricultural and Forestry
18-22 Cultural-Touristic

Taken from REBiMA Management Proposal, Tuxtla Gutierrez, Chiapas Government, 1990, p. 94

Figure 2:   Livelihood Planning in Management Programme REBiMA (adapted by [14]).

The above condition promotes conflicts and struggle among regular and irregular settlements and among the Lacandon people against the autonomy municipalities of Zapatist Army of National Liberation (EZLN). The first are the highest favored community in the Lacandon rainforest for their unequal right distributions. For instance, Lacanjá Chansayab and Emiliano Zapata (Miramar) are touristic places, first lacandon community, second zapatist filiation, and we can observe the following differences:

a) Access (state role): there is a railway that connects with the three most important touristic places in Lacanjá; on the other hand access to Miramar is more difficult, with unmade roads and touristic places are not connected.

b) Touristic dynamic (market role): there is less intervention by touristic agencies – with promotion and touristic affluence –in Miramar than in Lacanjá.

c) Livelihood (social dynamic importance): In Lacanjá, tourism is the main livelihood activity, in Miramar it is not so important.

In summary, the people of the Lacandon rainforest are not equal in their socio-environment because they live in ecological marginalization with exclusion, deprivation and displacement in the territory, and then they are in environmental poverty:

"The incapability to access to natural resources for to get environmental services and products for livelihood [16] caused by human activities over ecological detriment [17] inside a specific context with particular asset and rights to different places [18]". [sic]

4.3 Ecotourism in Lacanjá Chansayab

The analysis of sustainable indigenous policies in the Lacandon rainforest showed three important, interrelated findings. 1) The PNAs restricted the relationship between humans and nature and their nutritional and spiritual subsistence, and imposes a new economic order-reification and 'stigmatization' of their traditional rituals; 2) PES restricts Lacandon people's use of natural resources, generating lack of land and food insecurity; 3) ecotourism has promoted the Reserves' landscape valuation in monetary terms, underestimating the traditional ecological Lacandon knowledge. Therefore, encouraging political and economic benefits' atomization has prompted internal conflicts and marginalization. Thus, natural and cultural heritage became natural and social capital stock.

Field work results reveal that Lacandon people perceived that environmental subsidies achieve simultaneous economic and social benefits. They assert, retrospectively, that poverty is eradicated, there are employment opportunities and the jungle is safeguarded. Nevertheless, on the one hand despite multi-sectorial governmental intervention of twenty years, poverty and environmental degradation persist, and on the other hand, the Lacandon people strongly depend on the subsidies and their capabilities are not developed to safeguard themselves and their environment.

First, they have no sufficient income. Hence, they live in vulnerable and unstable conditions. Besides, land tenure is very important; being without land is linked to there being no chance of an owner's livelihood options [16, 18].

Since 1992, the communal property title connotes private property with the possibility that commoners can realize the legal trade of land with the State or Private Sector, a legal mechanism that safeguards the PES [19]. The Lacandon people say: "We believe that we are owners and guardians of the Jungle, however if we receive PESs, we are giving all our rights to the government and companies".

Second, transference streaming has diminished their human development and restricted their pursuit of a livelihood, and restricted community self-management [19]. However, it has prompted:

a) Consumption patterns are modified. From natural feed – self produced and expanded – to processed feed. This phenomenon is seen more in young people than elderly people.

b) Chronic-degenerative diseases increase. Mainly those related with stress and child malnutrition. Quality of life is depleted by the fact that physical activities are reduced. Diseases untreated by insufficient public service. Hence, the Lacandon people have to go out to other communities – using public or private services – or get no medical attention.

c) Null correlation between job and education. Streaming of multiple subsidies has not achieved favorable outcomes to motivate the youth to study in higher education and then diversify income source in large labor markets. This has recently happened and is contradictory to previous generations.

And, ecotourism has generated several problems.

a) Job and economic instability, unequal economic competition and there is job diversification.

b) In fact conventional mass tourism takes place with a negative environmental impact and trivializes indigenous culture [20].

c) There is no community model but rather private family monopolies [15].

Third, regarding the environmental aspects, the rainforest decreased by 72.5% in the last century [9]; from the perception of the Lacandon people, this phenomenon has generated environmental problems – climate variability and potential problems like air pollution, and a gradual decrease river levels – that generate impossible ecosystem resilience. Also the preservation strategies, PNAs, PES and ecotourism generated urban solid waste issues.

Last, gastronomic traditions, knowledge about the curative attributes of plants is being lost. Following the forced insertion to the international tourist market had led to the indigenous community meeting other lifestyles, exchanging behaviors and identities, in a reinvention form foreign to themselves, and from themselves to foreigners on how survivor strategically in a cultural heritage redimension [9], but always in a subordinate position [20, 21].

Consequently, cultural objects like vases, necklaces, drums, bags, robes and long hair that once were in daily use in Lacandon life no longer have this function. Instead they have acquired economic values by the Lacandon people and cultural values by tourists [21]. This culture of economic value is rejected by elderly people, who do not like to sell their traditions [1, 20].

5 Policies analysis: socio-spatial transformation

The research interprets the reproduction of socio-spatial transformations, meaning and re-signification that different actors connote to spaces and cultural, natural and urban sets, as well as territory planning [22]. Like part of a process of structural and institutional change expressed in daily realities [23], the discursive construction on different scales and spaces continues [24]. In this sense, socio-spatial transformation includes a global process constructed and represented with local realities.

Consequently, there are changes in social conditions, livelihoods, ancestral traditions, political organization, and the relation between human beings and their environment. This change underlies the power of unequal relations [25].

Hence, the relation among policies and socio-spatial transformation is about the institutional mechanisms that influence daily reality, in the lives of the Mayan people. Therefore, ecotourism policy implementation from regional to local level can be associated with:

a) Eco-territorial fragment in big way: nature preserved for ecotourism use in the global market; scientific bioprospection and energy use in PNAs; regularising an irregular settlement. In this way the most indigenous people have restricted use over natural space.

b) The restriction of natural resources represents socio-environmental inequality, because there are marginalizations: 1) ecological, since few people have or can use natural resources, the rest are displaced; 2) social, due to the same few people that can and have resources use, also can satisfy their basic needs – how food, dwelling and employment – are disposed through their livelihood; 3) economic, because tourism is a seasonal activity and touristic agencies are the most favored.

c) Symbolic representation of culture is resignified. First, the heterogeneity and diversity is replaced by homogeneity. Again, the most indigenous people are displaced. Second, bit by bit there are changes concerning the "use" in the iconographic sense of traditions; apparently those are more important to the tourist than for the Mayan people.

d) Finally, how the result of the three conditions described above, a struggling and fragmented community – ecological, social, economic and cultural – is in most cases evident or latent on the levels of inter-ethnic, intra-community, gender, and face to face. Also, social cohesion is limited.

Those situations are the effects of policies that combine the tourist market with a weakness in the political system. The tourist market is developed in a global logic, is a seasonal economic activity and is highly competitive. And the political system is related to the policies cycle:

1) Designed. For intrinsic features [26], the policies only include the solution of a little segment of the big spectrum of social and environment issues. The fact is that tourism is reified how operative panacea is only implemented from policies. This way, it is illogical.

2) Implemented. This step is characterized for a top-down mechanism, with diffuse and ambiguous aims, and disarticulated strategies and weakness normative.
3) Evaluated. Official institutions do not *ex-ante* and/or ex-post evaluate. And, there is little research about the negative impacts of information before and after implementation of policies.

6 Conclusions

In this research, the aim was not a policies evaluation about ecotourism in Southern Mexico. This paper showed a policies analysis in a wider sense in that structural policies function was contrasted with empirical evidence. The main explicative conceptual framework was the power of relations over control and access to natural resource use, which are developed in an upward and downward spiral to a global–local and local–global scale in three spheres: the tourist market, the political system and indigenous communities among themselves and within themselves.

For this reason, one alternative – in a strict analytical level sense – can be proposed, the deconcentration and decentralization of power at different scales, which implied [27]:

1) Macro level, rights transferences rather than power privileges toward a local level. Also, equilibrium and power security.
2) Micro level, local decision-making should include: economic capital conducive to well-being improved; solid political structure in design appropriate regulations and social and environmental common ideology.

The above means symmetry in macro-micro relations of power toward social and environmental justice in a democratic context and then, improving or eradicating the overexploitation and reappropriation of social and spiritual material objects – land use, raw material immaterial objects – recreational items – and intellectual – traditional knowledge – of the poorest people. However, decentralization is possible under the two premises outlined above; otherwise it can result in negative effects.

The community fracture in Mayan communities is due to the antidemocratic mechanism of governmental intervention and abrupt insertion into the tourist market. In the underlying discourse of land security and nature preservation, indigenous people have underestimated – in political and economic terms but not cognitive – their cultural and innate abilities for natural resource management, inadvertently reaffirming their inability to safeguard their environment and they have accepted instructions by the hegemonic State and Market. Hegemony accuses them of being invaders or thieves in their own land [1, 20].

Hence, the absence or little consideration of local dynamics in policy implementation has a high impact on heterogeneous reality, thereby the treatment of the homogeneous generates inequality, then exclusion and then poverty [28].

References

[1]   Coria, J. & Calfucura, E., Ecotourism and the development of indigenous communities: The good, the bad, and the ugly, Ecological Economics, 73, pp. 47-55, 2012.

[2]   Wearing S. y J. Neil, Ecotourism: Impacts, Potentials and Possibilities? Butterworth- Heinemann: Oxford, UK, pp. 1-286, 2009.

[3]   Weaver, D. B., Comprehensive and minimalist dimensions of ecotourism, Annals of Tourism Research, 32(2), pp. 439-455, 2005.

[4]   Cothran, D. A., & Cothran, C.C., Promise or political risk for Mexican tourism, Annals of Tourism Research, 2 (25), pp. 477-497, 1998.

[5]   Secretaría de Turismo (SECTUR) Programa Mundo Maya http://www.sectur. gob.mx/es/sectur/sect_Programa_Mundo_Maya. 2012.

[6]   Secretaría de Medio Ambiente y Recursos Naturales (SEMARNAT) http://www.conanp.gob.mx/acciones/pdf/, 2012.

[7]   Comisión Nacional para el Desarrollo de los pueblos Indígenas (CDI). http://www.cdi.gob.mx/programas/2012/cdi-reglas-de-operacion-.pdf, 2012.

[8]   Secretaría de Desarrollo Social (SEDESOL). Oportunidades para el desarrollo humano, http://www.oportunidades.gob.mx/Portal/work/sites /Web/resources/ArchivoContent/1783/Reglas_de_Operacion_Oportunidad es_2012_ (DOF050712).pdf, 2012.

[9]   Pastor Alfonso, M. A., Turismo y cambio en el entorno de los lacandones. Chiapas, México, PASOS. Revista de Turismo y Patrimonio Cultural, 10(1), pp. 99-107, 2012.

[10] Meyer-Arendt, K. J, Tourism development on the north Yucatan coast: Human response to shoreline erosion and hurricanes, GeoJournal, 4(24), pp. 327-336, 1991.

[11] Buzinde, C. N., Navarrete, D. M., Kerstetter, D. & Redclift, M., Representation and adaptation to climate change, Annals of Tourism Research, 3(37), pp. 581-603, 2009.

[12] Consejo Nacional de Población (CONAPO). Índice de marginación por localidad, http://www.conapo.gob.mx/es/CONAPO/Indice_de_Marginacion_por_Lo calidad, 2012.

[13] Durand S., L., Figueroa Díaz, F., G., Trench, T., Inclusión, Exclusión y Estrategias de Participación en Áreas Protegidas de la Selva Lacandona, Chiapas (Chapter 8). La Naturaleza en Contexto. Hacia una Ecología Política Mexicana, ed. L. Durand, F. Figueroa, M. Guzmán, CEIICH-UNAM, CRIM-UNAM, Colegio de San Luis: México, México, pp. 237-267, 2012.

[14] Vos, J., Camino del Mayab. Cinco incursiones en el pasado de Chiapas, CEICH-UNAM: México, pp. 1-299, 2010.

[15] Reygadas, L., Montoya, G., Hernández, F. y Velasco, F., Estilos de manejo y gestión de proyectos ecoturísticos en la selva lacandona de Chiapas,

México (Chapter 2). Estudios multidisciplinarios en Turismo, ed. Guevara Ramos, R., SECTUR, CEST y RICIT: México, México, pp. 71-100, 2006.

[16] Scherr, S. J., A downward spiral? Research evidence on the relationship between poverty and natural resource degradation, Food Policy, 25, pp. 479-498. 2000.

[17] Liu, L., Environmental poverty, a decomposed environmental Kuznets curve, and alternatives: Sustainability lessons from China, Ecological Economics, 73, pp. 86-92. 2012.

[18] Reardon, T. & Vosti, S. A., Link between Rural Poverty and the Environment in Developing Countries: Asset Categories and Investment Poverty, World Development, pp. 1495-1506, 1995.

[19] Rico García-Amado, L., Ruíz Pérez, M., Reyes Escutia, F., Barrasa García, S., & Contreras Mejía, E., Efficiency of Payments for Environmental Service: Equity and additionally in a case study from a Biosphere Reserve in Chiapas, México, Ecological Economics, 70, pp. 2361-2368, 2011.

[20] Machuca R., J. A., Estrategias turísticas y segregación socioterritorial en regiones indígenas (Chapter 3). Turismo, identidades y exclusión, ed. Castellanos Guerrero, A. & J. A. Machuca R., UAM-I/Juan Pablos: México, pp. 51-96. 2008.

[21] Van Den Berghe, P. L., Marketing Mayas. Ethnic Tourism Promotion in Mexico, Annals of Tourism Research, 22(3), pp. 568-588, 1995.

[22] Uribe, R., Paisaje, Narrativas y Experiencia: La Virtualización del Paisaje Maya, Estudios de la Cultura Maya, 40, pp. 227-265, 2011.

[23] Mc Lennan, C.J. Ritchie, B.W., Ruhanen L. M. & Moyle, B. D. An institutional assessment of three local government-level tourism destinations at different stages of the transformation process, Tourism Management, 41, pp. 107-118, 2014.

[24] Richardson, T. & Jensen, O. B., Linking Discourse and Space: Towards a Cultural Sociology of Space in Analyzing Spatial Policy Discourses, Urban Studies, 1(40), pp. 7-22, 2003.

[25] Durand S., L., Figueroa Díaz, F., G. Guzmán Chávez, M., La ecología política en México ¿Dónde estamos y para dónde vamos?, Estudios Sociales, 19(37), pp. 284-305, 2011.

[26] Aguilar Villanueva, L. F., La Hechura de las Políticas Públicas, Porrúa: México, pp. 1-442, 1992.

[27] Tacconi, L., Descentralización, forest and livelihoods: Theory and narrative, Global Environmental Change, 17, pp. 338-348, 2007.

[28] Sen, A., Nuevo examen de la desigualdad, Alianza: Madrid, España, pp. 1-37, 1992.

The cultural landscape as a cross-cutting resource for tourism products in low-density rural territories: diagnosis and guidelines for Alto Minho (NW Portugal)

A. Pereira
Faculty of Arts of the University of Coimbra,
Centre of Studies on Geography and Spatial Planning (CEGOT),
Portugal

Abstract

In Northern Portugal rural tourism is one of the most successful tourism sectors: the number of establishments rose by 30%, and the accommodation capacity registered a growth of 48% between 2002 and 2011. The evolution trends of rural and nature based tourism in Northern Portugal open new perspectives to the development of an integrative approach to tourism offer, where cultural landscape may be valued as a cross-cutting resource, as well as to the reinforcement of secondary demand.

Alto Minho (NW Portugal) is a predominantly low-density rural territory, with a rich cultural landscape shaped by agro-pastoral communities since the Neolithic. The concentrated diversity of potential tourism attractions and the combination of natural and cultural heritage stands as main distinguishing factors of Alto Minho as a tourism destination.

This research work aims to show how the acknowledgment of cultural landscape unities at a regional scale is as a crucial instrument for the conception of interpretative itineraries, joining different kind of tourism resources, from natural to cultural heritage.

Despite the short-term growth potential of rural and nature based tourism, its expansion may benefit from the development of a more integrated offer, widening the motivation spectrum. Heritage and cultural landscape touring may play a crucial role in the articulation of different tourism resources. This strategy proves to be the most advantageous one in the case of low-density rural areas.

Keywords: cultural landscape, nature based tourism, rural tourism, touring.

WIT Transactions on Ecology and The Environment, Vol 187, © 2014 WIT Press
www.witpress.com, ISSN 1743-3541 (on-line)
doi:10.2495/ST140201

1 Nature based tourism: trends and strategies

The Portuguese National Strategic Plan for Tourism (PENT [1]) establishes, for the period 2006–2015, that the products with potential to catalyse short-term growth in the region of Porto and North of Portugal, where Alto Minho is inserted, are *City Break*, *Touring* and *Nature Tourism*.

Nature based tourism is considered to be one of the fastest growing markets within the sector worldwide, with a growth rate between 10% and 12% per year (Tangeland and Aas [2]; Fredman and Tyrväinen [3]). Nevertheless the current economic frame prevented the confirmation of this numbers; the main evolution trend still is a meaningful indicator.

In Portugal, nature based tourism is expected an annual growth of 9% in a 10 year scenario, a value even higher than those estimated at a European level (AEP [4]). However, 96% of the demand corresponds to inbound tourism (THR [5]). Most of the outbound tourists are visitors who have travelled to Portugal for other reasons and that, once in the country, get interested in some form of nature tourism. This puts in evidence the weak position of Portugal as a destination for nature tourism trips in the international market (as main reason) and the importance of the concept of secondary demand.

Thereby, despite the short-term growth potential of nature tourism in North Portugal, its expansion may benefit from the development of a more integrated offer, widening the motivation spectrum through the combination of nature tourism, in a strict sense, with other branches of the tourism sector, taking advantage of the diversity of resources in the territory. Given the proximity and the intrinsic relation between the majority of natural environments, namely the protected areas, and the rural spaces in Alto Minho, *Heritage and Cultural Landscape Touring* may play a crucial role in the articulation of different tourism resources.

The gaps in the regional organization of nature based tourism induced the *Comunidade Intermunicipal do Alto Minho* (Upper Minho Inter-Municipal Community) to lead the development of a number of projects, coordinating the intents and efforts of the different municipalities.

The strategy for the sustainable and profitable management of the environmental resources of Alto Minho adopted by the Inter-Municipal Community establishes two main guidelines: the qualification of the greenways and the valorisation of the areas of environmental excellence. Aiming to create a backbone of the walking routes in Alto Minho, approaching the valley and the hilly areas, two new great routes are being implemented: the littoral and the mountain routes. The network of greenways in Alto Minho is due to be extended to 164 km long.

The global outlook of this strategy highlights the strong focus on pedestrianism as a way to promote leisure and tourism in natural areas. Thereby, aiming to achieve a deeper approach to this strategy, some important issues must be addressed:

- Which is the market of this type of nature based tourism in northern Portugal?

- What criteria are being observed in the restructuring of Alto Minho greenways, namely the projected great routes?
- Is natural and cultural heritage being properly considered in an integrative approach to tourism resources?
- May Alto Minho greenways' take advantage from exploring complementarities and synergies with heritage and cultural landscape touring?

The reflection on these questions may contribute to improve the regional nature based tourism strategy, enlarging the growth potential of this sector.

This research addresses the possibilities and advantages of integrating nature tourism with other products with strong synergies, such as rural tourism and touring. The definition, characterization and cartography of cultural landscape unities play a crucial role in the conception of tourism products based in the interpretation of the inter-relation between men and nature, bringing together natural and cultural heritage. Indeed, the acknowledgment of cultural landscape unities at a regional scale is as a crucial tool for the conception of interpretative itineraries.

An itinerary of cultural and landscape touring, linking the Arga ridge and the valley of Lima River will be developed, putting into practice the proposed strategy.

2   Upper Minho nature based tourism resources

The north-western region of Portugal, Alto Minho develops between the Lima River, its southern limit, and the Minho River that defines the boundary with North Spain.

More than inventorying the values that may support the development of nature based tourism products, it is important to stress how they can contribute to differentiate Alto Minho as a tourism destination. The concentrated diversity of potential tourist attractions and the combination of natural and cultural heritage elements, expressed in an evolutionary cultural landscape, stands as the main distinguishing factors.

Therefore, the nature based tourism resources of Alto Minho can only be understood in the frame of the interpretation of its cultural landscape, including the explanation of its physical and historical conditioning factors.

2.1 A complex and diversified landscape mosaic

The organization of the landscape of Alto Minho is defined by four main vectors: the contrast between lowlands and mountainous areas, more specifically between the alluvial plains and the surrounding hills and ridges, an agro-pastoral and forestry matrix built over several centuries, a scattered settlement pattern, where only stands some medium-scale centres and, at least, the strong fragmentation of rural property.

The complex organization of this territory results from the overlap of land occupation models and strategies from different historical periods. Indeed, the archaeological research conducted since the second half of the last century revealed that the regional landscape organization clearly shows the most important marks of the human presence. In this way, the archaeological remains offer meaningful evidences for the interpretation of landscape evolution.

The integrated study of natural and cultural heritage contributes to increase the knowledge about the options and strategies adopted in different periods in what concerns to the location of population centres, land use patterns, exploitation of natural resources, mobility networks or landownership models.

The landscape mosaic of Alto Minho highlights the crucial influence of the underling relief structure. The antagonism between the riverside and the mountain areas has a remarkable impact on the settlement models and on the distribution of the productive activities. In a closer look, the importance of tectonic valleys, granitic alveolus and natural terraces stands out. Similarly, the lithology strongly influences the landscape mosaic, conditioning the pedologic properties and the soil suitability. Its influence is particularly evident in the contact areas between granites and shales and in the alluvial plain of river Lima.

The terrain of Alto Minho is compared to mosaic of blocs (Ferreira [6]), defined by the intersection of tectonic lineations of the hercynian (NW–SE/NNW–SSE) and alpine (NE–SW/ENE–WSW) orogenies. The open valleys, conditioned by the betic direction, are delimited by a sequence of horsts, which elevation decreases from east to west. These mountain ridges are mainly constituted by granitic rocks, deeply cut by fracture alignments of late-hercynian (NNW-SSE) or alpine orogenies, whose directions determine the major rivers in the region and their main tributaries (Rebelo [7]). Despite the intense fracturing, it is still possible to identify several well preserved flattened levels in the mountain systems of NW Portugal – such as those of Gerês, at 1400 meters of height, Peneda about 1100–1200 meters, Cabreira around 900–1000 meters and Arga ridge at a 800 meters (Feio [8]). These levels correspond to conserved remains of extensive erosion surfaces (Martin-Serrano [9]). The tectonic action is patent in the orientation of the hydrographical network and in the enlargement of the main valleys. Consequently, the pre-ordovician schist-greywacke complex, the Ordovician quartzites and different types of hercynian granites stands out in the geological frame.

Three specific features of the regional morphology determine, at a great extent, the location of the rural settlements, as well as the distribution of the agricultural area: the cross-profile of the main valleys, the great number and remarkable dimension of granitic alveolus and the importance of natural terraces for the development of hilly villages.

Now we will present a synthesis of the main historical processes that influenced the evolution of the territory organization in Alto Minho. The Castro culture played a key role in shaping the landscape of the mountainous areas. During the early centuries of the first millennium B.C., Alto Minho landscape have been deeply transformed by the new agropastoral and forestry systems structured around the settlements fixed in middle slope. More than 31 hill forts were identified in the watershed of river Lima (Almeida [10]): fortifications that defined the concentration of the agro-pastoral communities on strategically defensive points of the hills and mountains. The demand for arable land and pastures in the area of influence of each hill fort triggered the deforestation and prevented the growth of shrubs in the highlands (Almeida [11]). The present mountain settlement may be regarded as an evolutionary heritage of the Pre-Roman land organization. Hill forts occupation persists under the Roman domain, being often continued until the Middle Ages.

Roman settlements established essentially on valley areas, with gentle slopes and more fertile soils. Romans were responsible by the deforestation the alluvium plains and drainage of marshy areas, modifying land occupation patterns and stimulating the evolution of agroforestry systems. The disperse settlement and strong parcelling that characterises the lowlands of Alto Minho finds its roots on the Roman period, whose land occupation matrix, agrarian organization and property division is rebuild over new power and social hierarchies during the Early Middle Ages. The Roman *villaes* consisted in agro-cattle proprieties, whose exploration was commonly carried out by slave or employed workmanship. The north-western settlement in the Roman period would lie on a *villae* network more or less scattered (Sampaio [12]). Summing up, the modern north-western rural landscape was shaped during Proto-History, with the Castro settlement model that occupied the hilly slopes of the major valleys. The subsequent settlement, Roman and Medieval, organized and increased the density of the occupation of the lowland areas (Martins [13]). Notice that the influence of the Castro settlement pattern still remains visible at the present, reflected in a system of isolated places of small dimension.

This summary of landscape evolution, combining natural and historical factors, contributes to the understanding of the present landscape mosaic.

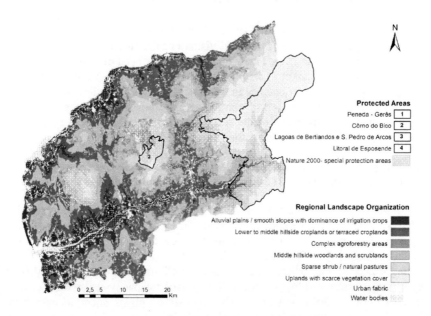

Figure 1:   Regional landscape organization.

The cartography of the main levels of landscape organization in Alto Minho, presented in figure 1, was based in the weighted correlation between elevation, lithology, slope and soil use, following a methodology similar to the one presented in Batista *et al.* [14]. The resulting map allows us to identify six main levels of landscape organization in Alto Minho, expressing the relation between the soil use and the biophysical support:

1) Alluvial plains / smooth slopes with dominance of irrigation crops,
2) Lower to middle hillside croplands or terraced croplands,
3) Complex agroforestry areas,
4) Middle hillside woodlands and scrublands,
5) Sparse shrub / natural grasslands or pastures,
6) Uplands with scarce vegetation cover.

The conservation areas present in this region, also represented in figure 1, includes the *National Park Peneda-Gerês*, the *Protected Landscape of the Lagoas de Bertiandos e S. Pedro de Arcos* and the *Protected Landscape of Corno do Bico*, as well as the sites of community importance and special protection areas of the rivers *Minho* and *Lima*, *Litoral Norte* and *Serra de Arga*, integrated in Nature 2000. Notice the strong diversity of habitats; including mountain areas, estuarine corridors and coastal environments that mark this network in Alto Minho. With more than 61200 ha included within the Nature 2000 network and 34300 ha of conservation areas, Alto Minho reinforces its potential for nature based tourism with a rich cultural landscape mosaic.

3 Taking advantage from cultural landscape as a cross-cutting resource for tourism products

In the Portuguese network of protected areas (ThinkTur [15]) spontaneous visitation largely overcomes structured visitation: the first represents over 80% and the second less than 20%. These figures stress the need of finding innovative ways to expand the market of nature based tourism in Alto Minho. Achieving this goal requires a greater balance in the tourism use of the different natural and rural areas and the integration of complementary tourism resources, aiming to stimulate and take advantage of the secondary demand. A practical example of this approach will be presented for the valley of the Lima River.

3.1 Integrating tourism offer in the valley of the Lima River: from high-quality rural tourism to cultural and landscape touring

The number of rural tourism establishments in Portugal increased by 33% between 2002 and 2011 (Turismo de Portugal [16]), while the accommodation capacity, measured in number of bed places, grew 58%. In the same period, the number of nights spent increase over 90%.

In northern region, where rural tourism has a longer tradition, the number of establishment rose by 30%, and the accommodation capacity registered a growth of 48% between 2002 and 2011. The number of nights spent increased by 83.62%. In 2011, this region gathered near 40% of the total accommodation capacity provided by rural tourism in the country and represented about 31% of the nights spent in this kind of lodgement.

The promising evolution trends of rural tourism in Portugal and the importance of the offer centred in northern region opens new perspectives to the expansion of nature based tourism trough the exploitation of secondary demand. The motivations and expectations of rural tourists and eco-tourists corroborate this point of view.   A survey on German tourists (European Commission [17]), one of the most important European outbound markets for nature based tourism, states that the four most important expectations for tourists seeking nature and culture orientated holidays are as follows:

- *"50% expect small accommodation businesses run by locals;*
- *45.6% want to go hiking by themselves and want to be furnished with good information;*
- *41.2% expect local cuisine with local ingredients;*
- *41.2% expect strong local hospitality; they want to feel welcome".*

This survey highlights how the conciliation of the offer of nature based tourism and rural tourism may fulfil the expectations of this market segment, valuing the combination of locally based hotel businesses, local productions and easy access to autonomous trekking.

An inquiry on the motivations of the guests of rural tourism establishments (Instituto de Estudos Sociais e Económicos [18]) pointed out that the discovery of a region and the contact with nature were the most cited reasons to choose this kind of accommodation.

The valley of the Lima River was the cradle of TURIHAB, a network of characterful rural properties, under the brand name *Solares de Portugal*, comprising small hotels, individual homes and apartments. This rural tourism network of excellence may be enriched by the integration with the regional offer of nature based tourism, specially by favouring the access to the more than 70 hiking treks spread all over the valley of river Lima, both inside and outside of the conservation areas.

3.2 Climbing the hill: understanding a cultural landscape

Aiming to demonstrate how the identification and cartography of cultural landscape unities may be a crucial tool for the conception of interpretative itineraries; a road route was developed in Arga ridge aiming to:
- Conceive an itinerary representative of the cultural landscapes mosaic,
- Stimulate the practice of hiking by rural tourism guests,
- Show how the interrelation between built heritage and cultural landscape may enrich the process of discovering a territory.

The *Cultural Itinerary of the Arga Ridge*, presented in the figure 2, consists of an open route of 34 km, meant to be done by car, which guides the visitor through a narrative of the man occupation of this territory and of the shaping of its landscape, taking advantage of an integrated analysis of the environmental and built heritage.

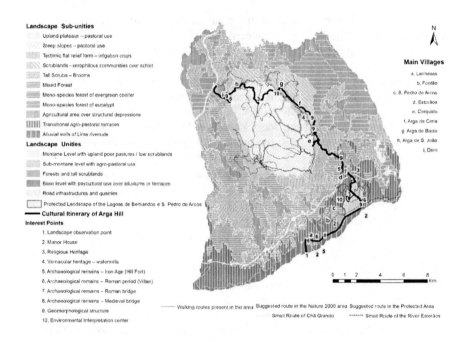

Landscape Sub-unities
- Upland plateaux – pastoral use
- Steep slopes – pastoral use
- Tectonic flat relief form – irrigation crops
- Scrublands – xerophilous communities over schist
- Tall Scrubs – Brooms
- Mixed Forest
- Mono-species forest of evergreen conifer
- Mono-species forest of eucalypt
- Agricultural area over structural depressions
- Transitional agro-pastoral terraces
- Alluvial soils of Lima riverside

Landscape Unities
- Montane Level with upland poor pastures / low scrublands
- Sub-montane level with agro-pastoral use
- Forests and tall scrublands
- Base level with polycultural use over alluviums or terraces
- Road infrastructures and quarries
- Protected Landscape of the Lagoas de Bertiandos e S. Pedro de Arcos
- ▬ Cultural Itinerary of Arga Hill

Interest Points
1. Landscape observation point
2. Manor House
3. Religious Heritage
4. Vernacular heritage – watermills
5. Archaeological remains – Iron Age (Hill Fort)
6. Archaeological remains – Roman period (Villae)
7. Archaeological remains – Roman bridge
8. Archaeological remains – Medieval bridge
9. Geomorphological structure
10. Environmental Interpretation center

N

Main Villages
a. Lanheses
b. Fontão
c. S. Pedro de Arcos
d. Estorãos
e. Cerquido
f. Arga de Cima
g. Arga de Baixo
h. Arga de S. João
i. Dém

0 1 2   4   6   8 Km

········ Walking routes present in the area   Suggested route in the Nature 2000 area   Suggested route in the Protected Area
Small Route of Chã Grande   ········· Small Route of the River Estorãos

Figure 2:   Cultural Itinerary of Arga Ridge exploring the classification of landscape unities.

It begins on the edge of river Lima, facing the so-called *Lugar da Passagem*: a river crossing site integrated in a pre-Roman route, later consolidated during the imperial occupation and continued to be used during the medieval ages. The antiquity of this route was attested by the discovery of two dugouts dated between the 4th and 2nd centuries BC. Then, the itinerary follows a national road, which develops along the fertile plain of the river Lima, a sediment deposition area intensively occupied by irrigated crops. The several archaeological remains that were identified nearby this section of the route prove the occupation of the alluvial plain and of the low hillside sectors by agricultural hill forts, during the High Empire, as well as the implementation of roman *villae* or even medieval agricultural exploitation unities based on family cells. This starting point provides a clear sight of the contrast between the alluvial plain of river Lima and the south-western slope of Arga ridge in terms of their morphology, vegetation and soil use (figure 3).

The route veers towards a secondary road that goes through the *Protected Landscape of the Lagoas de Bertiandos e S. Pedro de Arcos*, crossing the valley of Estorãos River and enabling the possibility of hiking in a small route that penetrates into this conservation area – the only wet zone that benefits of a special protection status in northern Portugal – conducting to its Environmental Interpretation Centre.

Figure 3: Landscape contrast between the alluvial plain and the Arga Ridge.

Following the road that climbs the southeast slope of the Arga Ridge, towards the small village of Cerquido (figure 4), one may observe a clear fault scarp. This village develops between 400 and 430 meters of height, in a well defined tectonic terrace. With a privileged geostrategic location, Cerquido has a unique visual *basin*, encompassing the valley of Estorãos River and the middle sector of the alluvial plain of the Lima River.

Climbing to the central granitic massif it is possible to observe the geological contact between the granite of Serra de Arga and black schists of the Unite of Minho. Following along the tectonic flat level we found the three main mountain villages of this route, surrounded by a complex agricultural area constituted by a mix of croplands and natural pastures. It is possible to have access to several small routes that leads us to the hilltop surface, area with a great diversity of granitic landforms.

Starting the way down, we will find an Early Middle Ages monastery that still is an important pilgrimage place: the Monastery of S. João de Arga, dated from the 13th century.

At least, the route meets the tectonic depression of Dem. This graben is marked by the agricultural use of the base of the slopes through archaic terraces. In a dominant elevation nearby the parish church we found the remains of a hill fort known as *Castro do Germano*, which probably has explored the fertile soils of the neighbour depression. The fertility of the soil of this graben is not due to the geological schist substrate but to sediment accumulation from upstream of slopes.

Figure 4:   Cerquido: a village and its agro-pastoral area in the Arga Ridge.

4   Final words: some advice on the promotion of nature based tourism

The exposed exercise aimed to show how the exploration of the concept of cultural landscape may contribute to a comprehensive interpretation of the territory and to the development of a space-based narrative to guide its discovery by the visitants.

The strategy based on the complementarities between rural tourism, nature tourism and cultural and landscape touring is the most advantageous one in the case of low density rural areas, with an ancient human occupation and high diversity of natural and cultural heritage, such as the region of Alto Minho.

The success of this approach may benefit from the following recommendations:

- Analyse the profile of the tourists that already visit the region, particularly at the segments of rural tourism and landscape and cultural touring;
- Design walking routes considering the demand of soft nature consumers, in order to satisfy the expectations of rural tourism guests;
- Pay special attention to the suitability of mobility solutions and meet the information needs of the target publics;
- Attract and guide potential hiking practitioners by the conception of interpretative road routes linking the existing footpaths;
- Diversify the scenic context of the walking routes, avoiding monotony, and the typology of interest points, offering a holistic overview of local environmental and cultural values;

- Take more advantage of the tourism infra-structures and services already available in the territory, promoting its use in the scope of integrated tourism products.

References

[1]   Turismo de Portugal, *Plano Estratégico Nacional de Turismo (PENT)*. Ministério da Economia e da Inovação: Lisboa, 2007, Online. http://www.turismodeportugal.pt

[2]   Tangeland, T. & Aas, Ø., Household composition and the importance of experience attributes of nature based tourism activity products – A Norwegian case study of outdoor recreationists. *Tourism Management*, 32(4), pp. 822-832, 2011. http://www.sciencedirect.com/science/article/pii/S0261517710001500

[3]   Fredman, P. & Tyrväinen L., Frontiers in Nature-Based Tourism. *Scandinavian Journal of Hospitality and Tourism*. 10(3), pp. 187–189, 2010. http://www.tandfonline.com/doi/abs/10.1080/15022250.2010.502365

[4]   AEP/Gabinete de Estudos. (2008). *Turismo de Natureza. Estudo de Mercado.* Lisboa: Turismo de Portugal. http://www.aep.org.pt/publicacoes/estudos-de-mercado-aep

[5]   *THR – Asesores en Turismo Hotelería y Recreación, S.A.* (2006). *Turismo de Natureza. 10 produtos estratégicos* para o *desenvolvimento* do *turismo em Portugal*. Lisboa: *Turismo de Portugal, IP*. http://www.turismodeportugal.pt/Portugu%C3%AAs/turismodeportugal/p ublicacoes/Documents/Turismo%20de%20Natureza%202006.pdf

[6]   Ferreira, A., *O Relevo de Portugal. Grandes Unidades Regionais*. Associação Portuguesa de Geomorfólogos: Coimbra, 2004.

[7]   Rebelo, F., Relevo de Portugal – uma introdução, *Inforgeo*, 4, pp. 17-35, 1992.

[8]   Feio, M., Reflexões sobre o relevo do Minho. *Notas Geomorfológicas*, 1, pp. 5-33, 1951.

[9]   Martin-Serrano, A. *El relieve de la región occidental zamorana. La evolutión geomorfológica de un borde del macizo Hespérico.*, Instituto de Estudios Zamoranos 'Florian de Ocampo': Zamora, 1988.

[10]   Almeida, C., *Povoamento Romano do Litoral Minhoto entre o Cávado e o Lima*. Ph.D. thesis., Universidade do Porto: Porto, 1996.

[11]   Almeida, C., Da pré-história à Romanização (vol. I), *Sítios que fazem história. Arqueologia do concelho de Viana do Castelo*, Câmara Municipal de Viana do Castelo: Viana do Castelo, 2008.

[12]   Sampaio, A. *Estudos históricos e económicos: As villas do Norte de Portugal*, Vega: Lisboa, 1979.

[13]   Martins, M., As vilas do norte de Portugal. *Revista de Guimarães*, 102, pp. 387-409, 1992.

[14]   Batista, T. *et al.*, Unidades Locais de Paisagem: ensaio aplicado à área Alentejo-Extremadura no âmbito OTALEX II /Unidades Locales de

Paisaje: ensayo aplicado al área Alentejo-Extremadura en el âmbito de OTALEX II., Batista, T, *et al.* (coord.), *OTALEX II – Resultado do Projecto – Resultado del Proyeto*. 81-96 s.l.: Ed. CIMAC e Dir. Gen. Urb. y Orden. Territ. 2011.

[15] ThinkTur Estudos e Gestão de Empreendimentos Turísticos, Lda., *Programa de Visitação e Comunicação na Rede Nacional de Áreas Protegidas*. Instituto da Conservação da Natureza: Lisboa, 2006, Online. http://www.icn.pt/portal/portal/cpublica/PVisitacao/visitacao_aps/relatorio 2fase/PVC_RNAP_R2_1.pdf

[16] Turismo de Portugal, Anuário das Estatísticas do Turismo 2011, 2012, Online. http://www.turismodeportugal.pt/Portugu%C3%AAs/ProTurismo/estat%C 3%ADsticas/an%C3%A1lisesestat%C3%ADsticas/oturismoem/Pages/OT urismoem.aspx

[17] European Commission. Tourism Unit. *Using natural and cultural heritage to develop sustainable tourism in non-traditional tourist destinations* (n.º 285). Enterprise Directorate General – Tourism Unit: Brussels, 2002. Online. http://ec.europa.eu/enterprise/sectors/tourism/files/studies/using_natural_c ultural_heritage/market_trends_en.pdf

[18] Instituto de Estudos Sociais e Económicos, *Estudo de Caracterização do Turismo no Espaço Rural e do Turismo de Natureza em Portugal*. Direcção Geral de Agricultura e Desenvolvimento Rural: Lisboa, 2008, Online. http://www.dueceira.pt/docs/publicacoes/99_estudo%20TER.pdf

Section 6
Heritage tourism

Historic cities and sustainable tourism: a configurational approach

V. Cutini
University of Pisa, Italy

Abstract

Tourism, as aimed at visiting and experiencing unknown places, obviously involves several questions regarding the use and management of urban space: where to locate bus terminals and car parking, how to guide and orient visitors in the grid of urban paths towards monuments and amenities, how to enhance their spatial comprehension, how (and where) to assist them with services and facilities, how (and where) to improve accessibility for all sorts of people, to mention the most evident. Such issues will be faced herein using a configurational approach, thus assuming the urban grid as the primary element in the phenomena along its paths, and in particular the distribution of movement and the location of activities. The configurational approach, whose reliability has been widely attested by a large number of studies in the last two decades, appears particularly suitable for supporting the touristic realization of cities, as a consequence of the fact that tourists are assumed to be non-expert urban users, generally unaware of the inner geography and of the functional features of a settlement and thus strongly moderating their behaviour from the perception and understanding of the surrounding spatial features. Furthermore, it ought to be noted that most of the historic centres of cities, renowned destinations of tourists from all over the world, are actually characterized by highly irregular and often labyrinth-like urban grids, sometimes confusing and barely accessible, so as to demand some comprehension and support during visits. The purpose of this research is to pinpoint the way a configurational approach can actually be used to improve touristic accessibility and to enhance the ease and safety in the realization of tourists visiting historic cities.

Keywords: tourism, orientation, accessibility, grid configuration.

WIT Transactions on Ecology and The Environment, Vol 187, © 2014 WIT Press
www.witpress.com, ISSN 1743-3541 (on-line)
doi:10.2495/ST140211

1   Introduction

The touristic visit of cities can actually be regarded as a peculiar urban experience, in that the presence of non-expert urban users aimed at exploring an unknown urban environment recalls and amplifies several questions concerning urban knowledge and management. First (and most obvious), how and where to locate tourist services and facilities (bus terminal and car parking, toilets, information points, etc.) in order to simplify visits and assist visitors. Then (and less obvious) how to facilitate and enhance an accurate comprehension of urban space, so as to make tourists well aware of the spatial consistency of the settlement and able to consciously choose their paths towards their chosen destinations, thus easily orienting within the urban grid. Moreover (not so obvious) how to improve urban accessibility for all sorts of people (including children, the elderly or single persons, etc.) so as to eliminate any discrimination and extend the potential range of visitors. Furthermore (and not obvious in the least) how the location and management of services and facilities can help to provide a key for the access and visit of cities, possibly modifying their intrinsic disposition. All these questions are generally faced by means of an interactional approach: given the position of tourist terminals (bus parking, railway station) and tourist attractions, the question is to allow/rationalize/optimize their mutual interaction. So far, several studies, recent and refined [1], have been carried out on these issues. Yet, this kind of approach has serious limits, in that it assumes that urban space is a mere object and can hence hardly account for the role that space itself plays in the distribution of tourist movement flows and in the location of any kind of activities. In other words, tourists are generally unaware of the inner geography and functional consistency of a settlement (distribution of activities and land use) and therefore strongly define their behaviour from what they actually perceive and understand of the surrounding spatial features; what an interactional approach can hardly appreciate, account for and manage. Moreover, in several cases tourist attractions can hardly relate to pinpoint destinations, rather appearing scattered all over a whole and wide historic context [2]. Furthermore, most of the historic cities, renowned touristic destinations, are characterized by irregular and often labyrinth-like urban grids, somehow confusing and hardly accessible, so as to strongly demand some understanding and support for the visit [3].

The perception of urban space does hence play a role, which can hardly be comprehended and managed by means of traditional interactional methods. This incapability is pretty clear in the actual accessibility and visiting potential of many Italian historic cities (Venice above others), which can hence be assumed to be persuasive examples. Other methods have been introduced and tested [4] in order to overcome such limits and to go beyond a mere deterministic approach, using multi-agent systems and agent-based modelling.

In the present research urban space comes into play. The above mentioned issues will be faced using a configurational approach, so as to assume the urban grid as the primary element in the phenomena along its paths, and in particular the distribution of movement and the location of activities [5]. It will be shown – and tested on several case studies – how a configurational approach can guide the location of services and facilities to improve urban accessibility and to enhance the ease and safety in the realisation of historic cities.

As a testing ground of such an approach, several Italian urban centres (Florence, Lucca, Pisa, Positano, San Gimignano, Siena, Venezia, Volterra), quite different from each other on any regard, were assumed as case studies, in order to highlight specific problems, to propose support tools and, even more, to apply and test a general operational method.

2 Tourism and configurational approach

The configurational approach to the analysis of urban settlements, introduced in the mid 1980s by Hillier and Hanson [6] and since then applied, improved and developed by large teams of researchers all over the world, is based on the role of the urban grid as the primary element in the phenomena occurring along its paths, in particular movement distribution and location of activities. The idea is that a portion of movement, called 'natural movement', does not depend on the presence and position of activities but only on the spatial relations between its elements, that is, the grid configuration [7]. It's the grid configuration that indicates and suggests the likely distribution of movement flows and hence the pre-condition for the use of urban land. On such basis, several operational techniques have so far been introduced and developed. The first, introduced by Hillier and Hanson in 1984 [6], is the axial analysis, which transforms the grid into a system, called an axial map, composed of the fewest and longest lines that cover all the grid, connecting all its convex spaces. Other techniques, including visibility graph analysis [8], angular analysis [9], segment analysis [10], mark point parameter analysis [11], sharing the same conceptual basis, differ from one another by the way of reducing the grid into a system, and actually present advantages and limits, so as to coexist, suitable for being used in different cases and with different purposes [12].

All those operational methods provide each element of the system with a full set of configurational variables. Among them, connectivity (the number of elements directly connected to the observed one) and integration (the mean depth of the observed element with regard to all the others) deserve particular consideration. The relevant significance of integration derives from several studies, which in the last decades have proved that it is suitable for narrowly reproducing the actual distribution of urban centrality, meant as the measure of attractiveness towards movement and activities [13]. Such notion of centrality can be said to be pure, in that it does not depend on the located activities, but is merely determined by the spatial relationships between the elements, that is by the grid configuration. In other words, the distribution of integration narrowly reproduces the distribution of the positional appeal of the spatial elements of the grid. Some peculiar features actually make the configurational approach specifically suitable for facing and overcoming the above mentioned questions regarding the touristic use of cities.

First, the assumption of the grid as the primary element of many urban phenomena actually provides the space of a settlement with a foreground role, and allows configurational analysis to face questions concerning the morphology of urban texture. In fact, configurational techniques assume the urban grid with its material consistency (from the pattern of the streets up to the shape of blocks and buildings) as their input variable, so as to provide results that regard several aspects of the working of the settlement. More concrete, such a feature makes them suitable for predicting the effects of any material transformation of the grid on a wide range of material and unimportant urban variables (distribution of flows, distribution of land values, accessibility, etc.).

The thesis is that urban space, by means of the visual perception of visitors, actually plays a role. It orients, guides and addresses the movement flows, enhances the positional value of single places while segregating and hiding others. Only a deep understanding of this role can hence support conscious and sustainable tourism. Tools for investigating this role are therefore definitely recommended: what configurational analysis precisely provides.

In further detail, the idea is that the distribution of some configurational indices can strongly support the touristic use of ancient urban centres in several respects: in order to locate information points and facilities, to select the paths to be made accessible [14], to match the visit of places with the presence and operation of local activities, so as to favour actual tourism sustainability.

3 Methodology

In this paper, three applications of configurational techniques, narrowly correlated and integrated one with another, are briefly outlined and proposed as suitable tools for supporting, improving and managing the touristic accessibility of historic centres.

A first application concerns the understanding of the degree to which an urban grid can be said to be labyrinthian, which actually confuses and disorients any visitor, making him need guidance and support. This aspect will hence allow us to understand (and comply with) the need for tourism assistance and support that an urban grid actually requires. Another application will then regard the location choice of services and facilities, in order to make accessibility cope with the actual distribution of movement and visitors. This aspect will therefore be aimed at rationalizing and optimizing resources for visits and tourism. The last one concerns the possibility of managing the distribution of touristic flows, influencing it by means of the location of touristic services, thus defining the distribution determined by the grid configuration.

Each of those three applications clearly focuses on urban space, recognizing it as the primary element in urban phenomena, including touristic visits to urban places and attractions. It's then the physical space of the settlement, assumed to be the main input variable of the model that is expected to provide information on its touristic accessibility. More generally, the city is examined on its availability to be visited, insofar as it results from the position, shape and relationships of its paths; as shown in the following.

A first, and somehow rough, indicator of the level of confusion and disorientation that a grid is actually likely to provide is the mean value of connectivity of its elements. Since connectivity varies from 1 (elements with a unique connection, that is cul-de-sac elements) and n-1 (element connected to all the other elements of the grid, being n its total consistency), a low value of connectivity is expected to stand for a strong presence of obliged paths, thus poorly depending on space perception. Conversely, high values of connectivity suggest a wide range of path choices, according to the perception of intermediate destinations. In this regard, the labyrinth (Figure 1) and the panopticon can be seen as opposite paradigms. Each step along a labyrinth is governed by the preceding one and governs the next step, no matter the destination, which cannot be seen. Conversely, each path on a panopticon is composed of a one-step path, from a source to the destination, which is in full view. The mean value of connectivity in a labyrinth is $C_M = 2(n-1)/n$, varying from 1 to 2 and approaching 2 as n grows, while in a panopticon $C_M = n-1$, thus approaching n. A panopticon is not really transferable into an urban grid, but can be somehow approximated by the fortress-city of Palmanova (Figure 1), provided with $C_M = 20.9$.

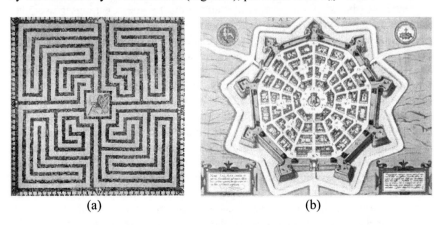

(a)   (b)

Figure 1:   The labyrinth (a) and Palmanova (b), opposite archetypes of intelligibility.

A further indicator of the same feature is the determination coefficient R^2 of the correlation of integration versus connectivity, in the literature generally called intelligibility. A high value of intelligibility means that the most connected spaces are also the most integrated, and hence that the more accessible spaces give access to a larger number of other spaces. Recalling the above mentioned references, a labyrinth is provided with a very low (almost zero) intelligibility value, while in Palmanova $R^2 = 0.98$.

A third indicator is then the correspondence of local integration with global integration, realised by the R^2 coefficient of radius 3 integration (computed taking into account the lines within a local area) versus radius n (extended all over the urban area). The idea is that the local spatial perception actually corresponds to the global geography of the settlement, and is hence suitable for guiding the paths all over the grid. Once more, the findings confirm such assumption, with $R^2 = 0.02\text{-}0.04$ in a labyrinth and $R^2 = 1.00$ in Palmanova.

Summing up, the three parameters indicated above can be used in order to evaluate the level of intelligibility with which an urban settlement is intrinsically provided, as a consequence of its spatial features, and hence the actual need of support and assistance to users and visitors. This application could be named 'configuration analysis for grid comprehension'.

The second application proposed herein is aimed at supporting the location of services and facilities, so that they correspond to the actual distribution of tourist movement flows. Generally, this question is faced by taking into account the specific position of tourist attractions as well as the location of transport terminals (railway stations, bus and car parking). Yet two aspects ought to be considered. First, tourism attractions rarely are concentrated and punctiform, so as to be regarded as pinpoint destinations. More often they are uniformly scattered all over the grid of the historic centre, so that it's actually difficult (when not actually impossible) to regard them as single pivot points in pedestrian touristic movement. Even in the particular case of Pisa, characterized by the presence of the singular worldwide attraction of the Leaning Tower, its assumption as a single terminal of movement paths could cause a failure to capture the actual visitor flows, as well as disregarding the whole historic context that surrounds it and the tourist attractions within the ancient town-walls. Something that unfortunately does occur in Pisa in the present distribution of touristic services. Within a historic city, therefore, the location of touristic services would better be located with reference to the distribution of natural movements (depending on the configuration of the grid) rather than on the mere basis of the position of a single attraction. It's then the distribution of the configurational indices of centrality that appears likely to reproduce the distribution of movement, and hence the indication for the location of services and facilities. Moreover, the same distribution of centrality can also provide a valuable hint concerning the location of touristic transport terminals and services, citing them (for instance, bus and car terminals, or public transport lines) near the most crowded areas of the settlement. This application could be named 'configuration analysis for grid accessibility' and also provides indications on the relationships between the distribution of natural movements and touristic flows, useful for managing the coexistence of tourism and ordinary economic activities.

The third application is subtler and apparently nearly opposite to the preceding one. It uses this approach not to more efficiently locate touristic services with reference to the touristic flows, but to locate touristic services (in particular transport terminals) in order to guide and manage the distribution of touristic flows. It is subtler, in that it is not aimed at enhancing the accessibility of areas visited by tourists, but at managing their magnitude, defining the movement distribution resulting from the configurational analysis of the grid. More generally, the use of configurational techniques highlights the distribution of natural movements, determined by the grid configuration, which will not overlap touristic movements, depending on the position of transport terminals, as sources, and touristic attractions, as destinations. The location of sources appears to be a tool for managing the relationships between natural movement and touristic flows (either making them coincide or separating them), therefore the relationship between the touristic realization of cities and the working of local activities. In other words, the grid configuration involves the distribution of touristic flows, which can be modified (for any reason, for instance, to guide tourists towards hidden or neglected areas) by the location of tourism services. For a better comprehension of this issue, a historic city can be usefully conceptualized as an open air museum. The internal organization of museums and exhibitions spaces has been widely studied and discussed, in order to increase their accessibility and to improve the realization of the collected pieces, and space syntax techniques have been tested and proved suitable for supporting it [15–17]. The obvious difference is that our open air museums generally don't allow the displacement of attractions, so that the only variables in their arrangement are the spatial grid and the location of services. That is precisely the purpose of this last application, which could be named 'configuration analysis for grid management'.

4 Case studies

The three operations so far presented were applied to several historic cities, corresponding to well-known Italian touristic destinations, taken as case studies. Here the outcome of such experimentations, with reference to the cases of Pisa, Lucca and Venice, will be presented and briefly discussed. What makes them suitable for a specific discussion is the fact that they are approximately a similar size (both physical and demographic) and conversely have radically different spatial features, with regard to the issue of accessibility and orientation. Such differences arise from the results of the grid configuration analysis, which will be here presented with reference to the three applications outlined above.

First, concerning the configurational analysis for grid comprehension, a comparison of the three parameters taken to reproduce the level of intelligibility is presented in Table 1, and appears worth discussing.

Table 1: Values of the three proposed parameters in Lucca, Pisa and Venice.

	Lucca	Pisa	Venice
C_M	5.53	7.43	2.71
$I_n/C \ R^2$	0.38	0.46	0.01
$I_3/I_n \ R^2$	0.64	0.63	0.06

The results clearly show that the two cases of Pisa and Venice can be taken to be paradigmatic. On the basis of the resulting values, Pisa appears highly understandable and Venice, on the contrary, markedly not understandable so as to confuse tourists and unfamiliar visitors. With regard to the other cities, Lucca appears in an intermediate position, in that all the parameter results are included between them. For a detailed view, the exponential correlation of connectivity versus integration is here represented in Figure 2, so as to highlight the differences above.

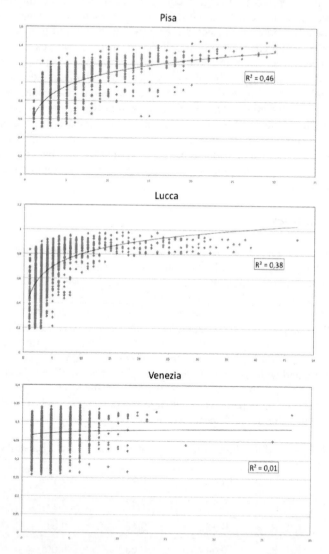

Figure 2: Connectivity versus global integration (intelligibility) in Pisa, Lucca and Venice.

Also the configuration analysis for grid accessibility provides interesting results when applied to the cities above. In the case of Pisa, shown in Figure 3, the lines providing the highest integration values (over the 95th percentile, comprising the so-called 'integration core') shape a rough cross centred on the main bridge (Ponte di Mezzo) and oriented north–south. This was proved [18] to narrowly correspond to the actual distribution of pedestrian movement.

Figure 3:   The distribution of global integration value in Pisa. The position of the Leaning Tower is circled.

The main attraction of Piazza dei Miracoli appears in contrast to be in a poorly integrated position. This result highlights two problems with tourism in Pisa. On one hand, tourists generally struggle to find the Leaning Tower, their main destination, as it is beyond the most crowded paths. On the other hand, most tourists that annually visit the Tower, reach it by coach or private car, and remain outside the historic centre of Pisa, thus missing its activities and disregarding a number of prominent attractions. In this regard the case of Venice (Figure 4) is quite different. Here the crowded touristic paths (mainly connecting Santa Lucia railway station, the Rialto and Piazza San Marco) appear to follow the routes to the centre, and visitors' movements hence coincide with the natural ones. These results show that, in Pisa, development in touristic information is strongly advised in order to address pedestrian flows towards the main attractions. In Venice, on the contrary, services are mainly demanded along the mentioned touristic axis, and services are advised in order to suggest and propose alternative targets as well as to orient visitors away from the main touristic flows [18].

Despite the differences so far discussed, in all the cases the use of configuration analysis for grid management is advised, for different reasons. In Venice the location of services (in particular transport services, such as *vaporetto* or *traghetto*) can usefully define the distribution of touristic flows so as to involve other destinations apart from the traditional targets of Piazza San Marco and the Rialto.

Figure 4:   The distribution of global integration value in Venice. The position of Piazza San Marco is circled.

In Pisa the present location of coach terminals and car parking, on the western edge of the city, actually confines most tourists to merely visiting the Tower, thus ignoring the remaining areas of the inner centre. Shifting that location could drive touristic flows to coincide with the distribution of natural movement, thus involving the whole historic city. In Lucca, which actually lacks a prominent touristic focal point, attractions are scattered all over the historic fabric. From a configurational point of view, Lucca appears (Figure 5) to be characterized by a general outward shifting of centrality, which in the last decades has gone, leaving the historic city to include the sprawled areas around the urban edge so as to progressively empty its inner centre. Here the purpose should be to promote easy access to the urban area encircled within the town walls, increasing the presence of parking and transport terminals in their close proximity. The density of touristic flows are hence expected to favour the persistency of economic activities and the survival of the ancient centre itself.

5   Conclusions

The results so far can be briefly summarized as follows.

In general a configurational approach appears to be a valuable key for taking into account the role of urban space in tourism management. The results of our case studies have proved that it is a reliable and suitable tool for supporting,

Figure 5:   The distribution of global integration value in Lucca.

improving and managing the touristic accessibility of historic centres. Furthermore, the configurational state of an urban grid concisely reproduces its actual intelligibility, thus proving that there is a real need for tourist information and services. Moreover, the distribution of configurational indices can support the supply and location of information points and facilities, making them able to cope with the actual distribution of tourist flows. Furthermore, it can also be useful for managing touristic usage of historic cities in order to match the visit of places with the presence and operation of local activities, so as to favour actual tourism sustainability.

References

[1]   Lew, A. & McKercher, B., Modeling tourist movements. A local destination analysis. In: *Annals of Tourist Research*, vol. 33, pp. 403-423, 2006.

[2]   Blank, U. & Petkovich, M., The metropolitan area: a multifaceted travel destination complex. In: *Tourism Planning and Development Issues*, Washington University, pp. 393-405, 1987.

[3]   Cutini, V. & Rabino, G., Searching for Ariadne's thread. Some remarks on urban resilience and orientation. In: *TEMA*, vol. 5, pp. 7-22, 2012.

[4]   Rabino, G. & Caglioni, M., Ontology and M.A.S. of pedestrian behavior: the case study of tourists in Lucca. In: *COST Action TU0801 Workshop*, Skopje, Macedonia, 2012.

[5]   Hillier, B., *Space is the Machine: a Configurational Theory of Architecture*, Cambridge University Press: Cambridge (UK), 1996.
[6]   Hillier, B. & Hanson, J., *The Social Logic of Space*, Cambridge University Press: Cambridge (UK), 1984.
[7]   Hillier, B., Penn, A., Hanson, J., Grajevski, T. & Xu, J., Natural movement: or, configuration and attraction in urban pedestrian movement. In: *Environment and Planning B, Planning and Design*, vol. 20, pp. 67-81, 1993.
[8]   Turner, A., Doxa, M., O'Sullivan, D. & Penn, A., From isovists to visibility graphs: a methodology for the analysis of architectural space. In: *Environment and Planning B: Planning and Design*, vol. 28, pp. 103-121, 2001.
[9]   Turner, A., Angular Analysis. In: *Proceedings of the 3rd Space Syntax Symposium*, Atlanta (GA), 7-11 May 2001, Alfred Tauban College of Architecture: University of Michigan, pp. 30.1-30.11, 2001.
[10]   Hillier, B. & Iida, S., Network and psychological effects in urban movement. In: Cohn, A. G. & Mark, D. M. (eds) *Spatial Information Theory: COSIT 2005, Lecture Notes in Computer Science*, vol. 3693, 475-490, Berlin: Springer-Verlag, 2005.
[11]   Cutini, V., Petri, M. & Santucci, A., From axial maps to Mark Point Parameter Analysis (Ma.P.P.A.). A G.I.S. implemented method to automate configurational analysis. In: *Computational Science and its Applications – ICCSA 2004 – Lecture Notes in Computer Science*, vol. 3044, pp. 1107-1116, 2004.
[12]   Cutini, V., Grilling the Grid: a Non-Ultimate (Nor Objective) Report on the Configurational Approach to Urban Phenomena. In: *The Dynamics of Complex Urban Systems*, Physica-Verlag: Heidelberg, pp. 163-183, 2007.
[13]   Cutini, V., Managing Accessibility – The Configurational Approach to the Inclusive Design of Urban Spaces. In: *Journal of Civil Engineering and Architecture*, vol. 6, pp. 444-456, 2012.
[14]   Tzortzi, K., Space. Interconnecting Museology and Architecture. In: *The Journal of Space Syntax*, vol. 2, pp. 26-53, 2011.
[15]   Hillier, B. & Tzortzi, K., Space Syntax: the language of museum space. In: McDonald, S., (Ed.) *A Companion to Museum Studies*, pp. 282-301, Blackwell Publishing Ltd.: Oxford (UK), 2006.
[16]   Tzortzi, K., Museum building design and exhibition layout: patterns of interaction. In: *Proceedings of the 6th Space Syntax Symposium*, pp. 72.1-72.16, 2007.
[17]   Cutini, V., Centrality and Land Use: Three Case Studies on the Configurational Hypothesis. In: *Cybergeo, Revue Européenne de Geographie*, n. 188, 26 mars 2001.
[18]   Coda, A., *L'analisi configurazionale a supporto dei servizi turistici. Una sperimentazione su Venezia*, Master of Science Thesis in Environmental and Land Planning Engineering, Politechnic of Milan, 2012.

The perception of gastronomic events within the framework of sustainable tourism development

N. Pavia[1], J. Gržinić[2] & T. Floričić[2]
[1]*Faculty of Tourism and Hospitality Management,*
University of Rijeka, Croatia
[2]*Faculty of Economics and Tourism,*
Juraj Dobrila University of Pula, Croatia

Abstract

Recognising modern tourist demands, tourist destinations perceive comparative advantages and potential available resources, placing them in the tourist market through selective tourist products and events. "How are gastronomic events perceived within the framework of sustainable tourist development?" is the research problem area, which leads to the definition of the paper's purpose and goal. It relates to the assessment of perception of the importance of organisation of gastronomic events within the framework of sustainable tourist destination development by the local producers of original tourist products and the local population.

The research includes an assessment of how many gastronomic events intensify gastronomic tourism and how they valorise the pre and post tourist season, which the Strategy of Development of Croatian and Istrian Tourism recognises as the terms which must be touristically intensified, strategically enriching the tourist offer. In the paper, the social component of sustainability is also perceived through the attitudes of gastronomic event visitors.

The research, which affirmed new scientific knowledge, was conducted by means of survey and interview methodology. For data processing, quantitative methods of analysis, synthesis, comparison, meta-analysis and other scientific and research methods were used. The generated knowledge confirms the purpose of the paper, which is channelled towards the determination of the importance of promotion of original products at gastronomic events, in accordance with the principles of sustainability. The research was conducted at the event Days of Fresh Olive Oil in Vodnjan, which was organised as a sustainable gastronomic tourist event.

Keywords: tourist event, social sustainability, gastronomic tourism, destination offer.

1 Introduction

The cultural landscape represents a spatial and natural correlation of the environment and human activity. Recognising the values of the cultural landscape as the world cultural heritage represents the recognition and preservation of a specific spatial "memory" of a particular way of living and an important part of social identity and quality of life of a community, which is in line with the concept of sustainable development.

The Master Plan of tourism development of Istria as a strategic document of future development stresses the importance of preservation of natural and cultural resources as a fundamental comparative advantage and a key element of the "brand" of Istria as a tourist destination. The Plan envisages improvement of the sector according to the natural (by 30%) and socio-cultural (by 40%) criteria, with the aim to achieve the vision of creation of the "tourist brand" of Istria as a "Green refuge of the Mediterranean" [1].

The Master Plan of tourism development of Istria attempts to provide diversity of offers for different guests, extend the season to nine months, raise the local population's quality of life, preserve the local culture, save the clean environment, open possibilities for a higher guest expenditure and develop high quality tourism, oriented towards the selective forms of offer (gastronomic tourism).

Given the recent uncontrolled development of mass tourism in the area of the Croatian Adriatic, thus equally in Istria, the total tourist destination offer is generally unrecognisable; unified segments in the sense of commercial offer (souvenirs), entertainment (music, dance, sports) and gastronomy (international cuisine) dominate. The same is related to the weakening of the cultural identity of the environment where guests come, uncritical acceptance of foreign values and models and misunderstandings between the local population and visitors.

The conducted research will examine how successful the model of valorisation of gastronomic resources and cultural heritage through traditional meals and provisions is.

2 Methodology

As an autochthonous provision, olive oil is the foundation of traditional gastronomy. It can be valorised through tourism by means of organised events, thus contributing to the development of sustainable cultural tourism.

For the purposes of testing of the hypothesis, three researches were conducted, the results of which synergically contribute to the derivation of conclusions. The first research is pertinent to examination of attitudes of the exhibitors – producers of olive oil at the event, followed by the research into the attitudes of event visitors and, finally, an interview was conducted with the President of the Hostelry Guild, which implements traditional gastronomy and provisions in tourist expenditure through the restaurant business. In the paper preparation, methods of data collection and creative thinking techniques, as well as other scientific and research methods were used. The statistical method includes processing and illustration of statistical information while meta-analysis and the historical method were used in the analysis of numerous scientific and professional works, with the aim of importance evaluation of sustainable tourism offer and events that support their marketing.

Research methods also include interviews, focus groups and questionnaires. Event exhibitors and tourists were asked to define the current state of development and to predict future potentials. Authors' arguments and predictions are also presented in the paper. Sustainable events that promote sustainable products are impetus for a qualitative response to globalisation processes (synergy of localisation, globalisation and sustainable development). Methodology is oriented to the research of the concept of sociological sustainability and the eco-oriented business philosophy on the repositioning of Istria tourist destination.

3 Conceptualisation of the social aspect of sustainable development and tourist valorisation of events: theory and literature review

There are relatively very few event researches in Croatia. Among the most important researches, chapters should be identified in books which, among others, clarify the phenomenon and significance of events in the improvement of tourist offer of receptive regions (Blažević [2], Pančić-Kombol [3]). In addition to these publications, also important are papers on the significance of particular sports events for tourism (Zekić [4], Skoko and Vukasović [5], Pranić et al. [6]), festivals in the Croatian part of the Adriatic coast (Škrbić Alempijević et al. [7]), as well as the influence and significance of urban festivals (Piškor [8], Kikaš et al. [9]).

Event tourism is the term used for all forms of tourist traffic motivated by the staging of various events (Vukonić and Čavlek [10]) and it includes visits to all planned events which have a tourist purpose and form a part of the attraction basis of a specific destination. There are eight main types of events: cultural, political, economic, entertainment, scientific and educational, sports competitions, recreational and private events. Getz [11] describes that cultural events include festivals, carnivals, commemorations and entertainment events include concerts and award presentations and economic events, trade fairs and markets, business gatherings and sale exhibitions. Festivals are the most frequent events according to Presbury and Edwards [12]. They can have different forms from cultural to gastronomy (wine, olive oil) and attendance may vary within the range of between around one hundred and several thousand visitors (Gelder and

Robinson [13]). Events are associated with the development of the special interest tourism and represent strength in the SWOT analysis of the tourism development of Istria (Stipanović *et al.* [14]).

The definitions of sustainable development as a concept which emerged at the turn of the 20th century are numerous and, in general terms, it can be defined according to WCED (1987) as "the development that meets the needs of the present without compromising the ability of future generations to meet their own needs" [15]. From each individual, the sustainable development policy requires sufficient responsibility to recognise what could be done and achieved once that individual recognises that his own interests are inseparably connected with the interests of the community, argue Pavić and Rogošić [16].

Sustainable development includes the change in the structure of global production and expenditure, while not disturbing eco systems. Črnjar [17] explains that it establishes a positive relationship between tourism development and the protection of the environment. It is the capacity of the environmental sustainability which determines the permitted scope of development, avoiding occurrence of unacceptable ecological and social impacts, by which it becomes a significant ecological and economic norm of natural resource management.

The sustainable tourism development was created as a counter-balance to mass, consumer and unsustainable tourism, whose goal is profit and that to the detriment of the local community environment and tradition. Modern trends of development of tourism of Istria, as a leading Croatian tourist region, rely on new technologies that provide lucrative marketing and on the concept of sustainable tourism and social responsibility (Grzinic and Floricic [18]). They include resource management in the manner that basic economic, social and aesthetical requirements are satisfied, at the same time preserving the cultural integrity, fundamental ecological processes and biodiversity defines Berger [19]. Klarić [20] explains that sustainable tourism development uses natural and cultural heritage to increase the number of visitors and profits, but in a way that it is saved also for future generations.

Socio-cultural sustainability represents a concept in which the population is the main factor of the geospatial system. It is characterised by the following existential functions: dwelling and life in the community, work, supply, education and use of free time. Črnjar [17] believes that education is becoming a global educational industry and science, prerequisite and starter of sustainable development. Developing tourism in tourist destinations impacts increase of local awareness about the financial value of natural and cultural resources. Developing it in sustainable way stimulates the feeling of pride for local and traditional heritage, as well as the interest in its preservation.

Considering the components of social sustainability, Klarić [20] lists: changes in the structure of population, migration movements, labour problems, change of cultural identity and quality of tourist experience. In tourist areas, the local population is employed in the tourism industry and other associated service businesses. Through the employment function, social development is initiated by means of creation of work posts, reallocation of income and removal of poverty and the destination management is incorporated in various destination subsystems in the sense of linking of economic subjects and tourist offer (Magas [21]). Within the framework of sociological sustainability, cultural sustainability is developed, which includes the method of cultural heritage utilisation and management. In defining cultural and historical heritage, according to UNESCO, Jelinčić [22] lists: monuments, groups of buildings and localities of historical, aesthetic, archaeological, scientific, ethnological or anthropological value. The main goals of cultural tourism include: prevention and preservation of local cultural heritage, encouragement of quality and diversity of cultural products, promotion of integrative culture and tourism policy, capitalisation of local particularities and advantages and assurance of quality of life and respect of local population's cultural identity. Synergical partnership among tourism and all professions dealing in protection and preservation of material and non-material cultural heritage is important for the sustainable development of cultural tourism. This also includes valorisation of folklore performances, autochthonous gastronomy, revitalisation and renewal of traditional crafts and traditional construction, as well as the overall cultural heritage.

Tourists have direct contact with unique social, historical and heritage characteristics of the destination they visit, as well as with its local lifestyle, which assists them with their perception of the present with a more complex understanding.

Sustainable tourism must be harmonised with the local community, i.e. the population of the locality in which tourist activity takes place (Swarbrooke [23], Weaver [24]) as well as sustainable management of festivals, congresses and events (Presbury and Edwards [12], Musgrave [25]).

Gastronomic diversity of particular tourist destinations and climates is subject to geographical and climatic conditions, historical circumstances and specific, radically different, customs and traditions of the people who live in particular areas. Križman Pavlović [26] quotes gastronomy as one of the variables which determine the tourist destination image as the fundamental receptive tourist unit.

The basis of Istrian gastronomy within the framework of the Mediterranean gastronomy is extremely healthy, natural ingredients, coming from ecological zones which are preserved and spared from excessive industrialisation and chemical treatments. Gastronomic elements, i.e. dishes and drink which are identified with the Istrian peninsula are based on fruit and ingredients from the sea and vegetable cultures characteristic for the Mediterranean climate, with strong presence of aromatic herbs and wild growing plants, such as asparagus or truffles. As Istria abounds both in autochthonous produce and characteristic specialities, the potential for their valorisation through thematic gastronomic events has been recognised. Some of them are: International Prosciutto Fair, Days of Istrian Asparagus, Mushroom Days and Istrian Truffle Days/Weekend, With Sausage to Europe, Oleum Olivarum and New Olive Oil Days. Illustration of tourist overnights, realised in the pre and post season periods follows, as well as the implication of importance of their intensification aimed at a more successful tourism development.

As autochthonous provisions form a base for the preparation of traditional folk dishes, they are also valorised through events, as a segment of non-material cultural heritage of the Istrian area: Festival of Istrian Manestra in Gračišće, Valbandon 'spod čripnje (dishes prepared under a baking lid "čripnja"), Polenta Festival and others. Events are usually held in the periods of tourist pre and post season and are the starters of rural tourism of municipalities in the sense of development of agrotourism households, traditional restaurants and taverns, as well as other selective forms of sustainable tourism.

Table 1:   Tourist overnights in Istria in pre and post season in the years 2007, 2008 and 2009.

Month	Years			Index	
	2007	2008	2009	2007/09	2008/09
March–April	601,439	405,893	492,802	122.0	83.0
May	1,098,884	1,305,625	1,105,969	99.4	118.1
September	2,049,774	2,001,787	2,092,101	97.9	96.0
October	310,254	352,844	331,991	94.0	106.3
Total	4,060,351	4,076,149	4,022,863	101.0	101.3
Overnights – Istria	17.63 mil	17.96 mil	18.13 mil	-	-
Share in overnights in Istria	23.05%	22.69%	22.19	-	-

Source: Authors' processing according to: Tourism of Istria in figures, County of Istria Administrative Section of Tourism, Poreč, September 2010, original data of the State Institute of Statistics, communications, [27].

While reviewing the out of season periods, considerable oscillations can be noticed in the pre-season periods of one year as opposed to another. This is the result of a changeable calendar of religious holidays in Western Europe. When considering the total number of indicators, it is evident that pre-season and post-season months of previous years were slightly better, which points to the need for improvement of offers by means of creative tourism projects and events. In these projects, the solution can be seen for an increase in the shares of the off-season months, as well as the total tourist season overnights.

4   Findings and discussion

Olive cultivation and production of olive oil in Istria marks a three thousand year-old tradition and boasts numerous monuments and artifacts from the Roman period. The remains of olive oil processing plants from the area of the National Park Brijuni and from Barbariga record evidence that olive oil was once produced for Roman emperors [28].

Today, Croatian olive cultivation includes 30,000 hectares of olive groves, of which 98 percent is privately owned and where 5 million olive trees are cultivated from a total of 60 acclimatised sorts. The annual olive crop of

38,000 tonnes of olives is processed in 180 specialised olive oil processing plants, yielding 51 hectolitres of oil [29]. Istria has 5,000 hectares of olive groves with 1,050,000 olive trees and listing in the Flos Olei Guide of best olive oils in the world speaks of the exceptional quality of the product [30]. The basic quality parameters of extra virgin olive oil, as the best, refer to the totality of properties and functions which can satisfy consumers' needs. They are free fatty acids, sensor grade and so-called peroxide number, K-numbers. The republic of Croatia adopted European Union regulations pursuant to the standards of the quality of olive oil and table olives; categories and market quality standards, as well as physical and chemical and sensory properties, are defined.

Olive cultivation and olive oil are promoted as an autochthonous business activity and a trade mark and olive harvest and oil production is increasingly becoming an attractive tourist product. Modern guests look for nature and want to be in touch with it, avoiding excessively built-up destinations of mass tourism, seeking exclusivity of experience which selective forms of tourism provide. Croatia aims to be perceived as a country of healthy, Mediterranean cuisine. In the aspiration to broaden knowledge about the gastronomic significance and healing properties of olives and olive oil, as well as to encourage gastronomic creations based on autochthonous resources, it is important to continuously advance experience about the gastronomic usability of olives. Ecologically produced olive oil, together with other ecologically produced autochthonous food, is being included in Croatian tourist offer and represents the potential for its comparative advantage. In this way, contributions are made to scientific and professional knowledge and to a higher quality and imaginative gastronomic offer of hostelry facilities.

Fresh Olive Oil Days is an event which takes place in mid-November in Vodnjan, lasting three days. In 2013, the 9th event was held, organised by the Town of Vodnjan, some eighty exhibitors, mostly from Istria, were presented with over two hundred olive oils and wine, brandy, honey, beer, truffles and numerous other autochthonous products. This represents growth in comparison with the last year and indicates that Fresh Olive Oil Days are becoming an important event for promotion of olive oil value in the region. Several thousand people visited the event and, on top of educational tasting sessions, took part in the gastro exhibition, competition, review, workshops and panel sections related to the offer of olive oil and other autochthonous Istrian products. At the event, also some innovative gastronomic products, based on olives, were presented: olive jam, chocolate with olives, desserts with olive oil, which have the potential to develop and be affirmed through sustainable development of tourism.

Within the event, a free educational tour by the tourist train 'Art and Oil Tour' also took place. It included visits to the mushroom exhibition, exhibition of four Vodnjan artists under the title 4in1 at the Town Palace and olive oil tasting at the San Lorenzo olive oil processing plant.

It was estimated through the media that the event contributes to the promotion of the values of olive oil and its use in everyday life and that, at the same time, it extends the tourist season, both in Istria and Croatia. The perception of sociological and economic sustainability as an impalpable value contributes to tourism development and attracts knowledgeable consumers to the destinations of sustainable and socially responsible tourism.

The study was conducted on the sample of 27 exhibitors at the event New Olive Oil Days, which was held in Southern Istria, in the Town of Vodnjan, positioned as the centre of Istrian olive cultivation. Out of the total sample, 19 exhibitors (70%) were entrepreneurs, olive oil producers, while 8 exhibitors (30%) presented gastronomic products related to olive oil and utensils made of olive tree wood as an autochthonous raw material. Development of olive cultivation is the interest sphere for all, as well as its valorisation through sustainable tourism.

As producers of olive oil, the exhibitors are placed into three categories: small, medium and large and the data in the sample points to the fact that, regardless of the company size, they valorise the promotion and placement of that autochthonous product through tourism.

Table 2: Participation of olive oil producers at the event according to total production.

Annual production	Number =N	%
Small producers – up to 1,000 litres of oil	10	52.6
Medium-size producers – up to 2,000 litres of oil	4	21.0
Large producers – over 2,000 litres of oil	5	26.3
Total	19	100.0

The research of the frequency of participation in gastronomic events shows that 7.4% of exhibitors took part in the event for the first time, 3.7% of exhibitors took part occasionally, while 88.8% of producers take part in the event every year.

To the question on production of varietal oils, as differentiation of quality and exclusiveness of specific sorts of olives, 63% of exhibitors confirmed the production of different sorted oils, while 37% of producers do not manufacture varietal oils, which is possibly conditioned by small production or by on-recognisability of the importance of product differentiation itself.

Table 3: Assessment of the influence of event organisation on gastronomic tourism sustainable development.

Question	YES		NO		TOTAL
	N	%	N	%	%
Do you think that the event encourages gastronomic tourism?	27	100	0	0	100
Do you think that olive oils are well presented through tourist offer?	21	78	6	22	100
Would you be prepared to invest in tourist marketing of olive oil?	25	93	2	7	100

In assessment of market recognisability of varietal olive oils as gastronomic brands, 70.4% of exhibitors believe that only certain consumers recognise and choose varietal oils, 22.32% of them believe that varietal oils are a recognisable gastronomic brand, while 7.4% of exhibitors believe that varietal oils are not recognisable. In consideration of the potential of valorisation of varietal oils as a gastronomic brand which contributes to sustainable tourism development, 26% of respondents recognise the possibility of development and 74% believe that the potential for this is great.

The analysis of the obtained results records that all exhibitors at the event believe that it stimulates the development of gastronomic tourism. To the question whether they believe that olive oils are well presented through tourist offer, 78% of them assess their tourist promotion as successful and 93% of respondents express their preparedness to further invest in tourist marketing of olive oil.

Aiming at getting a complex and comprehensive picture and assessment of the importance of gastronomic event organisation within the framework of sustainable development of destination tourism, attitudes of the event New Olive Oil Days in Vodnjan have also been examined. Using the random sample method, 60 visitors, of which 20% were tourists and 80% were local folk were asked the relevant questions. This points to the facts that the frequency of tourists in the post-season period (November) is low and that there is room for a stronger tourist promotion in the emissive markets. This data also points to the fact that the local population considers olive oil, as an autochthonous product, to be interesting, recognising the potential for its tourist valorisation and, at the same time, speaks of the awareness of the local population about their own values which need to be valorised, preserved and further sustainably developed.

The results of the research in the frequency of visits to gastronomic events show that 13.3% of respondents were visiting the event for the first time, 70% of them visit occasionally, while 16.7% visit the event every year. To the question about the recognition of varietal oils, 60% of respondents answered affirmatively to the question and, by further research into their opinion about the recognition of oils as a gastronomic brand in the market, 36.6 % of them believe that oils are not recognisable, 53.4% of the respondents occasionally choose and use varietal oils, while 10% recognise and specifically choose exact sorts of olive oil. This points to the fact that there is room for education of both tourists and local population within the framework of sociological sustainability. To the question about the influence of this gastronomic event on sustainable tourism of Istria, 96.7% of respondents believe that the event stimulates its development. In consideration of the current and future potential for the development of olive oil as a segment of sustainable tourist offer, 93.3% of respondents believe that olive oils are well presented through tourist offer, but that there is still further potential for the development of olive oil as a tourist brand. The share of 76.7% of respondents recognise certain opportunities for development, while 20% of respondents believe that the possibility for development is great, which represents the basis of future marketing activity and work in tourist markets with the aim to intensify sustainable valorisation and placement of the autochthonous product through tourism.

The third part of the research into the importance of organisation of gastronomic events for the purposes of sustainable tourist valorisation was conducted with the President of the Croatian Restaurant Guild [31], as an umbrella organisation which promotes autochthonous gastronomic offer in hostelry facilities, recording the economic impacts of its placement in tourism. The following attitudes and opinions were expressed:

- Istrian gastronomic specialities have been neglected and are not well presented in foreign markets; there is room for numerous marketing activities, events and different types of education.
- The rank of the quality level of Istrian gastronomic specialities is the following: (1) Olive oil, (2) Malvazija – Istrian white wine, (3) Prosciutto, (4) Cheese, (5) Truffles, (6) Manestra soup, (7) Homemade pasta (gnocchi/fusi). Poorer promotional activities and non-recognisability of the Istrian dishes are also conditioned by the organisation of restaurants in Istria, undermining of dishes and their classification into the offer of taverns and inns. This points to the need for education of hostelry workers themselves on the potentials.
- In principle, guests do not know and do not recognise traditional dishes in advance, although they accept the offer with quality presentation. They are also interested in tasting innovative dishes, as a fusion of traditional dishes and modern gastronomy.
- Although they recognise the quality of autochthonous provisions, they are not prepared to pay a slightly higher price for quality. This also refers to the choice of home-produced prosciutto or cheese from Istria, or the choice of a special, cold pressed extra virgin olive oil. The tolerance of the difference of price is a maximum of 10%.
- According to the perception of tourists, the Istrian cuisine and traditional provisions are seen as being of a high quality, ecologically acceptable and "healthy" (natural methods of cultivation, chemicals free).
- Istrian restaurants are not ready or educated to better evaluate autochthonous provisions in the tourist gastronomic offer. This is due to the non-existence of a common strategy for the restaurant business and systematic education of hostelry workers and DMC companies.
- The potential for branding and profiling of tourist destinations by means of sustainable projects (events), based on gastronomic offer, has been evident. Some examples are Vodnjan – Olive oil, Umag – "švoje" (sole fish) and tomato, Novigrad – mussels. The possibility of affecting the change of tourist destination image by implementation of innovative sustainable projects based on gastronomy by means of intensive marketing in both domestic and emissive markets, education of local population and tourists, as well as by the initiative of public and private partnerships, has been recognised.

- By the new innovative offer, organised on the principles of sustainability, new segments of consumers who appreciate and affirm new values in the tourist destination are attracted.

5 Conclusion

The strategic direction of development sustainability in Istria is defined as declarative and implementable at all executive levels. In accordance with the current long-term Croatian Tourism Development Strategy by 2010, based on sustainable development, all County of Istria administrative departments, as well as County developmental agencies with 94 implemented projects, support sustainable development, environmental protection, rural development, encourage small and medium entrepreneurships, tourism, culture and civil society.

The Regional Operational Plan of Istria represents an action plan for achievement of sustainability of tourism in Istria and is founded upon the bases and principles of sustainable tourism, namely: emphasising of the cultural and historical authenticity of Istria, one of the leading destinations of Croatian tourism; environmental protection of the Northern Adriatic, with encouragement of development of selective forms of tourism and promotion of the economic development by means of organising tourist visits to the authenticities of Istria.

When considering sustainable developmental directions, the potential for the valorisation of autochthonous gastronomy in the system of social and economic sustainability, has been evidenced. Valorisation is used to achieve economic benefits for producers and hostelry workers as economic subjects and, sociologically speaking, autochthonous products and dishes remain preserved in their original environment and form. The developmental potential of gastronomic valorisation, researched on the example of the event New Olive Oil Days, points to the need for strategic investment in the marketing and development of entrepreneurship with the aim to intensify future placement and promotion.

References

[1] THR in association with Horwath Consulting, *Master Plan of Tourism (2004–2012) Istria, Final Document,* Zagreb, 2003.
[2] Blažević, I., *Turizam Istre.* Zagreb: SGDH, 1984.
[3] Pančić-Kombol, T., *Kulturno nasljeđe i turizam*, Radovi Zavoda za znanstveni rad – Varaždin, No. 16–17 Listopad 2006.
[4] Zekić, J., Univerzijada '87. – drugi ilirski preporod, *Časopis za suvremenu povijest*, 39 (2), pp. 99–118, 2007.
[5] Skoko, B., Vukasović, I., Organiziranje međunarodnih sportskih događaja kao promotivni i ekonomski alat države. *Tržište.* XX, pp. 211–230, 2008.

[6]   Pranić, Lj., Petrić, L., Cetinić, L., Host population perceptions of the social impacts of sport tourism events in transition countries Evidence from Croatia, *International Journal of Event and Festival Management* 3(3), pp. 236–256, 2012.

[7]   Škrbić Alempijević, N., Žabčić Mesarić, R., Hrvatski priobalni festivali Sredozemlja, *Studia ethnologica Croatica*. 22 (1), pp. 317–337, 2010.

[8]   Piškor, M., Celebrate cultural diversity! Reading the discourses of world music festivals in Croatia. Narodna umjetnost, 43(1), pp. 179–201, 2006.

[9]   Kikaš, M., Mucko, B., Vukobratović, J., Kelemen, P., Urbano umjetnički festivali: kulturne politike i potencijali subverzivnosti, Studia ethnologica Croatica. 23 (1), pp. 67–92, 2011.

[10]   Vukonić, B., Čavlek, N. (eds). *Rječnik turizma*. Zagreb: Masmedia, 2001.

[11]   Getz, D., Event Tourism: Definition, Evolution, and Research Tourism Management. 29(3), pp. 403–428, 2008.

[12]   Presbury, R. and Edwards, D., Managing Sustainable Festivals, Meetings and Events, *Understanding the Sustainable Development of Tourism* Liburd J.J. and Edwards D. (eds). Goodfellow Publishers ltd., Oxford, pp. 163–187, 2010.

[13]   Gelder, G. and Robinson, P., Events, Festivals and the Arts, In: Robinson P., Heotman S. and Dieke P. (eds). *Research Themes for Tourism*. CAB International, Wallingford, 2011.

[14]   Stipanović C., Pavia N., Floričić T., Sustainable development in increasing competitiveness of hotel offer – Case study Istria County, Proc. of the 2nd International Scientific Conference *Tourism in Southern and Eastern Europe*, eds. Janković S., Croatia, pp. 279–294, 2013.

[15]   World Commission on Environment and Development (WCED). Our Common Future, Oxford, 1987.

[16]   Pavić, Rogošić, Održivi razvoj. Odraz, 2006.

[17]   Črnjar, M., *Menadžment održivog razvoja*. Sveučilište u Rijeci. Rijeka, 2009.

[18]   Grzinic J., Floricic T., Implementation of innovations in hotel offer promotion – case study of Istria as a tourist destination, Proc. of the 8th International Forum on Knowledge Asset Dynamics, eds. Schiuma G., Pulic A., Wellington C., Zagreb, Hrvatska, pp. 704–721, 2013.

[19]   Roland Berger, Strategy Consultants, *Studija o konceptu održivog razvoja – Hrvatska i svijet*. Zagreb, 2008.

[20]   Klarić, Z., *Elementi održivosti u turizmu*. Institut za turizam. Zagreb, 2011.

[21]   Magaš D., *Destinacijski menadžment – modeli i tehnike*. Sveučilište u Rijeci. Fakultet za hotelski i turistički menadžment Opatija, 2008.

[22]   Jelinčić D. A., Abeceda kulturnog turizma. Zagreb, 2009.

[23]   Swarbrooke, J. *Sustainable Tourism Management*. Wallingford: CABI publishing, 1999.

[24]   Weaver, D., *Sustainable tourism: Theory and practice*. Oxford: Elsevier, 2006.

[25]   Musgrave, J., *Moving towards responsible events management*. Worldwide Hospitality and Tourism Themes. 3 (3), pp. 258–274, 2011.

[26] Križman Pavlović D., *Marketing turističke destinacije*. Sveučilište Jurja Dobrile u Puli, Pula, 2008.
[27] County of Istria Administrative Section of Tourism, http://www.istra-istria.hr/fileadmin/dokumenti/turizam
[28] Agroclub Association, http://www.agroklub.com/vocarstvo/poticaji-za-maslinarstvo/2150/
[29] Croatia Chamber of Commerce, http://www.hgk.hr/wp-content/files_mf/maslinovoulje_web.pdf
[30] Istria Gourmet Association, http://www.istria-gourmet.com
[31] Černjul D., Personal Communication, 17 January 2014, President of the Croatian Restaurant Guild, Pula, Croatia.

Section 7
Climate change

Snow flakes and fates:
what hope is there for Alpine winter tourism?

A. Fischer
Institute of Interdisciplinary Mountain Research,
Austrian Academy of Sciences, Austria

Abstract

The rapid development of Alpine winter tourism and related infrastructures during the last century raises the question of development prospects against the background of climate change and sustainability. Today, amongst other macroscale forcings, snow is considered a precondition for winter tourism. The aim of this study is to investigate past climate change for four communities in Tyrol in relation to the number of overnight stays, and to compare the variability of the current climate with the bandwidth of future scenarios. This is done by analysing i) trends of air temperature, humidity and snow and ii) the statistical correlation of these parameters with the number of overnight stays. The height and duration of natural snow cover show high interannual variability. As a technical response, snow production has developed rapidly. Applying a Mann-Kendall test to the wet-bulb temperatures recorded at three Tyrolean climate stations reveals that the time frames when snow production is possible have changed most at medium elevations, but have so far not exceeded a few days at the beginning and the end of the winter season. In contrast to summer mean temperatures, winter mean temperatures have not changed significantly during the last 3 decades, and the range of interannual variability was about three times that of the most extreme temperature change calculated for future climate scenarios. Therefore it is very likely that the average future winter climate means will be within the range of the past century's records, and snow cover and temperature changes are minor macroscale forcings, so they are not factors that would delimit the future developments of Alpine winter tourism.

Keywords: climate change, winter tourism, snow production, ski tourism, snow cover.

WIT Transactions on Ecology and The Environment, Vol 187, © 2014 WIT Press
www.witpress.com, ISSN 1743-3541 (on-line)
doi:10.2495/ST140231

1   Introduction

After several thousand years of settlement history, the Alpine environment experienced its most significant changes in physical and human terms since the mid-19th century. The development of transport infrastructures and the transition from an agrarian society to a modern society left its traces not only by changing the landscape in the course of changing modes of land use, but also imprinted themselves on Alpine sociocultural and economical structures. These global changes coincided with climate warming after the Little Ice Age, which had made life difficult for the Alpine agricultural society for several hundred years, up to the glacial maximum observed around 1850.

With the development of roads and railroad connections, the increasing number of tourists, more and more physical and organizational tourist infrastructure developed, e.g. cable cars and travel agencies.

Today, tourism contributes 5.8% to the GDP [1], a significant share of the Austrian economy. If one includes indirect effects, these are estimated to be about three times the size of the direct effects [2]. Regionally and locally, the relative importance of tourism can be even higher, especially in peripheral, small mountain villages 'at the end of the roads', where other earnings are scarce and difficult to develop under a global trend to urbanization.

The macroscale drivers of tourism identified by Scott and Lemieux [3] include the economic situation, transport, political stability, technological and demographic change, exchange rates, travel limitations and climate change. As an additional factor, the amount of spare time can be considered. The rapid growth of the Alpine tourism industry within the last two centuries triggered the question of the limits of its growth, together with many centuries of discussions about the ecological, sociocultural and economic impacts and drivers.

In recent decades, a variety of concepts for sustainable tourism have been developed [4]. The World Tourism Organisation [5] defined sustainable tourism as tourism 'which meets the need of present tourists and host regions while protecting and enhancing opportunity for the future'. As this definition meets Heinz von Förster's ethical imperative [6] of increasing future possibilities, we will stick to this definition in this study.

Currently, and alongside socioeconomic, ecological and cultural impacts, the limitations of a sustainable development of tourism through climatic change are being discussed. Often, winter tourism is claimed as prime example for the climate sensitivity of tourism, although very different opinions exist on its role for sustainability [7, 8]. While first studies focused on the reliability of natural snow cover [9], more recent studies pay increasing attention to snow production as an adaption strategy to climate change [10]. Future perspective planning, including climate [11] and socioeconomic [12, 13] changes, and transition management [14] is often done using scenario analysis [15].

This study aims at sketching the status quo and recent developments in Tyrolean winter tourism together with the development of population, transportation capacities, and climatic parameters. Investigated climatic parameters are snow cover, snow production times derived from time series of air temperatures and humidity. This retrospective part of the study addresses the question if winter tourism in the past was correlated or causally related to climatological parameters. This is an important question for the development of future strategies. If no correlation between climate and tourism development can be found, there is no empirical evidence for an instantaneous appearance of such a relationship. This implies that the investigated data from the past cover most system statuses likely to occur in future. Therefore, the variability of the past system is compared to future climate scenarios, assuming that in a changing climate the absolute frequency of specific system statuses changes, so that the mean system status changes, whereas extreme events remain extreme events in a changed climate.

2 Status quo: winter tourism in Tyrol

In Northern Tyrol, 84 ski resorts have been operating (Figure 1) at altitudes between 460 m and 3,400 m a.s.l. 64% of the total ski resort area is located at altitudes between 1,200 m and 2,400 m a.sl., 9% below 900 m and 10% above 2,500 m a.s.l. Four communities representing different types have been selected for detailed investigations. The village of Neustift is located at the end of the Stubai valley, Schönberg at the entrance of the same valley, close to the city of Innsbruck. The villages of Ischgl and Galtür are located in the upper Paznaun valley, a rather peripheral area at the end of the Paznaun valley. The proportion of total area to permanent settlement area differs between these communities as does the share of ski resort area (Table 1).

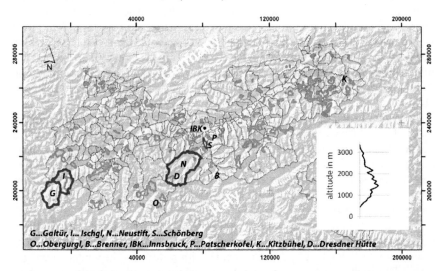

Figure 1:   Map of the province of Tyrol, ski resorts as defined by official spatial planning figures (red) and climate stations used in this study. The distribution of the ski resorts across the altitudinal range is shown in the insert.

The small community of Schönberg has no ski resort, and about one third of the area is permanent settlement area. In the three other communities, only a few percent of the area falls into that category. In Neustift and Galtür, less than 1% of the total area is used as ski resort, whereas Ischgl uses more than 3% of its area for skiing.

Table 1: Percentage of the total municipal and provincial area available for permanent settlements and used for ski resorts.

Municipality	Proportion of the total area	
	Ski	Permanent
Neustift/Stubaital	0.5	4.1
Schönberg/Stubaital	0.0	32.1
Galtür	0.4	2.7
Ischgl	3.4	4.3
Tyrol	0.6	12.4

After the Second World War rapid population growth set in (Figure 2). Today Galtür has the lowest number of inhabitants and the weakest growth, whereas Schönberg is subject to amenity migration from the nearby city of Innsbruck. The highest population growth is found in Neustift. All trends flatten in the last decade. The number of cable cars has been increasing by about 50% to 100% since the 1970s in Galtür, Ischgl and Neustift, but decreasing in Schönberg and in the province of Tyrol as a whole. As in Schönberg, where only one cable car existed, which was closed down, many of the smaller ski resorts in Tyrol with single cable cars shut down as bigger resorts emerged as a result of fusions between neighbouring smaller resorts. In 1992, a moratorium (cable car directive) was passed by the federal government of Tyrol, prohibiting the development of new ski lifts but allowing the replacement of old installations [16].

Transport capacities increased much more than the numbers of cable cars, as many T-bar lifts were replaced with chair lifts and gondolas. In contrast to surface lifts, transportation by chair lifts and gondolas does not rely on snow cover of the track, so that these cable cars can also be used as shuttles to higher parts of the ski resorts from the valley station, so that often the main ski runs are located at high to medium elevations in the resorts and the connection to the valley station is a single ski track.

The number of overnight stays decreased in Schönberg but increased the three other communities and for the province of Tyrol as a whole. The closing down of the ski lift in Schönberg did not coincide with a decrease in winter overnight stays. The highest increase in winter overnight stays was recorded in Ischgl, which also saw the sharpest increase in transport capacities. Winter overnight stays in Neustift and Galtür are increasing more slowly than in Ischgl. For the province of Tyrol, the growth in winter overnight stays flattens out after 2005, as is the case in Neustift and Galtür.

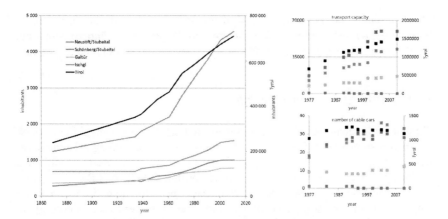

Figure 2: Development of the number of inhabitants, the number of cable cars and the transport capacity of the cable cars in the four communities and for the province of Tyrol.

Summer overnight stays in Tyrol reached a maximum in the late 1980s, exceeding winter overnight stays at the time, but with a decreasing trend since then. In the four communities of the study summer overnight stays have remained approximately at the same level. In Neustift the switch from summer to winter tourism occurred in the mid-1980s, about ten years earlier than for the

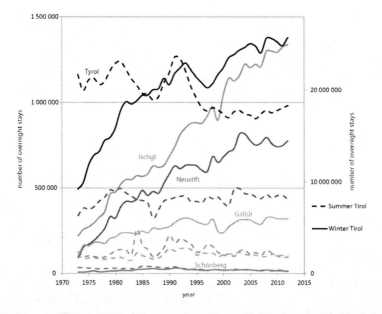

Figure 3: Development of the number of overnight stays for the summer and the winter season in the four communities and for the whole province of Tyrol.

whole province, in Galtür at the end of the 1970s. In Ischgl, the discrepancies between winter and summer overnight stays are largest. In Schönberg winter and summer converged after an overhang of winter overnight stays in the early years.

3   Climate and climate change

Climatic parameters recorded at stations located close to the main altitudes of ski resorts are shown here. Generally, long instrumental meteorological time series are available for a limited number of locations and need careful data homogenization to reflect climatic changes. Within the HISATLP data set, time series of temperature and precipitation have been homogenized. From the available stations, season means of air temperature time series for Obergurgl and Galtür are shown here, together with a pair of one valley and one mountain station in Innsbruck and at the nearby Patscherkofel summit to reflect temperature gradients.

Unfortunately, measuring snow cover is much more complex than measuring temperature in that the presence of an observer is needed. Therefore most records of snow cover are available for valley stations and there are very few places where snow cover and temperature time series are available. Therefore the locations of the specific records presented in these studies differ but have been selected for a climatologically similar setting and thus representative for the ski resorts.

Snow cover records are presented for Obergurgl and Galtür, Brenner and Dresdner Hütte. The calculation of potential snow production times in this study is based not only on daily air temperatures. As evaporation plays an important role for the freezing of the droplets, air humidity has also to be included. From six investigated Tyrolean stations [17], snow production times and their temporal changes are presented for the stations at Obergurgl, Patscherkofel and Kitzbühel, representing typical altitudinal ranges for Tyrolean ski resorts.

3.1 Temperature

The mean air temperatures [18] in the summer season (June, July and August) present an increasing trend from the 1970s onwards, but are close to stationary for the winter season (Table 2). As also evident from Figure 4, the temperature variability in winter exceeds the summer oscillations, and the temperature gradients between Patscherkofel summit station and the Innsbruck Valley Station are smaller in winter than in summer.

The long-term temperature lapse rate between Patscherkofel summit station and Innsbruck is $0.4 \pm 0.3°C$ per 100 m in winter and $0.6 \pm 0.1°C$ per 100 m in summer for the years 1991 to 2012. Thus temperature differences between different altitude levels are much smaller in winter than in summer, but show higher variability as a result of quite frequently occurring temperature inversions.

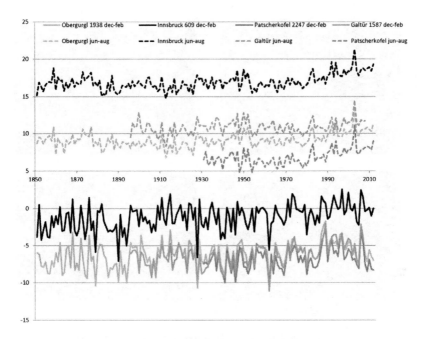

Figure 4:   Seasonal air temperature means at the four stations Obergurgl, Innsbruck, Patscherkofel and Galtür.

Table 2:   Decadal temperature trends for Obergurgl, Innsbruck, Patscherkofel and Galtür from 1970 onwards.

Station	Altitude m a.sl.	Winter °C		Summer °C	
Obergurgl	1938	-0.1	0.2	0.5	0.1
Innsbruck	609	0.1	0.2	0.6	0.1
Patscherkofel	2247	-0.1	0.2	0.4	0.1
Galtür	1587	0.4	0.2	0.5	0.1

3.2 Snow height

Snow height shows a quite high spatial and interannual variability [17], although mean snow height varies only between 42 cm at the Brenner station and 59 cm at the Dresdner Hütte. The maximum snow height ranges from 140 cm at Brenner to 215 cm at Dresdner Hütte. Figure 5 demonstrates that the high snow heights occur with great variability from year to year without following a general trend and varying from station to station.

The snow heights in Obergurgl are often in a similar magnitude as the ones in Galtür, although the station in Galtür is located 351 m lower than the one in Obergurgl. This indicates that altitude as a single parameter is not a good predictor for duration or height of snow.

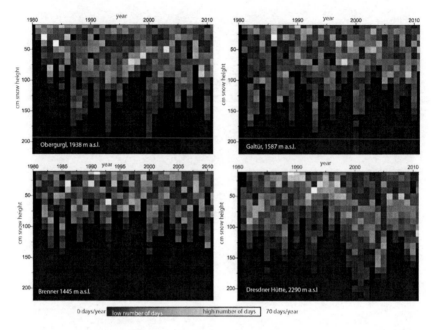

Figure 5:   Colour-coded absolute frequency (in days per year) of specific snow heights (black: no day of occurrence, white: 70 days of occurrence).

3.3 Snow production

Freezing liquid droplets in the air needs energy exchange between the droplets and the air, involving temperature gradients (air colder than droplet) but also evaporation as main drivers. The conditions for snow production at -2.0°C dry air temperature and 90% relative humidity and +1.0°C dry air temperature and 45% relative humidity, are similar, both corresponding to a wet bulb temperature of -2.5°C. Therefore, neglecting relative humidity and analysing dry air temperatures causes an uncertainty larger than the temperature trend to be expected for the next two decades. The potential snow production time was therefore calculated by Fischer *et al.* [17] from time series of temperature and relative humidity, which were converted into wet bulb temperatures. Fischer *et al.* [17] found a limit for snow production at a wet bulb temperature of -2°C.

Olefs *et al.* [18] investigated past changes in snow production days for six climate stations in Tyrol. They did not just include daily mean values, as today snow production often takes place over night, so that at the beginning of the season daily mean conditions are not good indicators of potential snow production times. In the study of Olefs *et al.* [18], interannual variability of snow production turned out to be high for most periods and most stations, while no statistically significant trend could be derived by applying a Mann Kendall analysis. Few changes in snow production times occurred during the main season, and the percentage of days suitable for snow production is high.

Snow production times changed most significantly at mid-range altitudes (~2000 m a.s.l.), with smaller changes at high and low elevations.

For Obergurgl (1953–2007), the potential snow-making days decreased by 22 days per season for Obergurgl, mainly in November (-12 days), and in April (-10 days). During the main season, December to March, the potential snow-making days decreased by only 2 days. Between mid-December and mid-February, the likelihood of snow production days is slightly above 80%. Between winter 2001/2002 and winter 2005/2006, a slightly positive trend in snow production was found.

At Patscherkofel (1948–2007), a positive trend in wet bulb temperatures has been recorded since the 1970s (+1.5°C), resulting in a significant decrease of 43 days/season in the snow-making days, mainly in November (-13 days) and April (-17 days). In the core season between January and late February, the likelihood for snow production is more than 90%.

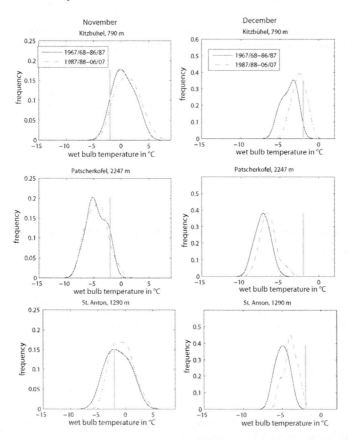

Figure 6:   Frequency of wet bulb temperatures for two different periods (1967/68 to 1986/87 and 1987/88 to 2006/07) for the months of November and December. The grey bar indicates the threshold temperature for snow production.

Early in the winter season, the hours when snow production is possible increase rapidly between the beginning of November and the end of December. Figure 6 shows frequency distributions of wet bulb temperatures for these months, with the area left of the grey bar representing times when snow production is possible. At all three stations, enough snow production hours occur in November to ensure piste preparation (3 days of snow making needed). In December, at all three stations, snow production is possible most of the time. Although the two periods shown by the red broken and the black solid line differ by the number of hours, no significant changes occur in terms of reduction of potential snow production times.

4 Comparison of climatological parameters and overnight stays

The number of snow days and mean annual snow heights for the stations Brenner and Dresdner Hütte were compared to the number of overnight stays in the communities of Neustift and Schönberg; ditto the snow days in Galtür to the overnight stays in Ischgl. As obvious from the comparison of Figures 3 and 5, overnight stays increase, whereas snow cover shows no significant trends, and thus no significant correlation between overnight stays and snow cover duration or snow height was found.

Therefore, the growth trends in overnight stays are very likely related to other factors than snow heights or the number of snow days. As the trends in winter temperatures are stationary, there is also no statistical correlation between the increasing numbers of overnight stays and seasonal temperature means.

5 Comparison of the past to the expected range of future climate change

The global climate scenarios show a general increase of the mean annual air temperature, but also a high range of variability regarding the quantity of this increase. For the period 2016–2025, temperature increases between about 0.3°C and 1.1°C have been calculated, for the period 2046 to 2055, the values range from 0.5°C to 2.3°C [19]. Even the maximum range of temperature increases is small compared to the observed ranges of seasonal mean temperatures of 7.7°C at Patscherkofel and 9.0°C in Galtür presented above. From this comparison we can conclude that very likely, apart from seasonal extreme values which can occur as a result of specific weather patterns fairly independently of the climatological mean, every future seasonal mean until 2055 is very likely to have occurred in the past century.

The future scenarios of snow cover extent have been calculated from the changes in precipitation and temperatures. The range of precipitation changes in the winter season is much higher than that for the temperatures. , Given an uncertainty range of future winter precipitation for the Alps of +/- 20%, it even remains unclear whether there is an increase or a decrease in precipitation [20]. Together with the variability of future temperature increases, snow cover trends for the Alps for the years until 2050 remain highly uncertain.

Assuming that extremes in every climate are outliers, it can be concluded that we will have already recorded most of the future winter snow cover durations and snow heights in the past, although possibly at different absolute frequencies.

6 Discussion and conclusions

The four selected communities are well spread around the Tyrolean average in terms of their proportion of area for ski resorts and they represent different types of communities from peripheral to quite central communities. The growth trends of overnight stays and the dominance of winter overnight stays over summer overnight stays occurred at different times. The comparison with the number of cable cars and the transport capacities shows that the increasing number of overnight stays coincides with increasing transportation capacity, notwithstanding the unclear causality. Ischgl and Galtür are basically located in the same climatological setting and have experienced very different developments in overnight stays.

Taking into account that snow production begun in the early 1990s and today covers about 70% of the total area of ski runs, it is no wonder that the overnight stays do not appear to depend on snow cover. The analysis indicates that within the last 50 years snow production did indeed change, but not in such a way that one could expect significant changes in the main season in the near future.

Past climate variability exceeds the scenarios of climate change for the next decades.

To sum up, a limitation of the still increasing winter tourism will very likely not be caused by climatic changes but by other macroscale forcings. As the effect of the cable car directive demonstrates, policy can play an important role in shaping future possibilities and in dealing with local resources. Sustainable development of winter tourism thus is more closely related to the clever use of local resources, such as settlement areas and business parks or water and energy consumption, than to climate change.

Acknowledgements

The Interreg project 3P CLIM is acknowledged for providing the data on snow cover, the HISTALP projects (www.zamg.ac.at\HISTALP) for providing the temperature time series. The data on the number of inhabitants, overnight stays, number of cable cars and transport capacities was provided by the Federal Government of Tyrol, Statistics Dept. and compiled from data of the regional statistics of the Sports Dept., and TIRIS and by Statistik Austria.

References

[1] Statistik Austria, 2012 http://www.statistik.at/
[2] Laimer & Ostertag-Sydler, *Tourismus-Satellitenkonto*, Statistik Austria, http://www.statistik.gv.at/web_de/statistiken/tourismus/tourismus-satellitenkonto/index.html
[3] Scott, D. & Lemieux, C., Weather and climate information for tourism. *Procedia Environmental Sciences*, **1**, pp. 146-183, 2010.
[4] Butler, R. W., Sustainable tourism: A state-of-the-art review, *Tourism Geographies: An International Journal of Tourism Space, Place and Environment*, **1(1)**, pp. 7-25, 1999. DOI: 10.1080/14616689908721291.
[5] World Tourism Organization, Sustainable Tourism Development: Guide for Local Planners. Madrid: WTO, 1993.
[6] Foerster, H. v., Understanding, Springer, 2003.
[7] Scott, D., Why sustainable tourism must address climate change, *Journal of Sustainable Tourism*, **19(1)**, pp. 17-34, 2011. DOI: 10.1080/09669582.2010.539694.
[8] Weaver D., Can sustainable tourism survive climate change? *Journal of Sustainable Tourism*, **19(1)**, pp. 5-15, 2011. DOI: 10.1080/09669582.2010.536242.
[9] Abegg, B., Agrawala, S., Crick, F., & de Montfalcon, A., *Climate change impacts and adaptation in winter tourism*. In S. Agrawala (Ed.), Climate change in the European Alps. Adapting winter tourism and natural hazards management, pp. 25-60, Paris: OECD, 2007.
[10] Scott, D., McBoyle, G., Minogue, A.& Mills, B., Climate Change and the Sustainability of Ski-based Tourism in Eastern North America: A Reassessment, *Journal of Sustainable Tourism*, **14(4)**, pp. 376-398, 2006.
[11] Steiger. R. & Stötter. J., Climate Change Impact Assessment of Ski Tourism in Tyrol, *Tourism Geographies: An International Journal of Tourism Space, Place and Environment*, **15(4)**, pp. 577-600, 2013. DOI: 10.1080/14616688.2012.762539.
[12] Müller, H., *Entwicklungsszenarien für den Alpenraum*. ed. Egger, R. & Herdin T., Tourismus: Herausforderung: Zukunft, Wissenschaftliche Schriftenreihe des Zentrums für Tourismusforschung – Salzburg, **1**, pp. 365-376, 2007.
[13] Steiger, R., Scenarios for skiing tourism in Austria: integrating demographics with an analysis of climate change, *Journal of Sustainable Tourism*, **20(6)**, pp. 867-882, 2012, DOI: 10.1080/09669582.2012.680464.
[14] Gössling, S., Hall, C. M., Ekström, F., Engeset, A. B. & Aall, C., Transition management: a tool for implementing sustainable tourism scenarios? *Journal of Sustainable Tourism*, **20(6)**, 899-916, 2012. DOI: 10.1080/09669582.2012.699062.
[15] Moriarty, J. P., Theorising scenario analysis to improve future perspective planning in tourism, *Journal of Sustainable Tourism*, **20(6)**, pp. 779-800, 2012. DOI: 10.1080/09669582.2012.673619.

[16] Amt der Tiroler Landesregierung/Abt. 1c – Landesplanung, *Seilbahngrundsätze des Landes Tirol mit Festlegung der Grenzen der Schigebiete in den Tourismusintensivgebieten*, 1992.

[17] Fischer, A., Olefs, M. & Abermann, J., Glaciers, snow and ski tourism in Austria's changing climate. *Annals of Glaciology*, **52(58)**, pp. 89-96, 2011.

[18] Olefs, M., Fischer, A. & Lang, J., Boundary conditions for artificial snow production in the Austrian Alps, *Journal of Applied Meteorology and Climatology*, **49**, pp. 1096-1113, 2010.

[19] Auer, I., Böhm, R., Jurkovic, A., Lipa, W., Orlik, A., Potzmann, R., Schöner, W., Ungersböck, M., Matulla, C., Briffa, K., Jones, P.D., Efthymiadis, D., Brunetti, M., Nanni, T., Maugeri, M., Mercalli, L., Mestre O., Moisselin J.-M., Begert M., Müller-Westermeier G., Kveton V., Bochnicek O., Stastny P., Lapin, M., Szalai, S., Szentimrey, T., Cegnar, T., Dolinar, M., Gajic-Capka, M., Zaninovic, K., Majstorovic, Z. & Nieplova, E., HISTALP – Historical instrumental climatological surface time series of the greater Alpine region 1760-2003. *International Journal of Climatology*, **27**, 17-46, 2007.

[20] Kirtman, B., Power, S.B., Adedoyin, J.A., Boer, G.J., Bojariu, R., Camilloni, I., Doblas-Reyes, F.J., Fiore, A.M., Kimoto, M., Meehl, G.A., Prather, M., Sarr, A., Schär, C., Sutton, R., van Oldenborgh, G.J., Vecchi, G. & Wang, H.J., *Near-term Climate Change: Projections and Predictability*. In: Climate Change 2013: The Physical Science Basis. Contribution of Working Group I to the Fifth Assessment Report of the IPCC, ed. Stocker, T.F., Qin, D., Plattner, G.-K., Tignor, M., Allen, S.K., Boschung, J., Nauels, A., Xia, Y., Bex, V. & Midgley, P.M., Cambridge University Press, Cambridge, United Kingdom and New York, NY, USA, 2013.

[21] Christensen, J.H., Hewitson, B., Busuioc, A., Chen, A., Gao, X., Held, I., Jones, R., Kolli, R.K., Kwon, W.-T. , Laprise, R., Magaña Rueda, V., Mearns, L., Menéndez, C.G., Räisänen, J., Rinke, A., Sarr, A. & Whetton, P., *Regional Climate Projections*. In: Climate Change 2007: The Physical Science Basis. Contribution of Working Group I to the Fourth Assessment Report of the IPCC, ed. Solomon, S., Qin, D., Manning, M., Chen, Z., Marquis, M., Averyt, K.B., Tignor, M. & Miller, H.L., Cambridge University Press, Cambridge, UK and New York, NY, USA, 2007.

Assessing knowledge of social representations of climate change and tourism

M. B. Gómez-Martín & X. A. Armesto-López
Department of Physical Geography and Regional Geographical Analysis, University of Barcelona, Spain

Abstract

The aim of this study was to explore how university students of Spain perceive climate change and its effects on and relationship to the Spanish tourism sector, and their attitudes towards this issue. This included the identification of the problem, the relative importance it was given compared to other problems, assessment of the potential threat it posed to the tourism sector and appraisal of the contribution made by the tourism sector to climate change. The methodology employed was a survey: 400 individual questionnaires were administered to university students. The exploitation of the information collected is performed by using univariate descriptive procedures. The results indicate a low level of awareness among this young segment of population of the risks associated with climate change, which is seen as representing little threat to the tourism sector and as being distant in time and space. Through our study, we aimed to contribute to filling the void which currently exists as regards to understanding how different segments of population construct their representations of the inter-relationship between climate change and tourism, since such knowledge could help improve the effectiveness of the adaptation and mitigation strategies which are being, or could be designed and implemented in both the public and private tourism sectors.
Keywords: tourism, perceptions, attitudes, climate change, adaptation, Spain.

1 Introduction

The evidence of sustained global warming of the Earth's surface throughout the last century has established climate change as one of the main subjects of debate and concern in the context of current global economic policies which will dictate the future of the planet in coming years [1, 2].

WIT Transactions on Ecology and The Environment, Vol 187, © 2014 WIT Press
www.witpress.com, ISSN 1743-3541 (on-line)
doi:10.2495/ST140241

The importance of tourism in the world economy, and the undeniable links which exist between tourism and atmospheric elements, suggest that climate change should be considered in all its aspects [3]. Accordingly, it is worth noting that weather and climate are important elements of many of the tourism products offered by tourist destinations and thus, any change in atmospheric conditions could have a considerable impact [4–9]. Similarly, it should not be forgotten that tourism has been, and is, one of the factors responsible for climate change: at present, tourism reflects the general energy consumption model of the industrial revolution, generating high carbon emissions. Indeed, on a global scale the tourism sector is responsible for 5% of greenhouse gas emissions [10–12]. Consequently, and given the importance of tourism to the economies of many countries worldwide, research into potential adaptation and mitigation measures in relation to climate change, are of prime interest [13–15].

For all strategies designed as a response to climate change, whether adaptation proposals or mitigation measures, consideration of the social factor is fundamental if an effective response is to be designed and implemented in order to avert the most pessimistic future scenarios [16]. Through our study, therefore, we aimed to contribute to enhancing knowledge of how citizens construct their representations of the inter-relationship between climate change and tourism, since such knowledge could help improve the effectiveness of the adaptation and mitigation strategies which are being, or could be, designed and implemented in the both public and private tourism sectors.

Few studies have examined the social representations of the inter-relationship between climate change and tourism. In other words, little research has been conducted into how citizens perceive this phenomenon, how it is identified, what beliefs and knowledge they hold about it, what importance they grant it compared to other decisions which may affect their purchase decisions, what their assessment is of the potential threat climate change poses for the tourism sector, what perceptions they have of their individual or collective responsibility for this phenomenon, etc. Becken [17] has highlighted the need for such studies, due to the significant contribution they could make in the preparation of effective communication campaigns for raising awareness among tourists of the importance of climate change and motivating them to take action.

Much of the research which has been carried out in this field has focused on exploring the importance of atmospheric variables when selecting destinations, with the aim of enabling assessment, a posteriori, of the impacts that future changes in these variables could have on tourism consumers' decisions and, consequently, on tourist flows. Thus, for example, Braun et al. [18] conducted a study to ascertain the socio-economical impacts on the tourism sector of climate change, assessing how tourists would behave under different future scenarios as regards selection of their destination. The study, which focused on the north coast in Germany, indicated that the phenomenon could have a significant influence on this process, potentially leading to a future change in the influx of tourists to this region. Also studies by Amelung and Viner [19], Amelung et al. [20], Bigano et al. [21], Hamilton et al. [22], Lise and Tol [23], Maddison [24] and Scott et al. [25] examine the changes that climate change could have on the current weather conditions for some destinations, and how those changes may impact on future tourism demand flows. To our study area, the results of these studies predict in most cases quite pessimistic future. These contributions, made with a quantitative approach (based mainly on the use of econometric techniques), rarely incorporate the social dimension and, therefore, these contributions do not consider some aspects that can influence the future tourist behavior and which have to do with perceptions, opinions and attitudes towards the phenomenon. Maybe working scales used and macromagnitudes considered in some of these works have hampered the introduction of this variable more "humane".

Qualitative approaches allow the introduction of the social dimension, however, these studies are fewer than quantitative approaches. Focusing on Zanzibar, Tanzania, Gössling et al. [26] studied tourist perceptions of climate change and the importance of climate in tourist decisions. Among other conclusions, the authors indicated that some of the changes associated with climate change (such as higher temperatures) were not perceived by tourists to be a significant problem, whereas others, such as increased rainfall and humidity, were, and that these latter could have a negative influence on choice of destination. The authors also explored the degree of awareness among tourists of how their tourism behaviour influenced, or could influence climate change, and found that tourists within the study area showed little awareness and assumed little responsibility. Similarly, Becken [27] took New Zealand as the study area and explored tourists' knowledge and awareness of the contribution made by air transport to climate change, their sense of individual responsibility and their reactions to specific climate change mitigation policies. The results indicate scant willingness on the part of tourists globally to change their tourism consumer habits, particularly with respect to transport, and revealed a disparity among those interviewed between their behaviour as tourists and their everyday behaviour (much more proactive and self-effective). Other studies, such as those by Dawson et al. [28] on long-distance tourists travelling to Canada to watch polar bears, or by Cohen and Higham [29] on tourists from the United Kingdom travelling to New Zealand, obtained similar results.

McKercher et al. [30] demonstrated the significant disparity between awareness and action, identifying different tourist profiles according to these variables and calling for governmental intervention to bring about a change in environmental attitudes among tourists. In an exploratory study, Becken [31] analysed how tourists and tourism experts perceived climate change and the carbon sinks provided by forests as a tool for offsetting carbon dioxide emissions. As regards tourists, the study identified five groups, each of which would require a different approach in order to ensure effectiveness of the educational campaigns which the sector could implement to address this phenomenon through adaptation or mitigation.

Marshall et al. [32] and Scott et al. [33] assessed awareness of and attitudes to climate change among tourists who had chosen diving in the Red Sea (Egypt). In this case, the study found a disparity in the results depending on whether those interviewed were the tourists (who reported high awareness and proactive attitudes), or the destination operators (who reported that their clients demonstrated moderate awareness and little evidence of proactive attitudes). This disparate perception hinders development and implementation by the sector of measures which could contribute to adaptation to, or mitigation of, climate change.

In this paper, we present the results obtained from a survey aimed at exploring how university students of Spain perceive climate change in relation to tourism, and their attitudes to it. Understanding how different segments of population construct their social representations of climate change and its consequences and risks for the Spanish tourism sector, and how such representations condition their attitudes and tourist behaviour, is a fundamental step in designing the education and communication campaigns necessary to ensure the success of the adaptation or mitigation measures which could be implemented by this sector. Consideration of these aspects could have a great significance for a country where tourism brings to the Spanish economy around 11% of GDP.

2 Method and data collection

The results of the present study are based on 400 questionnaires which were administered between 2008 and 2009. The reporting unit to which the study addressed was university students of Spain of both sexes over 18 years old. This is a segment of young population in educational / work transit that can provide valuable information for future action on climate change. The data collection method used was the classic collection called PAPI (Paper Assisted Personal Interviewing) that is personal surveys that are conducted by a pollster who uses the paper support.

The questionnaire was semi-structured (with open and closed questions) and it sought to explore how university students of Spain perceive the binomial climate-tourism. This included identification of the problem, the relative importance it was given compared to other problems, assessment of the potential threat it posed to the tourism sector and appraisal of the contribution made by the tourism sector to climate change. The exploitation of the information collected is performed by using univariate descriptive procedures.

41% of the college students interviewed were male, and 59% female; 43% were between 18 and 20 years old, 47% between 20 and 25 and only 10% were aged over 25 years old. As other authors, working with similar segments [33], have warned, one possible limitation of the study could be the homogeneity of the demographic, cultural and social variables presented by the section of the population analysed: the results are representative of young adult university students. Nevertheless, it is of particular interest to explore the public perceptions and attitudes regarding the effects of climate change on the tourism sector held by this section of the population which by 2025 and 2050, dates by which most of the climate scenarios will have become reality, will have attained maximum mobility.

3   Results

3.1   Identification of climate change as a problem

Subjects were asked about the future problems that concerned them, whether generic or specific (in this case, focusing on environmental issues and in climate change), and offered specific response options.

Thus, the sample was asked about their concern with a battery of basic questions. For the respondents, environmental issues occupied the first place in their scale of future concerns compared to other social or economic issues closely related to the everyday life of the section of the population surveyed. Thus, the environment scored 4.2 on a Likert scale of 1 to 5, followed by problems related to human rights (4.14), terrorism and citizen safety (3.61), the economy (3.51), technological development (3.21) and immigration (2.96) (Table 1). These results suggest that there is public awareness of environmental issues among this market's sector, in agreement with the cultural tendencies of industrialised societies. Nevertheless, the priority given to these issues over other problems which could have more relevance in the immediate future life of those surveyed is somewhat surprising: it may be relevant here to consider the possibility of social desirability bias, so frequent in studies of values, attitudes and perceptions regarding the environment [34–36].

Table 1:   Thinking about your immediate geographical surroundings in the future, to what extent are you concerned about the following problems?

	Weighted mean	Median	1 Not worried	2	3	4	5 Very worried	No opinion
Terrorism and citizen safety	3.61	4	5.70%	14.25%	19.37%	34.47%	25.93%	0.28%
Inmigration	2.96	3	15.95%	21.94%	24.22%	25.36%	12.25%	0.28%
Environment	4.26	4	0.85%	3.99%	11.11%	36.47%	47.29%	0.28%
Human rights	4.14	4	1.14%	2.28%	18.52%	37.32%	40.46%	0.28%
Technological development	3.21	3	8.55%	16.81%	30.77%	32.19%	11.40%	0.28%
Economy	3.51	4	5.13%	9.97%	31.34%	35.04%	18.23%	0.28%

When the sample is asked about his opinion regarding a battery of environmental problems, the issue of climate change is the aspect that received lower scores in the geographical area of study (albeit with minor differences compared to other items), compared with a wide range of other environmental problems. Thus, soil and water pollution obtained a mean score of 4.5 on a scale of 1 to 5, followed by the destruction and loss of species (4.37), atmospheric pollution (4.30), fires (4.29), exhaustion of energy resources (4.25) and, in last place, climate change (4.23). Note that all scores are high relative to the offered Likert scale (1 Not at all worried – 5 Very worried), including climate change score. However, in items like climate change and exhaustion of energy resources, the percentage of respondents who indicated a value of 1 and/or 2 of the scale is somewhat higher in relation to other items (Table 2). These results could show that on a regional or local level, climate change is perceived as a minor problem compared with other environmental issues. Various studies not specific to the tourism sector carried out in the last decade have reported the same tendency [37]: the phenomenon of climate change is perceived as relevant on a global scale, but loses precedence over other environmental issues as the perspective is reduced to a regional, and then local scale. This may possibly be due to the fact that our senses have great difficulty in detecting evidence of climate change in the present, to the widespread publicity given to reports on climate change or tourism published by different international organisations [38–42], where the results are systematically presented on both a global and specific macroregional scale for the medium and long term, to the scant publicity afforded to regional and local reports, and to insufficient efforts as regards providing information linking climate change with the everyday lives of tourists.

Table 2: Thinking about your immediate geographical surroundings in the future, to what extent are you concerned about the following environmental problems?

	Weighted mean	Median	1 Not worried	2	3	4	5 Very worried	No opinion
Atmospheric pollution	4.30	4	0.57%	3.13%	8.83%	40.46%	46.44%	0.57%
Exhaustation of energy resources	4.25	5	1.14%	5.13%	13.96%	26.78%	52.71%	0.28%
Climate Change	4.23	4	0.85%	4.84%	9.69%	39.60%	44.73%	0.28%
Fires	4.29	4	0.00%	3.42%	12.82%	35.33%	48.15%	0.28%
Destruction and loss of species	4.37	5	0.28%	1.99%	13.11%	29.34%	54.99%	0.28%
Soil and Water pollution	4.50	5	0.28%	1.42%	7.41%	29.63%	60.68%	0.57%

3.2 Perceptions of climate change and tourism

To investigate the level of awareness of climate change and tourism, two questions have been made. Thus, respondents were questioned about whether climate change will have an effect on tourism in the immediate geographical environment and how could be these effects on. In relation to the first question, only 86% answered in the affirmative, whilst 9% said no and 5% had no opinion. In response to how, those surveyed made particular mention of the negative effects on sun-and-beach tourism, highlighting the problems associated with pressure on water resources, loss of beaches and the degradation and diminishing attractions of tourism destinations due to loss of biodiversity. In no instance was an increase in temperatures and the effects of this on comfort levels mentioned as a serious problem by any of those surveyed. On the other hand, respondents repeatedly mentioned the consequences for Spanish tourism of other, competing destinations unaffected by the environmental impacts produced by climate change (Figure 1).

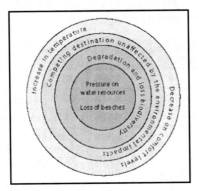

Figure 1: Perceived impacts of climate change on tourism.

Similarly, respondents were questioned about if tourism contributes in some way to climate change and how. In this case, 76% answered yes, 23%, no, and 1% had no opinion. Related with how, respondents who had answered in the affirmative way, placed more emphasis on the effects of tourism on environmental aspects such as degradation of water, coastal areas, pressure on resources, etc., than on the effects of tourism on climate (those surveyed tended to identify many of the environmental impacts generated by tourism with climate change, when in fact they are not always related). Of the 76% indicated, few emphasised the consequences for the atmosphere of air transport or the increase in energy consumption associated with tourism, to cite some examples. It seems that respondents perceive more easily the impacts of climate change on tourism, and have a greater difficulty to perceive tourism impacts on climate change.

To complete these questions, subjects were asked which aspects in the study area would be most affected by climate change, and offered specific response options. This inquiry into the situation of the tourism sector in the context of climate change, contrasting it with other sectors of the economy or strategic issues within the field of study, obtained a highly surprising result: the tourism sector reaches a 3.5 on a Likert scale of 1 to 5, the lowest score of the set (Table 3). Note for the tourism sector, the high percentage of answers that are at the value 1 and 2.

Finally, it is also interesting to examine the results obtained when respondents were asked to assess the immediacy of the effects of climate change at a generic and a specific (the tourism sector) level (Table 4). There appears to be little real understanding of the consequences of climate change for the tourism sector among respondents: low perceptions of threat due to difficulties in recognising the effects of climate change on the tourism sector at present evidences once again the difficulties encountered in relating this phenomenon (in special, tourism/climate change) to our immediate everyday surroundings.

Table 3: Thinking about your immediate geographical surroundings in the future, to what extent do you think the following aspects could be affected by climate change?

	Weighted mean	Median	1 Unaffected	2	3	4	5 Very affected	No opinion
Energy sector	3.60	4	2.28%	11.11%	28.77%	37.89%	18.52%	1.42%
Water resources	4.34	5	0.28%	3.70%	8.26%	36.47%	50.43%	0.85%
Human health	3.97	4	0.57%	4.27%	20.51%	46.44%	27.35%	0.85%
Tourism sector	**3.50**	**4**	**2.56%**	**12.25%**	**32.48%**	**36.47%**	**15.10%**	**1.14%**
Terrestrial ecosystems	4.19	4	0.57%	3.42%	14.25%	39.32%	41.60%	0.85%
Continental and marine aquatic ecosystems	4.20	4	2.28%	3.42%	13.68%	33.05%	46.72%	0.85%
Fishing sector	3.89	4	2.56%	5.13%	22.22%	39.89%	29.06%	1.14%
Plant and animal biodiversity	4.29	4	0.28%	2.28%	11.97%	38.75%	45.87%	0.85%
Agricultural sector	4.19	4	0.85%	1.42%	16.81%	39.03%	41.03%	0.85%
Coastal areas	4.06	4	2.56%	4.56%	15.10%	39.32%	37.61%	0.85%

Table 4: When do you think the effects of climate change will begin to have an impact? When do you think the effects of climate change will begin to have an impact on the tourism sector?

	Generic	Tourism sector
It is causing impacts at the moment	5.41%	2.56%
It is causing impacts at the moment and will also cause them in the future	90.03%	56.13%
It will only cause impacts in the future, in the short term (10-20 years)	2.28%	19.37%
It will only cause impacts in the future, in the long term (20-50 years)	0.85%	17.38%
It will not cause any impacts	0.57%	3.13%
No opinion	0.85%	1.42%

3.3 Valuation of information provided on climate change and tourism

Two questions have been raised regarding the level of information: 1) Do you believe the information provided by the media about climate change is adequate in quantity and quality? Why? and 2) Do you believe the information provided by the media about the impacts of climate change on the tourism sector is adequate in quantity and quality? Why? Those surveyed reported that the information they received on the general effects of climate change is insufficient in terms both of quality and quality, an inadequacy which intensified as regards specific information concerning the effects of climate change on the tourism sector (Table 5). Respondents did not give a positive assessment of information provided about the general or specific effects of climate change, and reported having received generalised information with a clearly catastrophic and alarmist bias, rendering it less credible or resulting in attitudes of stoicism.

Thus, as regards the level of basic information that this section of the population possessed about climate change in the study area, our findings indicate that their knowledge was quite biased. When asked about the nature of the possible impacts of climate change on the study area, a catastrophic vision predominated: 53% of those surveyed believed that the impacts would be very negative, and 34%, negative. Only 2% felt that the effects might be positive, 0% very positive, and 9% thought that the effects would be neutral. 1% had no opinion.

Table 5:   Information provided by the media on the general impacts of climate change, and impacts on the tourism sector in particular.

	Climate Change		Climate Change and Tourism	
	Quantity %	Quality %	Quantity %	Quality %
1 Inadequate	21.94	27.92	29.06	31.34
2	35.04	37.04	35.04	37.89
3	21.94	22.51	23.36	25.07
4	15.95	10.26	9.97	3.13
5 Adequate	3.99	1.42	0.85	0.85
No opinion	1.14	0.85	1.71	1.71

3.4 Different modes of tourism and climate change

When respondents were asked about the degree and nature of the effects of climate change on different modes of tourism, it became apparent that an implicit understanding existed of how these modes indicated varying degrees of awareness of or dependence on atmospheric elements and, consequently, how they would be affected in different ways: similarly, the responses once again showed low perception of the beneficial effects of some of the direct impacts of climate change (for example, increased duration of inter-seasonal periods, potentially leading to longer tourism seasons and reduced importance of the marked problem of seasonality, did not appear to be perceived by the respondents). Of all the modes of tourism, the one which was perceived to be most susceptible to being affected by climate change in our study area was snow tourism (4.10 on a scale of 1 to 5), followed by sun-and-beach (3.76) and nature tourism (3.56): those perceived to be least susceptible were nautical tourism (3.32), adventure sports tourism (3.14) and cultural tourism (2.39). The potential effects were perceived as positive as regards cultural tourism, negative for snow tourism and predominantly negative for nature and sun-and-beach tourism (Table 6). It should be noted that there were a high percentage of "no opinion" responses, perhaps reflecting the level of disinformation.

When asked who they thought was most aware of the impacts climate change could have on the tourism sector, respondents' answers clearly indicated the low level of concern among tourists as regards this issue. Tourists are not perceived to be the group which is most concerned about the consequences that climate change might have for the tourism sector: according to those surveyed, it is scientists and tour operators or agents in the sector who display higher levels of awareness (Table 7). Respondents indicate that tourists can modify their behaviour in response to climate change by choosing new destinations capable of satisfying their climatic preferences or by changing when they take their holidays, as long as these options do not involve significantly greater expense.

Table 6: Thinking about your immediate geographical surroundings in the future, to what extent do you think the following modes of tourism could be affected by climate change?

	Weighted mean	Median	1 Not at all	2	3	4	5 Very much	No opinion
Cultural tourism	2.39	2	22.79%	34.76%	24.79%	14.53%	2.56%	0.57%
Sun and beach tourism	3.76	4	7.12%	11.40%	15.38%	29.63%	35.90%	0.57%
Nautical tourism	3.32	3	9.69%	15.10%	25.36%	32.48%	16.81%	0.57%
Snow tourism	4.10	5	8.26%	3.99%	7.41%	29.63%	50.14%	0.57%
Nature tourism	3.56	4	3.42%	11.40%	28.21%	39.32%	17.09%	0.57%
Adventure sports tourism	3.14	3	8.26%	17.95%	34.19%	29.91%	9.12%	0.57%

	Weighted mean	Median	1 Negatively	2	3	4	5 Positively	No opinion
Cultural tourism	2.96	3	4.27%	19.94%	54.70%	12.25%	6.27%	2.56%
Sun and beach tourism	2.27	2	33.05%	27.35%	19.66%	12.25%	5.13%	2.56%
Nautical tourism	2.55	3	17.95%	25.36%	39.03%	11.40%	3.13%	3.13%
Snow tourism	1.70	1	53.56%	25.64%	11.97%	3.70%	1.71%	3.42%
Nature tourism	2.26	2	21.94%	38.18%	29.06%	5.41%	2.28%	3.13%
Adventure sports tourism	2.54	3	10.26%	33.62%	47.58%	6.55%	1.14%	0.85%

Table 7: Who do you think is most aware of the impacts climate change could have on the tourism sector?

	%
Tourists	9.11
Tour operators and the main agents involved in the tourism sector	27.78
Politicians	7.33
Scientists	37.11
None of the above	6.22
All of the above	6.22
Others	6.22
No opinion	0.00

4 Conclusions

Respondents understanding of the risks associated with climate change suggest a low level of perception of the possible effects of this phenomenon on the tourism sector (Figure 2). Our findings indicate that the media and educational campaigns implemented in recent years regarding environmental issues have had a profound effect on young people: degradation of the environment appears to be their prime concern for the future. However, of the many environmental issues raised, climate change is not their main concern. Although they are conscious that the problem is already having an impact and that, above all, it will continue to do so in the future, climate change is perceived as an issue of great interest on a global scale, but not at local or regional levels. In other words, our findings indicate a low perception of the risks associated with climate change, which is perceived to be distant and unrelated to the everyday life of individuals. This perception is clearly related to the enormous difficulty our senses encounter in detecting the subtle manifestations of climate change in the present, and to the kind of information provided about this phenomenon. Thus, those surveyed did not give a positive assessment of the information provided as regards either general or specific effects of climate change, and reported having received generalised information of an evidently catastrophic and alarmist nature. Maybe that helps explain the low ability to perceive positive impacts of climate change on the tourism sector. The information provided by the media is fundamental for correct transmission of the evidence for global warming and associated impacts. The contents of such information contribute to creating public opinion, and should therefore be rigorous, responsible and associated with the everyday surroundings of the individual.

To a certain extent, the tourism sector is perceived as less susceptible to being affected by climate change than other sectors of the economy or strategic issues, and the effects were also perceived to be less apparent and immediate. This surprising situation may be related to the insufficient information provided by the media on the inter-relationship, mentioned earlier, between climate change and tourism: the rare headlines which appear tend to reflect generalised and sensationalist treatment of the issue, while the conditional and uncertain nature of long-term forecasts for the complex tourism system and the use of examples depicting distant geographical scenarios, all encourage the population to dismiss the problem and its consequences. Nevertheless, there are certain indications which suggest that this low perception is not merely the result of a lack of knowledge, or "ignorance": the vested interests evidenced by respondents in their possible role as tourism consumers condition their perceptions of the situation. They see what they want to see, enabling them to maintain and justify their own lifestyles and their personal, and often "unsustainable", forms of tourism consumption. This would explain why they do not see tourists as the group which is most concerned by climate change, but are aware of the concern of scientists, tour operators and agents in the tourism sector.

Scale	Climate change is a major problem in the global scale. Climate change is a minor problem in the local scale.
Vulnerability	The tourism sector is not perceived as one of the most vulnerable sectors to climate change.
Direction	The impacts of climate change on tourism are becoming more visible than the impacts of tourism on climate change.
Kinds of impacts	The negative impacts of climate change on the tourism sector are displayed more than the positive. Indirect impacts of climate change on the tourism sector are seen as more negative than the direct impacts.
Timeframe	The impacts of climate change on the tourism sector are displayed in medium and long term.
Actors	Tourists are not perceived to be the group which is most concerned about the consequences that climate change might have on tourism sector.

Figure 2: Perceptions of climate change and tourism.

Low perception of the effects of climate change on the tourism sector, and of the tourism sector on climate change, may contribute to reduced awareness of personal and collective responsibility and, above all, demotivate present action, which is postponed until the future. For any climate change policy or strategy, whether adaptation or mitigation, consideration of the social factor will be fundamental in design and implementation of effective responses to avert the most pessimistic scenarios. It is therefore crucial for the tourism sector to provide truthful, close-to-home and scientifically correct information on the contribution of the tourism sector to climate change and vice versa. Cross-disciplinary educational and awareness raising campaigns on climate change are not sufficient: what is needed are specific campaigns that, led by the sector itself (from both the public and private sectors), will influence tourism consumers, rendering them aware and active. The great challenge: to increase environmental awareness among tourists and involve them in environmental action.

Acknowledgement

This study was conducted within the framework of a Plan Nacional de I+D+I research project sponsored by the Spanish Ministerio de Economía y Competitividad, reference number CSO2011-23404.

References

[1]   IPCC, *Climate Change 2013: The Physical Science Basis.* Contribution of Working Group I to the Fifth Assessment Report of the Intergovernmental Panel on Climate Change. Cambridge University Press: Cambridge, 2013.

[2]   Stern, N., *The Economics of Climate Change: The Stern Review.* Cambridge University Press: Cambridge, 2006.

[3]   Scott, D., Amelung, B., Becken, S., Ceron, P., Dubois, G., Gössling, S., Peeters, P. & Simpson, M., *Climate change and tourism. Responding to global challenges.* United Nations World Tourism Organization: Madrid, 2008.

[4]   Becken, S., *The importance of climate and weather for tourism: literature review.* Lincoln University, LEaP, Land Environment and People Miscellaneous Publications: Lincoln, 2010.

[5]   Becken, S. & Hay, J., *Tourism and climate change – risks and opportunities.* Channel View Pub: Cleveland, 2007.

[6]   Gómez-Martín, M.B., Weather, climate and tourism. A geographical perspective. *Annals of Tourism Research,* 32(3), pp. 571-591, 2005.

[7]   Hall, C.M., Tourism and Climate Change: Knowledge Gaps and Issues. *Tourism Recreation Research,* 33, pp. 339-350, 2008.

[8]   Smith, K., The influence of weather and climate on recreation and tourism. *Weather,* 48, pp. 398-404, 1993.

[9]   Wall, G. & Badke, C., Tourism and Climate Change: an international perspective. *Journal of Sustainable Tourism,* 2(4), pp. 193-203, 1994.

[10]   Scott, D., Amelung, B., Becken, S., Ceron, P., Dubois, G., Gössling, S., Peeters, P. & Simpson, M., *Climate change and tourism. Responding to global challenges.* United Nations World Tourism Organization: Madrid, 2008.

[11]   Lyle, C., *Discussion Paper on Climate Change Mitigation Measures for International Air Transport.* United Nations World Tourism Organization: Madrid, 2009.

[12]   Peeters, P., Tourism and Climate Change Mitigation – Methods, Greenhouse Gas Reductions and Policies. *NHTV Academics Studies,* 6. NHTV. Breda University: Breda, 2007.

[13]   Simpson, M.C., Gössling, S., Scott, D., Hall, C.M. & Gladin, E., *Climate Change Adaptation and Mitigation in the Tourism Sector: Frameworks, Tools and Practices.* UNEP, University of Oxford, UNWTO, UNWMO: Paris, 2008.

[14]   UNWTO, *From Davos to Copenhagen and Beyond: Advancing Tourism's Response to Climate Change.* UNWTO Background paper, UNWTO: Madrid, 2009.

[15]   WTTC, *Leading the Challenge on Climate Change.* World Travel & Tourism Council: London, 2009.

[16]   Meira Cartea, P.A., *Comunicar el cambio climático. Escenario Social y Líneas de Acción.* Organismo Autónomo Parques Nacionales, Ministerio de Medio Ambiente y Medio Rural y Marino: Madrid, 2009.

[17] Becken, S., How Tourists and Tourism Experts Perceive Climate Change and Carbon offsetting Schemes. *Journal of Sustainable Tourism,* 12(4), pp. 332-345, 2004.

[18] Braun, L, Lohmann, M., Maksimovic, O., Meyer, M., Merkovic, A., Messerschmidt, E., Riedel, A. & Turner, M., Potential impact of climate change effects on preferences for tourism destinations. A psychological pilot study. *Climate Research,* 11(3), pp. 247-254, 1999.

[19] Amelung, B. & Viner, D., Mediterranean tourism: exploring the future with the tourism climatic index. *Journal of Sustainable Tourism,* 14(4), pp. 349-366, 2006.

[20] Amelung, B., Nicholls, S. & Viner, D., Implications of global climate change for tourism flows and seasonality. *Journal of Travel Research,* 45(3), pp. 285-296, 2007.

[21] Bigano, A., Hamilton, J.M., Maddison, D.J. & Tol, R.S.J., Predicting Tourism Flows under Climate Change. *Climatic Change,* 79(3-4), pp. 175-180, 2006.

[22] Hamilton, M., Maddison, D.J. & Tol, R.S.J., The Effects of Climate Change on International Tourism. *Climate Research,* 29(3), pp. 245-254, 2005.

[23] Lise, W. & Tol, R., Impact of Climate on Tourist Demand. *Climatic Change,* 55(4), pp. 429-449, 2002.

[24] Maddison, D., In search of warmer climates?. The impact of climate change on flows of British tourists. *Climatic Change,* 49(1-2), pp. 193-208, 2001.

[25] Scott, D., McBoyle, G. & Schwartzentruber, M., Climate change and the distribution of climatic resources for tourism in North America. *Climate Research,* 27(2), pp. 105-117, 2004.

[26] Gössling S., Bredberg, M., Randow, A., Sandström, E. & Svensson, P., Tourist Perceptions of Climate Change: A Study of International Tourists in Zanzibar. *Current Issues in Tourism,* 9(4-5), pp. 419-435, 2006.

[27] Becken, S., Tourists' Perception of International Air Travel's Impact on the Global Climate and Potential Climate Change Policies. *Journal of Sustainable Tourism,* 15(4), pp. 351-368, 2007.

[28] Dawson, J., Stewart, E.J., Lemelin, H. & Scott, D., The carbon cost of polar bear viewing tourism in Churchill, Canada. *Journal of Sustainable Tourism,* 18(3), pp. 319-336, 2010.

[29] Cohen, S. & Higham, J., Eyes wide shut? UK consumer perceptions on aviation climate impacts and travel decisions to New Zealand. *Current Issues in Tourism,* 14(4), pp. 323-335, 2011.

[30] McKercher, B., Prideaux, B., Cheung, C. & Law R., Achieving voluntary reductions in the carbon footprint of tourism and climate change. *Journal of Sustainable Tourism,* 18(3), pp. 297-317, 2010.

[31] Becken, S., How Tourists and Tourism Experts Perceive Climate Change and Carbon offsetting Schemes. *Journal of Sustainable Tourism,* 12(4), pp. 332-345, 2004.

[32] Marshall, N.A., Marshall, P.A., Abdulla, A., Rouphael, T. & Ali, A., Preparing for climate change: recognising its early impacts through the perceptions of dive tourists and dive operators in the Egyptian Red Sea. *Current Issues in Tourism,* 14(6), pp. 507-518, 2011.

[33] Scott, D., Gössling, S. & De Freitas, C.R., Preferred climates for tourism: cases studies from Canada, New Zealand and Sweden. *Climate Research,* 38(1), pp. 61-73, 2008.

[34] Beckmann, S.C., In the eye of the beholder: Danish consumer-citizens and sustainability. *Consumers, policy and the environment: a tribute to Folke Olander* (ed) K.G. Grunert, & J. Thogersen, Berlin: Springer, pp. 265-299, 2005.

[35] Meira, P.A., Arto, M. & Montero, P., *La sociedad ante el cambio climático.* Fundación MAPFRE: Madrid, 2009.

[36] Milfont, T.L., The effects of social desirability on self-reported environmental attitudes and ecological behaviour. *Environmentalist,* 29, pp. 263-269, 2008.

[37] Meira, P.A., Arto, M. & Montero, P., *La sociedad ante el cambio climático.* Fundación MAPFRE: Madrid, 2009.

[38] IPCC, *Climate Change 2013: The Physical Science Basis.* Contribution of Working Group I to the Fifth Assessment Report of the Intergovernmental Panel on Climate Change. Cambridge University Press: Cambridge, 2013.

[39] Stern, N., *The Economics of Climate Change: The Stern Review.* Cambridge University Press: Cambridge, 2006.

[40] UNWTO, *Climate Change and Tourism. Proceedings of the 1st International Conference on Climate Change and Tourism (Djerba, Tunisia, 2003).* UNWTO: Madrid, 2003.

[41] UNWTO, *From Davos to Bali: A Tourism Contribution to the Challenge of Climate Change.* UNWTO: Madrid, 2007.

[42] UNWTO, *From Davos to Copenhaguen and Beyond: Advancing Tourism's Response to Climate Change.* Background paper, UNWTO, UNWTO: Madrid, 2009.

Section 8
Marine and
coastal areas tourism

The evaluation of the present anchorage condition and the development tendency in Zadar County

M. Kovačić[1] & S. Favro[2]
[1]Faculty of Maritime Studies, University of Rijeka, Croatia
[2]Adriatic Expert, Croatia

Abstract

As result of consistently more rigorous and demanding regulations on the protection of marine environment and coastal landscape, as well as following the requirements for integral management of coastal area and sustainable development of nautical tourism, any new intervention in the highly sensitive littoral area is subject to strict assessments. Accordingly, the development of new infrastructure objects of nautical tourism is frequently questioned.

Due to the continual increase of nautical vessels that sail and permanently or temporarily stay at the east coast of the Adriatic Sea, the reception capacity of nautical ports is limited and consequently navigators, especially those with bigger vessels, deploy anchorages as their destination points. Respecting the current reality and the necessity to develop nautical tourism as an important economic function in Croatia this paper gives a systematic analysis of the anchoring issue. The authors research the method and the need for anchoring on free and institutional anchorages and evaluate the role of anchorages in the economy. The aim of the paper is to analyze the current situation based on the example of the Zadar County, especially the spatial-geographical conditions for the development of anchorages in the Zadar County. The goal of the paper is to establish the interdependence between the institutional anchoring and development of nautical tourism in the Zadar County.

Keywords: anchorage, institutional anchoring, nautical tourism, Zadar County.

WIT Transactions on Ecology and The Environment, Vol 187, © 2014 WIT Press
www.witpress.com, ISSN 1743-3541 (on-line)
doi:10.2495/ST140251

1 Introduction

The Croatian coast of the Adriatic Sea is a paradise for navigation experts, with more than one thousand islands and well-indented coasts, clear sea and favourable climatic conditions. As the navigation experts' interest in the coast grew, so did the required infrastructure develop, as well as marinas and ports for residing, moorings were arranged, anchorages organised as well as facilities for vessels and yachts' supply and maintenance. Every year, the number of vessels is in the increase and so is the demand for berths. Many small ports, marinas and piers are desirable destinations for moorings during the summer season and every protected bay becomes a mooring.

The coastal waters of Zadar County comprise of an attractive part of the Croatian coast set between the foothills of Velebit Mountain on the coast and Silba and Olib islands in the NW, and Vrgara, Murvenjak and Murter in the SE. Besides natural beauties and a quality tourist offer, the area has a favourable climate for ship accommodation. There is a growing need for new nautical moorings in Zadar County, especially for the ones that could accept larger nautical vessels, and the boaters evaluate it as favourable for navigation and ship accommodation.

The subject of author's research is nautical anchorages of Zadar County. The aim of this research is to get known with the importance of nautical anchorages, and their role in sustainable development of nautical tourism in Zadar County.

The purpose of this research is to explore and analyse nautical anchorages of Zadar County and point to their role in economic development of Zadar County.

2 Theoretical guidelines and analysis of the issue

The research of scientific literature that thematically analyses nautical anchorages indicates a very small number of scientific papers as well as to a modest official range of pieces of information about registered physical traffic in organized nautical anchorages, especially of the ones of Zadar County and of the type, scope and service quality provided.

Nautical tourism is a specific form of tourism based on recreation activities related to the sea, lake and river navigation [1]. The motive for a trip is recreation and pleasure on the vessel and the sea and it is the key criterion to distinguish nautical tourism among other tourism forms. Nautical tourism has a complex structure and heterogeneous nature. Besides its own specific features, it also has elements of health, sport, excursion, cultural and other similar forms of tourism.

Anchorage is a part of water area equipped for the mooring of vessels in a bay protected from any bad weather. Safe anchorages are located in water area of the port or bay, and open anchorages are located in the unprotected water area and are intended for a short stay of vessels (overnight stay/several days). These anchorages aren't equipped with commercial infrastructure. From the nautical aspect, anchorages that are charted and marked with clear signs should be differentiated from the ones intended to vessels that are subjects to payment system.

2.1 The analysis of anchorages' effects on the economy

There are numerous bays favourable for anchoring along Croatian islands and coast. Many of them are still intact, un-built, and the others are periodically inhabited, and along some coasts are old insular places.

Anchorage managing is under the authority of regional government in accordance with acts and ordinances that regulate that area [2–5]. It implies granting the concession and monitoring due to which a part of maritime domain is excluded from public use and is given to the authorized concessionaire to be used. The authorized concessionaire is in charge for keeping the order on organized anchorages in accordance with the Concession contract. A person operating a yacht or a boat shall be responsible for safety of the vessel while at anchorage, and shall be obliged to follow instructions of the concession holder and the competent harbourmaster's office. When anchored, a person operating a vessel shall ensure that the vessel is sufficiently removed from the nearest vessels in all directions and all weather conditions. When anchored, a vessel shall exhibit day signals and lights according to the "International Regulations for Preventing Collisions at Sea". The fee for anchoring depends on the location and anchorage organisation, and it is additionally regulated by provisions. A concession holder of a special purpose port – anchorage shall issue to a person operating a vessel a receipt for dues paid. If dry waste was collected, the concession holder shall issue a receipt for collection of the waste from the vessel. The dues charged shall include the service of collecting dry waste from the vessel. A person operating a ship, a boat or a yacht shall keep on the vessel the invoice and the receipt until leaving the territorial sea of the Republic of Croatia. The concession holder shall present, at the navigator's request, the price list of dues charged for mooring, certified by the County Office. According to Tomas Nautica Yachting Survey 2012 [6], an organised anchoring attracts boaters. Only the cognition that there is an organized system, gives a sense of security to the crew and the vessel overcomes the expense of anchorage fee.

According to Tomas Nautica Survey 2012 [6], Yachtsmen realized 12 overnights on average during their journey; of those, 7 overnights on average in marinas, and 1 to 2 overnights on average in town ports and on corpo-morto and moorings outside marinas/ports; yachtsmen in Croatian charter realized 9 overnights on average, while on vessels of personal ownership, ownership of friends/relatives and foreign charter they realized 16 overnights. Average number and distribution of overnights by location is shown in the Table 1.

A small number of yachtsmen realized overnights in accommodation facilities on shore. The number of overnights moored out of town ports and marinas by vessel ownership is shown in the Table 2.

Table 1: Average number and distribution of overnights by location.

Number of overnights	Average number of overnights	%
On corpo morto out of town ports and marinas	1.5	11.7
Moored out of town ports and marinas	1.7	13.3
In accommodation facilities on shore	0.2	1.4
TOTAL	12.4	100.0

Source: [6].

Table 2: Number of overnights moored out of town ports and marinas by vessel ownership.

Number of overnights moored out of town ports and marinas	Total	Croatian charter	Other
0	62.9	62.8	63.1
1 to 3	20.8	25.2	16.5
4 to 7	11.5	10.4	12.6
8 to 14	3.2	1.5	4.9
15 to 21	1.0	0.1	1.9
22 and more	0.5	.	1.0
TOTAL	100.0	100.0	100.0

Source: [6].

The biggest number of overnight stays on average was realized by charters from Russia (10), and between 9 to 10 overnights were realised by Frenchmen, Germans, British and the Dutch. More than the average overnight stay in marinas was realized by Russians (70% of all overnight stays was realized by Russians), Italians have realized a relatively smaller number of overnight stays (50%) and they have realized overnight stays in ports above the average (20%) and on buoys outside local ports and marinas (14%).

Domestic charters realized overnight stays on buoys more than others (14%), while most Slovenians stayed overnight on the anchor outside marinas and local ports (18%). The biggest share of charter carriers, who during the navigation visited four or more marinas, was among the Swedes (45%), Russians (43%) and British (40%) [6]. Vessels longer than 12 meters in Croatian nautical tourism ports have an insufficient number of berths. The number of overnights moored out of town ports and marinas by length of vessel is shown in Table 3.

With the increase of vessel's length, the share of navigations with 15 and more overnight stays was decreased (29% for vessels up to 9 meters and 16% for vessels longer than 13 meters). The smallest share of overnight stays in marinas was recorded among boaters with vessels up to 9 meters (54% of all overnights), while boaters on longer vessels more than 60% of all overnights realized on average in marinas. Boaters on vessels up to 9 meters stayed overnight on anchors outside local ports and marinas more often than average boaters (17% of all overnight stays).

Table 3:   Number of overnights moored out of town ports and marinas by length of vessel.

Number of overnights moored out of town ports and marinas	Total	Up to 9.0 m	9.1 to 11.0 m	11.1 to 13.0 m	13.1 m and longer
0	62.9	58.0	64.5	62.9	64.6
1 to 3	20.8	20.2	21.2	22.2	19.4
4 to 7	11.5	14.9	11.4	10.0	10.9
8 to 14	3.2	5.5	1.8	2.9	3.6
15 to 21	1.0	0.5	0.7	1.6	1.0
22 and more	0.5	0.8	0.4	0.3	0.5
TOTAL	100.0	100.0	100.0	100.0	100.0

Source: [6].

2.2 The effect of anchorages on marine environment

Under the development pressure, many bays have changed their indigenous shape during the last decades and they have become apartment resorts and nautical marinas, moorings and anchorages. Motives for mooring have significantly changed due to sport and entertainment with the development of nautical tourism and in the last thirty years with the development of navigation. While anchorages were a necessity to professional navigators and fishermen due to the lack of ports or while they were waiting to enter the port, anchoring is often both the purpose and the aim of the navigation for boaters. Boaters often use anchorages for the following purposes: planned due to the way they use their vacations (swimming, fishing, diving, ...), as a shelter from wind and sea during the storm or a malfunction on the vessel, as a necessity due to the shortage of berths. Due to a large number of vessels during summer there is often a shortage of berths in ports or moorings so anchorage becomes a necessary choice to many boaters. Many boaters, who navigate on their own vessels with a smaller budget, visit isolated bay because they don't have to pay a berth there or if there is an organized anchorage, the berth is much cheaper than the one in marinas.

Natural resources are still the main motivational factor for the arrival and stay of tourists in Croatia. The negative influence of tourism on the area and the environment can be reduced to the minimum only by regulating its development, which presumes the planning of a rational and controlled [7], that is, limited and directed use of space for the building of accommodation, and the implementation of all environmental protection measures. The main precondition for a sustainable coexistence among certain activities is their appropriate locating and responsible management [7]. Garbage is regularly gathered and taken on organized anchorages, and other activities with the aim to protect maritime environment are as well carried out. The garbage is sorted and taken to an appropriate place provided for disposal.

It is particularly significant because of two invasive green algae *Caulerpa taxifolia* and *Caulerpa racemosa*, which represent the biggest threat to biological diversity and, in the long-term, can adversely make damages. *Caulerpa taxifolia* is particularly dangerous. It is known for a long period of time in the Adriatic. It has been proved that from the area where it settles, it extrudes all other algae and animals, especially sponges, corals and sea urchins. *Caulerpa taxifolie* is spread by transport on anchors and nets. The spreading can only be prevented by physical removal, and by prohibition of anchoring and fishing at places where it was discovered. That is why it is recommended the use of buoys for a safe anchoring and sea bed protection from the above mentioned invasive alga.

3 Methodological approach to the issue

Maritime region of Zadar County outshines in comparison to other areas of Croatian coast thanks to insular groups with its distinct degraded, scattered, indented coastal line and specific parallel spread in several lines that follow the direction of spreading basic geological and geomorphologic structures on the nearby land. A large number of bays protected from the wind and storms are natural shelters. Once were a salvation for fishermen, labourers and passengers, and now are safe retreats for nautical tourists who use them more and more due to the lack of berths and moorings in nautical tourism ports.

3.1 The analysis of spatial and geographic features of the Zadar County

Zadar County spreads over 7.276,23 km^2 and it is situated in the central part of Croatian coastal area. Due to its natural location, Zadar County is a significant transport connection; it is connected by state roads and Zagreb-Split highway, airlines (Zadar airport), and ferry lines with Ancona in Italy (departure from the City of Zadar) and rail routes with the rest of Croatia.

The main characteristics of Zadar sea waters are numerous islands and islets set in several lines that aren't significantly distant and that are partly connected with slit channels. Coastal area of Zadar County is relatively lowland coast and somewhere it is also sandy. The coast is more indented in the Velebit Channel. Zadar archipelago is the most indented Adriatic archipelago with numerous beauties of nature and 4 lines of islands: 24 big ones and 300 smaller islets and cliffs, out of which only 17 ones are inhabited.

With 1,300 km long costal line (island included), it is the most indented coast in the whole Mediterranean. Sea and offshore zone of Zadar County are considered to be particularly sensitive resource and it is enclosed with special regulations from the Strategy and the Programme of Physical Planning of the Republic of Croatia [8].

3.2 Oceanographic features of Zadar County archipelago

Main oceanographic features of Northern Dalmatian waters coincide with average values of the entire Croatian coast with appropriate particularities that derive from the geographic position, geomorphological segmentation and climate features.

The deepest parts of Zadar County waters are NW part of Silban channel (116 m), western entrance to Maknare passage (98 m), Murter sea (94 m), and the area between Žirje and lines of islets and reef (Blitvenica, Kosmerka, Vrtlac and others) up to 108 meters deep. The sea bed near the coast is mostly rocky and sandy (especially in bays and vast shallows), and deeper parts of sea bed are covered with silty sediments on which in some places are deposited thinner layers of different mollusks shells [9]. More important areas with sandy sediments are on the sea bed between Vir and Privlaka and along the coast around Olib Island. Sea temperatures on the surface of internal part of Northern Dalmatian waters (according to the data for Zadar and Veli Rat, for which a continuous statistical line for more years doesn't exist) are from the lowest average of 10.8°C in February and the highest one of 23.6°C in August. Sea transparency is significant. It is mainly over 10 meters, and often is around 20 meters. It is bigger along islands of the middle and outer line and in the areas of rocky sea bed. There is less transparency in the internal channels which are influenced by various forms of pollution from the nearby mainland, especially in the area of Zadar and Šibenik. During the summer, long-periodical gradient streams of the SW or S directions prevail in some channels, especially in those closer to the open sea. The average speed of surface currents in the Vir Sea is 11 cm/s (0.21 knots), and in Zadar Channel only 8 cm/s (0.15 knots) [10]. Maximum current speeds in northern part of Šibenik archipelago are relatively large (up to 61 cm/s or 1.2 knots in Žirajski Channel), and the average speeds (17.9 cm/s or 0.34 knots Kaprijski channel and 16.1 cm/s or 0.31 knots in Žirajski channel) are above the average Mediterranean Sea channels. Tidal currents are very expressed in the internal channels. The average speed of tidal currents is 20.5 cm/s (0.4 knots). The current is intensified, especially during live tides on the full moon and the new moon, when the speed can reach up to 154 cm/s (3 knots). The average difference between high and low water is 29 cm, and the average extreme amplitude is 38 cm [11]. There is a greater difference between high and low waters when the sea level is influenced not only by tides but also by greater changes in air pressure. The average sea salinity is approximately 38%. In general, the annual fluctuations are mostly expressed in Velebit Channel and Pag Bay. The lowest degradated in these waters are in February and May, primarily due to the influx of fresh water from the mainland and occasional flows on the island of Pag during winter months, and due to snow melting from Velebit during the spring. The quality of sea water in Zadar County waters is marked by the second grade quality, which, among other things, makes it suitable for various forms of economic evaluation (fishing, aquaculture, tourism, etc.) Since the installation of a collector is only a partial solution, the construction of the device for waste water purification has largely been completed in Zadar, which significantly affects the increase of sea water quality in Zadar Channel.

3.3 Analysis of nautical tourism in Zadar County

Tourism is one of the strategic development guidelines [12] of Zadar County that is based on a significant tourist potential and resources [13] such as: attractive coastal area (beaches, anchorages, etc.), vast areas of protected natural heritage (National Park Velebit, Nature Park Telašćica, etc.), cultural heritage (town of Zadar, Nin, Pag, etc.), medicinal mud (Pag, Nin, Karin, Posedarje, etc.), and a geographic location that is relatively close to one of the most important tourist generating areas.

The most important form of tourism in Zadar County is nautical tourism [14]. According to typology, with the reference to the motive of the subjects in the area of North Dalmatia there is mobile, navigational and sunbathing nautical tourism. From the aspect of the size and type of vessels, there is yachting and motorboat nautical tourism. From the aspect of share, volume and area of navigation, there is "small" nautical tourism, and from the aspect of the organisation of navigation there is individual nautical tourism. According to the purpose of navigation there is excursion, cruising, sailing, and navigation for sports and entertainment. According to areas where it takes place, nautical tourism is divided in coastal and insular nautical tourism.

Data indicates that Zadar County was visited by a total number of 1119,119 guests in 2010, thus realizing 7,973,587 overnight stays. In average, duration of stay was 7.1 day and most foreign guests arrived from Germany (144,426 guests) who realized 1219,278 overnight stays. They were followed by guests from Slovenia (130,464 guests) who realized 1009,765 overnight stays and 82,770 guests from Austria who realized 539,643 overnight stays [15]. Tourism in Zadar County has seasonal character, 34% of the total arrivals are recorded in July. Also, 75% of overnight stays is realized in July and August. The total income from tourism in Zadar County was 696.075.899 Kuna in 2010. The same year, investments in tourism were in total 117.605.188, 00 Kuna [15].

In 2012, there were 19 ports, 7 anchorages, 2 moorings and 10 marinas (of which two land marinas and eight marinas categorised in categories: 4 in the 2nd category and 4 in the 3rd category) in Zadar County. The capacities in Zadar County include 828,000 square meters of water surface area, or 25% of such surfaces in the country. There are 3,557 moorings or 20% of moorings in the country or more than 25% of such areas in the country. More moorings than the Zadar County has only the County of Istria. The profit realised by nautical ports in 2011 and 2012 is shown in the Table 4.

Table 4: Profit realised by nautical ports in 2011 and 2012 in 000 HRKa.

	2011	2012	Indices 2012/2011
The County of Zadar	137,731	141,689	102,9
Renting of moorings	101,657	105,256	103,5
Stationed	90,675	94,696	104,4
In transit	10,982	10,560	96,2
Maintaining services	12,112	9,057	74,8
Other income	23,962	27,376	114,2

Source: [15].

There were 3,031 of vessels permanently moored in Zadar County that is about 20% more of such vessels in Croatia. Istria with 3,500 and the Primorsko-Goranska County with 3,100 vessels had more permanently moored vessels than Zadar County. The total income realised in nautical ports in 2012 in Croatia amounted to 660 million Kuna, out of which 487.8 million Kuna was realised through the renting of moorings that is 73.9% of the total realised income. As compared to 2011, the total profit increased by 10%, while the income gained through renting of moorings increased by 11%. These indicators show that the income realised through moored vessels amounted to 105.3 million Kuna, and through other marina services (maintaining services and other services) 141700,000 Kuna in Zadar County that is 23% of the total income of all nautical ports. The income increased by 2.9%, out of which for the moorings 3.5%.

During the summer, the density of vessels in northern waters of Zadar County often surpasses permeable power of small inter-islands water and narrow straits. Boaters then join various participants of already intensified maritime traffic in the part of the year with the most favourable meteorological and oceanographic conditions. Numerous fishing boats and excursion vessels sail out then from island's bays and the nearby mainland even without boaters, and the frequency of marine lines that connect islands to the mainland is increased.

The most important centre of nautical tourism in the region is Zadar with the surrounding neighbourhood. There are several marinas in Zadar (*Zadar – Tankerkomerc* with 300 berths and 200 dry berths in Vrulja bay, *Uskok* with 500 berths and 50 dry berths and *Borik* with 220 berths and 50 dry berths in the western part of the city), and on the border of Bibinje and Sukošan is the biggest Croatian marina *Dalmacija* with 1200 berths and 500 dry berths.

Big marinas are also located in Biograd *(Kornati* with 500 berths and 60 dry berths and *Šangulin* with 150 berths and 10 dry berths), Tribunj *(Tribunj* with 260 berths and 150 dry berths), Vodice *(ACI Vodice* with 415 berths and 90 dry berths), Skradin *(ACI Skradin* with 200 berths), Šibenik *(Mandalina* with 280 berths and *Solaris* with 320 berths), Primošten *(Kremik* with 393 berths and 150 dry berths) and Rogoznica *(Frapa* with 300 berths and 150 dry berths in *Soline bay).*

Zadar County has launched the organization of moorings with buoys on favourable locations along the Zadar archipelago which are granted in a concession usually to the islanders themselves.

3.4 The analysis of receptive capacities of organized anchorages in Zadar County

In 2013, Zadar County has granted 30 concessions for anchorage management. The total area of concessional organized anchorages is 369,511 m^2. There were 607 buoys while the average price per day for one meter in length was 12 Kuna.

Economic effects of concessions on nautical anchorages are visible through financial results and employment [13, 16, 17]. Direct financial effects of granting a concession on maritime domain are: fixed fee of the concession fee, and variable fee of the concession fee. Indirect financial effects of granting a concession are: income tax, contributions from salaries, and Value-added tax.

Investment in anchorages brings positive effects for employment. It is foreseen that at least 3 workers during the season (2 months) will be employed on one anchorage. The structure of persons employed is the following one: diver (1), maintenance worker (1) and worker on the dock (1). That system doesn't require large investments (it is necessary to set buoys, concrete weights and build moorings on the coast), and it allows boaters a safe berth without the need of anchoring, and an organized waste collecting. In that way, the possibility for "a black berth" is minimized, and boaters are gathered in local ports where it is increased the spending possibility, on average, of wealthy tourists in local restaurants and other existing service facilities (shops, rarely souvenir shops, etc.). Moorings motivate smaller investors to build supporting facilities (restaurants, cafes, etc.) that is an additional confirmation of successful model of adjustment of the existing modest infrastructure to the needs of boaters and the local community.

4   Results and discussion

The development of the coastal area must be sustainable for a longer period of time because the preserved area is the most important resource. Sustainable development includes the fulfilment of human needs without reducing the possibility to meet the needs of future generations [18]. Sustainability, when it comes to nautical tourism, implies the balance between reducing possibilities for economic development and permissible reduction in the quality of coastal ecosystems. Therefore, future development has to be based on the policy of nature preservation, in order to ensure socio-economic prosperity of locations and areas where the activity is being performed. Particularly important segment of sustainable development is the creation of economic and social preconditions for the life of local population employed in service sector of nautical tourism.

Management and use of integrated approach in the development of coastal area implies significant evaluations, aim defining and management of coastal systems and resources, and at the same time take care about traditional, cultural and historic interests. It should be a constant evaluation process.

Inshore and maritime area of Zadar County offer significant possibilities for economic growth, entertainment and life. There is also a rich but very fragile biodiversity that requires a transparent management, maintenance and protection. Organised anchorages have a significant development potential that wouldn't significantly violate maritime environment. Practically it can be discussed about monitoring the sea water by not violating the freedom to navigate. Every partial management of nautical tourism subjects and objects, organised anchorage system included, should be harmonized with specificities and demands of local community [19–21].

Organised anchorages increase the supply and complementary services based on boaters' demands, and its purpose should be to create competitive position on the market and improve socio-economic indicators in those areas, including indirect and direct factors. Prospects for the development of economy from the aspect of the development of organised nautical anchorages with its direct and indirect complementary activities and their effects can be analysed through the expected growth of: catering capacities, services, employment.

Effects that nautical tourism can have on economic activities can be direct and indirect. Direct effects of nautical tourism are primarily connected to local labour employment, stimulation of different service activities important for boaters (vessel and engine servicing, equipment, catering, supplies). There are also many indirect effects of nautical tourism, for example boaters are interested in visiting cultural events in coastal towns and sightseeing local cultural and historical monuments [9, 22]. The development of organized nautical anchorages cannot be seen only as a process of social change of living conditions in nautical destinations but also as an incentive process that can influence the change of social and economic structure of services and activities on islands and coast.

Increasing the number of organized anchorages, it is possible to expect positive results of the process of employing local inhabitants that are not in the direct relation with the anchorage. This primarily relates to the employment related to the offer from local food products, restaurants and other services.

5   Recommendations and possibilities for further development

The development of nautical tourism in primarily conditioned by boaters' demand that refers to the formation of new capacities, i.e. berths in marinas and tourist ports but also by the demand of vessels on the mainland. It is expected that with the assumption of general economic and social development, a significant potential demand will be formed in Europe.

The demand for nautical anchorages is inversely proportional to the demand for berths in nautical tourism ports. More berths in marinas means also a lower demand for anchorages, i.e. lack of berth in marinas increases the demand for organised and unorganized anchorages.

Taking into account that nautical tourism still has a seasonal character in the area of Zadar County, the need to construct new nautical tourism ports is questioned here. The offered solution is in ecological-acceptable system of organised anchorages that would satisfy the nautical demand. At the same time, nautical tourism of Zadar County would increase its berths' offer by an appropriate control and monitoring of anchorage use. When planning new anchorages or spreading the capacities of existing anchorages, the total receptive capacities of Zadar County's sea water should be taken into account. Zadar County, as the area with great potential, for the establishment of organized anchorages should continue to operate in the way to issue concessions on attractive but also on less attractive locations.

6   Conclusion

Great landscape diversity of County's mainland part, a combination of the mountain, valley, sea and numerous islands make Zadar County extremely attractive for the development of elite and selective form of tourism. The main feature of Zadar archipelago are numerous islands and islets situated in a few lines, that aren't significantly distant, and are partly interconnected with narrow passages. The coastal area of Zadar County is relatively low land coast, somewhere also sandy. Among significant socio-economic effects of organized anchorages on the local community and beyond, their biggest contribution is the sea protection. It becomes an integral element of coastal zone management, it reduces "wild anchoring", uncontrolled waste dumping into the sea, it increases safe navigation and completes tourist offer. Although nautical tourism still isn't a major polluter, a constant increase in the number of vessels, tendency of the arrivals of larger nautical vessels, multiplies the amount of produced waste (biodegradable but also non-biodegradable) that should be gathered and properly treated. Organized anchorages protect the environment through the proper waste disposal. The construction of new anchorages should be viewed as an important part of nautical tourism that contributes to social and economic development of coastal areas and island in Zadar County. It is also a form of the offer that opposite to marinas includes simple services with an emphasis on boaters' safety and the safety of their vessels.

References

[1]   Act of services in Tourism. Zagreb: Official Gazette, 88/10.
[2]   Environmental Protection Act. Zagreb: Official Gazette, 110/07.
[3]   Law on Maritime Domain and Seaports. Official Gazette, 158/03, 100/04, 141/06, 38/09.
[4]   Ordinance on amendments to the Ordinance on the conditions and methods of maintaining order in ports and other parts of internal waters and territorial sea of the Republic of Croatia. Zagreb Official Gazette, 80/12.
[5]   Regulation on the procedure for granting concessions in the maritime domain. Zagreb: Official Gazette, 102/11.
[6]   Marušić, Z., Horak, S., Sever, I., Stavovi i potrošnja nautičara u Hrvatskoj Tomas Nautika Jahting 2012, Zagreb: Institute for Tourism, 2012.
[7]   Kovačić, M., Dundović, Č., *Planning and design of nautical tourism ports.* Rijeka: Pomorski fakultet Sveučilišta u Rijeci, 2012.
[8]   Ministry of Sea, Transport and Infrastructure. 2008, Strategy for the Development of Croatian nautical tourism for the period 2009 to 2019, Zagreb.
[9]   Faričić, J., *Geography of Northern Dalmatian Islands.* Zagreb: Školska knjiga, 2012.
[10]   Buljan, M., Zore-Armanda, M., Oceanographical Properties of the Adriatic sea, *Oceanogr. Mar. Biol. Ann. Rev.*, 14, Harold Barnes, Ed., Aberdeen University Press, 1976.
[11]   Riđanović, I., *The Geography of the Sea.* Zagreb: Publishing House Fletar, 2004.
[12]   Zrilić, S., Peričić, S., Lonić, D., Kevrić, V., County Development Strategy, Zadar: Zadar County, 2011.
[13]   Karlić, B., *The most beautiful Adriatic anchorages.* Library Sea, 2010.

[14] Kovačić, M., Favro, S., Possibilities for nautical tourism development in Zadar County. *Pomorstvo*, 26(1), pp. 151-164, 2012.

[15] Croatian Bureau of Statistics www.dzs.hr.

[16] ZADRA, Feasibility study for granting concessions and valuation of the concession to exploit anchorages: Zadar County Development Agency, 2010.

[17] Kundih, B., Srabotnak, N., Anchorages and moorings. webpage: http://www.pomorskodobro.com/hr/sidrista-i-privezista.html, 2012.

[18] Kovačić, M., The development of nautical ports in terms of sustainable development of nautical tourism. *Pomorski zbornik*, 41(1), pp. 135-154, 2003.

[19] Gračan, D., Strategic planning development of nautical tourism in Croatia. *Tourism and Hospitality Management,* 12(1), pp. 111-117, 2006.

[20] Luković, T., Bilić, M., Nautical tourism ports in Croatia and the local development strategy. *Naše more*, 54(3-4), pp. 114-122, 2007.

[21] Žuvela, I., The concept and strategy development of the maritime economy of Croatia, Rijeka. *Pomorski zbornik*, 38(1), 2002.

[22] Favro, S., Saganić, I., Natural features of Croatian littoral area as a comparative advantage for the development of nautical tourism. *Geoadria* 12(1), pp. 59-81, 2007.

[23] MPPI, Popis koncesioniranih sidrišta za potrebe brodica i jahti u unutarnjim morskim vodama Republike Hrvatske u 2013. Webpage: http://www.mppi.hr/.

The feedback between a tourism model and urban planning in La Manga, a mass tourist destination on the Spanish coast

S. García-Ayllón[1] & J. L. Miralles[2]
[1]Technical University of Cartagena, Spain
[2]Polytechnic University of Valencia, Spain

Abstract

The urbanization process that shapes the current Mediterranean coast started in Spain with mass tourism, encouraged by the National Law of Tourist Interest Areas in 1963 as a strategic investment. Fifty years after its implementation, it is necessary to conduct a retrospective analysis of the results, for the evaluation of the goals set in the 60s. The evolution of the economic, political and legal parameters show certain deviations from the initial forecasts of many urban plans carried out in coastal places created from scratch.

The case of La Manga del Mar Menor is certainly an enlightening example of the results that have been achieved on a mass tourist destination. La Manga, located in the coastal Region of Murcia (south-eastern Spain), is a destination of 250,000 holidaymakers in summer which was a desert dune in the 60s. The study of feedback between a tourist model and urban planning reveals the problems of a tourist product to maintain its attractiveness in the long term. The short-term benefit of second homes versus hotels, the cost of maintaining the locations with high seasonality in demand or the target customer in a tourist destination are elements heavily influenced by urban planning in coastal cities. In this paper, all these elements will be distributed to either side of the balance, in order to evaluate the validity of the La Manga model.
Keywords: tourism strategies, urban planning, La Manga, Mar Menor, National Law of Tourist Interest Areas.

WIT Transactions on Ecology and The Environment, Vol 187,© 2014 WIT Press
www.witpress.com, ISSN 1743-3541 (on-line)
doi:10.2495/ST140261

1   Introduction: La Manga del Mar Menor and Spanish tourism policy

La Manga del Mar Menor, is now the main tourist attraction of Murcia, a coastal region in southeastern Spain. These ancient dunes hosts during the summer months more than 250,000 tourists attracted by the uniqueness of enjoying beaches washed by two seas: the Mar Menor to the west and the Mediterranean Sea to the east (Fig. 1).

Figure 1:   La Manga view from the south, between the Mar Menor (left) and the Mediterranean (right). Source: Atlas of Murcia.

The project for La Manga arises in the 60s as part of development plans that enhance tourism as the main economic activity in Spain. The National Law of Tourist Interest Areas and Centres creates in 1963, out of nowhere, many coastal tourist resorts such as La Manga. This plan is undertaken thanks to the substantial public funding that granted interest-free loans to private promoters for developing urban plans aimed at quality tourism of sun and beach in parts of Spain without tourist activity [1].

The results at the macroeconomic level for the country thanks to this policy shift towards tourism have been unquestionable. Tourism has grown from a residual sector until becoming the main source of income of Spain (Fig. 2). However, the results obtained in different resorts on the Spanish coast have been very heterogeneous. The case of La Manga is a very illustrative example of how wrong urban planning decisions can lead to premature obsolescence of a tourist destination as a product market.

2   A successful tourism project initially

During the making of La Manga as a tourist destination, businessman Tomás Maestre received in the 60s 11,000 million pesetas to develop a dune ridge nearly 20 km in length and make it a world-class tourist resort that houses up to

60,000 visitors [2]. The business model was simple and Tomás Maestre based it on an urban masterplan developed in different phases and oriented to foreign and domestic customers with high purchasing power (Fig. 3).

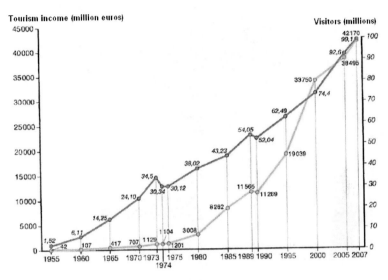

Figure 2:   Evolution of the number of visitors (dark) and income (light) for tourism in Spain between 1955 and 2007. Source: [1, 2].

Figure 3:   La Manga in 1956 (left) and model of the tourist project of Tomas Maestre in 1961 (right). Source: [2].

With state funding the development works of La Manga (roads, electricity, water, etc.) are undertaken and major facilities (marinas, casinos and hotels) are constructed. Revenues come from the management of hotels and sale of plots for large houses or second homes apartment buildings (Fig. 4). La Manga soon turns into an international-class destination, get great benefits that serve to further the development works and create new facilities that make it grow rapidly. The success of La Manga attracts VIPs and tourists with high purchasing power worldwide, which provide luxurious mansions on its beaches (Fig. 5).

Figure 4:   Infrastructure works and buildings in La Manga in 60s (2nd homes, left and hotel in right). Source: [2].

Figure 5:   Luxury 2nd homes in La Manga. Source: [2].

3   Oil crisis and the changing model of tourism in La Manga

Certainly a point of inflection in the urbanization process of La Manga was the 1973 oil crisis, which hit all developed countries including (albeit with some delay), Spain [3]. The effects of the crisis were felt at all levels in the case of La Manga. On the one hand, the financial crisis ended soft loans provided by the government for the execution of the works, which now had to be financed by market conditions and with higher energy costs. On the other hand, the global economic crisis caused a sharp drop in demand for hotel occupancy and plot sales [3].

Crisis and the difficulty of access to finance forced the promoter Tomás Maestre to continue works paying multiple contractors with plots designed for housing and hotels. Thus, the tourism project of La Manga until then governed by a single masterplan of a promoter, becomes many small real estate projects that aim to make money in the short term with maximum building houses on the plots.

This causes a change in business model and the tourism project. Small developers do not want to manage hotels or sell plots to build single family homes, but to build apartment buildings for second homes, with the maximum number of dwellings (often illegally or exploiting loopholes). Works that were started in the first ten kilometres of La Manga (half length) are continued, but under these new criteria from the mid-70s. This new tourism planning leads to a new urban landscape in La Manga.

The original masterplan had built in 1975 hotels and facilities in the first half of La Manga. The original tourism project planned that most of the apartments were put on the market once the hotels had consolidated La Manga as an international destination. Thus, foreign customers who already knew La Manga for coming to their hotels at different times might feel interested in acquiring home ownership. The unexpected situation caused two major changes in the development process of La Manga: on one hand, second residence apartments multiplied in the first half (south of La Manga area), and on the other hand, most hotels and equipment planned in the second half (north area) were not executed, whose plots were finally destined to second homes (Fig. 6).

This situation had important consequences in La Manga as a town and as a tourism product. First, the visitor population of the new city grew by leaps and bounds from the 70s.

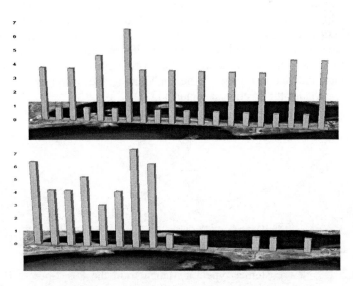

Figure 6:   Geographical distribution of hotels planned in the original project (top) and final distribution today (below). Source: [2].

In 1984, the supply of hotel accommodation and second homes already exceeded the 60,000 total seats which provided the whole starting project. In 1988 reached nearly 100,000 and more than 200,000 in 2005. Nevertheless, if we analyze the figures in detail we can see how the real growth was occurring only in second homes, which multiplied exponentially. The hotel accommodation began to grow more slowly from 1975 to stagnate in the 80s (Table 1).

Table 1: Evolution of hotel beds vs. 2nd homes in La Manga. Source: modified from [3].

Year	2nd homes	Hotel beds	TOTAL	Year	2nd homes	Hotel beds	TOTAL
1965	820	0	820	1977	40,727	1,586	42,313
1966	1,528	217	1,745	1978	42,272	2,521	44,793
1967	3,193	563	3,756	1984	62,110	2,521	64,631
1972	18,228	563	18,791	1988	97,004	2,577	99,576
1973	23,180	1,586	24,766	2005	202,177	2,965	205,142
%	93,5%	6,5%	100%	%	98,6%	1,4%	100%

These changes led to a significant metamorphosis in La Manga as a tourism product. The new business model aimed at selling more accommodation but more affordable, and based on the sale of second homes. These ones produced more rapid economic returns compared to hotels, inputting a new customer profile. This new costumer was a more local tourist, usually national but less purchasing power, and wanted to buy a house for the summer. This new lower added value client cohabited between the late 70s and early 80s, with the former one, which was foreign or domestic but with high purchasing power. This cohabitation did not last long, "expelling" finally the overcrowding of local client in La Manga the foreign customer (Fig. 7).

Figure 7: New customer type La Manga from the 80s. Source: Blanco y Negro Magazine, No. 24, 2001.

This "mutation" in the target customer was soon reflected in the urban landscape of La Manga. Some equipment projects that began to be built in the 70s in the north area, as the expansion of Casino Dos Mares, were never completed (in fact, the casino itself finally closed). Others like the shooting club were substituted by 2nd home buildings (Fig. 8), because this new client did not consume that kind of product. In fact, it was a customer with little added value, since it was actually a tourist who consumed little since their substantial financial investment was made in the purchase of the second residence. To This question is now added another, which was the deepening of the seasonality in tourism demand, which was concentrated in the months of July, August and September, with a very tight supply generating thousands of empty homes the rest of the year as if it was a ghost town. This caused problems in services management (waste collection, police or street lighting) and a significant oversizing of infrastructure (roads, water systems, etc., Fig. 9).

Figure 8:   Abandonment of Casino Dos Mares (left) and disappeared shooting club (right). Source: Authors and archive VECOS promoter.

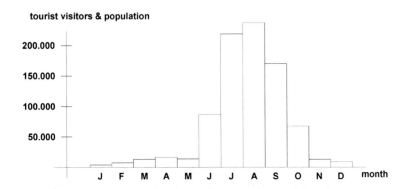

Figure 9: La Manga visitor's annual distribution in 2012. Source: [5].

4 Current analysis of changing model consequences: feedback of urbanization and tourist model

Inertia initiated in the mid-70s will be consolidated in the 80s. In the early 90s, the tourism model seems to be exhausted (Fig. 10). However, with the beginning in the mid-90s of the housing bubble (half of the homes built in Spain were located on the Mediterranean coast, see [6] and [7]), the sale of plots and apartments construction are not completely stopped.

Figure 10: Criticism of the tourism model in La Manga in the late 80s. Source: La Verdad y La Opinión de Murcia journals, years 1987, 1988 1991.

Looking at La Manga as a tourism product market from the perspective of supply and demand for land, we can show the depletion of La Manga as a tourism product and its premature obsolescence as product market due to wrong planning policy implemented.

The tip of La Manga visitor population has grown to nearly 250,000 visitors in recent years (Fig. 11). However, this growth has not been uniform nor continuous, but reveals own deficiencies of La Manga as a tourism product. This tourist population remains constant these latter years despite the global economic crisis, because most of these tourists are 2nd home owners.

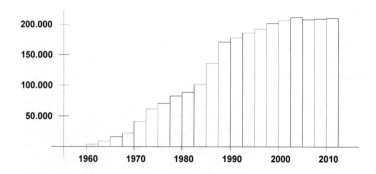

Figure 11: Evolution of peak tourist population in La Manga. Source: [2].

If we compare the first half of La Manga (south) and the second half (north) we notice a very different urban appearance. In the south, which was urbanized (and where hotels and facilities were built) before 1973, we found a clogged building environment (Fig. 12, left). Nevertheless, in the north, the urban built-up area has numerous voids (even in privileged surroundings of the beach) without any presence of hotels and equipment (Fig. 12, right). Looking at the graphs of house building intensity (directly linked to the sale thereof) we see continued growth of urban area until stagnation in the early 90s in both north and south half of La Manga. However, it should be stressed that this urban surface reaches 100% in the first one but does not exceed 66% in the second one (Fig. 13).

Figure 12:   Southern half (left) and northern half (right). Source: authors.

The graphs analyzed show that La Manga clogging as a tourism product in the south (by overcrowding) contributed to a loss of value in the set of the tourist destination.

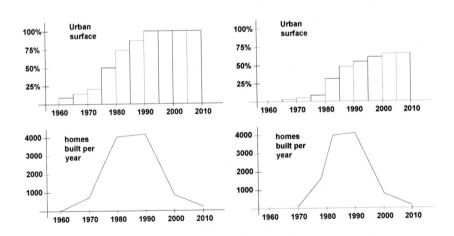

Figure 13:   Evolution of artificial surface and build construction in south (left) and north (right) zone of La Manga. Origin: modified from [3].

This situation leads in the north to a fall in demand for plot sales and housing construction. If we translate this in terms of economic returns of tourism product generating an index of average expenditure per tourist in La Manga (updated over time in line with inflation), we can see how this tourist destination has grown from a destination with high added value to what is now called a "mature" destination (Fig. 14). Being this a consolidated basis, only by adding value with urban renewal projects, we can achieve to increase attractiveness [8].

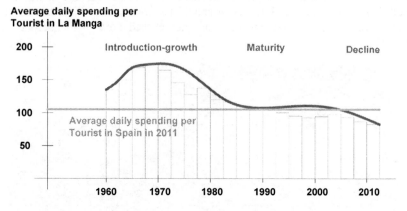

Figure 14:   Life product model of La Manga as tourist market product. Source: modified from [3].

5   Conclusions

–   There is a strong feedback between the urban model of La Manga and its profitability as a tourism product. The urbanization process developed after the oil crisis changed a successful product in the 70s to a product currently with low value-added and major problems of seasonality demand.
–   The wrong policy of favouring urban second homes versus hotel equipment produced a strong economic return in the short term, but contributed to overcrowding. This overcrowding "mutated" the type customer of La Manga, deteriorating profitability and long-term tourism product.
–   It should be noted that the final model, based on a local and national tourism with low added value, seems paradoxically be quite resistant to the effects of the economic crisis gripping Spain since 2008.
–   The solutions of urban problems in currently model are very complicated. No room to expand infrastructure and equipment or to introduce new ones. The changing of the model may be possible rethinking local situation by long time projects to improve the attractiveness [9] or introducing new cultural forms such as low carbon landscapes [10].

References

[1] Galiana L. & Barrado D. *Los centros de interés turístico nacional y el despegue del turismo de masas en España.* Investigaciones Geográficas n° 39, pp. 73-93. ISSN: 0213-4691, 2006.

[2] García-Ayllón S. En los procesos de urbanización del mediterráneo: el caso La Manga. PhD thesis, Polytechnic University of Valencia, 2013.

[3] Miralles i Garcia, J.L., García-Ayllón S. The economic sustainability in urban planning: case La Manga. *WIT Transactions on Ecology and The Environment,* Vol. 173, WIT Press: Southampton, pp. 379-389, 2013.

[4] López-Morell M., Pedreño A. y Baños P. *"Génesis y trayectorias del desarrollo turístico del entorno del Mar Menor".* VIII Congreso de la Asociación Española de Historia Económica, 2006.

[5] Statistics of 2012 in www.murciaturistica.es. Region of Murcia (Spain).

[6] Rullán, O. *La regulación del crecimiento urbanístico en el litoral mediterráneo español.* Ciudad y Territorio n° 168. M° de Fomento, 2011.

[7] Miralles i Garcia, J.L. Real estate crisis and sustainability in Spain. *WIT Transactions on Ecology and the Environment,* Vol. 150, WIT Press: Southampton, pp. 123-133, 2011.

[8] Miralles J.L., Díaz S. & Altur V.J. Environmental impact on the Mediterranean Spanish coast produced by the latest process of urban development. *WIT Transactions on Ecology and the Environment,* Vol. 155, WIT Press: Southampton, pp. 379-389, 2012.

[9] Scott, A. & Ben-Joseph, E. Renewtown. Adaptive urbanism and the low carbon community. Routledge: New York and Oxon, 2012.

[10] Fraker, H. The hidden potential of sustainable neighbourhoods. Lessons for Low-Carbon Communities. Island Press: Washington, Covelo, London, 2013.

Author index

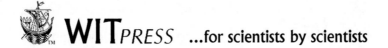

Island Sustainability II

Edited by: S. FAVRO, Hydrographic Institute of the Republic of Croatia, Croatia and C.A. BREBBIA, Wessex Institute of Technology, UK

Containing the papers presented at the second conference organised on island sustainability by the Wessex Institute of Technology, the book addresses the massive scale of seasonal population mobility that has such a profound effect on coastal regions and islands. The problems that result from large temporary increases in population are especially serious for islands and archipelagos, which have limited resources and possibilities of developing supporting infrastructures.

Most islands cannot provide all the resources required by a large seasonal tourist population; in many cases basic requirements such as water and energy, as well as agricultural produce, must therefore be imported. Authorities need to carefully evaluate the impact of large seasonal population increases on the community and the resulting socio-economic factors, as well as issues related to transportation and communication, all of which should be part of an overall strategy. They must also ensure year-round economic activity in order to achieve true sustainability.

The topics covered include: Tourism Impact and Strategies; Community Issues; Changing Climate and Environment; Infrastructure; Transport Issues; Natural Resources; Energy Issues; Risk and Safety; Waste Management; Island Services.

WIT Transactions on Ecology and the Environment, Vol 166
ISBN: 978-1-84564-618-9   e-ISBN: 978-1-84564-619-6
Published 2012 / 228pp / £98.00

*All prices correct at time of going to press but
subject to change.
WIT Press books are available through your book-
seller or direct from the publisher.*

Tourism and Environment

Edited by: F. D. PINEDA, Universidad Complutense de Madrid, Spain

The contributions contained in this volume deal with two perspectives of 'tourism and environment'; the 'role of the environment in tourism' and 'environmental tourism'. The same message would be expected in both cases. The environment comprises the set of biophysical and cultural events surrounding us and influences the activities developed depending on time and site.

Certain places in the world captivate visitors who flock to them in large numbers. Local people recognise the benefit of this, employers become interested in the economic aspects and so the tourism infrastructure develops.

The appeal of 'good climate' has led to a change from a rural subsistence culture to a lucrative services economy in some areas. Unfortunately, however, in many cases short-sightedness and corruption can lead to the ruin of the natural landscape. Situations like this are now common throughout the world due to the environmental mismanagement of tourism. Local populations within emerging tourism-based economies should learn this lesson.

The edited papers included in this volume address important issues related to tourism and the environment and offer a better understanding of some of the current challenges.

Tourism Today, Vol 2
ISBN: 978-1-84564-808-4   e-ISBN: 978-1-84564-809-1
Published 2014 / 164pp / £84.00

WITPRESS ...for scientists by scientists

Tourism and Natural Protected Areas

Edited by: **M.F. SCHMITZ**, *Universidad Complutense de Madrid, Spain*

Yellowstone National Park spans the states of Montana, Wyoming and Idaho in the USA. It is famous worldwide. Since their creation in 1872, most 'protected natural areas' have been considered as probably the greatest achievement of nature conservation. Many countries have such spaces within their territories and many visitors, native or foreign, use some of their free time to get to know them. In this sense these spaces undertake to conserve nature and educate society and give us a kind of cultural tourism that has grown considerably in recent decades.

Cultural tourism today specifically includes, along with cities, museums, monuments and rural traditions, the aim of 'getting to know nature'. Protected natural areas are ideal for this. The tourism industry has realised this and so the value of the landscape and natural resources is becoming increasingly recognised. This is a welcome development and represents a challenge for tourism management, for environmental education and for dissemination of nature and conservation.

This volume of the series Tourism Today considers the evolving relationship between tourism and protected natural areas. The contributions selected are papers that were presented at relevant conferences organised by the Wessex Institute of Technology.

Tourism Today, Vol 3
ISBN: 978-1-84564-810-7   e-ISBN: 978-1-84564-811-4
Published 2014 / 152pp / £84.00

WIT Press is a major publisher of engineering research. The company prides itself on producing books by leading researchers and scientists at the cutting edge of their specialities, thus enabling readers to remain at the forefront of scientific developments. Our list presently includes monographs, edited volumes, books on disk, and software in areas such as: Acoustics, Advanced Computing, Architecture and Structures, Biomedicine, Boundary Elements, Earthquake Engineering, Environmental Engineering, Fluid Mechanics, Fracture Mechanics, Heat Transfer, Marine and Offshore Engineering and Transport Engineering.

Lightning Source UK Ltd.
Milton Keynes UK
UKOW05n1403050614

232920UK00001B/22/P